T0133732

Games User Research

A CASE STUDY APPROACH

Games User Research

A CASE STUDY APPROACH

Edited by **Miguel Angel Garcia-Ruiz**

CRC Press
Taylor & Francis Group
Boca Raton London New York

CRC Press is an imprint of the
Taylor & Francis Group, an **informa** business

AN A K PETERS BOOK

CRC Press
Taylor & Francis Group
6000 Broken Sound Parkway NW, Suite 300
Boca Raton, FL 33487-2742

© 2016 by Taylor & Francis Group, LLC
CRC Press is an imprint of Taylor & Francis Group, an Informa business

No claim to original U.S. Government works

Printed on acid-free paper
Version Date: 20160405

International Standard Book Number-13: 978-1-4987-0640-7 (Hardback)

Library of Congress Cataloging-in-Publication Data

Names: Garcia-Ruiz, Miguel A., 1970- editor.
Title: Games user research : a case study approach / Miguel Angel
Garcia-Ruiz, editor.
Description: Boca Raton, FL : Taylor & Francis, 2016. | Includes
bibliographical references and index.
Identifiers: LCCN 2015043400 | ISBN 9781498706407 (alk. paper)
Subjects: LCSH: Video gamers--Research. | Video games--Design. | User
interfaces (Computer systems)
Classification: LCC GV1469.3 .G434 2016 | DDC 794.8--dc23
LC record available at https://lccn.loc.gov/2015043400

Visit the Taylor & Francis Web site at
http://www.taylorandfrancis.com

and the CRC Press Web site at
http://www.crcpress.com

This book is dedicated to my wife Selene and our son Miguel,
who are the spice of my life. I love them both.

Contents

Foreword

GUR is a field that emerged from a practical stance: making games better to ultimately improve players' experience. With such a goal, GUR has been actively fostered by professionals in the game industry and academics since the early stages of this discipline. Practitioners had to demonstrate and evangelize how UX contributes toward a better product, which helped to shift many companies' design philosophies toward user-centered design. Academics push methodological boundaries and have developed the university courses that shape the newest cohorts of GURs.

This book brings together the roots of this field combining practical components with academic relevancy. Even though GUR is a young discipline, a substantial amount of work has been done on adapting a collection of research techniques to this interactive entertainment industry. This effort has created a foundation of knowledge and paved the road for best practices. Understanding strengths and limitations of methods is important. However, I always emphasize that there is no wrong or right method; the ultimate method is the one that answers the research question.

Being able to scope the research issue at hand and choose the suitable methodology for execution is actually a skill that distinguishes a junior researcher from a seasoned one. There is no best way to showcase this skill than a case study. Thus, this book serves as a compilation of exemplifying critical thinking within GUR.

At Electronic Arts (EA), we design games as an iterative process in which GUR is an integral part. We execute multiple players user experience (UX) research studies to improve the game and the players' experience. Each study is a case study in itself, even when looking at the same title on different occasions because the game has changed, evolved, and research questions might have also shifted. The day to day of a practitioner is a collection of case studies.

Among the utmost qualities that I seek in all research studies at EA are scientific rigor and actionable results. I believe this conveys the common ground of academics and practitioners, and it also helps to demystify that academics are in ivory towers and practitioners just need to make it quick. For me, each GUR study needs to be solid in terms of defining research goals and the suitable method applied. We wear "scientists' hats" when it comes to designing and executing the study. The other side of the coin is that we also have a clear connection to the product and how findings are going to help shape the design. What happens in the "lab" has a clear connection to design elements.

Games are designed in collaborative, multidisciplinary environments. As UX researchers, we interact on a daily basis with producers, designers, executives, artists, quality analysts (QAs), and marketers, just to name a few. This highlights the importance of being able to work in a setting that brings together multiple perspectives and touching on themes that are in the fringe areas of our expertise. Fundamentally, making games is designing with others, everyone contributing from different angles toward the best-possible product. Conclusively, Garcia-Ruiz has chosen a collection of articles that demonstrates several different aspects of working in gaming and working with others that stands to raise the level of expertise in the field.

Veronica Zammitto
Sr. Lead Games User Researcher
Electronic Arts, Inc.
Redwood City, CA, USA

Preface

I was motivated to edit this book by the desire I share with other colleagues to further the evolution of games user research (GUR), in particular to improve the teaching of inquiry, inspection, and user-testing methods applied in the video game development process, as well as to convey the importance of improving the human–computer interfaces of video games, including UX. I was also motivated to compile academic yet practical case studies on GUR that could serve as effective study materials for usability and video game design students, as well as valuable references for researchers and practitioners interested in these topics. Computer science students, lecturers, instructors, and researchers from video game design, programming, and related areas, as well as people from the gaming industry will find the book illuminating. All those engaged in fields such as information technologies, software engineering, human–computer interaction, usability, UX, and human factors will find ideas of value in the chapters.

The objective of this book is to present the latest interdisciplinary research and applications on GUR in the form of case studies to provide students, researchers, lecturers, and practitioners the necessary background in theory and practice to pursue this endeavor. Case studies can be beneficial in GUR because they present an analysis and an intensive description of practical and special situations where users are involved in analyzing and testing video game user interfaces. In addition, case studies provide a good source of ideas, innovative technical insights, "war stories," and proven techniques that students, researchers, and practitioners can understand, adapt, and use in further academic and professional activities related to video game development.

Games User Research: A Case Study Approach is a comprehensive—yet specialized—compendium of case studies using state-of-the-art GUR methods and investigations. Writing case studies on GUR should require the "coming together" of science, technology, and social knowledge in an interdisciplinary manner, since GUR is supported by a number of knowledge areas. This book includes new perspectives from academics and practitioners from around the world on how and why GUR can support the design and development of video games. The book presents comprehensive case studies to be used as learning and teaching materials in video game design and development, usability, human–computer interaction, software engineering, and related undergraduate and graduate courses.

Practitioners will benefit from this book by developing and applying usability and player-testing methods and techniques for improving software interfaces and the human–computer interaction of video games. Practitioners will also benefit from the pragmatic techniques, implementation guidelines, and case discussions that this book contains. Undergraduate-level and graduate-level students will find the case studies useful in their course work and research. Also, this book will be a welcome addition to academic libraries' research collections for further consultation in this particular topic. There are many technical books about the theory, principles, and the general impact of usability and books that include case studies on video games research, but this is not particularly the case with this book. For example, many of the books or websites I found with case studies on usability of video games are somewhat outdated; most of them do not include important and recent topics, such as video games in mobile computing. Thus, this book will be distinguished from existing titles on usability testing of video games.

Games User Research: A Case Study Approach is a valuable supporting book for video game development courses because the case studies cover important aspects on the game interface design, for example, the usability of sounds from a video game. Usability is a very important topic that should be part of all game design courses. The potential audience for this book is very large. There are hundreds of colleges and universities around the world that offer video game design and development courses that can benefit from this book. A Google search found more than 3500 links related to video game design courses from universities and colleges worldwide. The website http://www.gamecareerguide.com/schools/ shows more than 140 featured universities and colleges from around the world with game design courses. A website on gaming careers (http://www.gamecareerguide.com/schools/) shows a list with almost 280 colleges and universities from the United States and Canada that offer video game development courses (25 universities and colleges in Ontario, Canada alone that offer video game design courses). The website http://education-portal.com/game_design_universities.html shows a list of the 21 largest schools by student enrollment that offer video game design courses in the United States. I teach video game design courses at Algoma University, Canada, with group sizes of 40+ (our university is small), and the number of students who are taking a minor in Computer Games Technology is growing each year. A typical video game minor may contain over five specialized game design and development courses and generally belong to Computer Science Departments/Colleges. A number of video game development instructors have used case studies in their classes. The video game industry is growing every year and has high demand for competent game designers and usability/UX specialists.

I am deeply indebted to a number of colleagues and peer reviewers who have read this book and given me and the chapter coauthors many valuable suggestions for improving the contents. I owe a special debt of gratitude to Silvia Gabrielli, Genaro Rebolledo-Mendez, Pedro Santana, Zeno Menestrina, Karyn Moffat, Bill Kapralos, Jaime Munoz, Cynthia Putnam, Claudia Hernandez Luna, David Golightly, Stuart Cunningham, Hakan Tuzun, Gavin Sim, David Murphy, Victor Gonzalez, and Michael DiSanto.

Miguel A. Garcia-Ruiz
Sault Ste. Marie, Canada
September, 2015

Editor

Miguel A. Garcia-Ruiz graduated in computer systems engineering and earned his MSc in computer science from the University of Colima, Mexico. He earned his PhD in computer science and artificial intelligence at the University of Sussex, UK. Dr. Garcia-Ruiz took a virtual reality course at Salford University, UK, and a graphics techniques internship at the Madrid Polytechnic University, Spain. Dr. Garcia-Ruiz is an assistant professor with the Department of Computer Science and Mathematics, Algoma University, Canada. He has published scientific papers on usability and UX in major journals, book chapters, and a number of books, and directed an introductory video on virtual reality. His research interests include educational virtual environments, usability of video games, and multimodal human–computer interaction.

Contributors

Ronald M. Baecker
Department of Computer Science
University of Toronto
Toronto, Ontario, Canada

Fatma Bayrak
Faculty of Education
Hacettepe University
Ankara, Turkey

Michele Bianchi
Point Grey Italy S.r.l.
Trento, Italy

Jeremy Birnholtz
Department of Communication Studies
Northwestern University
Evanston, Illinois

Barbara Chamberlin
Learning Games Lab
New Mexico State University
Las Cruces, New Mexico

Jinghui Cheng
College of Computing and Digital Media
DePaul University
Chicago, Illinois

Andrea Conci
Department of Information Engineering
    and Computer Science
University of Trento
Trento, Italy

Stuart Cunningham
C.A.R.D.S.
Glyndŵr University
Wales, United Kingdom

Antonella De Angeli
Department of Information Engineering
    and Computer Science
University of Trento
Trento, Italy

Esin Ergün
Computer Technology Department
Karabük University
Karabük, Turkey

Michelle Coles Garza
Learning Games Lab
New Mexico State University
Las Cruces, New Mexico

Laura S. Gaytán-Lugo
School of Mechanical and Electrical
    Engineering
University of Colima
Colima, Mexico

David Golightly
Faculty of Engineering
University of Nottingham
Nottinghamshire, United Kingdom

Claudia Lucinda Hernandez Luna
Faculty of Engineering
University of Nottingham
Nottinghamshire, United Kingdom

Matthew Horton
School of Physical Sciences and
    Computing
University of Central Lancashire
Lancashire, United Kingdom

Aidan Kehoe
Logitech
Munster, Ireland

Ayşe Kula
Ministry of National Education
Ankara, Turkey

Blair MacIntyre
School of Interactive Computing
Georgia Institute of Technology
Atlanta, Georgia

Raul Masu
Department of Information Engineering
    and Computer Science
University of Trento
Trento, Italy

Zeno Menestrina
Department of Information Engineering
    and Computer Science
University of Trento
Trento, Italy

Karyn Moffatt
School of Information Studies
McGill University
Quebec, Canada

Amy Smith Muise
Learning Games Lab
New Mexico State University
Las Cruces, New Mexico

David Murphy
Computer Science Department
University College Cork
Munster, Ireland

Fatih Özdinç
Selçuk University
Konya, Turkey

Richard Picking
C.A.R.D.S.
Glyndŵr University
Wales, United Kingdom

Cynthia Putnam
College of Computing and Digital Media
DePaul University
Chicago, Illinois

Janet C. Read
School of Physical Sciences and Computing
University of Central Lancashire
Lancashire, United Kingdom

Miguel A. Rodríguez-Ortiz
School of Telematics
University of Colima
Colima, Mexico

Pedro C. Santana-Mancilla
School of Telematics
University of Colima
Colima, Mexico

Nicholas Shim
Sago Sago Toys
Toronto, Ontario, Canada

Adriano Siesser
Department of Information Engineering
    and Computer Science
University of Trento
Trento, Italy

Gavin Sim
School of Physical Sciences and
    Computing
University of Central Lancashire
Lancashire, United Kingdom

Jesús H. Trespalacios
Department of Educational Technology
Boise State University
Boise, Idaho

Hakan Tüzün
Faculty of Education
Hacettepe University
Ankara, Turkey

Jonathan Weinel
Glyndŵr University
Wales, United Kingdom

Yan Xu
Intel Labs
Santa Clara, California

Gareth W. Young
Computer Science Department
University College Cork
Munster, Ireland

José P. Zagal
Entertainment Arts & Engineering
University of Utah
Salt Lake City, Utah

CHAPTER 1

Practical and Ethical Concerns in Usability Testing with Children

Gavin Sim, Janet C. Read, and Matthew Horton

CONTENTS

EXECUTIVE SUMMARY

It is a common practice to evaluate interactive technology with users. In industry, usability companies typically carry out these evaluations and the participants in the evaluation are usually adults. In research studies, researchers who do not do this sort of work on a daily basis, typically perform the evaluation. Complexity can be increased if the researcher is also the developer of the software and if the users are children. This case study explores that space, the evaluation of software with researchers/developers with children. The chapter describes the evaluation of an educational game that was designed to teach Spanish to children. The chapter outlines the planning for, and the execution of, a usability study of the game with 25 children aged 7–8 years in a school in the United Kingdom. The study used two methods to try and discover usability problems; direct observation and retrospective think aloud, and also gathered user experience data using the Fun Toolkit. The focus in this chapter is less on the results of the evaluation (although these are presented) but more on the practical and ethical concerns of conducting usability evaluations of games with children within a school setting. Those reading the chapter will gather hints and tips from the narrative and will understand better the use of the three methods included in the study. In addition, the researcher/developer role is discussed and it is shown that the methods used here enabled children to make judgments without the ownership of the product being an issue. To make the main points more concrete, the chapter closes with a set of "key points" to consider when doing usability testing with children in schools.

ORGANIZATION/INSTITUTION BACKGROUND

The study described in this chapter took place in the United Kingdom and involved children from a primary school in a semi-rural area of Northern England. The work was carried out by members of the ChiCI (Child Computer Interaction) research group at the University of Central Lancashire (UCLan)—a modern University with over 30,000 students. The ChiCI group was formed in 2002 when a group of the four researchers at UCLan came together around a shared interest in designing for, and evaluating with, children. The group has since grown and at the time of writing this chapter was made up of eight academics, five PhD students, and four students on specialist masters courses. ChiCI receives funding from the European Union (EU), the UK research councils, and industry.

The ChiCI group has a long tradition of working with school children from around the region. The group has a dedicated PlayLab within the university and uses this to hold MESS days (Horton et al. 2012), which are structured events that bring a whole class of children (25–30) at a time to the university to rotate through a variety of activities aimed at evaluating and designing technologies for the future. The overarching aim of the ChiCI group is to "develop and test methods that facilitate the design and delivery of highly suitable technologies for children." These technologies may be for fun, learning, the benefit of children in communicating with others, or for recording their thoughts or ideas. Innovations to date have included a handwriting recognition system designed for children aged between 5 and 10 years, a tabletop game for kindergarten children, a specialized pod for use by teenagers to identify with domestic energy use, and a mobile game for use with children aged between 5 and 11 years with communication difficulties.

CASE STUDY DESCRIPTION

The case study described in this chapter concerns the processes and outcomes around the evaluation, by children, of an educational game. The evaluation took place in a UK primary school and took the form of a usability test that was carried out to identify usability problems and also capture satisfaction metrics. The aim was to improve the design of the game but in the process the research team also sought to investigate several elements of school-centered evaluation. The authors developed the game that was used in the study; it took the form of a medium to high fidelity prototype that included all the required functionality and had suitable graphical elements. The game met the appropriate educational objectives for children who would be evaluating the game. The educational merit of the game was not going to be examined in this case study. It is noted however that usability can be examined from a pedagogical perspective focusing on the user interface, design of the learning activities, and the determination of whether learning objectives have been met (Laurillard 2002).

The case study provides the reader with a clear narrative that explains how different tools can be used to capture both usability problems and user experience data from children within a school setting. The use of two different evaluators, one with a personal tie to the game (the developer) and the other looking at the game from an impartial view (the researcher), is also explored to see whether the investment of the evaluator may affect how the children respond to the user study and what they report.

Usability testing with children has been the subject of many academic papers with researchers focusing on the development and refinement of tools and techniques that can help children engage with researchers to evaluate products and systems. Various adult methods have been explored including think aloud, interviews, and the use of questionnaires (Markopoulos and Bekker 2003, LeMay et al. 2014). Using these, and other methods, it has been shown that children can identify and report usability problems. For example, direct observation has been shown to identify signs of engagement or frustration along with the ability to identify usability problems (Sim et al. 2005, Markopoulos et al. 2008). Think aloud has been used effectively by children to identify usability problems (Donker and Reitsma 2004, Khanum and Trivedi 2013). Hoysniemi et al. (2003) found that children were able to detect usability problems which would aid the design of a physically and vocally interactive computer game for children aged 4–9 years. However, when conducting usability research with children, there are still a number of challenges that need to be considered, with one example being the impact of children's less mature communication skills. Several studies have identified that younger children, especially when using the think-loud technique, are less able to verbalize usability problems than older children. Despite the apparent success of the think aloud method, it still comes under some criticism. There is concern that the think aloud method is quite challenging for children due to its cognitive demands (Donker and Reitsma 2004), especially for younger children (Hanna et al. 1997) as they could forget to think aloud unless being prompted (Barendregt et al. 2008). One study by Donker and Reitsma (2004) found that out of 70 children only 28 made verbal remarks during a user test—this is a low number and could be considered hardly representative of that group. Where think aloud has been shown to be taxing for children, the use of retrospective methods, where the child describes what happened after the usability test has ended, have shown some promise. Kesteren et al. (2003) found that with retrospective techniques children were able to verbalize their experiences. It has been suggested that children may be less communicative, not because of a lack of skill in communicating but rather as a result of personality traits. Barendregt et al. (2007) showed that personality characteristics influenced the number of problems identified by children in one usability test. Research is still needed to understand usability methods and to identify and catalogue their limitations in order to ascertain which can be reliably used with children. The literature provides guidance on how to perform usability studies in Hanna et al. (1997) and Barendregt and Bekker (2005) but these are somewhat dated, are restricted to the studies being performed in usability labs, and do not take account of recent research in the field.

For user experience, similar to usability, many methods for children have emerged over the years. These include survey tools (Read 2008, Zaman et al. 2013) and specialized verbalization methods (Barendregt et al. 2008) that have typically focused on measuring fun within the context of game play or with children using interactive technology. The survey tools that are widely used with children, including the Fun Toolkit (Read and MacFarlane 2006) and the This or That method (Zaman 2009), capture quantifiable data relating to user experience. Research that has compared the results from the Fun Toolkit and the This or That method has shown that they yielded similar results which can be taken as evidence that they are, when used appropriately, collecting useful data (Sim and Horton 2012, Zaman et al. 2013). The literature on the use of survey methods with children highlights that gathering opinion data is not without difficulties as the younger the children are, the more immature they are at understanding the question—answer process. Children are generally unused to giving opinions in this sort of context and this gives rise to problems including suggestibility and satisficing (Read and Fine 2005). These two problems are related but come from two sides—suggestibility is seen where a question might be phrased a certain way in order that the child is "more minded" to answer a particular way. An example might be a question like "Do you like this game more than that hopeless one you just played?"—satisficing is more about answers than questions and is more difficult to deal with in survey design as it is really a process problem. Satisficing is where a child seeks to give an answer that he or she thinks the adult wants to hear. It is born out of the imbalance in the relationship between the child and the evaluator and is inherent in all evaluation studies.

One of the aims of the case study presented here is to explore satisficing as a known issue within usability and user experience studies with children. Another aim is to consider the effectiveness of the three different evaluation methods. The study presents data relating to identified usability problems and reported satisfaction, and this is critiqued to understand the limitations of the process and methods, and to offer suggestions for further research. The main lessons from the case study are used to generate a set of guidelines for carrying out usability and user experience testing in school settings. These guidelines will follow the same structure as those presented by Hanna et al. (1997).

Method

As described earlier, for this study, children were being asked to evaluate the usability and user experience of a medium to high fidelity prototype educational game. Each child would play the game and data would be collected using three different methods; the Fun Toolkit, direct observation, and retrospective think aloud. The researchers carrying out the study had experience of carrying out observations and capturing usability problems (Sim et al. 2005)—had this not been the case, video recording might have been considered an option for this work to ensure events were not missed whilst notes were being taken. It is quite feasible that some events may have been missed as a result of not recording the screen, but if there were severe problems or obvious problems it was anticipated that several children would experience this and so it would be captured.

Satisficing was examined at the level of "who made the game." The use of two adult evaluators acted as "developer" and "researcher" in order to explore how the children reported on, and talked about, the software that they saw. This presentation was controlled for in a between subjects design so that the "developer" was a different person for half the children than for the other half. The usability study was also controlled with half the children being told extensively about the ethics of their inclusion and the other half getting only a brief explanation before being told afterwards. The case study will focus mainly on the qualitative data that was gathered and will give examples of how children spoke to the two adults and the impact of the ethical information had on the results.

The Game Prototype

The study used a game that had been developed to help the children learn Spanish in the school. The children testing the game had recently begun to learn Spanish in school and so the game fitted in well with the school curriculum. The game is shown in Figure 1.1.

The game was a platform game set in Gibraltar. The storyline featured a pesky Gibraltarian ape stealing a bag from a tourist and then throwing all the contents of the bag off the rock. The (human) player had to retrieve all the items and then return to the top of the rock. Each time an item was found, the game presented a feedback message showing the name of the item in English and Spanish; it also played Spanish audio, speaking out the name of the object, to accompany the message. Whilst navigating around the platforms looking for the missing objects, the pesky apes at the top of the rock threw down bananas that the player had to avoid. Once three bananas had hit the player it was the end of the game. As the game was a prototype, only one level of the game was playable for the purpose of the evaluation. The game was functional but did have some "built in" usability problems, for example, the feedback messages staying on the screen until they were clicked, the lack of instructions on how to control the character, and a known problem with the collision detection at the end. The rationale for leaving these problems in was to see whether children would notice them and would talk about them in the retrospective think aloud; this process of deliberatively incorporating usability problems into games has been used in other research (Sim 2012).

FIGURE 1.1   Screenshot of the game.

Study Design

Usability and user experience were both being measured in this study. There are numerous evaluation methods that could be used for measuring user experiences, however, few have been extensively validated with children, and therefore, for this reason, the Fun Toolkit was selected (Read 2008). This tool has predominantly been used for comparative analysis of technology or games with children and it includes three tools, one of which (the Fun Sorter) is only meaningful in comparative studies. As the study described here was only evaluating a single game that tool, the Fun Sorter was omitted. Thus, the Smileyometer and the Again Again tables were used in this study. The Smileyometer is a visual analog scale that is coded using a 5-point Likert scale, with 1 relating to "Awful" and 5 to "Brilliant" (see Figure 1.2).

The Smileyometer is intended to be used both before and after the children interact with technology. The rationale in using it before is that it can measure a child's expectations of the product, whereas using it afterwards it is assumed that the child is reporting experienced fun. The Smileyometer has been widely adopted and applied in research studies (Read 2012, Sim and Horton 2012) to measure satisfaction and fun as it is easy to complete and requires no writing by the child. The Again Again table is a table that requires the

FIGURE 1.2   Example of the Smileyometer.

Again Again

Would you like to play it again

	Yes	Maybe	No
	✓		

FIGURE 1.3   A completed Again Again table.

children to pick "yes," "maybe," or "no" for each activity they have experienced. In this study, the children were asked "Would you like to play this game again?" and they had to respond accordingly. A completed Again Again table is shown in Figure 1.3.

There are many methods available for evaluating the usability of software for children, including think aloud and observations. The decision was made to use direct observation to capture any problems the child had whilst playing the game as this approach has been used effectively in evaluating educational games with children (Diah et al. 2010). The problems observed would be captured on a preformatted sheet documenting both the problem found and the location in the game where it occurred—see Figure 1.4.

Chil   _2N_

Observation sheet

Screen codes

1	First page	4	Game play
2	Instructions 1	5	End screen fail
3	Instruction 2	6	End screen win

Comments:	Screen
Had to be told to move to the next screen	2
Did.'t know to remove the message	4.
Had to be told about double jumping	4
Kept falling off the platforms. Seemed to get frustrated.	4

FIGURE 1.4   Completed observation form.

To ensure the child remained anonymous, as there was no need to record names, each child was given a unique code. In this instance this was child 2 and the N referred to the fact that the role taken by the evaluator in this instance was that of "not" the developer.

In addition to direct observation, a decision was made to use an adaptation of retrospective think aloud. On finishing the game, each child was shown paper screenshots of different parts of the game and asked to recall any problems he or she had experienced within that part of the game. These problems were then recorded on a separate data capture form similar to the one used for the observation. The screens are shown in Figure 1.5; when these were presented to the child each screen was printed in color on a separate sheet of A4 paper to ensure that the child only focused on the screen of interest rather than getting distracted by multiple images. One of the screens that was included in the original study has been removed for illustration purposes as none of the children managed to complete that level and therefore never saw the screen. The screens were presented in the order as shown in Figure 1.5.

In a traditional retrospective think aloud, the player would normally watch a video of himself or herself playing and comment on the interaction. It was felt that this might be difficult for children, time consuming, and not very engaging for the child, which is why the decision was made to use just screenshots. This worked in the context of this game as there were not many different screens but it is acknowledged that had the game had lots of levels or screens, then the use of video would possibly be a more practical solution. Using video has many drawbacks especially when it comes to tagging reported problems to a moment in the video and dedicated software may be useful to speed up the process (Kjeldskov et al. 2004).

Ethics

In the view of the ChiCI team, ethics is much more than just obtaining consent for participation in a research study especially as, with children, there are questions about their

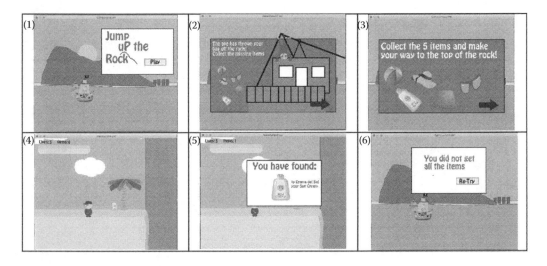

FIGURE 1.5 (1–6) Screenshots of the game.

ability to understand what they are consenting to. Within a school context the teachers typically give consent to involve the children from a class in an "out of curriculum" activity. In that set up, it is believed that if a child did not want to take part in the activity then he or she might find it hard to say so as school is not an environment where children pick and choose to do things. Researchers need to be mindful of this and need to explore ways of empowering children to make informed decisions about their participation in evaluation studies. The CHECk tool was developed to facilitate good ethical practice when working on design and evaluation studies with children (Read, Horton et al. 2013) and has been subsequently used to aid the development of applications to address bullying (Mechelen et al. 2014). The main principle behind the CHECk tool is that it leads the researcher or designer to examine his or her own priorities and beliefs. CHECk consists of two checklists, CHECk1 and CHECk2. The first tool CHECk1 focuses on examining values by asking six questions to be answered prior to any activity. The questions challenge the designer or researcher to consider the appropriateness of both the technical solution and the involvement of children. The aim is to become more explicit about the values that drive the work, pushing designers, developers and researchers to be honest; the six questions and answers from CHECk1, within the context of this study are presented in Figure 1.6.

The second tool is referred to as CHECk2 and aims to examine the value of participation to the child. In completing CHECk2 the intention is to look before and beyond the activity in order to better frame, for the children, the landscape of the work in order that they can better consent to participate. The second aspect of information that has to be conveyed to children is about the data the children contribute. CHECk2 provokes discussion about children being informed about what they will be doing, understanding how their contributions will be disseminated, and, although difficult, considering who would get credit for any ideas that come out of the activity. The main goal of CHECk2 is to achieve an ethical symmetry, that is, full consent from the children instead of consent only by adults (Buckingham 2009). The CHECk2 questions are stated in Figure 1.7.

These tools, and the completion of the tools, enabled the researchers in this study to reflect on the process prior to carrying out the evaluation. This helps in being critical of the study design, ensuring that the methods planned for use are suitable. The process also encourages research teams to think about how to explain concepts in a way that children can understand.

Participants

The children who took part in this study were all from a class 3, aged 7–9 from a UK primary school. On the day, five of the children in the class were absent and so only the remaining 25 children participated in the study. The children who took part did so during their normal school day coming out of regular classes to play the game. Three researchers were involved; all had experience of working, and conducting evaluations, with children of these age groups.

Procedure

The children came to the study in groups of two according to selections from the teacher. The study room used was the school library where the researchers used two tables, one

CHECk 1 questions

1. What are we aiming to design?

A Spanish game.

2. Why this product?

Excuse: We want to understand the problems of the game in order to make it better and enjoyable for children.

Honest: We want to write a book chapter on game usability.

3. What platform or technologies are we planning to use?

Flash based game running on a laptop.

4. Why this platform or technology?

Excuse: Tablet devices are widely used within educational settings and second language learning is often neglected within UK schools until high school.

Honest: Flash was an easy platform for use to create the game. We knew someone who could speak Spanish.

5. Which children will we design with?

Year 3 (i.e., 7- to 8-year-olds) in the UK.

6. Why these children?

Excuse: Second language learning is often neglected within UK schools until high school, Spanish is not widely taught within the UK compared to French and German. The children will not be familiar with the subject.

Honest: It is the age range of the children we decided to study and could get access to.

FIGURE 1.6 CHECk 1 questions and answers.

at each end of the room; as the children came in, they were asked to go to one of the two tables—they made that decision themselves in terms of which table they went to. Ensuring adequate spacing between participants is required to help ensure that the children do not get distracted by each other or by other equipment. On each of the desks there was a laptop that had the prototype of the game being evaluated preloaded. Each table had an adult evaluator sitting at it. The two evaluators used a script to introduce the activity to ensure that each child received the same information. The evaluators took on the role of developer or

CHECk 2 questions

1. Why are we doing this project (i.e., summary of CHECk 1)?

For publication purposes and to refine and better understand evaluation methods.

2. What do we tell the children?

(Two scripts would be produced one for the person acting as developer and another for the none developer.)

Developer

I am developing a game that I want to put on the app store. The game is set in Gibraltar were they speak Spanish and English. I would like you to play the game for me and tell me what you think. Whilst you are playing the game I will be making notes of any problems that you encounter. I would like you to play the game for 5 minutes but feel free to stop at any point.

Researcher

I am looking at games that teach Spanish and I have found this one. The game is set in Gibraltar were they speak Spanish and English. I would like you to play the game for me and tell me what you think. Whilst you are playing the game I will be making notes of any problems that you encounter. I would like you to play the game for 5 minutes but feel free to stop at any point.

3. Who is funding the project?

The University of Central Lancashire, where we work, is funding this research.

4. What do we tell the children?

The university that we work at.

5. What might happen in the long term?

We plan to update the guidelines on usability evaluations and improve the quality of the game and making this available to download.

6. What do we tell the children?

We write advice for other people about working with children. We hope to create better games for you to play.

7. What might we publish?

A book chapter relating to usability and children.

8. What do we tell the children?

We hope to write a book chapter on the work we are doing today.

FIGURE 1.7   CHECk 2 completed questions and answers.

researcher, as described earlier, and they switched these roles half way through the evaluations to reduce bias in the results.

Once the children were settled at one of the two tables, before playing the game, each was shown the first screen of the game and then asked to complete the first Smileyometer; this was intended to measure expectations of the game before playing. Following this, children played the game for between 5 and 10 min; but this was flexible to allow children to stop earlier if they were bored or were not enjoying the experience and also to let them continue longer if they were engaged. Whilst each child played the game, the evaluator documented any usability problems observed using prepared data capture forms.

Once the child had played the game a number of times or the session had finished, the child was asked to complete the Again Again table and a second Smileyometer. Following this they were then shown each of the main screens within the game and were asked if they recalled any problems or difficulties within each of these sections of the game. The responses were captured on a separate sheet of paper. The children were then thanked for their help and then went to another activity being run by the third researcher attending the day.

This third researcher had two pairs of Google Glasses and showed the children how to interact with these, having them take photos and videos. They played with the glasses for about 5–10 min before returning to the classroom. The rationale for including this activity was the fact that this would be a new technology for the children and it was conjectured that, upon returning to the classroom, the children would talk about the glasses rather than the game, thus minimising chatter about the game in the classroom that could have an effect on the subsequent children's responses. It is acknowledged, that even with the Google Glass intervention, the children in this study may well have discussed the game with their peers during the day; this is one of the limitations of running a study like this within a school context.

Analysis

All children managed to complete the Smileyometers before and after they played the games. These were coded from 1 to 5, where 1 represented "awful" and 5 represented "brilliant." In line with other studies using this scale, arithmetic averages have been derived from these scores (Read 2012). The Again and Again table, resulted in a single numeric score with yes being coded as 2, maybe as 1 and no as 0.

During the observation, the problems encountered by the children that were observed by the evaluator, were recorded into an Excel spreadsheet. The problems were then merged, by the two researchers carrying out the work, into a single list of usability problems; this list included the frequency of discovery (in other words a count of the number of children who met that problem). This required each researcher to look at each recorded problem and determine if it was the same as another problem in the list. Problems were treated as separate if they occurred in different locations within the game. In coding problems one approach taken in work with children has been to code the problems based on the behaviour of the child. This was first used by Barendregt and Bekker (2006) who coded problems to identify a number of breakdown indicators. This form of analysis was also used when comparing the usability problems of three prototype games with children (Sim et al. 2013) and was used in this current study both for the observed problems and also for the comments from the retrospective think aloud. In the think aloud, although the children were meant to be reporting the problems they encountered, several children made generic statements about the game or game elements. For example, one of the children stated that he *Liked the Monkey* and another child, when considering the first screen, simply remarked that it was hard, without any reference to why it was hard. These statements were removed from the list of usability problems and so are not included in the results.

RESULTS

The results will be discussed in three parts, the first relates to the use of the Fun Toolkit to capture the user experience, then followed by the results from the two usability methods, direct observation and retrospective think aloud. In each case, results are broken up by the role of the evaluator—as developer or researcher as explained earlier in this chapter. This data feeds into discussion about the use of the ethical checklists and about the effect of satisficing.

Use of the Fun Toolkit to Capture User Experience

The results from the Smileyometer are shown in Table 1.1. Arithmetic averages have been used in line with other studies that have used this tool.

Results from the Smileyometer show that children were not disappointed with the game. Scores were higher after play than before and this indicates that the product was, in the main, a good experience. To determine whether the children satisficed in their responses on account of the role of the evaluator the mean scores were compared, for the nondeveloper when compared to the developer, a Mann–Whitney test revealed no significant difference between the results before $Z = -1.156$, $p = 0.320$ or after $Z = -1.156$, $p = 0.852$. This would suggest that the role of the evaluator did not significantly impact on satisficing, it is assumed that the children rated the game highly to please the adults irrespective of their role.

Table 1.2 shows the difference between the children's scores from the Smileyometer both before and after they played the game, highlighting the difference between their

TABLE 1.1   Results of the Smileyometer before and after Play

Role	Before		After	
	Mean	SD	Mean	SD
Developer	3.50	0.798	3.75	1.138
Researcher	3.92	0.954	3.92	0.954
All children	3.72	0.891	3.84	1.028

TABLE 1.2   Frequency of Change between the after and before Scores of the Smileyometer

	Difference in Rating of the Smileyometer				
	−2	−1	0	1	2
Developer	0	5	2	2	3
Researcher	1	3	6	1	2
All children	1	8	8	3	5

TABLE 1.3   Frequency of Response to
Whether the Child Would Play It Again

Role	Yes	Maybe	No
Developer	9	2	1
Researcher	9	3	1

expectations and experiences. In total, nine of the children's score decreased after they had played the game suggesting that for them, their initial expectations had not been met. The split between the number of children reporting a positive, negative, and no change was relatively equal, showing that a third of the children did not enjoy the game.

The Again Again table that forms part of the Fun Toolkit was also used to establish if the children wished to play the game again and the results for this are shown in Table 1.3.

It is clear that the majority of children in both conditions stated that they would like to play the game again, suggesting that they have enjoyed the game. It was interesting to note that the two children who did not want to play again, and three of the five children who said they maybe would, were the last five children who participated in the study. These lower scores may have been down to the fact that, for these children, the evaluation was being carried out at the end of the school day, and maybe they were fatigued after a long day, and so did not really enjoy the experience.

Direct Observations

From the direct observation, a total of 112 problems were observed. The fewest observed problems for a single child were two and the highest eight. These problems were aggregated based on the location in which the problem occurred within the game; this left 25 "unique" problems. Seven of the problems in this list were only seen once—that is, only one child had each of these difficulties, 14 problems were seen by a few children, and four problems were encountered by 10 or more children. Two problems were observed on the start page, with three children not knowing how to start the game, and another not knowing how to use the mouse pad on the laptop. On the two instruction screens, that followed the start page, five problems were observed. The two problems with the highest frequency were that the child did not know how to move to the next screen, which was observed five times and that children tried to click items that were simply images; this was observed four times. The vast majority of the problems were observed within the actual game play, where 18 problems were observed. The five problems with the highest frequency in the gameplay were:

- Didn't know how to jump or double jump (18 times)
- Unsure how to remove message (18 times)
- Struggled to get onto platforms (12 times)
- Not sure of controls (11 times)
- Tried to collect bananas (10 times)

Although some of these problems appear very similar the decision was made to treat them separately. For example, the problem of the children getting onto platforms was not because they did not know how to jump, it was that they struggled to jump at the correct moment or landed on the platform but immediately fell off. Similarly, not being sure of the controls related to the beginning when they did not know whether to use the keyboard or mouse pad and which buttons to press rather than knowing how to make the man jump.

Within the context of analyzing results from usability tests to make improvements to the game, frequency of discovery should not be the only criteria. The persistence of the problem with regard to whether it is first encountered or whether it can be overcome later could be another factor (Donker and Reitsma 2004). As an example, although 18 children were initially unsure how to remove the message, once informed, only one child struggled with the message after the first play. Another consideration that needs to be taken is on how many children may have progressed to a certain part of the game, in this study two of the unique problems relating to game play were:

- Got to the top, thought they had won and lost, they did not collect all the items

- Go to top and collision detection did not work they fell off the rock and then endlessly fell

Although these two problems had a low frequency it should be noted that these were the only two children who managed to complete the level, which suggests the level was quite hard. These problems might have had a higher frequency if more children had managed to complete the level.

The problems that were "built in" by the developers prior to conducting the evaluation were all encountered but problems such as the children's inability to get onto platforms was not anticipated. This would provide useful data for the redesign of the level, simplifying the game mechanics, and enabling an understanding of how to make the progression through levels challenging.

Other observations, which were not formally documented at the time, relate to the children's participation in the process. All children appeared to come to the activity with enthusiasm and appeared engaged throughout, however, a small number did show signs of frustration during a game play.

Retrospective Think Aloud

For the retrospective method the children had to report any problems they recalled for the various sections of the game. As none of the children successfully completed the level no feedback was obtained on this part of the game and this screen was omitted. Of the 25 children, seven of them claimed to have had no problems, this will be explored further in the next section. Of these seven children, three of them were discussing the game with the developer and four of them are the nondeveloper. This would suggest that the role of the facilitator did not impact on their reluctance to talk about problems and satisficing in this

TABLE 1.4   Number of Problems Found by Each Child

	Frequency of Problems Reported						
Problems found	0	1	2	3	4	5	6
Number of children	7	6	5	5	1	0	1

TABLE 1.5   Number of Usability Problems Reported by the Children for the Various Screens

	Screens					
	1 Start	2 Instruction	3 Instruction	4 Game	5 Feedback	6 End
Number of problems	4	5	1	10	2	2

form may not have occurred. A further six children only reported one problem using this method, and the total number of problems found by each child is shown in Table 1.4.

In total, 47 problems were reported by the children and only 11 of these problems were communicated to the developer. This may suggest that children were reluctant to talk about problems to the developer and felt more comfortable talking to someone impartial. After the problems were aggregated, there remained 24. The number of problems reported by the children for each of the screens is shown in Table 1.5.

Of the 24 problems reported, 15 of the problems were unique in that only one child reported it as a problem. Similar to the direct observation, the majority of problems related to the actual game play, as might have been expected. Only five of the children reported a problem understanding how to jump or perform a double jump and six stated it was hard to get onto the platforms. Eight children indicated a problem in removing the feedback message once an item had been collected. On the final screen, they were asked if they had any problems and knew why the game ended, four of the children after playing the game several times, had not realized that the bananas killed you.

Direct Observation Compared to Retrospective Think Aloud

After aggregation there were 25 problems identified via direct observation whereas 24 were reported using the retrospective think aloud method. How many problems were unique to a particular method and how many were identified in both methods are shown in Figure 1.8.

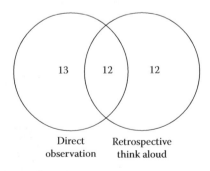

FIGURE 1.8   Usability problems in each method.

For the retrospective think aloud, all the problems that were only seen using this particular method were unique problems in that only one child reported each. Some of the examples of the unique problems are

- Did not know there were lives

- Hard to try again

- Did not understand the Spanish

For the problem "hard to try again," this was not observed, the child reporting this did not appear to have any difficulty when on this screen. It may have been that the facilitator had missed this and if screen capture software had been used this could have been further analyzed. Alternatively, and perhaps more plausible is the suggestion that the child had to "think" of a problem, in order to "help" the evaluator and so came up with this response. This is an example of potential satisficing.

The five problems with the highest frequency within the direct observation method were all identified as problems whilst using retrospective think aloud, but the frequency of verbal report, as opposed to observed activity, was a lot lower. For example, in direct observation, 18 children had been seen to have problems jumping whilst only five children reported this problem in retrospective think aloud. Of the 13 problems that were unique to the direct observation all of the seven problems with a frequency of one were unreported via retrospective think aloud. Examples of the problems with a higher frequency that were unique to direct observation include:

- Opened Flash menu (4)

- Tried to click items (4)

- Got stuck inside hill (2)

In both methods the problems reported by a single child were unique to that method, it would appear that the more obvious and potentially severe problems are identifiable within both methods. These conflicts across the methods are interesting as they show that the two methods are collecting different stories. It could be that some of the observed problems, like the Flash menu opening, were indeed problems but were such that the children could not explain them. These might have been the more implementationally focused problems.

CHALLENGES

In carrying out usability evaluations with children, there are a number of challenges that researchers and practitioners face. Additionally, the practical side of carrying out evaluations with children there is the challenge of obtaining useful data.

Methodological Challenges

It has been shown with adults and children that different evaluation methods yield different results (Desurvire et al. 1992, Markopoulos and Bekker 2003). Within this case study, the two usability methods yielded different results. Although a comparison was made between the two usability methods presented in this case study, this mainly focused on the reported problems. Other metrics for comparing usability methods have been established, for example Markopoulos and Bekker (2003) identified the three criteria:

- Will they be able to apply a particular usability testing method for their problem (robustness)?

- How good are the results that the usability testing produce (effectiveness)?

- How expensive it is to apply a usability testing method in terms of time or other resources (efficiency)?

Robustness was concerned with the feasibility of applying the method in different contexts and highlighted the importance of understanding the suitability of the methods at different stages of the life cycle and use in different locations. Within this case study the evaluations methods were only used in one location and for one game but the results can be used to offer further evidence to the robustness of these methods within a school context.

To determine the effectiveness of an evaluation, Hartson et al. (2003) proposed quantified criteria based on the work of Sears (1997). This looks at the three criteria, thoroughness, validity, and effectiveness where success is defined as the extent to which actual problems are found. This approach is problematic as it requires there to be a known set of problems that can be listed as otherwise a number, which is simply a total has no meaning. In this case study, the practical aspects of carrying out the evaluations was the main concern and thus the decision was made not to calculate this value.

For the final criteria efficiency, this can be a simple measure of the resources required to perform the evaluation, the time to complete the study, and analyze the data. Mathematical models have also been used to determine the efficiency of a method based on the number of participants (Nielsen and Landauer 1993). There may be conflict between these three criteria, for example, video analysis can be time consuming, meaning it may be less efficient than the use of other methods such as the retrospective think aloud as used in this case study. However, there may be a trade off in the fact it is inefficient but is more effective and researchers need to establish the priority before selecting a suitable method.

The results of the retrospective think aloud method within this case study, showed that of the 25 children used, seven of the children claimed to have no issues. However, all the children were observed having problems. These children may have been reluctant to talk about the problems with an adult which might imply satisficing occurred, that they just wanted to go back to class, or genuinely could not remember any problems. For example, child 3 in this study stated that they had no problems within the retrospective method but the following problems were observed:

- Kept pressing shift key by mistake

- Struggled to remove message

- Showed signs of frustration

- Struggled to get to the platforms

Child 9 also stated no problems but the following were observed:

- Flash menu appeared

- Not sure how to remove message

- Right clicked menu to try and remove it instead of just left click

- Character appeared in the middle of the mound and they struggled to move it

If relying on this method alone then the selection of the children may be important as in this case 28% of the children did not report any problems and there may be a need to recruit more children to overcome these difficulties.

The variability of evaluator performance has also been highlighted in studies with adults (Hertzum and Jacobsen 2001). In both the direct observation and retrospective think aloud methods there were a large number of unique problems. It is clear that the different usability evaluation methods used within this case study yielded slightly different results, and this is in line with other studies examining usability methods with children (Markopoulos and Bekker 2003, Als et al. 2005). It is unlikely that all the problems within a game would be captured through a single usability study, inevitably a number of problems may go undetected.

In this case study, gender was not considered although this has also shown to effect results when performing usability studies with children (Markopoulos and Bekker 2003). Further research is still required to fully understand the effect gender has on the results of usability studies.

This case study has highlighted a number of challenges faced when performing usability evaluations with children, yet there are still a vast amount of unanswered questions and limitations. For example, in this study, only one game was tested and this was a platform game. This is true in many other studies where only a limited number of games, or game genres, are evaluated (Edwards and Benedyk 2007). It is unclear whether a particular method is more suited to one genre of game over another.

Further work is needed to understand how usability and user experience change over time. Within this game only one level was examined, if there had been multiple levels then it would not have been possible to evaluate the entire game in the time available. New methods and techniques are thus needed to understand the persistence of problems throughout a game and to capture longitudinal user experience. Vissers et al. (2013) proposed the MemoLine, which is a tool for capturing long-term user experience of a game and help facilitate interviews about game experience. This type of data would be useful to assist in the prioritization of the most severe problems as part of a redesign of a game.

The usability studies performed in this case study were carried out by academics and more input is needed from industry to enable methods to be created that are useful for development teams to make informed decisions about the usability of a game. The actual hardware game is running on and may also affect the suitability of the method. Within this case study, the game was running on a laptop and therefore the interaction could easily be observed. If the children were using a mobile device such as a phone, then observing the game play may not be feasible. With the advancement of technology, methods may need to be established or existing methods analyzed to determine their effectiveness within new contexts such as games developed for the Oculus Rift (Dufour et al. 2014).

Challenges of Conducting Evaluation Studies with Children

There are many practical challenges that are faced when conducting usability studies with children. Children's lives are predominantly situated into two locations; the home and school. These provide a child with a sense of safety and comfort, which is almost impossible to replicate within the context of a usability laboratory. Taking children out of their natural environment will have an effect on their emotions and perceptions, and therefore could affect their participation in an evaluation study. The effect may not necessarily be negative and may differ for each individual child; where one child is excited about coming to a research laboratory and therefore very positive in their contribution, another may be scared or nervous about the unfamiliar surroundings. There is a strong focus on the use of field studies in child research with the apparent need to keep children in a natural environment evident (Jensen and Skov 2005) but as yet very little in the way of guidance in working with children outside of the laboratory setting. If an evaluation has to be carried out outside of a natural environment such as in a research lab, making the lab more child-friendly can help put the children at ease. However, any such interventions do need to be designed in such a way as to not cause too much distraction from the task at hand (Hanna et al. 1997). The case study presented here offers guidance on performing usability evaluation studies within the field.

Owing to the natural unequal power relationship between adults and children, researchers themselves can unintentionally affect an evaluation study (Read and MacFarlane, 2006) due to:

- Increased possibilities of researcher bias

- Children trying to please, or not to upset, the researcher

- Not building up a relationship with the child participants

Children spend the majority of their time with adults who are in a position of power over them. Spending most of their time at home and at school, it is the children's parents and teachers who they interact with the most and these are the adults who children have become accustomed to; taking instruction from and being disciplined by. This is why the presence of parents and teachers during evaluation studies is questioned. The power imbalance can be minimized when only a researcher is present as the relationship has not already been formed. However, there is some evidence to suggest that the influence of a teacher has little impact on the results of the evaluation (Pardo et al. 2006).

Researcher bias is where the views and opinions of the researcher can affect the answers given by a child in a variety of ways. These include: the biased wording of a question, positive or negative wording, or gestures toward a specific answer, and probing answers for more information that gives off the perception that the researcher does, or does not, agree with the answer of the child. Children in their very nature want to please adults making it important that the researcher shows neutrality toward any answers given and thinks carefully about the wording of questions so as not to lead a child to a particular answer. If a child is of the belief that a researcher wants him or her to answer a specific way, or feels the researcher is not happy with the answer that has been given, then there is a tendency for the child to answer in a manner which will be designed to please the researcher. It is to this point that we decided to see if the perceived investment by the evaluator, with the two distinct roles (developer vs researcher), would have an effect on the children's responses. In this case study, there seemed to be very little difference between the two roles on the children's responses to both the survey and usability methods.

Building relationship is a vital role to reduce issues associated with satisficing, as the more comfortable children are with an evaluator, the more likely they are to provide opinions and useful feedback. Different approaches have been used to try and break down unequal power balances such as getting to know the children well before the study by working with them on nonresearch related activities (Alderson 2001), engaging in small talk (Hanna et al. 1997), playing games, and team building activities (Druin 2002), all of which are designed to get the children used to being around the adults and allow the researchers the opportunity to prove that they are not teachers and to build up a rapport with the children talking to them on their own level about their own interests. Punch (2002) notes that researchers also need to build up a rapport with the adult gatekeepers of the children and not just the children themselves.

In a study considering participatory design with children, Kam et al. (2006) found children to be extremely nervous having their class teachers present, to the extent that this hindered the different relationship the researchers were trying to build with the children. Their solution was to, politely, ask the teachers to leave the room where the study was being conducted. This issue could also be prevalent when conducting usability studies with children. However, when evaluating the involvement of teachers in usability testing, Pardo et al. (2006) found that teachers' involvement, as an obstacle in this regard, was not critical and did not inhibit children's participation. Teachers, and parents, are more likely to introduce their own biases into a study through interventions such as assisting the children to answer questions, rather than affect the relationship between the children and the researcher. It is important to ensure that it is not the views and ideas of the adult that are being recorded through the child. In the case study here the decision was made to use a quiet room within the school to minimize external influences that might bias the results.

Language skills are an important challenge, particularly when working with younger children and carrying out evaluation studies with children of different ages. Children develop their reading and writing skills at different speeds, therefore, the abilities of children of the same age group could differ significantly (Markopoulos and Bekker, 2003; Read and MacFarlane, 2006). Researchers need to ensure the language used in an evaluation is age appropriate and if necessary provide instructions in more than one format to assist and support the children as much as possible. When working with children of different age groups the gulf in ability may be sufficient to require different language and different methods to be used even though the researcher is trying to gather the same information from both. Children use language differently to adults, they use slang words and terminology that may have different meanings to adults. Listening to children interacting with each other and discussing language, and methods, with the children and their gatekeepers, can help researchers choose the right techniques to ensure children have the best chance of participating properly and provide more valid and reliable data.

When carrying out any research with children, it is important for the researchers to be flexible and creative in the methods used. Children are still developing their capacity to concentrate and therefore tasks of different size and complexity should be used with children of different age groups (Markopoulos and Bekker, 2003). There is an agreement that research studies involving children should not last too long but not on what this length of time should be. Hanna et al. (1997) state that activities should last around 30 min, which is in line with the recommendation of Barendregt et al. (2007), that they should be less than 1 hour, but ultimately not the same. There may also be instances where parts of a study require adapting or changing due to unforeseen circumstances or unexpected responses (Darbyshire et al. 2005). With children, particularly when working with (school) classes or groups, the right to participate can be equally important. It may be the case that a study requires a certain number, or sample, of children but the opportunity to take part should be given to all, even if the results from some children are not actually used. Children are used to inclusion and the exclusion of some in a group can lead to undue stress on children who are not even participating in the study. This is discussed in more detail in the next section.

Ethical Challenges

Ethical challenges are widely regarded as one of the major differences and most important factors of doing research with children as opposed to research with adults (Punch 2002). There are three major ethical factors that should be taken into account when carrying out research with children, these being informed consent, confidentially/privacy, and vulnerability, although in this research it is informed consent that we have focused on.

Informed Consent

Informed consent is a much-debated area of ethics with children. In essence, it is an agreement by the child or suitable parent/carer that they are happy to take part in a research study and that this consent has been given freely. This involves the subject, or person responsible for giving the consent, receiving as much information about the research that is taking place to be able to make an informed decision as to whether they wish to take part.

The choice to participate in a research study is quite often not down to the child themselves but comes from an adult gatekeeper (parent, teacher, etc.) who is responsible for the child at the time the research is being conducted (Mauthner 1997). Often, it is not that the child has not been given the right to choose, more that the child feels they do not have the right to refuse. At school, children are used to following instructions given by their teacher and participating in activities as a group and also at home they are used to obeying the directions of their parents (Backett-Milburn and McKie 1999).

Whether or not a child should receive the right to give their own consent often comes down to the beliefs of the researchers involved in a study with some believing that children are the property of their parents and therefore devoid of any right to choose (Morrow and Richards 1996) or not competent enough to give their consent and this must be sought by a more competent adult (Fargas-Malet et al. 2010). This view is not supported by all with more and more researchers beginning to understand the importance of giving each child the choice to take part in their research whether consent has been sought from an adult gatekeeper or not (Horton and Read 2008).

The ability to retract this consent at any time during the study should be seen as equally important as the concerns over gaining consent in the first place but is often not considered by researchers. A child should have the right to withdraw from a research study at any time whether it is because they are uncomfortable with the study or simply uninterested in continuing with it. Even if it was an adult that gave consent in the first place, the child should be able to revoke it. Often young children are uncomfortable withdrawing their consent and, particularly with younger children, it is the job of the researcher to identify when a child may wish to withdraw. Cree et al. (2002) note that when carrying out research with young children, it is possible to identify whether or not they wish to take part in the research as they are capable of showing it in different ways such as crying or refusing to engage with the research. In this case study, signs of frustration and anxiety were looked out for by the facilitator and if any signs of distress were shown then intervention would occur.

Whatever method is chosen to obtain informed consent it is the quality of the information given about the study that is most important. All involved should receive simple and concise information about the study, the participation level required, how the outcomes of the research will be used along with information about privacy and data security. It may be a case of this information being created more than once to cater for different audiences (Fargas-Malet et al. 2010). More often than not, consent gained is not "informed" appropriately, particularly with the children participating compared to their adult gatekeepers. It is for this reason that we use, and recommend, the CHECk tool (Read, Horton et al. 2013) to ensure the important issues are considered and answered truthfully. This will help address some of the many issues that can arise when conducting usability studies with children.

SOLUTIONS AND RECOMMENDATIONS

For inexperienced researchers and practitioners guidelines for carrying out usability evaluations with children have been studied and several publications offer ideas including the CHECk tool (Read, Horton et al. 2013), the book on evaluation by Markopoulos et al. (2008), and papers that include direct reference to school situations like MESS days (Horton et al. 2012). Adding to this literature and using the experience gained in conducting the studies here, evidence from previous studies, and knowledge from the literature, the following modifications to the guidelines found in Hanna et al. (1997), are proposed with the aim of helping researchers and developers carry out effective evaluations in schools.

Set Up and Planning

- It is important to know the school day, when the scheduled break times are and any other scheduled activities that may impact on the study. This will prevent children needing to stop part way through the evaluation for a scheduled break, or an in class test, for example. In the case study presented here, we had to work around a class test. This enabled us to determine the duration for each session and when children would be available during the day. It is also important to plan for the unexpected and be flexible with the schedule as there are occasional unforeseen events that will occur within the school day.

- Hanna et al. (1997) recommended to use laboratory equipment as effectively yet unobtrusively as possible and this is still important within a school. However, the equipment has become less obtrusive with cameras and MP3 dictaphones becoming smaller. Within a school setting, it is important to consider the placement of equipment as access to power sockets, for example, could lead to trip hazards with cables needing to cross busy classroom floors. It is up to the researcher to ensure the equipment is safe and not hazardous to the children.

- It is important to know the physical location that the evaluation will take place within the school. This will have an impact on the study design and whether it is feasible to use recording equipment. In this case study, the study was conducted in the library and occasionally throughout the day children would come in and out to get books. If video equipment was being used, other children may be accidently captured and this may have ethical implications, as they have not consented. People coming in and out of the room may also influence the behavior of the child during the session, distracting them, so it is important to try and minimize any disruptions.

- In the original guidelines, it is recommended that the duration of the session is 1 hour and for preschoolers this should be reduced to 30 min. The times should be influenced by the school day and in our study here and previous studies (Horton et al. 2012) we tried to keep activities to about 20 min, although other research studies have been slightly longer (Vermeeren et al. 2007). Taking children out of the class for 1 hour at time may be difficult and would require the researchers to be in school over a number of days if the whole class is to be used, which is a good practice. It is unfair if only a subset of the class get to play on the game or take part in the evaluation. There may not be a requirement to use the results from everyone but it is important the children do not feel excluded from the activity, unless of course they opt out.

- If a number of tasks are being performed then it is important the order of these is counterbalanced to avoid fatigue and any possible ordering effect (Markopoulos et al. 2008). It is also important that the tasks are in different locations in order not to distract the children, especially if one task is perceived to be more interesting or engaging than the other. In this case study, the decision was made to use Google Glass as another activity after they had performed the main study and this was conducted in a separate location.

- Most children within western schools will have some experience of computers, for example, a European Commission report found that there are between 3 and 7 children for every computer in a school and 9 out of 10 children are in schools with broadband (European Commission 2013), so screening for computer experience may not always be necessary. It may be important to screen children in certain situations, for example, if they had played a particular game before as this could influence the results (Sim and Cassidy 2013). Screening may also help identify which children are likely to verbalize problems (Barendregt et al. 2007). Children should not be omitted from a study due to their expertise, or lack of it, unless the study specifically requires it.

- A checklist can be used to ensure that you take all the equipment that is required to the school, including data capture forms and pens (Markopoulos et al. 2008). It is sensible to have backup or spare kit just in case the laptop breaks down or runs out of power for example. Within this study, we were reliant on the battery of one of the laptops and the Google Glasses. When the equipment is not in use for a period such as school breaks, then the equipment should be charged.

- The CHECk tool could be used to help consider any ethical implications for the study and how this could be communicated to the children. This should be completed at the planning stage.

Introduction

- It may be easier to explain the ethics, any confidentiality agreements, and consent before the session starts to the whole class (Read, Sim et al. 2013), however, this is not always possible. In the study presented here this was our original intension but was not feasible on the day therefore the discussion took place on a one to one basis.

- It is important to establish a relationship with the child when you first meet, asking them their name and having some small talk is recommended as a good way to put them at ease (Hanna et al. 1997).

- Having a script to introduce the children to the evaluation process is important to ensure all the children are getting the same information. It is not possible to account for all the possible questions that children may ask, but it is important to answer these ensuring that the child understands and is comfortable taking part in the study. It has been recommended not to refer too strictly to the protocol (Barendregt and Bekker 2005) to ensure you sound natural.

- Try and motivate the child and highlight their importance in this process (Hanna et al. 1997). Younger children are often highly motivated because they are doing something new, and in the context of this study they get to play games, which is usually a motivational factor (Habgood and Ainsworth 2011).

- If any equipment is being used to record audio or video, children should be informed of this and be told how the data will be used (Read, Sim et al. 2013). These devices can sometimes be embedded within the equipment, for example, a laptop with a webcam could be used to capture the children during an evaluation. It is important that the children are made aware of this prior to the study.

- It is usually good practice to have a facilitator present to explain the purpose of the study, help the children if they have any difficulties with the technology or software irrespective of their age or experience (Markopoulos et al. 2008). For example, in this study a number of children accidentally opened the Flash menu and needed assistance. Having a facilitator present to fix and explain this type of issue would help alleviate any anxieties or fears of breaking damaging the game or technology.

During the Study

- If the child really does not know what to do, it is then useful to intervene. This will alleviate any stress or anxiety and enable them to continue playing the game. In this study, a number of children struggled on the first screen and also did not know how to double jump. They were told the actions by the facilitator to enable them to play the game, it is important that the child has a positive experience and if they are showing signs of confusion then you should ask them if they are ok. These problems can be recorded through observation so there effects on a study can be documented.

- If children cannot understand the information on the screen, or read the, words, then it is advisable to read them out or rephrase if asked. In the guidelines proposed by Barendregt and Bekker (2005), they suggest that children should be encouraged to try and read the instructions and Edwards and Benedyk (2007) also suggest that the facilitator should read out all the instructions.

- Hanna et al. (1997) suggested that you should not ask the children if they want to play the game again as this presents them with an opportunity to say no. Saying no should be a perfectly acceptable response. If a task is enjoyable to the child then they will want to do it again, they should not be forced or feel pressured to participate in the study. In this case, the last child struggled to play the game and it was apparent after the second try that they were not enjoying the game and they wanted to stop, so at this point, the facilitator ended the session having confirmed with the child that they wanted to stop.

- Try and encourage the child to remain on task if they are looking around or appear distracted. It is important to take into account the fact they might be looking around due to anxiety and want to stop participating in the task or study. It is the facilitator's job to recognize the reasons for a distracted child and deal with this in the appropriate manner.

Finishing Up

- Once the child has finished participating in a study then you should present them with any survey questions (Hanna et al. 1997). For young children it might be useful to read out the questions and complete the forms for them. In this study, the questions and information were read out to the children and a method that has proved useful in other studies (Sim et al. 2013).

- Once complete you should thank the child for their help, explain to the child what the data collected will be used for, and reconfirm that they are happy for you to use it (Markopoulos et al. 2008). The children may have given consent at the beginning before they understood the process and therefore it is good practice to ask again at the end.

- Once the activity is complete you can escort the child back to the classroom or to another activity. Once the session has finished and all the children have completed the evaluation, you should go into the classroom to thank all the children again for their assistance and thank the teachers.

- When possible you should share the findings of the study with the children so they understand how their input has helped in the design of the game or product (Read, Horton et al. 2013). It might be that you go back to the school at a later date with a new version of the game for the children to play.

CONCLUSIONS

The case study aimed to examine the usability of an educational game. A variety of methods was used to explore whether satisficing was an issue dependent upon the role of the facilitator and understand ethical issues. In total, 25 children took part in the study over the course of a day. Direct observation was used along with an adaptation of the retrospective think aloud method to capture usability problems within a game. A similar number of usability problems was documented in both methods but approximately 50% of the problems were unique to a single method, suggesting that multiple evaluation methods may be necessary to capture all the problems. However, a large number of the problems that were unique to a specific method were only observed or reported by one child. Using the Fun Toolkit to capture satisfaction metrics, the children reported a positive experience of playing the game despite the observed problems. It is unclear whether the children were being overly generous in their scores, given the fact that all of the children experienced some difficulty in playing the game and no one actually completed the level. From our experience of conducting usability evaluations within a school context, guidelines were produced that complement and update the existing guidelines present in the literature. Researchers or practitioners could use these guidelines to help plan and carry out usability evaluation studies within a school context.

REFERENCES

Alderson, P. 2001. Research by children. *International Journal of Social Research Methodology* 4 (2):139–153.

Als, B.S., J.J. Jensen, and M.B. Skov. 2005. Comparison of think-aloud and constructive interaction in usability testing with children. *Proceedings of the 2005 Conference on Interaction Design and Children*, Boulder, Colorado, pp. 9–16.

Backett-Milburn, K. and L. McKie. 1999. A critical appraisal of the draw and write technique. *Health Education Research* 14 (3):387–398.

Barendregt, W. and M.M. Bekker. 2005. Extended guidelines for usability (and fun) testing with children. *Proceedings of SIGCHI Conference*, The Hague, the Netherlands.

Barendregt, W. and M.M. Bekker. 2006. Developing a coding scheme for detecting usability and fun problems in computer games for young children. *Behavior Research Methods* 38 (3):382–389.

Barendregt, W., M. Bekker, and E. Baauw. 2008. Development and evaluation of the problem identification picture cards method. *Cognition, Technology and Work* 10 (2):95–105.

Barendregt, W., M. Bekker, D.G. Bouwhuis, and E. Baauw. 2007. Predicting effectiveness of children participants in user testing based on personality characteristics. *Behaviour & Information Technology* 26 (2):133–147.

Buckingham, D. 2009. Creative' visual methods in media research: Possibilities, problems and proposals. *Media, Culture & Society* 31 (4):633–652.

Commission, European. 2013. *Survey of Schools: ICT in Education.* Belguim: European Commission.

Cree, V.E., H. Kay, and K. Tisdall. 2002. Research with children: Sharing the dilemmas. *Child & Family Social Work* 7 (1):47–56.

Darbyshire, P., C. MacDougall, and W. Schiller. 2005. Multiple methods in qualitative research with children: More insight or just more? *Qualitative Research* 5 (4):417–436.

Desurvire, H., J. Kondziela, and M. Atwood. 1992. What is gained or lost when using evaluation methods other than empirical testing. *Proceedings of CHI*, Monterey, pp. 125–126.

Diah, N.M., M. Ismail, S. Ahmad, and M.K.M. Dahari. 2010. Usability testing for educational computer game using observation method. *Information Retrieval & Knowledge Management*, Shah Alam, Selangor.

Donker, A. and P. Reitsma. 2004. Usability testing with children. *Interaction Design and Children*, Maryland.

Druin, A. 2002. The role of children in the design of new technology. *Behaviour & Information Technology* 21 (1):1–25.

Dufour, T, V. Pellarrey, P. Chagnon, A. Majdoubi, T. Torregrossa, V. Nachbaur, C. Li, R.I. Cortes, J. Clermont, and F. Dumas. 2014. ASCENT: A first person mountain climbing game on the oculus rift. *Proceedings of the First ACM SIGCHI Annual Symposium on Computer–Human Interaction in Play*, Toronto, Canada, pp. 335–338.

Edwards, H. and R. Benedyk. 2007. A comparison of usability evaluation methods for child participants in a school setting. *International Conference on Interaction Design and Children*, Aalborg, Denmark, pp. 9–16.

Fargas-Malet, M., D. McSherry, E. Larkin, and C. Robinson. 2010. Research with children: Methodological issues and innovative techniques. *Journal of Early Childhood Research* 8 (2):175–192.

Habgood, M.P.J. and S.E. Ainsworth. 2011. Motivating children to learn effectively: Exploring the value of intrinsic integration in educational games. *The Journal of the Learning Sciences* 20 (2):169–206.

Hanna, L., K. Risden, and K.J. Alexander. 1997. Guidelines for usability testing with children. *Interactions* 4 (5):9–14.

Hartson, H.R., T.S. Andre, and R.C. Williges. 2003. Criteria for evaluating usability evaluation methods. *International Journal Human–Computer Interaction* 15 (1):145–181.

Hertzum, M. and N.E. Jacobsen. 2001. The evaluator effect: A chilling fact about usability evaluation methods. *International Journal of Human–Computer Interaction* 13 (4):421–443.

Horton, M. and J.C. Read. 2008. Interactive whiteboards in the living room?—Asking children about their technologies. *22nd British HCI Conference*, Liverpool.

Horton, M., J.C. Read, E. Mazzone, G. Sim, and D. Fitton. 2012. School friendly participatory research activities with children. *CHI 12 Extend Abstracts*, Austin, Texas.

Hoysniemi, J., P. Hamalainen, and L. Turkki. 2003. Using peer tutoring in evaluating the usability of a physically interactive computer game with children. *Interacting with Computers* 15 (2):203–225.

Jensen, J.J. and M.B. Skov. 2005. A review of research methods in children's technology design. *Proceedings of the 2005 Conference on Interaction Design and Children*, Boulder, Colorado, pp. 80–87.

Kam, M., D. Ramachandran, A. Raghavan, J. Chiu, U. Sahni, and J. Canny. 2006. Practical considerations for participatory design with rural school children in underdeveloped regions: Early reflections from the field. *Proceedings of the 2006 Conference on Interaction Design and Children*, Tampere, Finland, pp. 25–32.

Kesteren, I.E.H. van, M.M. Bekker, A.P.O.S. Vermeeren, and P.A. Lloyd. 2003. Assessing usability evaluation methods on their effectiveness to elicit verbal comments from children subjects. *Proceedings of the 2003 Conference on Interaction Design and Children*, Preston, England, pp. 41–49.

Khanum, M.A. and M.C. Trivedi. 2013. Comparison of testing environments with children for usability problem identification. *International Journal of Engineering and Technology* 5 (3): 2048–2053.

Kjeldskov, J., M.B. Skov, and J. Stage. 2004. Instant data analysis: Conducting usability evaluations in a day. *Proceedings of the Third Nordic Conference on Human–Computer Interaction*, Tampere, Finland, pp. 233–240.

Laurillard, D. 2002. *Rethinking University Teaching: A Conversational Framework for the Effective Use of Learning Technologies*, 2nd edition. London: Routledge.

LeMay, S., T. Costantino, S. O'Connor, and E. ContePitcher. 2014. Screen time for children. *Proceedings of the 2014 Conference on Interaction Design and Children*, Aarhus, Denmark, pp. 217–220.

Markopoulos, P. and M. Bekker. 2003. On assessment of usability testing methods for children. *Interacting with Computers* 15:227–243.

Markopoulos, P., J.C. Read, S. MacFarlane, and J. Hoysniemi. 2008. *Evaluating Children's Interactive Products: Principles and Practices for Interaction Designers*. San Francisco: Morgan Kaufmann.

Mauthner, M. 1997. Methodological aspects of collecting data from children: Lessons from three research projects. *Children & Society* 11 (1):16–28.

Morrow, V. and Richards, M. 1996. The ethics of social research with children: An overview. *Children & Society* 10 (2):90–105.

Nielsen, J. and T.K. Landauer. 1993. A mathematical model of the finding of usability problems. *Proceedings of the SIGCHI Conference on Human Factors in Computing Systems*, 206–213. Amsterdam, Netherlands: ACM Press.

Pardo, S., F. Vetere, and S. Howard. 2006. Teachers' involvement in usability testing with children. *Proceedings of the 2006 Conference on Interaction Design and Children*, Tampere, Finland, pp. 89–92.

Punch, S. 2002. Research with children the same or different from research with adults? *Childhood* 9 (3):321–341.

Read, J.C. 2008. Validating the Fun Toolkit: An instrument for measuring children's opinion of technology. *Cognition, Technology and Work* 10 (2):119–128.

Read, J.C. 2012. Evaluating artefacts with children: Age and technology effects in the reporting of expected and experienced fun. *14th ACM International Conference on Multimodal Interaction*, Santa Monica.

Read, J.C. and K. Fine. 2005. Using survey methods for design and evaluation in child computer interaction. *Interact 2005*, Rome.

Read, J.C., M. Horton, G. Sim, P. Gregory, D. Fitton, and B. Cassidy. 2013. CHECk: A tool to inform and encourage ethical practice in participatory design with children. *CHI '13 Extended Abstracts on Human Factors in Computing Systems*, Paris, France.

Read, J.C. and S. MacFarlane. 2006. Using the Fun Toolkit and other survey methods to gather opinions in child computer interaction. *Interaction Design and Children*, Tampere.

Read, J.C., G. Sim, P. Gregory, D. Xu, and J.B. Ode. 2013. Children designing serious games. *EAI Endorese Transactions on Serious Games* 13 (1):e5.

Sears, A. 1997. Heuristic walkthroughs: Finding the problems without the noise. *International Journal Human–Computer Interaction* 9:213–234.

Sim, G. 2012. Designing the anti-heuristic game: A game which violates heuristics. *11th International Conference on Interaction Design and Children*, Bremen, Germany.

Sim, G. and B. Cassidy. 2013. Investigating the fidelity effect when evaluating game prototypes with children. *Proceedings of the 27th International BCS Human Computer Interaction Conference*, London, UK, pp. 1–6.

Sim, G., B. Cassidy, and J.C. Read. 2013. Understanding the fidelity effect when evaluating games with children. *Interaction Design and Children*, New York.

Sim, G. and M. Horton. 2012. Investigating children's opinions of games: Fun Toolkit vs This or That. *Interaction Design and Children*, Bremen, Germany.

Sim, G., S. MacFarlane, and M. Horton. 2005. Evaluating usability, fun and learning in educational software for children. *World Conference on Educational Multimedia, Hypermedia and Telecommunications*, Montreal.

Van Mechelen, M., G. Sim, B. Zaman, P. Gregory, K. Slegers, and M. Horton. 2014. Applying the CHECk tool to participatory design sessions with children. *Proceedings of the 2014 Conference on Interaction Design and Children*, Aarhus, Denmark, pp. 253–256.

Vermeeren, A., M.M. Bekker, I.E.H. van Kesteren, and H. de Ridder. 2007. Experiences with structured interviewing of children during usability tests. *Proceedings of the 21st British HCI Group Annual Conference on People and Computers: HCI…but not as we know it—Volume 1*, University of Lancaster, United Kingdom.

Vissers, J., L. De Bot, and B. Zaman. 2013. MemoLine: Evaluating long-term UX with children. *Proceedings of the 12th International Conference on Interaction Design and Children*, New York, pp. 285–288.

Zaman, B. 2009. *Introduction and Validation of a Pairwise Comparison Scale for UX Evaluations and Benchmarking with Preschoolers*. Interact, Uppsala.

Zaman, B., V.V. Abeele, and D. De Grooff. 2013. Measuring product liking in preschool children: An evaluation of the Smileyometer and This or That methods. *International Journal of Child–Computer Interaction* 1 (2):61–70.

LIST OF ADDITIONAL SOURCES

Journal of Children Computer Interaction http://www.journals.elsevier.com/international-journal-of-child-computer-interaction/.

IFIP Working Group on Interaction Design and Children (Online Resource) http://www.idc-sig.org/.

Evaluating Children's Interactive Products (Book) https://www.elsevier.com/books/evaluating-childrens-interactive-products/markopoulos/978-0-12-374111-0.

Interaction Design Foundation (Online Resource) https://www.interaction-design.org.

Guidelines for Successful Online Resource: Mobile Interactive Apps for Children (Video) http://www.gdcvault.com/play/1015634/Guidelines-for-Successful-Mobile-Interactive.

Guidelines for Usability Testing with Kids and Teens (Online Resource) http://www.usability.gov/get-involved/blog/2015/02/working-with-kids-and-teens.html.

Game Usability (Book) https://www.crcpress.com/product/isbn/9780123744470.

Designing Games for Children Developmental, Usability, and Design Considerations for Making Games for Kids (Book) http://www.tandf.net/books/details/9781315851259/.

ChiCI Group (Online Resource) http://www.chici.org/.

Testing by Teaching: Peer Tutoring, a Usability Evaluation Method for Children (Online Resource) http://uxpamagazine.org/testing-by-teaching/.

BIOGRAPHIES

Gavin Sim is a senior lecturer in human computer interaction at the University of Central Lancashire. His research interests are in the board area of human–computer interaction and child–computer interaction where he is a member of the ChiCI group. His main research areas are in usability, user experience, and interaction design with over 50 peer-reviewed publications in this area. He is the secretary of the British Computer Society Interaction Group, was co-chair for the British HCI Conference in 2014, and will be co-chair of the 2016 Interaction Design and Children Conference. He actively reviews for a wide range of journals and conferences relating to HCI and Educational Technology.

Janet C. Read is a professor of Child Computer Interaction (CCI) at the ChiCI group at the University of Central Lancashire in Preston, UK. She has a general research interest in understanding how best to design and evaluate interactive technologies for children and has authored the textbook *Evaluating Interactive Technologies for and with Children* as well as organized a series of courses and master's classes across the globe on doing research, design, and evaluation with children. She is the editor in chief of the *International Journal for Child Computer Interaction* and also the chair of the IFIP TC13 Working Group on Interaction Design and Children. Her most cited work is work relating to measuring fun and the associated "Fun Toolkit" is the single most used evaluation tool in CCI.

Matthew Horton is a lecturer in computing at the University of Central Lancashire. He specializes in organizing and carrying out design sessions with children and in gathering information about technology use from children in a way that is robust and reliable. He is a member of the Child Computer Interaction Group (ChiCI Group), secretary of the TC13-IFIP Working Group on Interaction Design and Children, and co-chair of the 2016 Interaction Design and Children Conference. He has over 50 peer-reviewed publications in CCI and HCI and is a regular reviewer for leading conferences and journals in this field.

KEY TERMS AND DEFINITIONS

Child computer interaction: ChiCI is an area of scientific investigation that concerns the phenomena surrounding the interaction between children and computational and communication technologies.

Direct observation: Relies on an individual observing and documenting a user interacting with a system or product.

Ethics has many definitions and interpretations: Ethics is associated with ensuring protocols and processes are in place to protect participants, researchers, and their affiliations.

Fun Toolkit: Is a set of child-appropriate survey tools designed to measure the construct of Fun. This consists of three tools: the Smileyometer, Again Again table, and the Fun Sorter.

Retrospective think aloud: A retrospective thinking aloud test is an adaption to the think aloud method where you ask test participants to use the system while continuously thinking out loud. The retrospective think aloud asks the participants to recall their thoughts whilst watching a video or viewing the system after the interaction.

Usability: ISO 9241 defines usability as the "Extent to which a product can be used by specified users to achieve specified goals with effectiveness, efficiency, and satisfaction in a specified context of use."

User experience: ISO 9241-210 defines user experience, or UX, as "a person's perceptions and responses that result from the use or anticipated use of a product, system, or service."

CHAPTER 2

You Are Not the Player

*Teaching Games User Research
to Undergraduate Students*

Cynthia Putnam, José P. Zagal, and Jinghui Cheng

CONTENTS

EXECUTIVE SUMMARY

Games user research (GUR) has become an important part of designing and developing games. We present a case study of an 11-week undergraduate course focused on GUR, titled "Game Usability and Playtesting," taught at DePaul University, Chicago, Illinois. The course was designed to provide students with the opportunity to practice and develop skills in GUR as it is done in industry; methods discussed and practiced include competitive review, heuristic evaluation, usability, and GUR playtesting.

While the course has been generally well received by students, we have made some modifications after teaching the course three times to address major challenges, including: (a) creating templates to scaffold student writing of research findings (see the Appendices); (b) developing tools and methods to help with recruitment and scheduling for GUR playtesting; and (c) reducing class and project team size.

This case study is intended to be a nuts-and-bolts discussion aimed at instructors to help them set up an undergraduate GUR class (and lab) at their institutions. As such, we describe our equipment and labs, game selection, the week-by-week course curriculum, and recommendations to address some of the challenges we have encountered.

ORGANIZATION BACKGROUND

DePaul University's College of Computing and Digital Media houses both graduate and undergraduate games programs. The graduate game program, focused on computer game development, started in 2009 with one student and has grown to 62 students (32% American minorities, 16% foreign students, and 6% female) in the 2014–2015 school year. The undergraduate program, started in 2007 with 137 students and has grown to 332 students (28% American minorities, 3% foreign, and 10% female) in the 2014–2015 school year. The undergraduate program has three concentrations: (1) Systems programing which is focused on the internals of computer games, including game engines; (2) Gameplay programming which focuses on level design, game scripting, computer graphics development, game physics, and artificial intelligence programming; and (3) Game design where students focus on ideation and iteration through the creation of multiple playable game builds (including prototypes). The GUR course, targeted at 3rd year undergraduate students ("juniors" in the US higher education system), has been required for the Game Design concentration since 2012. The course is now offered twice a year and, as of this writing, has been taught three times by two of this chapter's authors.

INTRODUCTION

We present a case study of an 11-week undergraduate course focused on GUR, titled "Game Usability and Playtesting," taught at DePaul University, Chicago, Illinois; this chapter is an extension and elaboration of previous work (Zagal and Putnam 2013; Putnam and Zagal 2014). Broadly, GUR is concerned with the systematic measurement of players' behaviors and opinions in order to evaluate and gain insights that can be used to improve the design of games (El-Nasr et al. 2012); i.e., the goal is to collect unbiased data to provide better player experiences. We argue that an understanding of GUR has become more important in recent years to prepare students to work in and contribute to the game industry. One key reason for emphasizing GUR is that videogames are enjoyed by a diversity of people and there are increasingly more types of games to meet this wider audience. For example, a recent report by the Entertainment Software Association (ESA) noted that "women age 18 or older represent a significantly greater portion of the game-playing population (36%) than boys age 18 or younger (17%)" (ESA 2014). In other words, it is no longer the case that students will be expected to design and develop games that should appeal to stereotypical game players (i.e., players much like themselves), and will need to have the tools to understand their audiences (Sotamaa et al. 2005; Jørgensen 2011).

Unlike productivity tools, in which users are expected to produce tangible outcomes (e.g., reports), the user outcome of playing a game is usually entirely experiential (Pagulayan et al. 2003). Accordingly, user experience (UX) considerations are quite different in games; e.g., while productivity tool UX is concerned with decreasing the challenges of use, successful games require an understanding of the appropriate level of challenge for their intended audience (Pagulayan et al. 2003; Jørgensen 2004). By helping games achieve an optimized player experience, GUR affords greater player enjoyment. Examples of GUR improving games include Thompson's (2007) description of how Microsoft Studios User Research improved the UX of Halo 3 (Thompson 2007). Good UX also leads to better reviews and higher ratings. That is, product reviews have a significant effect on videogame sales (Zhu and Zhang 2006) and games with the best reviews (highest rated) were those with fewer reported usability problems (Bromley 2014).

GUR is a growing concern in industry because of the relationship between a game's success and the use of GUR methods. For example, the 2014 game industry's flagship event, Game Developers Conference (GDC), featured several talks on game user research (e.g., Griffiths 2014; Henderson 2014; Livingston 2014). In further evidence, the GUR special interest group (SIG) of the IGDA has over 900 members on Linkedin (GUR SIG of the IGDA) and their own dedicated conference titled "Games User Research Summit," which was started in 2009 (see http://www.gamesuserresearchsig.org).

To summarize, there are three reasons for including GUR in students' game design and development education: (1) it helps game creators better understand their widening audiences; (2) it leads to better and more successful games; and therefore (3) it is a growing concern in industry. In this chapter, we share materials we have created and knowledge gained through teaching our GUR course three times over 3 years. We will present syllabi, lab design details, challenges we have encountered, student responses to the course, and how we iterated upon and improved the course to address challenges and student input. This case study is intended as a nuts-and-bolts discussion aimed at instructors to help them set-up a GUR class (and lab) at their institutions.

CASE STUDY DESCRIPTION (COURSE DESCRIPTION)

The course was designed as an "authentic learning" experience (Shaffer and Resnick 1999); i.e., we were concerned with (a) making the course personally meaningful to students; (b) ensuring it related to the real-world outside school; (c) providing opportunities for students to think about GUR in multiple ways; and (d) using means of assessment that reflected the learning process. Specifically, we wanted to ensure students tested professionally produced games and used software and equipment common in industry. We also wanted to provide students with the opportunity to practice and develop skills in GUR as it is done in industry. As such, we designed the course to be hands-on; i.e., focused more on performing evaluations than on reporting findings. In the next sections, we describe course details, equipment and labs, game selection, and the topics and methods covered.

Course Details

There are two prerequisites for the course: (1) basic statistics and (2) certification of training in the ethical concerns of conducting research with human subjects (e.g., a CITI certificate, see https://www.citiprogram.org). The course meets once a week for 3 hours with a 15-minute break. The term is 10 weeks long with an additional 11th week for exams. We have used two texts: (1) *Handbook of Usability Testing* by Rubin and Chisnell (2008) and (2) *Game Usability* by Isbister and Schaffer (2008). We supplement the text readings with other academic and industry/trade articles (e.g., Fulton 2002; Pagulayan et al. 2003; Lazzaro 2004; Spanner 2006).

There are three primary course objectives, giving students the opportunity to: (1) acquire knowledge of several methods used to evaluate games, which includes an understanding of their strengths and weaknesses and when each method is ideally used in the development cycle; (2) have hands-on experience performing four common GUR methods (competitive review, heuristic evaluation, usability, and GUR playtesting); and (3) learn and practice how to present research findings effectively.

Equipment and Labs

We use two labs for the course in the College of Computing and Digital Media's main building located in the Loop Campus in downtown Chicago. One is focused on GUR playtesting, and the other is used by multiple courses for usability and other game play studies.

GUR Playtest Lab

The GUR lab consists of 10 playtest/usability stations separated by movable dividers (see Figure 2.1). Each station consists of an Xbox360 Console, a Mac Mini running Bootcamp for

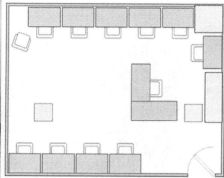

FIGURE 2.1   GUR playtest lab.

Windows 7, a monitor, HDMI switch, and headphones; all computers have Morae Recorder installed. Morae is a software designed for UX and market research and is comprised of three primary components: (1) "Recorder" that records users actions on a desktop and can also be set up to record users' facial expressions and verbalizations; (2) "Observer" where members of the research team can observe a session, log details about a session, and send surveys (although Recorder can be set-up to automatically serve surveys); and (3) "Manager" where researchers can combine data from Recorder and Observer (for more see Techsmith's website at http://www.techsmith.com/morae.html). In our lab, one station has a game screen capture device installed between the Xbox and the computer for usability. This set-up allows students to monitor game play in the usability lab through the screen capture device, which is set to monitor game play (not record). However, because the screen capture device combined with Morae causes gameplay lag, we have the research participant play the game through the Xbox display; i.e., the computer is monitoring and projecting the slower gameplay images to the observers in the upstairs lab, but the participant does not experience any of the lag.

Usability and Game Play Lab

The usability and motion game lab (see Figure 2.2) includes a living room set-up (large screen TV, couch, coffee table, etc.), adjustable cameras on tripods, and two workstations. We have multiple game consoles set up for group and motion gaming, including Xbox One with Kinect, Nintendo Wii U, and Sony PlayStation 4. The workstations and large TV are configured for remote viewing (through Morae Observer) of any of the stations in the GUR playtest lab. Both workstations in the usability and gameplay lab have Morae Manager installed.

Game Selection

Since we could not assume access to games currently under development, we realized that we would have to use commercially available games. However, we needed to select titles that were "big" enough to provide rich-opportunities for formulating research questions, but were also somewhat obscure so as to minimize the chance that students would have significant prior experience with the games used in class; i.e., we wanted to minimize the chance that students would be biased by their prior knowledge and experience. As a rule of thumb,

FIGURE 2.2   Usability and game play lab.

we decided to use relatively recent (<10 years old) mainstream commercial games that were not high-profile releases and whose review scores were average (6–7 on a 10-point scale). For practical (time and scheduling) reasons, we also tried to select games that were quickly playable upon start-up—providing plenty of gameplay in the first 30 minutes. This tended to rule out story and cut-scene heavy games (e.g., many role-playing games (RPGs)). We note that an ideal game for learning about GUR is probably not the same as a poorly rated buggy game. Our rationale for choosing average games is that students need to have the opportunity to tease out subtle problems or issues. Our ideal game, therefore, was one with several issues (targetable by different teams of students), but not so many as to be overwhelming.

Other considerations included platform (our labs were set up with Xbox 360s), availability (we wanted 10 copies because our lab has 10 stations), and cost (we aimed for under US $10 each). Additionally, to maximize recruitment, we desired games that did not require specialized knowledge. Games that have worked well include:

"Baja: Edge of Control" (THQ 2008), "Homefront" (THQ 2011), "Lost Planet: Extreme Condition" (Capcom 2007), and "Star Wars; Force Unleashed" (LucasArts 2008). Games requiring too much specialized knowledge include games in the Madden Football series (Electronic Arts 2000–2016) and "World Series of Poker: Tournament of Champions" (Activision 2006).

Topics and Methods Covered

People who practice GUR use multiple (and evolving) research methods; in the course, we focus on specific variations of four methods (1) competitive reviews; (2) heuristic evaluation; (3) summative usability; and (4) GUR playtesting. Students are introduced to the methods following a four-part schedule: (1) introduction, early methods, and statistics review (2 weeks), (2) summative usability (3 weeks), (3) GUR playtesting (3 weeks); and (4) guest speakers, final presentations, course review and a final (3 weeks). Throughout the course, the students are working in groups and iterating the same report by adding findings from each new method; see appendices for the reporting templates.

Part One: Introduction, Early Methods, and Statistics Review (Two Weeks)
In the first week of the course, students form teams. We have learned that three-person teams are ideal (see challenges and solutions for more discussion on team size). Students are first asked to either (a) form their team on their own or (b) identify as a free agent. All student names are then drawn from a hat; if their name is selected they choose the game that they would like to work on for the quarter. They are encouraged to select a game they are not familiar with. If a free agent's name is drawn, then other free agents are asked to join that team. Each team then selects a team captain.

In the introductory class, we also emphasize the need for GUR; we approach this by conducting an activity to reinforce the human–computer interaction mantra "you are not your user," or in this case "you are not the player" (Norman 2013). Students take the Myers–Briggs type indicator survey which places people into one of sixteen temperament types based on four dichotomies: (1) introversion (I) versus extroversion (E); (2) how people take on information as either a sensor (S) (e.g., someone who needs tends to base decisions more empirically through their senses) or as an intuitor (N) (e.g., someone who follows their intuition); (3) how people make decision as either a thinker (T) (detached and objective) or as a feeler (F) (attached and subjective); and (4) how people manage their life activities as either a judger (J) (having a definite plan of action) or as a perceiver (P) (being more adaptable and open to serendipity) (Bates and Keirsey 1984). Therefore, someone who tests as an introvert-sensor-thinker-judger would be considered an ISTJ. We then use work presented by Bateman and Boon (2006) that associated Myers–Briggs temperament types with game play habits through a cluster analysis using data from over 400 participants; the findings resulted in the DGD1 (Demographic Game Design 1) model (Bateman and Boon 2006). The DGD1 model describes four general play types:

1. **Conquer** who finds winning to be the most important goal and enjoys first-person shooters (FPSs) and RPGs. This type includes all ISTJ, introversion, intuition, thinking, judgment (INTJ), extraversion, sensing, thinking, judgment (ESTJ), and extraversion, intuition, thinking, judgments (ENTJs).

2. **Manager** who prefer mastering the game and learning how to play well (not necessarily winning). This type includes introversion, sensing, thinking, perception (ISTP), introversion, intuition, thinking, perception (INTP), extraversion, intuition, thinking, perception (ENTP), and extraversion, sensing, thinking, perceptions (ESTPs).

3. **Wanderer** who enjoys exploration and includes introversion, intuition, feeling, perception (INFP), extraversion, intuition, feeling, perception (ENFP), introversion, sensing, feeling, perception (ISFP), and extrovert, sensing, feeling, perception (ESFP) types.

4. **Participant** who prefers to watch the game and includes extraversion, sensing, feeling, judgment (ESFJ), introversion, sensing, feeling, judging (ISFJ), extraversion, intuition, feeling, judgment (ENFJ), and introversion, intuition, feeling, judging (INFJ) types.

By having the students identify their own play type, and then presenting play types unlike themselves, we hope to reinforce the need for GUR and encourage enthusiasm about the course.

In the first week's homework (and first assignment), students are asked to perform a competitive review. Specifically, they are asked to (a) identify the major competition for the game, (b) determine dimensions they will use to compare the competitors to their game, e.g., graphics quality might be a dimension, and (c) compare the competitors to their game. See Appendix A for a template of the report students are asked to complete.

The second week of class takes place in a computer lab for a statistics review. Major topics include descriptive statistics (e.g., measures of centrality), how to create simple bar graphs using Excel, and how to perform univariate tests for group comparisons (which they are required to do later in the quarter in their playtest reports). We discuss both parametric tests (t-tests and ANOVAs) and nonparametric tests (Kruskal–Wallis and Mann–Whitney U).

We also present a lecture about heuristic evaluations. In a heuristic evaluation, a user researcher analyzes a user interface and interaction design through the lens of a list of best practices, i.e., a sort of checklist of known usability issues (Nielson 1993). We start by discussion the most well-known set of heuristics; these are the 10 heuristics Jakob Nielson created primarily for productivity tools (Nielson 1993; Nielson 2015). However, many game-centric heuristics have also been developed to better address games. Game heuristics focus on different attributes than those in productivity tools, e.g., pace, game mechanics, heads up display, and gameplay. Game-specific heuristics we discuss include: (a) Federoff's 40 heuristics covering three categories (interface, mechanics, and play; Federoff 2002), (b) Heuristic evaluation for Playability (HEP), which includes 43 heuristics in four categories (play, story, mechanics, and usability; Desurvire et al. 2004), and (c) Schaffer's heuristics from the textbook which includes 29 heuristics over three categories (general, GUI, play; Isbister and Schaffer 2008).

As their homework for the second week, students are expected to do a heuristic evaluation of their game individually, and then combine their findings with their teammates'. The writing template (see Appendix B) includes a summary table that follows the format presented in the textbook (Isbister and Schaffer 2008); see Table 2.1 for a student example. The report is added on to the competitive review previously submitted; students are expected to iterate on their competitive reviews based on instructor feedback.

TABLE 2.1   Student Example of Summary Table of a Heuristic Finding

Heuristic	Provide clear goals, present overriding goal early as well as short-term goals throughout play
Severity	Important
Description	The game does not provide clear goals. While the game describes what the possible goals are, it is hard to find the current goal because players must search for the goal on a cluttered screen
Actionable recommendation	Clearly shows what the goal is prior to the start of the race

Part Two: Usability (Three Weeks)

In week three we introduce usability. We emphasize that in the context of games, usability is about player behavior and understanding (not opinions). Research questions in usability might include, can the player equip their weapon? Or does the player understand how to navigate through the level? Students are instructed to use the findings of their heuristic evaluation to write their research questions. We include a mix of lecture and workshops to instruct and prepare students to conduct their own usability tasks.

In this course, we focus on teaching task-based summative usability tests. This method requires participants to complete a set of required tasks; while tasks vary from game to game, an example initial task might be to modify your player character or set up closed captioning.

To introduce the concept of usability, students list out what a player must understand and be able to do to successfully play their game; i.e., the tasks that are required to play the game. We use the example of Tetris to help students understand these concepts; for example in Tetris, a player must understand how to rotate blocks and know which buttons they need to press to rotate a block clockwise and counter-clockwise.

We also model a think-aloud protocol (TaP) in the classroom; in TaP participants are asked to tell moderators what they are thinking as they complete tasks (Nielson 2014). To give the students hands-on practice as participants and moderators, students work in two-person teams with one student playing the part of the usability participant and the other the moderator. The student in the "participant role" is tasked with recreating a Lego object from a picture of a finished object and to practice think aloud. Meantime, the student playing the "moderator role" is tasked with identifying difficulties in recreating the Lego object and encouraging the participant to think aloud. The students then switch the roles. The Lego objects we used were a turtle and a guitar; both can be built using 20–30 bricks.

Much of the third week's class is focused on helping students create their test plan. Again, we created templates for them to use (see Appendix C); the template is adapted from the Rubin and Chisnell 2008 textbook. Sections include: (1) their objectives for conducting the usability test; (2) their research questions; (3) the measure they will collect (e.g., number of errors, nature of the errors, and/or points of confusion); (4) recruitment inclusion and exclusion criteria; and (5) and the study procedures (consent, pretest interview, performing the tasks, posttest debrief).

Students work in their groups to create all of their test materials, including their set of tasks using the template. Students are expected to use the same consent form that DePaul University requires for exempt studies. We also discuss the dos and don'ts of moderating usability tests; e.g., the participant is not being tested, do not rescue the participant (except as a last resort), and react to "mistakes" as you would "correct" behavior.

In the fourth week of class (week two of the usability section) we meet in the playtest lab to have students set up their tests and survey questions in Morae. We then have students practice setting up their tests. Teams are expected to trial one task as the rest of the class observes.

In the fifth week, each team reserves the labs for one day to conduct three to five usability tests; there is no class meeting. All students are required to participate in another group's usability test and receive extra credit for participating in more than one study. Students submit their usability report (which is added to the competitive review and heuristic evaluation) and present their findings to their peers in week six.

Part Three: Playtesting (Three Weeks)

In week six of the course, we introduce GUR survey-based playtests; we emphasize that unlike usability, playtests are concerned with participants' attitudes and opinions. Therefore, we need a much larger sample of participants (ideally 30 participants for parametric statistics of group differences). Much like in the usability preparation, the first class is a combination of lecture and hands-on workshops to help them prepare for their playtest studies.

The lecture focuses on procedures similar to those developed by Microsoft studios (Pagulayan et al. 2003). Playtest participants are asked to (a) play for a specific amount of time or until a specific in-game event occurs and (b) answer survey questions about their experience. To accommodate limitations of our labs, we have participants play to a time or goal on the Xbox, stop and switch to the computer (using an high-definition multimedia interface (HDMI) switch), and complete an online survey, and then switch back to resume play, repeating the process two to three times.

A very important concept students learn in the class workshops is the difference between a research question and a playtest question. Research questions are what the researcher wants to know; for example, how fun is the level, is the pace appropriate, and what participants thought of the graphics. Playtest questions are what the participant is asked; we discuss both closed and open questions. A closed question for a graphics research question might be "How satisfied were you with the artistic style of the graphics?" And include Likert scale answers from "very dissatisfied" to "neither satisfied or dissatisfied" to "very satisfied." An open question might ask "what did you LIKE MOST about the graphics?" and "what did you LIKE LEAST about the graphics?"

In week six, students workshop their playtest research questions by playing their games in the lab as a team. They are instructed to think about what things are important for the game at a general level and to list things other people (their target player) might like and dislike, find easy or difficult, or be frustrated with.

After the research question workshop, we give a short lecture on the dos and don'ts of writing questionnaires. For example, not asking compound questions. Because good questionnaire writing is a complex topic that we do not have enough time to properly cover in the course, we give students a list of well-structured questions. Additionally, students submit their research questions and questionnaires for our feedback prior to their playtests.

In week seven, we have students setup their playtests in the labs. This includes creating their online surveys. We also discuss data analysis; e.g., what kinds of group comparisons they hope to make and expectations for the final report. We again provide templates for the playtest plan and report; the playtest report is the last added section to the report that they started with the competitive review.

In week eight, students reserve the playtest lab for an entire day and run four playtest sessions; there are no class meetings. Since our lab has 10 stations, students can run 10

TABLE 2.2 Summary of the 11-Week Schedule Has Been Keyed

Section	Week	Topics
Introduction, early methods and statistics review	1	Introduction, you are not your user, competitive review
	2	Statistics, heuristic evaluation
Summative usability	3	Usability introduction and workshops
	4	Setting up usability tests
	5	No class: performing usability tests
GUR playtests	6	Introduction to GUR playtests
	7	Setting up GUR playtests
	8	No class: performing playtests
Guest speakers, final presentations, review, and final	9	Guest speakers
	10	Final presentations and review
	11	Finals

participants in a session. Again, students are required to participate in at least two peer playtest studies. Participation in the usability and playtests provides an additional learning experience.

Part Four: Guest Speakers, Final Presentations, Course Review and Final (Three Weeks)
In week nine, we have invited guest speakers and discuss a special topic, for example, game accessibility. Guest speakers have included people from industry who act as user researchers and people from academia who include games in their research and people who are concerned with game accessibility. Week 10 is set aside for students' final presentations and a course review for the final exam. Week 11 is finals week; the course final is an open-book test. See Table 2.2 for a summary of the week-by-week schedule.

STUDENT FEEDBACK

We have had 64 students take the course over the three times it was taught (14 in winter 2012, 32 in winter 2013, and 18 in fall 2014). For all courses at DePaul, students are asked to complete an evaluation questionnaire about their courses and instructors in the last few weeks in the quarter. We have received a total of 32 course evaluations; eight (57% of students) for winter 2012, eighteen (56% of students) for winter 2013; and six (33% of students) for fall 2014. Feedback from students has been helpful in both modifying the course and helping us understand what we are doing well.

The questions that we have summarized in Figures 2.3 through 2.8 are: (a) The course objectives were met (strongly disagree to strongly agree), Figure 2.3; (b) The assignments for this course contributed effectively to my overall learning experience, Figure 2.4; (c) I found the course material to be (not as challenging to more challenging), Figure 2.5; (d) The amount of work I performed outside scheduled class time was (less than other courses to much more than other courses), Figure 2.6; (e) I found this course was valuable for my career development, Figure 2.7; and (f) this course increased my knowledge and skills, Figure 2.8.

Overall, this course increased my knowledge and skills (less than almost all courses to more than almost all courses), Figure 2.8. In most cases, students rated the course highly.

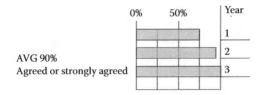

AVG 90%
Agreed or strongly agreed

FIGURE 2.3   Were objectives met?

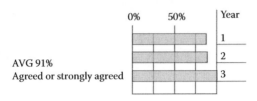

AVG 91%
Agreed or strongly agreed

FIGURE 2.4   Assignments contributed to learning.

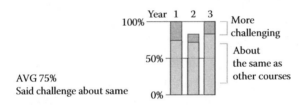

AVG 75%
Said challenge about same

FIGURE 2.5   How was the challenge level?

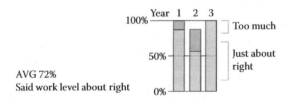

AVG 72%
Said work level about right

FIGURE 2.6   How was the work level?

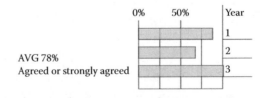

AVG 78%
Agreed or strongly agreed

FIGURE 2.7   This course was valuable for your career.

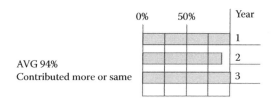

FIGURE 2.8   Course increased knowledge/skills.

Students were also asked two open-ended questions about the course (and an additional three about the instructor): (1) What aspects of this course were most beneficial to you? and (2) What do you suggest to improve this course?

The most salient beneficial aspect was the hands-on nature of the course; most of the students who completed the open-ended response focused on the benefits of doing the studies. For example, one student wrote, *"Being able to actually do some playtests and usability tests was great because I would have never gone through anything like that before leaving DePaul unless this class existed."* One student felt that the focus on different types of players was most beneficial, writing *"The discussions about different types of players and people."* Last, one student felt that the complexities of interacting with participants in the usability and playtests were a beneficial learning experience: *"I think the time management of other people. This class was primarily a 'go out and forge your own grade' type of class because we relied on a MASSIVE group of outside help. It allowed us to exit our comfort zones and not wait for results, but go out and get them."*

Suggestions to improve the course included a smaller class size; this was a common response in the second year when we had 32 students in the course. However, the most common theme to improve the course was a desire to work on their own games or run studies for other student groups, rather than commercial games. For example, once student wrote, *"Let us play-test our own capstone games, tie it to capstone."* Another wrote, *"Maybe team up with a more advanced gaming class and do some research with that, as a lot of the things covered in class were hypothetical since we studied with games that were already out."*

MAJOR CHALLENGES

There were six major challenges that we have encountered in our time teaching this course: (1) moderating class size and smaller groups; (2) student bias; (3) integrating the course into the game design curriculum; (4) recruitment and scheduling for the GUR playtest studies; (5) supporting student writing; and (6) short academic term (11 weeks):

Challenge 1: Moderating Class Size and Smaller Groups

The second year the course was offered, 32 students were enrolled; this was much too large to run this kind of hands-on course. This was reflected in the student feedback; year two had the lowest scores.

Challenge 2: Student Bias

Prior work in games education has shown that students often have problems stepping back from their identity as "gamers" and have trouble assuming different viewpoints on games

(Zagal and Bruckman 2007). Helping students begin to understand how to evaluate games for others and to realize their personal preferences and intuitions on games may be "incorrect" for certain audiences is an important challenge.

Challenge 3: Integration into the Curriculum

The concept of GUR is not currently very well integrated into the game design curriculum at DePaul. Some courses covered the concept of playtesting with players but in a much less formal way. Many students have also told us that the course is very different from other courses they have taken in the program. Some students mentioned that they were surprised how rigor and planning are needed to conduct a usability test or playtest. In other words, it was challenging to help students overcome a "mental gap" of including scientific methods in game design and stimulate their interest of learning about these methods. For some, bringing this level of "rigor" and "science" seems contrary to their notions regarding the "purity" of game development as an artistic and creative process; artists and creators should be free to follow their passion and vision in their creations and this kind of research is equated to marketing research groups that "remove the soul" of creative projects. To be fair, this is a conversation that is also part of the broader game industry where there is a rich and on-going discussion regarding the nature of game design: is it an art, a type of engineering, or a craft that combines them (e.g., Adams 2010, Koster 2011, and Neil 2012). As such, the validity and value of different methods and tools for assisting in the process of game design is constantly being developed and challenged.

Challenge 4: Recruitment and Scheduling for the GUR Playtests

While recruiting for usability was not a problem, recruitment and scheduling for the GUR playtests has been difficult. Usability test recruitment has not been an issue because student groups only need 3–5 participants (6 groups × 3 = 18 participants) and all students in class were expected to act as participants; several studies have found that a relatively small sample (3–7) will find at least 80% of the usability problems (Barnum 2002).

However, when trying to assess opinions and attitudes, which is the goal of GUR, playtests requires a much larger sample; ideally teams would recruit 30 participants from different user groups (e.g., novice versus expert) so they can make group comparisons using parametric statistics (6 groups × 30 = 180 participants). We have found that undergraduate game design students do not have access to a diverse user pool nor have the ability to manage their own scheduling.

Challenge 5: Student Writing

The first time we taught the course, students were expected to write their reports from scratch. It became obvious after the first two reports (competitive review and heuristic evaluation) that this was not a tenable assumption for undergraduate game design students.

Challenge 6: Short Academic Term (11 Week Quarter System)

We feel this class would ideally be taught in a semester system (15 weeks), where students could spend the last 4 weeks evaluating a peer team capstone project. This would also address the major student critique (in response to how the course could be improved) of wanting to work on either their own projects or those of their peers. While we would never recommend having students evaluate their own projects because of bias, we really wish that we could extend the course so that they could apply what they learned from the commercial game experience to evaluating a peer's game; this would also give students an additional cycle to practice the methods and would reinforce their learning.

SOLUTIONS TO ADDRESS MAJOR CHALLENGES

In the next sections we present our solutions for addressing the first five challenges presented in the previous section.

Solution 1: Moderating Class Size and Smaller Groups

To address the challenge of overly large project groups, we reduced the cap to 18 students for the third year it was taught. Consequently, this meant the class had to run two times a year. Additionally, we learned that the ideal group size for the projects is three (for a class of 18 this would mean six groups); however, in the two instances teams lost one member (i.e., became a team of two) the teams did extremely well in the course.

Three person teams have several advantages. First, three people work well for running the usability because as one team member plays the moderator, one can play the observer, and that allows for one student to act as a note-taker. (Also note that all students are expected to play the moderator role for at least one usability test.) Second, during GUR playtests, students could take shifts running the studies; as such, it was easier for teams to manage the four sessions in one day. Third, we found it was difficult for students to socially loaf in three-person teams; i.e., everyone has to pitch in and work. We found that four-person teams were much more likely to have at least one noninvolved member. To encourage involvement, we provided a means to assess team contribution.

As part of the final, students were asked to rate their group peers on a scale of 0–5 on several dimensions: (a) initiative, (b) reliability, (c) amount of work, (d) quality of work, (e) supported learning (e.g., providing constructive feedback), and (f) specialized contributions. A score of 3 is considered average. The averaged scored acted as a multiplier to the final grade. Receiving an average total score of 20–30 from teammates resulted in 100% of the team project scores; scores of 18–19 resulted in 95% of the team project scores; scores of 15–17 = 90%, 12–14 = 85%; 9–11 = 80% of team project scores; 6–8 = 75%, and an average of 6 or less = 70% of the team project scores. One team member per group could also get an extra credit; i.e., their multiplier would be 105%. Extra credit was given if the average was 28 or over, and only one team member had a score of 28 or over.

Solution 2: Addressing Student Bias

We addressed student bias by encouraging students to reflect on their identity and preferences as gamers and compare them to those of their peers in week one. Throughout the course, we also remind students that "they are not the player." In addition, the hands-on experience of interacting with participants with diverse backgrounds helped to reinforce this notion. As we will discuss in a later section, we help recruit participants through our participant pool that includes diverse players. In informal conversations, some students mentioned that interacting with diverse participants helped them better understand players of different types; several students commented on the benefit of including participants from outside of the game design program.

Solution 3: Integration into the Curriculum

To combat the initial resistance of GUR from our students, we have tried to emphasize the importance of these methods and stimulate students' interest by (1) inviting guest speakers from industry and academia to discuss how GUR methods are used in practice and (2) asking the students to focus on how data they gathered from the studies can help improve the game from a game designer's perspective. We also include (through readings and guest speakers) industrial examples and in-class demonstrations of how the GUR methods can help identify problems and help improve the game. The result has been positive, as one student wrote to one of the instructors: *"As naïve as it sounds, I would always think that it took a great team and a great idea to make successful games, but I know now that playtesting and getting user feedback is just as important as well."*

Solution 4: Recruitment and Scheduling for the GUR Playtests

To address the challenge of recruitment we used the Sona System (see http://www.sona-systems.com/default.aspx) in the third year to create a participant pool. Sona System is a web-based participant management software created for universities that many psychology departments use for recruiting human subjects among the student body; establishing the tool required review and approval by DePaul's ethics review board (i.e., Institutional Review Board [IRB]). Before the beginning of the quarter, we asked all instructors in the College of Computing and Digital Media to offer an incentive (e.g., extra credit) for signing up for the participant pool, which required completing a screening survey (e.g., for our studies all participants had to have some familiarity with Xbox 360 controllers).

While eight instructors participated, and we had over 200 students complete the screener, only a fraction had enough (a) game experience, (b) time or ability to come into the labs to complete a study, or (c) interest in participating. We hope that we have more enthusiastic participation from instructors and students in the future.

We also found that winter quarter can be more difficult than fall or spring for recruitment in Chicago. There were two GUR studies in winter 2013 affected by weather issues that disrupted transportation (e.g., in our case, heavy snowfall). We are now running the course in the fall and spring quarters.

Solution 5: Student Writing

To address the challenge of student writing, we have developed writing templates for all the assignments, study plans, and study materials (see Appendices). We have continued to refine the templates and have found that the templates allow students to focus on doing the research, rather than reporting the research. Additionally, the templates were designed based on reports and materials used in industry; as such, students are exposed to formats similar to what they will encounter in industry.

RECOMMENDATIONS

Based on our experience teaching this course we have five top recommendations: (1) to encourage authentic learning, the course should be taught as a "hands-on" experience where time practicing GUR methods is maximized and writing/reporting results is minimized; (2) class size needs to be minimized to help students get this "hands-on" experience; (3) it is important to actively discuss research bias throughout the term focusing on student biases about gamers and emphasize that they are not the users; (4) with an understanding that game design students typically do not have experience doing user research, emphasize the importance of GUR in industry with guest speakers and additional readings; and (5) because there is a need to help students recruit diverse participants for their studies, it is important to set up a recruitment mechanism (in our case we used Sona Systems).

CONCLUSIONS

GUR has become an important part of designing and developing games. As educators, we are concerned with how to teach GUR and encourage our students to consider an audience beyond themselves. We have presented our 11-week hands-on course that introduces students to GUR methods and hope to continue to evolve the course to better meet student needs. Of course, many of the materials would need to be adapted based on the context and situations faced by educators in their own institutions. For instance, some students may not need the statistics "refresher" and may be able to go into greater detail in some of the methods that are covered. Similarly, there is room to explore GUR in play contexts and platforms that are different from the traditional home console experience (e.g., social and mobile gaming, location-based gaming). As a nuts-and-bolts discussion, we consider hope this case study helps others set up an undergraduate GUR class (and lab) at their institutions.

ACKNOWLEDGMENTS

We would like to thank our students and their study participants for their feedback. We also thank the attendees of the 2014 Game Developers Conference and 2013 CHI GUR workshop for their suggestions, ideas, and insights.

REFERENCES

Activision. *World Series of Poker: Tournament of Champions.* [Xbox 360], 2006.
Adams, E. *Fundamentals of Game Design,* 2nd Edition. Berkeley, CA: New Riders, 2010.
Barnum, C. M. Usability testing and research. In S. Dregga (ed.) *The Allyn & Bacon Seiries in Technical Communication.* New York, NY: Longman, 2002. Barr, P., J. Noble, and R. Biddle. Video game values: Human–computer interaction and games. *Interacting with Computers* 19, 180–95, 2006.
Bateman, C. and R. Boon. *21st Century Game Design.* Hingham, MA: Charles River Media, 2006.
Bates, M. and D. Keirsey. *Please Understand Me: Character & Temperament Types.* 5th Edition. Del Mar, CA: Prometheus Books, 1984.
Bromley, S. *How Important Is Games Usability to Reviewers?* http://www.stevebromley.com/blog/2014/02/24/how-important-is-games-usability-to-reviewers/. Last Accessed: January 12, 2015, 2014.
Capcom. *Lost Planet: Extreme Condition.* [Xbox 360], 2007.

CITI Program. Available at: https://http://www.citiprogram.org. Last Accessed: January 14, 2015.

Desurvire, H., M. Caplan, and J. A. Toth. Using heuristics to evaluate the playability of games. In *CHI '04 Extended Abstracts on Human Factors in Computing Systems (CHI EA '04)*. Vienna, Austria: ACM, 1509–12, 2004.

Electronic Arts. *Madden Football NFL.* [Xbox 360], 2000–2016.

El-Nasr, M. S., H. Desurvire, L. Nacke, A. Drachen, L. Calvi, K. Isbister, and R. Bernhaupt. Game user research. In *CHI '12 Extended Abstracts on Human Factors in Computing Systems*. Austin, Texas: ACM, 2679–82, 2012.

Entertainment Software Association: Sales, Demographic and Usage Data. *Essential Facts About the Computer and Video Game Industry.* Available at: http://www.theesa.com/wp-content/uploads/2014/10/ESA_EF_2014.pdf. Last Accessed: January 26, 2015, 2014.

Federoff, M. A. *Heuristics and Usability Guidelines for the Creation and Evaluation of Fun in Video Games.* Indiana University, 2002.

Fulton, B. Beyond psychological theory: Getting data that improves games. Paper presented at *the Game Developer's Conference (GDC)*, San Jose, CA, March 2002.

Games User Research SIG of the IGDA. Available at: https://http://www.linkedin.com/groups/Games-User-Research-SIG-IGDA-1873014/about. Last Accessed: January 12, 2015.

Games User Research Summit. Available at: http://www.gamesuserresearchsig.org. Last Accessed: January 12, 2014.

Griffiths, G. Child's play: Playtesting with children in the world of skylanders. Paper presented at the *Game Developer Conference (GDC)*. San Francisco, CA, March 17–21, 2014.

Henderson, D. Using user research to improve game narratives. Paper presented at the *Game Developer Conference (GDC) Game Narrative Summit*. San Francisco, CA, March 17–21, 2014.

Isbister, K. and N. Schaffer. *Game Usability.* Burlington, MA: Elsevier, 2008.

Jørgensen, A. H. Marrying HCI/usability and computer games: A preliminary look. In *Proceedings of the Third Nordic Conference on Human–Computer Interaction (NordCHI '04)*, Tampere, Finland, 393–96, 2004.

Jørgensen, K. Players as co-researchers: Expert player perspective as an aid to understanding games. *Simulation & Gaming* 43(3), 374–90, 2011.

Koster, R. *The Case for Art.* Available at: http://www.raphkoster.com/games/essays/the-case-for-art/. Last Accessed: January 26, 2015, 2011.

Lazzaro, N. Why we play games: Four keys to more emotion in player experiences. Paper presented at the *Game Developers Conference*, San Jose, CA, 2004.

Livingston, I. Where are the sharks? User research in the far cry production pipeline. Paper presented at the *Game Developer Conference*, San Francisco, CA, March 17–21, 2014.

LucasArts. *Star Wars: The Force Unleashed.* [Xbox 360], 2008.

Neil, K. Game design tools: Time to evaluate. Paper presented at the *DiGRA Nordic 2012 Conference*, Tampere, Finland, 2012. Available at: http://www.digra.org/wp-content/uploads/digital-library/12168.46494.pdf.

Nielson, J. *Usability Engineering.* Cambridge, MA: Academic Press, 1993.

Nielson, J. *Thinking Aloud: The #1 Usability Tool.* Available at: http://www.nngroup.com/articles/thinking-aloud-the-1-usability-tool/. Last Accessed: July 7, 2014.

Nielson, J. *10 Usability Heuristics for User Interface Design.* Available at http://www.nngroup.com/articles/ten-usability-heuristics/.Last Accessed: January 26, 2015.

Norman, D. *The Design of Everyday Things: Revised and Expanded Edition.* New York, NY: Basic Books, 2013.

Pagulayan, R. J., K. Keeker, D. Wixon, R. L. Romero, and T. Fuller. User-centered design in games. In *Handbook for Human–Computer Interaction in Interactive System*, edited by J. Jacko and A. Sears, 883–906, Mahwah, NJ: Lawrence Erlbaum Associates, Inc. 2003.

Putnam, C. and J. Zagal. Setting up and Running a Games User Research Class. Paper presented at the *Game Developer Conference (GDC) Education Summit*, San Francisco, CA, March 17–21, 2014.

Rubin, J. and D. Chisnell. *Handbook of Usability Testing*, 2nd Edition. Indianapolis, IN: Wiley, 2008.

Shaffer, D. W. and M. Resnick. "Thick" authenticity: New media and authentic learning. *Journal of Interactive Learning Research* 10(2), 195–215, 1999.

Sona Systems. *Cloud-based Subject Pool Software for Universities*. Available at: http://www.sona-systems.com/default.aspx. Last Accessed: January 26, 2015.

Sotamaa, O., L. Erm, A. Jäppinen, T. Laukkanen, F. Mäyrä, and J. Nummela. The role of players in game design: A methodological perspective. Paper presented at the *6th DAC Conference, IT University of Copenhagen*, Copenhagen, 2005.

Spanner. The perception engineers. *The Escapist Magazine* 73, 2006. Available at: http://www.escapistmagazine.com/articles/view/video-games/issues/issue_73/423-The-Perception-Engineers.

TechSmith. *Moraie*. Available at: http://www.techsmith.com/morae.html. Last Accessed: January 14, 2015.

Thompson, C. Halo 3: How Microsoft labs invented a new science of play. *Wired* 2007. Available at: http://archive.wired.com/gaming/virtualworlds/magazine/15-09/ff_halo?currentPage=all.

THQ. *2XL Games Baja: Edge of Control*. [Xbox 360], 2008.

THQ. *Kaos Studios, Homefront*. [Xbox 360], 2011.

Zagal, J. and A. Bruckman. From gamers to scholars: Challenges of teaching game studies. In *Proceedings of the Digital Games Research Association International Conference (DiGRA) 2007*. Tokyo, Japan, 575–582, 2007. Available at: http://www.digra.org/digital-library/publications/from-gamers-to-scholars-challenges-of-teaching-game-studies/.

Zagal, J. and C. Putnam. Teaching games user research. In *Games User Research Workshop at CHI 2013*. Paris, France, 2013.

Zhu, F. and Zhang, X. The influence of online consumer reviews on the demand for experience goods: The case of video games. In *Proceedings of the International Conference on Information Systems, (ICIS)*, Milwaukee, Wisconsin, Paper 25, December 10–13, 2006.

ADDITIONAL RESOURCES

Bernhaupt, R., (ed.) *Evaluating User Experience in Games: Concepts and Methods*. London: Springer-Verlag, 2010.

Blythe, M., K. Overbeeke, A. F. Monk, and P. C. Write, (eds.) *Funology: From Usability to Enjoyment*. Dordrecht, The Netherlands: Kluwer Academic Publishers, 2004.

Chandler, H. M. Testing. In H. M. Chandler (ed.) *The Game Production Handbook*, Burlington, MA: Jones & Bartlett, 233–54, 2014.

El-Nasr, M. S., A. Drachen, and A. Canossa. *Game Analytics: Maximizing the Value of Player Data*. London, UK: Springer-Verlag, 2013.

Flanagan, M. and H. Nissenbaum. Verification. In *Values at Play in Digital Games*, edited by M. Flanagan and H. Nissenbaum, Cambridge MA: MIT Press, 119–38, 2015.

Fullerton, T. *Game Design Workshop: A Playcentric Approach to Creating Innovative Games*, 2nd Edition. Burlington, MA, USA: Elsevier, 2008.

Gibson, J. *Introduction to Game Design, Prototyping, and Development: From Concept to Playable Game with Unity and C#*. Crawfordsville, IN: Pearson Education, 2015.

Goodman, E., M. Kuniavsky, and A. Moed. *Observing the User Experience: A Practitioner's Guide to User Research*, 2nd Edition. Waltham MA: Morgan Kaufmann, 2012.

Levy, L. and J. Novak. *Game Development Essentials: Game Qa & Testing*. Clifton Park, NY: Cengage Learning, 2010.

Schultz, C. and R. Bryant. *Game Testing: All in One*, 2nd Edition. Dulles, VA: Mercury Learning and Information, 2012.

APPENDICES

Appendix A: Competitive Review Report Template
Appendix B: Heuristic Evaluation Report Template
Appendix C: Usability Test Plan and Moderator Guide
Appendix D: Usability Task Sheets
Appendix E: Usability Report Template
Appendix F: Playtest Plan and Moderator Guide
Appendix G: Playtest and Final Report Template

BIOGRAPHIES

Cynthia Putnam is an assistant professor at DePaul University where she teaches in the Human–Computer Interaction (HCI) and Games programs. Her primary research is focused on game approaches to rehabilitation therapies; this project includes a creation of a case-based reasoning (CBR) system prototype that helps therapists learn about and choose games to use with patients who have had a brain injury. CBR system data will be leveraged to identify therapy-centered game design patterns and user requirements to create tools that support game designers who want to create games for rehabilitation. Putnam earned her PhD in human-centered design & engineering in 2010 and her master's in technical communication in 2007 from the University of Washington, located in Seattle, Washington.

José P. Zagal serves on the faculty at University of Utah's Entertainment Arts and Engineering (EAE) program where he teaches courses on game design and analysis. His research explores the development of frameworks for describing, analyzing, and understanding games from a critical perspective to help inform the design of better games. He is also interested in supporting games literacy. His book on, *Ludoliteracy: Defining, Understanding, and Supporting Games Education* was published in 2010. More recently, he edited *The Videogame Ethics Reader* (2012), a collection of writings that provide an entry point for thinking, deliberating, and discussing ethical topics surrounding videogames. Zagal is the vice president of the Digital Games Research Association (DiGRA). He earned his PhD in computer science from Georgia Institute of Technology in 2008, MSc in engineering sciences, and a BS in industrial engineering from the Pontificia Universidad Catolica de Chile in 1999 and 1997.

Jinghui Cheng is a PhD candidate in computer science at DePaul University, focusing on human–computer interaction. Prior to pursuing his PhD, he earned an MS in electrical engineering and has been working as a game developer in industry for 2 years. His research interest is focused on examining game design principles and methods to support game design for diverse players. He is currently working on a project that aims at supporting the use and creation of games for brain injury rehabilitation and is leading a subproject examining game design patterns and design tools that can help game designers understand the needs in brain injury rehabilitation.

KEY TERMS AND DEFINITIONS

Authentic learning: As defined by Shaffer and Resnick (1999) is concerned with creating learning experiences that (a) are personally meaningful to students; (b) are related to the real-world outside school; (c) provide opportunities for students to think about a topic in multiple ways; and (d) use means of assessment that reflected the learning process.

Competitive review: Is the practice of identifying and profiling the competition to compare competitors on a key set of dimensions; competitive reviews are usually conducted early in a development cycle in order to discover a niche to exploit.

GUR: Is concerned with the systematic measurement of players' behaviors and opinions in order to evaluate and gain insights that can be used to improve the design of games; i.e., the goal is to collect unbiased data to provide a better player experience.

Heuristic evaluation: Is a type of expert review in which a researcher checks the system against a known list of usability issues and best practices.

Task-based usability testing: In task-based usability testing, participants are asked to complete specific tasks in the game and typically asked to "think aloud." Measures might include completion rates, points of frustration, frequency, and nature of errors. Usability in the context of productivity software is traditionally concerned with learnability, efficiency, memorability, error reduction, and satisfaction. Usability in the context of games has the same concerns, but is most focused on the learnability aspects of games; i.e., the "can" and "understand." For example, can users equip their weapons? Do they understand how to complete a level?

CHAPTER 3

User Testing in the Learning Games Lab

Getting Valuable Feedback through Frequent Formative Evaluation

Barbara Chamberlin, Jesús H. Trespalacios,
Amy Smith Muise, and Michelle Coles Garza

CONTENTS

EXECUTIVE SUMMARY

Several logistical issues can make formative testing problematic, such as getting access to testers and finding the best location and equipment for the right type of testing. In addition, learning games—also called educational, serious, or transformational games—present additional challenges to user testing. Developers and researchers at New Mexico State University (NMSU) have created a unique program to combat these problems. Researchers offer ongoing, year-round *Game Design Think Tanks* where testers participate in activities to build their reviewing skills, test games regularly during the design process, engage in a variety of feedback methods, and gain valuable media skills. Through this Learning Games Lab model, professional game developers have easy access to testers at any stage of game development and can build their design intuition through frequent contact with members of the target audience. This case study looks at how the Learning Games Lab operates, including processes for recruiting subjects, collecting data, and sharing that data with the development team.

ORGANIZATION/INSTITUTION BACKGROUND

Developers at the New Mexico State University (NMSU) Learning Games Lab have been creating educational games, animations, and videos for more than 20 years with partners and funders including major research universities, the U.S. Department of Agriculture, the National Science Foundation, the Bureau of Land Management, the Foreign Agricultural Service, the Federal Bureau of Investigation, and the National Parks Service. The nonprofit design studio maintains stand-alone production facilities at NMSU, a public, land-grant research university in Las Cruces, New Mexico (NM), including all hardware and software resources needed for game design, programming, production, and usability research. The research space is outfitted for flexibility in conducting interviews, observations, focus groups, and design activities, and includes computers, mobile devices, and other equipment for users/testers. The space offers three distinct game testing areas as well as a video closet that facilitates collecting qualitative feedback from research subjects and participants.

Testing has always been a critical part of the *Learning Games Lab Design Model* (Chamberlin et al. 2012, 2014), and Learning Games Lab user-testing protocols were created specifically to conduct research on games *in development,* as part of the development process. With this model, developers prioritize establishing access to target users early in the process to facilitate frequent testing throughout development. The overall approach resembles the backward design method outlined in *Understanding by Design* (UbD): designers focus on what students need to know and emphasize helping students uncover ideas through learning (Wiggins and McTighe 2005). They use key design questions to define what activities will lead learners to perform expected outcomes. Important to this process is the integration of content specialists, learning experts, teachers, and learners with the creative team, throughout the design process. Rather than designing an educational tool in isolation and then contracting out development, the Learning Games Lab Model involves all team members in asking the guiding questions, reflecting on expected evidence of learning, and suggesting engaging and meaningful learning experiences. This team might include programmers, illustrators, project managers, instructional designers, scriptwriters, youth Game Lab consultants, and human–computer interaction (HCI) professionals. These interactions—along with first-hand observations from formative testing—help team members stay focused on learning outcome targets with each product iteration.

CASE STUDY: FACILITATING FREQUENT TESTING

Game design, like any instructional design project, relies on the evaluation phase as a component of the design process (Hirumi et al. 2010). Formative evaluation is an ongoing activity during design, development, and implementation activities (Larson and Lockee 2014). As described by Corry et al. (1997), formative evaluation is often considered the backbone of usability testing in the field of HCI (Booth 1989; Hix and Hartson 1994; Nielsen 1994). However, user testing is typically done at just a few key review points during development (DuVerneay 2013).

One important characteristic of formative evaluation is the need for representative target populations from which to collect data on user experience, to improve the design quality of learning games/serious games (DeSmet et al. 2015; Fulton and Medlock 2003; Schell 2015; Sykes and Federoff 2006). By establishing easy access to testers, developers at NMSU are able to test much more frequently, and on a wider range of concepts than they otherwise would. They train users as *expert consultants*, building their abilities in providing valuable feedback. Several different strategies for collecting information from users—from observation to creative design activities—help provide meaningful input, and any given testing session usually includes various ways to collect information. Finally, Learning Games Lab personnel have refined specific processes for including developers in the testing stage and for documenting results.

To place this in context, during the 4-year development process of the five games in the *Math Snacks* suite (available at mathsnacks.org), youth consultants in the Learning Games Lab provided feedback on character development, gameplay, and learner guides at all stages of development, from paper prototype through final playable versions. Most of the games underwent 40–60 user testing sessions, including title discussion through level balancing. This case study documents how the Learning Games Lab gains access to testers for such projects, the methods used by researchers, and the process for documenting findings to shape development.

CHALLENGES

As in most studios, Learning Games Lab designers often work on several projects concurrently, with different target audiences, and designed by different teams. As summarized by Isbister and Schaffer (2008), game developers ideally collect play feedback as early as possible to correct usability issues (playtesting) and/or fairly late in the design process to catch bugs (quality assurance). Thus, at any given time, games need to be tested in different stages: one game may be in early development of characters and story, whereas another requires level balancing. In addition, testing any learning or transformational game presents additional demands: while they must be as usable, accessible, appealing, balanced,

FIGURE 3.1 Developers test with a variety of methods in the Learning Games Lab, including direct observation.

and playable as any video game, learning games have to also effectively communicate the correct concepts and enable specific content learning (Figure 3.1).

The challenges of testing may be due in part to the widely different elements to be considered during game testing—the experiences of test users and evaluators, instruments to evaluate and record data, and play-session scripts (Moreno-Ger et al. 2012). The Learning Games Lab user-testing model evolved to solve specific challenges: developers need frequent, reliable access to testers who are approved through the University Institutional Review Board and have consented to participate in research; those testers needed to be able to articulate their preferences and use of the games; and assessment had to be integrated with development through a consistent process for testing and documentation.

An additional challenge is the use of youth in the testing process. Game designers need to consider age, since it is one of the most significant demographic variables in a game design (Schell 2015). There is considerable recognition of the relevance of using children as participants in the design and the evaluation of applications for children (Hanna et al. 1997; Markopoulos and Bekker 2003; Read et al. 2002). However, usability methods employed for adults, or for older children, should be different from those for younger children. Based on cognitive development, techniques that work with 14-year-olds will not work for 4-year-old children without modifications (Guha et al. 2004). Research shows that age is an important variable in usability testing. For instance, in one study (Gilutz and Black 2006), researchers used 39 preschoolers divided in two groups according to their age. Results showed that in the group with older children, those players with more experience using technology succeeded better in the game challenges. In a second study, 115 children aged 3–5 years interacted with four interfaces: familiar simple, familiar complex, unfamiliar simple, and unfamiliar complex. Results showed that both child factors (age and technology experience) and design factors (complexity and familiarity) were relevant variables that need to be considered.

SOLUTIONS AND RECOMMENDATIONS

Setting up a user-testing situation with youth consultants presents challenges associated with recruitment and consent, providing participants with a meaningful and enjoyable experience, and developing methodologies for training and reporting. Table 3.1 summarizes needs, challenges, and recommendations for those considering setting up a Learning Games Lab-like environment.

Recruiting Subjects and Obtaining Consent

Regular and consistent contact with youth during a testing cycle creates a relaxed and productive atmosphere and helps set expectations among the consultants and product team. To accommodate this need, the Learning Games Lab begins by bringing participants in over the summer for a series of 2-week sessions, referred to as Think Tanks. Participants may come in for half days or full days and for 1 or 2 weeks. Developers and other staff

TABLE 3.1 Development Needs, Challenges, and Solutions in a Youth Game Consultant Program Integrated with an Educational Media Development Studio

Development Needs		Challenges	Solutions
Feedback on games at multiple stages	Age-appropriate characters and storyline Clean user interface "Fun factor": Motivation to play the game	Recruiting an appropriate pool of game consultants (target age, demographics) and getting proper consent from their parents.	Establish ongoing opportunities for meaningful, educational experiences during the summer and school year, so consultants are in the pipeline and have paperwork completed.
Specific, detailed responses from users.		Getting youth to articulate their experiences clearly and with sufficient detail.	*Blogging* (Reviewer prompts consultant for more detail if necessary) *Video closet* (Provides privacy and space to reflect) *Focus groups* (Helps to generate ideas and start reflection)
Retesting with new users after changes are made.		Bringing in new groups of game consultants frequently.	Schedule game consultant sessions (*Think Tanks*) with small groups, changing weekly. Groups can recur on rotation.
Building design intuition for specific target audiences		Putting developers and researchers in close contact with game consultants.	Have developers and researchers serve as reviewers and teachers for game consultant sessions. Showcase youth consultants' own media production work in end-of-week sessions (parents invited), so developers can see which storylines and platforms appeal to which age groups.
Nimble changes in ongoing development		Gathering observations and feedback efficiently and communicating it with developers and client.	Use direct observation, including one-on-one and one-on-two observations (i.e., one reviewer and one or two consultants). Use video clips from video closet, when needed, to convey user responses to developers and clients.

members get to know them better and the youth get a chance to relax in the environment. Researchers have continual access to the target audience during the summer, and summer participants make up teams of consultants they can call on to test games when needed during the school year. Changing the group every 2 weeks creates flexibility for testing; for example, middle school students for one session, then high schoolers when testing a game for older audiences. For *Math Snacks* (which targeted content crucial for learners in the sixth grade, but which is often taught in younger grades), testers included students in grades 4–8. The schedule also gives developers a window in which to identify problems in games, fix them, and test with a fresh set of users. The strategy has helped to improve consistency and continuity over the product cycle in the Learning Games Lab and dramatically increased how much testing gets done. It is also fun and rewarding for both the researchers and the team of consultants, who build an ongoing relationship. Usually, 12–18 youth are selected for each Think Tank; this number could change depending on how many are comfortably accommodated in other design spaces (the Learning Games Lab fits around 20 people).

Key to the Learning Games Lab process is reframing participants' involvement: in the Think Tank they are called *game consultants*, not "kids," "users," or "gamers." Researchers and developers listen to and honor their input as consultants who are helping refine the products being worked on. When researchers emphasize their role to them, youth testers take their role more seriously. At the beginning of the process, researchers tell them, "I need you as an advisor. I'm not a 12-year-old; help me understand what 12-year-olds are thinking." Participants report this made the role of expert advisor feel real for them. More than a club, class, or focus group, it is an invitation to join the team and help to build something valuable. Participants who have returned to visit years later report that this opportunity to do something real, at a young age, felt incredibly empowering.

Youth are invited to apply to be consultants through a simple one-page form asking them about their favorite games and why they want to be consultants. Because it is generally free to participate in Think Tank sessions, it is easy for parents to treat it as a summer camp, pulling their children out for appointments or travel. To counter this, researchers strive to make the process of applying and acceptance feel a bit more formal—not everyone who applies is accepted. The sessions are balanced to ensure a healthy diversity of ages and mix of genders, and youth are selected based on the desired target audiences for games in development. As part of their application process, prospective consultants must complete (and their parents must sign) photo and video consent documents as well as a consent form approved by NMSU's Institutional Review Board. Other records, such as emergency contact and food allergy forms are completed at this time as well.

All participants in the games lab provide consent to participate in the research. Being located at a university, the Learning Games Lab enjoys access to an Institutional Review Board to review all research and to approve the consent process. While much of the research is exempt from a full review because it is simply gathering opinions from users without tracking data or tying that data to an individual, the lab asks all participants to provide consent anyway. Consultants sign a consent form acknowledging that they can leave the process at any time, noting possible benefits (such as learning more about a specific topic, or getting better at analyzing media), and stating that there are no possible risks. Because most of the Learning Games Lab consultants are 18 years old or younger and the consent form also requires signature from an adult guardian. Before participating, consultants are also given the opportunity to sign a photo release and are encouraged to list any food allergies relevant to snacks that may be offered.

Game Lab Activities

Creating a stimulating daily routine for participants is a crucial part of the process. Developers do not need youth to be testing in-house products *all the time*: the value of this approach is in having access *whenever it is needed*. To make sure each session feels meaningful for participants, a Games Lab teacher and manager lead them in engaging activities daily, regardless of testing schedules (Figure 3.2). These activities vary and may include learning to code, developing collaborative spaces in Minecraft, learning animation techniques, or even designing math learning games. One of the significant outcomes of the Learning Games Lab model is that, in addition to the important role participants play in testing games in development, youth gain a valuable experience with a wide range of digital technology. Activities include plenty of exploration with content, development of specific products (such as a game design document, or an animated movie), and reflection with developers. To make this work, the schedule must be flexible enough that developers can have access to youth consultants for a 1- to 2-hour test session at any time. On the last day of each session, Learning Games Lab developers join parents of participants to see demonstrations of products youth consultants have created. This provides another valuable outcome—developers build design intuition for each age group by seeing what youth create on their own.

Tester Training

During each session, Game Lab Consultants also go through a training procedure to learn some basics about game dynamics and establish a common vocabulary for talking about games. The training program includes activities where consultants learn about the different types or genres of games and come to understand *challenge* or *flow* in a game. This builds their vocabulary and helps them articulate their preferences: for example, rather than saying the game just did not seem fun, they may recognize that it did not keep up the degree of challenge needed through all levels. Consultants engage in additional critical and reflective activities to help them build their vocabulary and evaluation techniques, such as development and storyboard creation for the redesign of a popular game for a new version, or the use of a specific game device for a different kind of interaction. While these game design activities may not be structured evaluation techniques, they build the capacity in the consultant for more complex reviews in the future. Other activities include character customization and designing for specific audiences. Consultants also design paper prototypes of games, and in doing so access a different perspective on evaluating a game (Figure 3.3).

Every day, participants build their analysis skills by playing and reviewing games, including commercial entertainment titles, apps, and other educational or serious games. This

FIGURE 3.2   Game Lab Consultants engage in different review, planning, and development activities as part of their work. This may include coding on the computer, collaborative design activities, and reviewing different types of games. Here, they play a card game whereas an observer makes notes on their behavior.

process lets them practice the reviewing protocols, refine their vocabulary, and develop skill in articulating preferences. This is a valuable life skill for youth to gain in determining what gives a game quality or makes it engaging: why it is worth purchasing. It also helps them learn how to identify their own feelings about a game, which makes them more valuable in reviewing in-development games for the studio.

FIGURE 3.3   In the *Genre* activity, each consultant writes the name of different games on 12–15 cards. The group then organizes all of the cards into groups, defining genres of games. This activity helps reviewers understand that there are different types of games, and each is reviewed differently.

Testing Methodologies

Depending on what type of feedback is needed and the state of the game being tested, researchers apply different methods. Usually, more than one method is used to ensure validity and to give consultants multiple ways to think through and express their ideas. Additionally, participating via one method usually prompts more thoughtful reflection in the next; for example, consultants generally provide richer feedback in the video closet if they have participated in a group discussion beforehand. They are able to think better and express their ideas, confirming shared ideas or expressing things they did not have a chance to say during group discussion.

Often, methods are used simultaneously. For example, the four different consultants could be testing a game, while each has their own reviewer conducting a one-on-one interaction, and other testers are using the video closet. Often, the reviewers will communicate during testing via computer-based chatting or phone texting prompting each other with specific questions or concerns. This allows for some discussion among reviewers without disturbing the testers. Specific testing methodologies are described next.

One-on-One Interactions

One-on-one interactions take place with paper prototypes and working and interactive versions. Usually, one reviewer interacts and observes with only one consultant. In the Learning Games Lab, this is usually done in groups, with two to five testers and two to five reviewers. This is particularly valuable when a product is in the early prototype stage: testers interact directly one-on-one with reviewers so that reviewers can explain missing details of the products for better utilization and testing. For example, a button that says *more* may open a screen without any text. The observer could then explain to a user what kind of text *would* appear there. It is helpful when proposing different types of instructions, or when a game in its early versions is so open-ended that a user would have difficulty moving through it alone.

In one-on-one interactions, it is common for the reviewers to talk directly with the consultant throughout, with open-ended prompts like, "What do you think would happen if you were to click that button?" or "Tell me what you are trying to do here." They also test sample prompts. For example, if a user demonstrates an inability to use a specific tool, the tester would try different verbal prompts that might be used in the game, such as, "Place the cursor on the grid," to see what could be implemented in the next version.

Reviewers generally end each one-on-one interaction with a short discussion or interview of the consultant (Figure 3.4).

One-on-Two Observations

Requiring fewer testers, *one-on-two observations* are particularly useful when reviewers need to see how users play. Here, one reviewer observes two consultants interacting with the prototype. The Learning Games Lab team found it problematic to use video of players, because it took too much time to review the footage and extract findings. With one-on-two observations, reviewers are able to observe two players and draw conclusions more efficiently.

FIGURE 3.4 In the *one-on-two observation*, each reviewer can easily watch two players play a game, and make notes. Here, one observer would track the two consultants on the left and another would watch the two on the right.

Direct observations offer a reliable way of understanding interactivity with a product because observers are able to watch what testers are doing. This is often done with more than two consultants; for example, a table may seat four consultants with two observers watching silently.

Generally used for more complete or usable versions of a game, one-on-two observations involve prompting users only when they are struggling or ask a question. Observers take detailed notes on how the product is used, where users have difficulties, and perceived level of engagement. Often, observers will refer to printed screenshots of game levels to note problems users have, or they will sit with a laptop and type notes during observations. After each user session, observers ask open-ended questions to elicit additional feedback from users.

This method of immediate documentation minimizes the time between testing and communicating recommended changes to the development team.

Focus Group Discussions

During *focus group discussions,* one or two reviewers interact with four to twelve consultants. In a group setting, observers ask specific questions related to the game in development: these may involve graphics or character sketches, scripts, general theming, or even existing level of knowledge on content. Users are asked to share their thoughts, feelings, attitudes, and ideas on certain subjects. Focus group discussions allow for peer interactions, which can be fruitful. Unfortunately, other social dynamics also come into play, and this type of discussion often produces a groupthink rather than just individualized responses, so it is rarely used as the *only* method to evaluate a game. It is most helpful in providing initial feedback on preferences or knowledge level. Researchers also use it to set the stage for a review session. A short group discussion helps prime consultants to understand what issues they will be addressing, the stage of the game, or what aspects of the game developers need feedback on. In the Learning Games Lab, focus group discussion is usually used in concert with another method.

Video Closet

Inspired by the recorded testimonials on television reality shows, the *video closet* was designed to give individuals a private and low-pressure way to reveal their thoughts and ideas.

In a small closet space with a mounted video camera, specific question for the consultant are written on a whiteboard. When ready, the consultant uses the remote control to turn on the camera and responds on video. The video closet is an excellent way to get detailed feedback from consultants, particularly those who are introverted or uncomfortable speaking in groups. Used in conjunction with other methods, it gives the consultant time to reflect and really think about the question posed. Videos are collected by the testing manager and shared only with other researchers or reviewers. Reviewing the data takes time, but Learning Games Lab researchers rarely transcribe the interviews. Instead, they use the videos as a powerful tool to communicate testing results with clients or to clarify observations made by reviewers. To share these, the testing manager usually places each video on an internal website and gives developers or clients access to videos relevant to their projects (Figure 3.5).

During Learning Games Lab Think Tanks, consultants use the video closet every day, even when not testing games in development. Consultants are asked to review other games, provide feedback on various activities, or propose new ideas for games. It is important that the consultants feel comfortable in the video closet and get a chance to build their verbal review abilities.

Consultant Blogging

In early days of the Learning Games Lab, users were asked to complete forms or write comments on a clipboard. Consultants consistently ranked this as their least favorite method and the feedback was often jumbled, too short to be of value, or irrelevant to the testing.

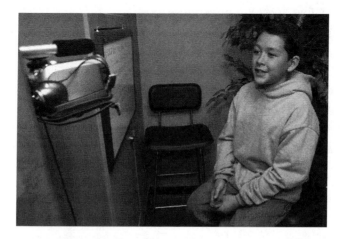

FIGURE 3.5 The *video closet* is a small room where consultants can sit and reflect on a specific question written on a small board. When ready, the consultant turns on the camera and records feedback.

FIGURE 3.6   By creating a space that felt creative and special, researchers were able to encourage more written feedback through a *consultant blog*.

Eventually, this evolved into the more helpful practice of blogging, where consultants use computers in the lab and a web blog to respond in writing to specific questions. A teacher reviews posts before submission to be sure the writing is clear and provides enough detail to be useful. Blog posts are only made available to researchers and reviewers (Figure 3.6).

Blogging serves as a great way for consultants to organize their thoughts. Even when written responses do not provide the level of detail preferred by reviewers, they serve as a prompt to help students prepare for other types of testing. This has been particularly useful in concert with the video closet. It seems that by organizing their thoughts first in writing, youth are more articulate and detailed in the video closet when asked to respond to a related question.

Process for Conducting and Documenting Testing

Documenting testing procedures and results are both important for keeping records and communicating findings. In the Learning Games Lab, in-house game developers serve as testers (also called *observers* or *researchers)*, interacting or simply observing consultants and taking their own notes. Table 3.2 lists names and responsibilities for various roles in the Learning Games Lab. Before any testing session, testers meet briefly to agree on desired questions for that session and on the methods that will be used. These are noted in the testing journal and should be specific. They may include overall playability, specifics on usability, questions regarding content understanding, or even general perceptions. One session for *Ratio Rumble*, a *Math Snacks* game about creating equivalent fractions, included these specific outcomes:

- What kinds of instructions help youth understand the point of the game?

- Where are the youth in terms of their understanding of expanding a 2:3 ratio to, for example, a 4:6 ratio or a 6:9 ratio?

TABLE 3.2   Roles in the Learning Games Lab

Title	May Also Be Called	Function
Consultant	Subjects, youth, gameplayers, experts	These members of the target audience play the games, interact with the apps, and engage in game lab activities.
Teacher	Coordinator	Usually someone with classroom management experience, the *teacher* coordinates daily activities as part of the daily schedule (such as the design activities youth consultants engage in when not testing games). The teacher is not necessarily involved in user testing.
Game developer	Programmer, artist, animator, game designer	Game developers serve two functions in the lab. 1. Developers mentor youth *consultants* (such as when they discuss careers or give feedback on projects) and interact with them casually, either through testing or for fun. 2. Developers regularly take part in testing, serving as *testers*.
Tester	Reviewer, observer, server, researcher	Usually one of the game or app *developers*, the *tester* conducts the testing with the *consultant*: observing activities, interviewing consultants, or interacting with the group.
Testing manager	Documenter, lead researcher	The *testing manager* sets up testing and documents findings. The *testing manager* works with developers to articulate what questions each testing session needs to answer, establishes which methods will be used, and sets up the room and users for the test. During testing, the *testing manager* observes the *testers* to document how they interact with the *consultants*. Immediately after each session, the *testing manager* works with the *testers* to document findings, updating the testing document.

- What kinds of in-game mechanics motivate them (or could motivate them) to create more complex ratios?

- What kind of thinking do they have about the gameplay as well as the process of making ratios?

- Did they understand the fail condition (that skulls hitting bottom ended the game)? How did that impact play?

While other studios often conduct external testing, where developers are not part of the testing process, the Learning Games Lab model actively involves developers as testers. Doing so brings a specific bias to the process and it takes developers practice and training to participate in testing without guiding the behavior of the testers. However, we have found it valuable to include them because *witnessing player issues* gives them nuanced and first-hand knowledge. While a researcher could simply share findings with developers in a cut-and-dried format, in seeing specifically *how a player struggles* with a specific mechanic, or the *extent to which a player is frustrated*, developers are better positioned and motivated to arrive at a creative solution to the problem.

In addition to the testing reviewers, the Learning Games Lab also includes an additional observer in their testing process, one who observes the testers: a *testing manager*. The testing manager is considered necessary to detect complex interactions between tester and user and to record all. In every session, a testing manager watches the session and observes the testers, taking notes regarding *their* actions: questions they ask, biases they demonstrate, etc. As Hornbaek and Frokjaer (2005) point out, usability testing, although it appears objective, is not always so, because interpretation ultimately shapes what gets reported. By including a testing manager in testing sessions, some of this interpretation can be mitigated (Figure 3.7).

Another important aspect of the NMSU Learning Games Lab testing process is the systematic analysis that occurs with testers and the testing manager immediately after the testing sessions occur. It is important for this discussion and analysis to take place while the results of the testing are fresh in the mind. According to Norgaard and Hornbaek (2006), testing reviewers rarely check whether they agree on the most important observations, which can weaken the process. Furthermore, Hertzum and Jacobsen (2001) point out that reviewers observing the same test can find substantially different usability problems, which makes collecting and discussing main observations important. The cooperative process designed at NMSU seeks to avoid such problems. Immediately following each testing session, testers compare written notes and observations and discuss with each other. They agree on what was observed, making specific notes about conflicting perceptions of what happened or inconsistent responses of consultants (Figure 3.8).

After a group analysis of the user testing, the testing manager records agreed-upon outcomes, particularly testers' consensus about the testing and recommendations. The testing manager compiles his or her notes, coordinates and stores other sources of data (such as video from the video closet or consultants' blog entries), and completes the *testing journal* for each project. The testing journal serves as a primary form of communication among developers, the testing manager, and clients. With NMSU's testing process, the testing journal generally includes a description of the user-testing audience, the version tested, the objectives of the user test, findings and recommendations, and a testers' consensus, which includes a compilation of all recommendations for change. Team members refer to the testing journal to ensure they address all relevant changes in future versions. Evaluating the testing journal throughout the design process helps developers review the changes that have taken place over various versions.

Expanding the Model to Other Studios

Learning Games Lab activities have evolved based on what is useful and doable in this specific environment. The research group had access to a fairly large space to create the lab and had the support of administration to engage in ongoing activities in that space. The primary goal of the Learning Games Lab is to provide feedback and access for regular testing, not to offer camp-like or hands-on learning activities to youth. However, by creating an ongoing program for youth, the developers solved the problem of having access to users to test programs, the most significant obstacle in previous testing work. The costs of such a program include maintaining the space and equipment used (including a suite of mobile devices and computers) and personnel costs for the teacher who manages the program. All other costs (such as the research manager and the observers) are the same as they would be if testing was done in other ways, say, in classrooms.

Potion Mixer Testing Journal, page 14

Potion Mixer Testing Journal, page 15

Project: Math Snacks – Potion Mixer

Testing:

Date: July 27, 2012

Consultants: 16 Middle School Consultants (all girls)
4 groups of 4 (Consumer acceptance IRB)

Group 1: Cecilia (12)
Nicole (13)
Natalie (13)
Melissa (13)
Group 2: Sonya (13)
Zeena 9(13)
Anisa (13)
Becca (12)
Group 3: Leah (11)
Emily (11)
Yasmene (12)
Victoria (12)
Group 4: Melody (11)
Annie (11)
Elizabeth (13)
Naomi (11)

VERSION: Unity #22, 7-27-12 version
Added to the new version
• Defeat the enemy's mechanics
• Hearts
• Swords
• Bombs
• Special Abilities

4 rounds of One-on-two protocol (2 observers, 16 kids… in four rounds)… Observer gives some general instructions on how to play at beginning, then as needed during game play. Instructions included:

• This is a game about making ratios (for almost all, this was enough explanation to get them quickly into the basic gameplay.)
• The goal of the game is to get rid of your enemy's heath before the enemy gets rid of your health. (All seemed comfortable with this.)
• Include swords in your ratios to damage the enemy. Put hearts in your ratios to heal yourself.
• The enemy damages you with bombs. Include bombs in your combinations to defuse them. When a bomb counts down to zero you will lose health. Bombs count down every time you take a turn.
• You double or triple your ratio combos you'll get a bonus for any swords or hearts in your combo. Every time you make a double or triple combo you will earn an ability point. You can spend the points on different abilities.

Objective:

• Observe overall impression of the game

Methods:[6]

o One-on-Two Observations

Observers: Michelle Garza, Game Lab Coordinator and Research Scientist; James McVann and David Abraham

Findings/Recommendations:

• Observations
  o Players seemed to enjoy this version much more than the previous versions.
  o Several players commended how much fun the game was.
  o All the game mechanics up at the beginning seemed to be a bit overwhelming for most.
  o The bombs seemed to be the only item that needed to be explained more than once to each group. (Players didn't get that they were supposed to use the bombs.)
  o Most players seemed to get the general gameplay mechanics on their own.
  o Most players (11/16) changed over to consistently using multiples once they were told about them.
  o A few players died once but none seemed to die more than once.
• Reviewers' consensus was
  o Add skill descriptions
  o Spread out instructions over the course of several levels

[6] Methods used are described in Appendix

FIGURE 3.7 The *testing journal* is an internal document used to track all testing. Each game has one document, which includes—for every testing session—version tested, goals for testing (what questions need to be answered), agreed upon observations, and final recommendations for the development team.

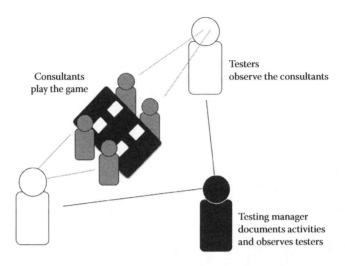

FIGURE 3.8   In a one-on-two observation, four consultants play the game, with each tester observing two consultants. The testing manager observes the entire process, watching the activities of the testers and documenting findings.

In importing or translating this model, some design studios have adapted it to provide frequent access to teachers for the development team, without the larger commitment of an ongoing program. Alternative strategies include

- After-school program at the design studio, where consultants come once in a week for a couple of hours at a time. In one example, the consultants rarely engage in any activities outside of testing, and spend approximately 2 hours per week reviewing games in development.

- Monthly evening family meetings at the studio, where parents of toddlers come in to interact with developers and new apps. This is ideal for building design intuition regarding apps for young children, as developers can see how the children interact with apps when they are with their parents, and observe how adults feel about the apps as well.

- Scheduled test sessions at the studio, where members of a testing club are alerted in advance of the specific time, and given an open invitation to stop by. With this model, kids and families are excited to contribute and participate, and develop a sense of ownership in the studio when they feel they can shape the final product.

While the Learning Games Lab model may not be specifically replicable in any design environment, researchers have identified the four key components to consider when creating a similar program:

- *Establish an ongoing program, with an ongoing group of testers.* All of your testers may not be available every time, but by creating a recurring event, or a special list of testers, you help create a club-like feeling, where your users feel as though they are part of something important (not simply one-time guinea pigs).

- *Create an environment for testing that is comfortable and consistent with the desired use of the product being tested.* If testing a game will be used in classrooms, design a process through which several users come in at the same time, sit at tables, and can interact with each other while playing. If working on apps that will likely be used by teenagers at home on their own, conduct testing with couches in a comfortable environment, where a couple of kids can come in at the same time, but each has their own space. If it is likely family members will be using a product together, utilize your program to bring the family in at the same time.

- *Establish buy-in from your target users.* Give target users ownership in your studio and your product. Most users find it tremendously gratifying to be asked to review and contribute and to know their recommendations have been heard. Offer benefits to your testers that others do not have (such as a short talk from developers on "selecting the best apps for your toddlers," or a special animation class for kids where animators walk kids through an hour lesson on animating a ball drop and bounce). The Learning Games Lab does not pay their consultants to participate, but each consultant gets to choose a t-shirt with logos of characters from in-house games. Other studios have had success with treasure chests, where kids get to pick an inexpensive toy or set of stickers. Treat your users as valuable consultants by providing snacks and reinforcing their value to your product development. Often, this is even more powerful than simply paying them for their input.

- *Involve developers in the testing process.* Researchers bring specific knowledge to user testing and should be included in the process, but developers often have to see testing in progress to really understand the nature of any problems. When simply reading a summary from a nondeveloper, it is easy for programmers, artists, and animators to doubt the authenticity of the recommended fix or to misunderstand what the problem is. When developers are involved, they are better able to identify what the problem is and design specific fixes in the weeks following any test.

- *Document immediately and succinctly, and focus on problems (not solutions).* Findings from any user session have to be summarized immediately after, so that the design team can immediately begin the process of fixing any problems. If there is a delay waiting for video to be transcribed, or for a researcher to summarize notes, observers may forget the nature of what they saw. After every test session, a Learning Games Lab testing manager meets briefly with the observers, and discusses everyone problems till they agree on the key challenges, documenting them before the session is over. These notes are then easy to read and immediately accessible to the entire team the next day.

CONCLUSIONS

The effectiveness of this approach is measured through the development of the product. The design methods and processes continue to evolve as different products are developed and the design team changes. While the studio places heavy emphasis on the value of testing, the value of testing is most accurately reflected in a product that is usable, engaging, and effective. While researchers use different methods to formally assess the educational value of the games developed, the studio does not release a game or app until the team has seen users successfully navigate and play through the games. Any developer in the studio has stories of successful changes made to games as a result of the testing and multiple versions of any game—each with changes and improvements—is perhaps the best testament to the value of the established process.

An ongoing games consultant program can be a powerful response to the challenges of conducting research on game usability, such as getting specific feedback on games at multiple stages, retesting with new users after changes are made, and putting developers and researchers in close contact with their target audiences to build design intuition. Assessment techniques that encourage both reflection and articulation of specific feedback—and build reviewing skills in testers—can inform nimble changes in ongoing development and enable researchers to gather valuable feedback quickly when needed.

Interactive programs and games are complex and multifaceted. Especially when including educational content, these tools offer many ways to engage the user, including sound, animation, story, characters, and effective interfaces for interacting with the program. This diversity demands testing of various factors to help ensure a given program will be effective: age-appropriate characters and storylines, clean user interface, and motivation for users to play the game long enough to benefit from the educational content. Extensive user testing throughout the development process has the potential to prevent development of ineffective materials, yet the user testing process can be onerous due to scheduling, and it can provide inaccurate information if the testers are not adequately prepared and are not able to articulate their feelings. The Learning Games Lab has developed specific procedures and methods to mitigate each of these difficulties; yet, significant commitment from institutions, funders, and researchers is required in order to put these procedures in place and maintain physical space, logistical expertise, an appropriate pool of game consultants, and accompanying educational programs. At its most active, the Learning Games Lab held 10 sessions in one summer, with additional sessions monthly throughout the year. Costs for managing the program include a teacher and assistant to manage the Think Tanks, laptops, tablets, additional gaming systems, and other resources. The NMSU Learning Games Lab estimates the cost of the program at $35,000–$40,000 annually, recognizing that—in addition to providing valuable input to the games, they are offering a service to approximately 30–200 youth that participate annually. The Learning Games Lab protocol is a powerful, though demanding, method to facilitate high-quality, nimble testing of games, and educational multimedia.

ACKNOWLEDGMENTS

The research in the Learning Games Lab at NMSU has evolved over many years, many researchers, hundreds of testers, and several developers. Special thanks are due to all of those who guided development of these protocols and shaped this research. *Math Snacks* materials were developed with support from the National Science Foundation (0918794). Any opinions, findings, and conclusions or recommendations expressed in this material are those of the author(s) and do not necessarily reflect the views of the National Science Foundation.

REFERENCES

Booth, P.A. 1989. *An Introduction to Human–Computer Interaction*. East Sussex, UK: Lawrence Erlbaum Associates Ltd.

Chamberlin, B., J. Trespalacios, and R. Gallagher. 2012. The learning games design model: Immersion, collaboration, and outcomes-driven development. *International Journal of Game-Based Learning* 2 (3): 87–110.

Chamberlin, B., J. Trespalacios, and R. Gallagher. 2014. Bridging research and game development: A learning games design model for multi-game projects. In *Educational Technology Use and Design for Improved Learning Opportunities*, 151–171, M. Khosrow-Pour (Ed.). Hershey, PA: IGI Global.

Corry, M. D., T. W. Frick, and L. Hansen. 1997. User-centered design and usability testing of a website: An illustrative case study. *Educational Technology Research and Development* 45: 65–76.

DeSmet, A., A. Palmeira, A. Beltran et al. 2015. The Yin and Yang of formative research in designing serious (Exer-)games. *Games for Health Journal* 4: 1–4.

DuVerneay, J. 2013. When to test: Incorporating user testing into product design. *User Testing*, accessed May 13, 2015, http://www.usertesting.com/blog/2013/03/04/when-to-test-incorporating-usability-testing-into-product-design/.

Fulton, B. and M. Medlock. 2003. Beyond focus groups: Getting more useful feedback from consumers. *Game Developer's Conference Proceedings*, San Jose, CA.

Gilutz, S. and J. B. Black. 2006. Young children's comprehension of a novel interface: How cognitive development and previous computer experience come into play. *Paper presented at the 28th Annual Conference of the Cognitive Science*. Vancouver, BC, Canada.

Guha, M. L., A. Druin, G. Chipman, J. A. Fails, S. Simms, and A. Farber. 2004. Mixing ideas: A new technique for working with young children as design partners. *Proceedings of the Conference on Interaction Design and Children: Building A Community*. Baltimore, MD.

Hanna, L., K. Risden, and K. Alexander. 1997. Guidelines for usability testing with children. *Interactions* 4: 9–14.

Hertzum, M. and N.E. Jacobsen. 2001. The evaluator effect: A chilling fact about usability evaluation methods. *International Journal of Human–Computer Interaction* 13: 421–443.

Hirumi, A., B. Appelman, L. Rieber, and R. van Eck. 2010. Preparing instructional designers for game-based learning: Part 1. *TechTrends* 54: 27–37.

Hix, D. and H. R. Hartson. 1994. *Developing User Interfaces: Ensuring Usability through Product and Process*. New York, NY: John Wiley & Sons, Inc.

Hornbaek, I. and Frokjaer, E. 2005. Comparing usability problems and redesign proposals as input to practical systems development. *Proceedings of the Conference on Human Factors in Computing Systems (CHI)*, 391–400, Portland, OR.

Isbister, K. and N. Schaffer. 2008. *Game Usability: Advice from the Experts for Advancing the Player Experience*. Burlington, MA: Morgan Kaufmann Publishers.

Larson, M. and B. B. Lockee. 2014. *Streamlined ID*. New York, NY: Routledge.

Markopoulos, P. and M. Bekker. 2003. On the assessment of usability testing methods for children. *Interacting with Computers* 15: 227–243.

Moreno-Ger, P., Torrente, J., Hsieh, Y. G., and W.T. Lester. 2012. Usability testing for serious games: Making informed design decisions with user data. *Advances in Human–Computer Interaction*. Retrieved from http://dx.doi.org/10.1155/2012/369637.

Nielsen, J. 1994. *Usability Engineering*. Boston, MA: AP Professional.

Norgaard, M. and K. Hornbaek. 2006. What do usability evaluators do in practice? An explorative study of think-aloud testing. *ACM Symposium on Designing Interactive Systems (DIS 2006)*, 209–218, New York, NY.

Read, J., S. MacFarlane, and C. Casey. 2002. Endurability, engagement and expectations: Measuring children's fun. *Proceedings of the Conference on Interaction Design and Children*, Eindhoven, Netherlands.

Schell, J. 2015. *The Art of Game Design: A Book of Lenses*, 2nd ed. Burlington, MA: Elsevier.

Sykes, J. and M. Federoff. 2006. Player-centered game design. *Extended Abstracts on Human Factors in Computing Systems*, 1731–1734. New York, New York.

Wiggins, G. P. and J. McTighe. 2005. *Understanding by Design*, 2nd ed. Alexandria, VA: Association for Supervision & Curriculum Development.

LIST OF ADDITIONAL SOURCES

Baauw, E. and P. Markopoulous. 2004. A comparison of think-aloud and post-task interview for usability testing with children. In *Proceedings of the 2004 Conference on Interaction Design and Children: Building a Community*, 115–116. ACM, Baltimore, MD.

Hourcade, J. P. *Child–Computer Interaction*. University of Iowa. http://homepage.cs.uiowa.edu/~hourcade/book/child-computer-interaction-first-edition.pdf.

Pinelle, D., N. Wong, and T. Stach. 2008. Heuristic evaluation for games: Usability principles for video game design. In *Proceedings of the SIGCHI Conference on Human Factors in Computing Systems*, 1453–1462. ACM.

BIOGRAPHIES

Barbara Chamberlin, PhD, is an extension educational technology specialist, professor at NMSU, and director of the Learning Games Lab. She currently leads the instructional design for development of educational games, websites and mobile apps, including interactive virtual lab modules, educational videos, and online learning tools, including for Science, Technology, Engineering, and Mathematics (STEM) education, financial literacy, nutrition, and food safety. She developed the NMSU Learning Games Lab for research on effective learning through games and interactive programs. Her dissertation evaluated youth learning through interactive video games and their potential to engage audiences to effectively teach content. She led the development of award-winning math education games in the *Math Snacks* series (2014 Best in Show and multiple Gold awards 2012–2014 at International Serious Play Conference; finalist status at the Serious Games Showcase and Challenge). She frequently speaks to national audiences about developing effective and inspiring educational media tools.

Jesús H. Trespalacios, PhD, is an assistant professor in the Educational Technology Department at Boise State University, where he teaches online graduate courses on instructional design and research methods. As part of his work designing instructional environments, he is currently working on the implementation of case-based reasoning in distance education. Additionally, he is interested in exploring and promoting the use of technology in mathematics learning at upper elementary grades. For 3 years, he was part of the *Math Snacks* project at NMSU exploring the design of serious games and animations and their implementation in the classroom. He earned his PhD in instructional design and technology from Virginia Tech.

Amy Smith Muise is an editor and partnerships manager at NMSU Media Productions/ Learning Games Lab. She supports dissemination and promotion of the studio's educational tools, including games, animations, web modules, and mobile apps with content in STEM education, agriculture and natural resources, nutrition, and food safety. Previously, she worked on educational modules for general education astronomy, including stand-alone laboratory exercises for distance learners.

Michelle Coles Garza is a research specialist and coordinator for the Learning Games Lab. Garza managed day-to-day operations, designed curriculum and ran programs with youth, and conducted research with many of the user testing methods described here. She is pursuing her PhD in curriculum and instruction at NMSU.

KEY TERMS AND DEFINITIONS

Formative testing: Testing throughout development, including at early and intermediate stages.

Game-based learning: Often used to contrast a type of gameplay that is different from *gamification*, game-based learning reflects learning that occurs when immersed in gameplay, usually specific to a content area or type of behavioral change. Gamification is the application of game-like mechanics to provide incentives for doing a certain type of behavior (such as awarding points in a frequent flier program or having friends compete to complete the most steps on their motion tracker). Game-based learning reflects deeper learning and transformation and generally includes an immersive environment in which learners solve problems, explore, and reflect. It can include both the game and companion activities that build on what the game introduces.

Game consultants: Members of a target audience who give feedback about games and multimedia in development, and who have undergone training in reflective techniques and articulating their responses via various media.

Game Design Think Tanks: Groups of game consultants who work together on various projects during multiple sessions to develop skills in evaluating games.

Learning games: Games that increase learners' knowledge and understanding by harnessing the inherent fun in learning. Also frequently called serious games, educational games, or transformational games, these are games designed to change learners' knowledge, understanding, or behavior.

Learning Games Lab Design Model: A model for conducting research on games *in development*, as part of the development, using key design questions to define what activities will lead learners to perform expected outcomes.

Video closet: Secluded space where a game consultant can give audio-visual feedback captured by a recording device.

Youth: Children aged 9–14 years.

CHAPTER 4

Usability Testing of a Three-Dimensional Library Orientation Game

Fatih Özdinç, Hakan Tüzün, Esin Ergün,
Fatma Bayrak, and Ayşe Kula

CONTENTS

EXECUTIVE SUMMARY

Games require constant interaction, which makes usability one of the fundamental elements of the game development process. A high level of usability in games developed for educational purposes is important for sustaining the user's game experience. Orientation is crucial for freshmen at universities. Performing orientation in a three-dimensional virtual and gamified environment enables users to feel like they are in a real environment and to experience an entertaining and sustainable process. With this aim, the Hacettepe University Beytepe Campus Library Orientation Game was designed and created in a three-dimensional virtual environment. This study conducted two different usability studies of the three-dimensional library orientation game based on user participation. The first asked users to fill out a survey after their gaming experience to collect their subjective data. In the second, a usability evaluation was done to collect objective data based on the users' eye tracking. This study presents the results of these two approaches.

ORGANIZATION BACKGROUND

University orientation is among the initial steps students take to get to know the university. Orientation informs them about the psychological counseling and guidance provided for freshmen in order to help them to adapt to this new environment and cope with any difficulties they may encounter. It also informs them about the university's facilities and services as well as its principles and rules, and allows them to explore the campus, departments, dormitories, libraries, and the city (Kutlu 2004).

The introduction to the library, which the students will frequently visit during their education, is also part of orientation. The primary purpose of the library orientation is to let students know about the resources that will contribute to their studies. The second purpose is to encourage students to do research to acquire the information related to their general education and professional formation (Walsh 2008).

Research on orientation programs indicates that they are useful and necessary (Sevim and Yalçın 2006). Different environments are used for orientation, most commonly traditional physical environments. Yet there are also web-based virtual and online orientation environments (Çukurbaşı et al. 2011; Özdinç 2010). The traditional physical environment is an interactive environment and allows students to meet faculty members and other students (Forgues 2007). Considering its cost in money and time, physical orientation programs may not be most appropriate and flexible (Granholm 2007). Three-dimensional multiuser virtual environment (MUVE) orientation services that are delivered over the Internet save the students from the obligation to be physically present in this environment. Thus, students may be offered the flexibility of time and students are able to visit the unit when they need to learn about it.

Holding orientation in a three-dimensional virtual and gamified environment ensures that users feel like they are in a real environment and experience a sustainable process. The aim of this case study is conveying the practice of participatory usability methods, with subjective and objective data, through an authentic project as a means to address the usability-related challenges faced in computer games.

CASE STUDY DESCRIPTION

To stimulate users and improve user experience, gamification, which is the addition of game components into an application, has become a growing trend (Fitz-Walter et al. 2011). Gamification has been defined as the use of game design components within a nongame context (Deterding et al. 2011). Prensky (2001) lists the structural elements required for an environment to be deemed a game: (1) rules, (2) goals and objectives, (3) outcomes and feedback, (4) conflict/competition/challenge/opposition, (5) interaction, and (6) representation or story. In this study, the components suggested by Prensky have been taken into consideration during the gamification process of virtual library orientation. These elements informed the design of the Hacettepe University, Beytepe Campus Library Orientation Game in a three-dimensional virtual environment.

The three-dimensional library orientation game was developed using the game engine, Active Worlds, which is a MUVE. Maher et al. (1999) defined MUVE as an environment which enables the users to navigate and accomplish activities in a virtual environment where users can also communicate with each other at the same time. In recent years, MUVEs such as Second Life and Active Worlds have become popular and have been used in a variety of fields by users. MUVEs allow for navigation, exploration, and communication, and they may be more helpful for acquiring reliable and permanent information than real life experiences (Jones and Warren 2008). MUVEs can also be used to animate real environments in virtual worlds. Data are kept on a server in the MUVE environment, and users access their virtual worlds through interface software. After users install the interface software on their online computers, they must be authorized by the administrators of the virtual world to be able to access the virtual world where the game is located (Tüzün 2010).

To provide maximum design usability, system flexibility, and optimal feedback for users, the coherence of the systems must be in line with design principles (Dix et al. 2004). This study implemented the user-centered design principles suggested by Norman (2002) during the development of the Hacettepe University Beytepe Campus Library Orientation Game. Norman's seven principles (Dix et al. 2004) are: (1) use both knowledge in the world and knowledge in the head, (2) simplify the structure of tasks, (3) explain and show what is to be done and how to do it, (4) include the user within the system, (5) define system controls clearly, (6) organize feedback for errors made by users, and (7) there may be small differences in the interface, but critical control elements must be standardized.

The library orientation game, which was created in the Active Worlds environment as the learning product of graduate and undergraduate design students in accordance with these design principles has been revised and a redesign process was carried by following these guidelines:

- First, exterior photos were taken to be able to replicate the library building

- Photos were taken inside the library for interior design

- Interface design documents were prepared for design guidance

Design was initiated using these data.

There are several tasks that the users are asked to accomplish in the game. These tasks were created to help individuals understand the functioning of the library and engage in more efficient learning. Users are provided with an environment that includes both two-dimensional (within the web browser) and three-dimensional elements. In order for the users to make progress within the game, they must follow the instructions in the two-dimensional browser. Users that complete the tasks are given a certificate of achievement. Here are the tasks:

Task 1: Locate the bulletin board and find out the hours during which you can study at the library

Task 2: Locate the bulletin board and find out the general rules to be followed in the library

Task 3: Click on the marked computer and search for the book *Good-bye Panic* in the pop-up window

Task 3.1: Find the marked computer

Task 3.2: Search for the book in the pop-up window

Task 4: Take the book you searched for from the shelf

Task 5: Explore the book you retrieved in the marked carrel

Task 6: Borrow the book you searched for from the first floor

Task 7: Retrieve the dictionary from the reserve and study room

Task 8: Photocopy any page of the dictionary in the photocopy room

The game was developed as part of graduate and undergraduate courses. The development of the game by a group of five took 10 weeks. Updates in the game, arising from changes in the real environment, have been completed by two people in 2 weeks. In total, the development of the game took 12 weeks.

Usability is one of the fundamental elements of the game development process. This is because games require constant interaction. Thus user interfaces should not be just entertaining, but also functional and user friendly. Illegible text on the screen and hard-to-use controls are usability problems. Game designer, Chris Crawford, says: "If the game interface is distorted or confusing, the user will quit the game." This means that usability testing is important to ensure playability and learning outcomes (Olsen et al. 2011). The required measures should be taken in advance to improve the design process and develop a successful learning tool.

Game designers need methods to define usability problems both at the initial and prototype stages of the design. Some research are based on experts (Federoff 2002; Pinelle et al. 2008), and others are based on user participatory evaluation (Barendregt et al. 2006; Moschini 2006; Tüzün et al. 2013; Virvou and Katsionis 2008). User participatory evaluation may be done either in laboratories or in users' working environment. Variables are defined, participants are selected, hypotheses are constructed, and the research is designed. Finally, statistical evaluations are made. Interviews, observations, surveys, or scales can be used to gather information from the users. But none of the evaluations conducted by designers or experts can replace usability tests with real users. Therefore, the usability of a game in this study was evaluated based on user participatory evaluation. A prerequisite for this type of evaluation is the need for a working prototype.

Two separate techniques were used to evaluate the usability of the three-dimensional library orientation system. The first was realized in a computer laboratory, and the other in a Human–Computer Interaction Laboratory with an eye-tracking device.

One of the important principles in usability studies is testing with people, tasks, and environments that correspond to the real target audience (Çağıltay 2011). For this reason, in both studies, people who use the library or potentially may use the library were selected, and the tasks in the game match real tasks in the library. The design process of the game environment attempted to animate the authentic library environment.

In both usability tests, users were briefly informed about the game they would play and the purpose of the test. However, related to the Human–Computer Interaction Laboratory, users were also informed about the laboratory environment (eye-tracking technology and cameras). These stages are explained in more detail in the following section.

Usability Test 1

A total of nine people, one woman and eight men, attended the usability test of the Beytepe Library Orientation Game. In these studies, just 5–15 participants are sufficient for finding 85%–100% of the usability problems (Nielsen 2000). Of the participants aged between 19 and 25, one is a graduate student and the others are undergraduate students. Five of the participants stated that they had been in such virtual game environments before. Being familiar with the game environment may have made participants feel comfortable playing and evaluating the Library Orientation Game.

The first five users did the test one by one, and the rest did it in pairs. Two people playing the game simultaneously allowed the multiuser affordance to be evaluated. Participants were observed while using the system by researchers using observation forms.

After their participation the participants were asked to fill out a survey prepared by researchers to measure the system's usability. It includes one multiple-choice question, an open-ended question, and seven items of Likert type. The Likert-type items were scaled from 1 (completely disagree) to 5 (completely agree). The score average for each question was calculated based on the responses (Table 4.1).

The averages calculated for each Likert-type item show that

1. The three-dimensional orientation game introduces the library adequately (4.22).

2. Users can navigate the system easily (4.56). However, observation revealed that, at first, users had the tendency to use the keys A–W–S–D, which are used in game environments.

3. Users have difficulty understanding the tasks given to them in the library game (2.67). Observations showed that they had problems with the catalog search, the first stage of the book search task.

TABLE 4.1   Score Average of the Answers to Survey Questions Given by Participants

		Mean
1	I think the three-dimensional library game introduced the Beytepe Library adequately.	4.22
2	I was able to navigate in the three-dimensional library game.	4.56
3	I understood the tasks given to me in the three-dimensional library game.	2.67
4	I found the instructions of the two-dimensional web environment clear and understandable for use in the three-dimensional library game.	4.33
5	The three-dimensional library game was adequately realistic.	4.22
6	The three-dimensional library game made me feel like I was actually there.	4.56
7	Environments similar to the three-dimensional library game should be developed for other units of the university as well.	4.78

4. Users were able to understand the instructions in the two-dimensional web area (4.33). Participants suggested that instructions should help the users to complete the tasks.

5. Users find the game adequately realistic (4.22). Users who knew the real environment found the objects in the game a bit different from the actual library (for example, the game environment was wider, and its doors and tables were a bit different).

6. The game has virtual reality (4.56). Virtual reality is a three-dimensional simulation model that gives the participants the feeling of reality, and allows for communication in a dynamic environment created by computers. Virtual reality will increase our ability to comprehend and perceive the systems we design to a considerable extent (Bayraktar and Kaleli 2007). If the three-dimensional library game has virtual reality, then this game prepared as an introduction to the Beytepe Library could increase the ability of the user to comprehend and perceive.

7. When users were asked about introducing similar programs for other university units, a vast majority (4.78) were in favor. This means that users found this three-dimensional library game useful and beneficial.

Users fulfilling tasks successfully were indicated by a "1" and users who experienced problems while performing the task were indicated by a "0" in Table 4.2.

It was found that the most challenging task was T4. All users experienced a problem in this task except for a single participant. T1, T6, T7, and T8 were all successfully completed by all participants. The open-ended question asked users of the three-dimensional environment whether they saw the links that guide and help them to complete the tasks while navigating in the game and if they did, whether they understood that these were intended to help them. They stated that they either did not pay attention or look at the help option showing how to change camera angles even though they saw it. This was because they did not need help with camera angles. They made suggestions about other help links that would contribute to the completion of the task. They criticized the help links lack of clear explanations. For example, a user looking for a marked object had a hard time figuring out what kind of mark to seek. After finding the first marked object, the user expects the same

TABLE 4.2   Task Completion Results

Participants	Tasks							
	T1	T2	T3	T4	T5	T6	T7	T8
P1	1	0	0	0	0	1	1	1
P2	1	0	0	0	0	1	1	1
P3	1	1	0	0	0	1	1	1
P4	1	1	0	1	1	1	1	1
P5	1	1	1	0	0	1	1	1
P6	1	1	1	0	1	1	1	1
P7	1	1	0	0	0	1	1	1
P8	1	1	0	0	1	1	1	1
P9	1	1	0	0	0	1	1	1

kind of mark again. However, since the objects are marked in different ways, the user had a hard time finding marked objects. During the usability test they said, "Why are we looking for the marked computer or carrel when we can complete the task with any computer or carrel?" Suggestions for the help links concerned the content of help (help topics), the form of help (location, appearance, etc.), and the timing of help.

Similarly, regarding the design of the game tasks Rouse (2005) stated that accomplishing the task should be meaningful for the players. Otherwise, players are affected by this situation negatively. Kumar (2013) states that players will be worried about fulfilling the task when they face difficulties.

Users who used the chat module reacted positively to the help provided by other individuals in the game, while users who could not do this since no other individuals were online with them stated that they would have preferred getting help from other people. When these players were observed in the game, it was found that they followed other players' avatars to perform the tasks.

Usability Test 2

Visual information processing is one of the most important components of how a user perceives a gaming experience (Kenny et al. 2005). One of the methods used to measure the usability is through eye tracking. Studies with eye-tracking devices are more useful than the other techniques in terms of providing more accurate and detailed data. Thanks to the usability studies with eye-tracking technology (Goldberg and Kotval 1999; Goldberg et al. 2002; Pernice and Nielsen 2009) the system can be evaluated through the eyes of users, readability of text can be tested, and difficult and easy tasks can be determined.

Over-gazing and selective attention become apparent in the eye-tracking process. In this way, what interface elements are misused can easily be revealed. Therefore, the second usability test used an eye-tracking device in a Human–Computer Interaction Laboratory. Three people participated in this test, one of whom was a student at Hacettepe University and knew the actual environment of the Beytepe University Library, and two of whom had never seen the actual environment of the Beytepe University Library. Eye tracking conducted with only three people may be considered a limitation of this study. Therefore, the think-aloud technique is used together with the eye-tracking method in order to obtain more data.

Laboratories are special places where eye-tracking studies are conducted. A unique monitor, cameras, and audio recorders are located in laboratories. Therefore, environmental conditions within the laboratory must be controlled before making the study that may cause problems. Prior to the implementation, each user was calibrated with the eye-tracking device. Calibration of the eye-tracker and the introduction of the game environment took approximately 6 minutes. The users were taken into the Human–Computer Interaction Laboratory one by one and navigated the orientation system on their own. The first user was familiar with the real library environment and the game was completed in 21 minutes and 12 seconds by the first user. The other two users were not familiar with the real library environment. One of these users completed the game in 53 minutes and 9 seconds and the other user in 48 minutes and 55 seconds.

Users played the three-dimensional library game, and these sessions were recorded by the eye-tracking device. Due to the inability of one user to fixate on the screen, that user's data has been omitted from the evaluation. Users were given tasks to complete in the game. The eye movements of users were examined while they were performing the tasks.

The eye-tracking device reveals where and how long users focus during task completion, the elements that attract their attention, and the elements that fail to attract their attention. Data were analyzed using the Tobii Studio (version 1.3.14) program. In addition to recording eye movements, fixation points, case history, screen content, user voice and image, keys pressed, and mouse clicks as well as replaying all these operations, Tobii Studio can also produce statistical data for finding fixation points and densities. This study's parameters include eye movements, fixation lengths, and heatmap during the tasks.

Fixation Length

In their eye-tracking analysis, Just and Carpenter (1986) claim that long fixation of the eyes indicates that users are either having a hard time extracting information or have found an object that attracts their attention. With this in mind, the areas in the system that will enable users to complete their tasks were marked or rendered distinctively to try to attract users' interest. Data analysis indicates that fixation length increases when users encounter objects that will enable them to complete their tasks. As Figure 4.1 shows, when the user finds the computer that will enable completion of the task, the user becomes fixated on that computer and clicks on it. Thus objects provide clues for task completion.

Similarly, the system indicates an increase in attention span when users get closer to their goal, the intensity of which increases gradually. However, it was observed by the cameras located in the laboratory that during the book finding task, users fixated on the illuminated object offered as a clue near the book, and for this reason had a hard time finding the book itself. Regarding this situation, Albert (2002) claimed that when users fail to fixate on an area that is considered to be important in the system, that area must be relocated or made more distinctive.

FIGURE 4.1   Areas of eye fixation.

Eye Movements

Goldberg et al. (2002) determined that short eye movement indicates that the users are not focusing on a particular point. Their study also observed that eye movements are longer when users are looking for their targets. Figure 4.2 shows that a user scans all parts of the three-dimensional screen to find out which direction to take. Fixation counts rise with the difficulty of the task.

Fixation Count

Depending on the difficulty or ease of the task, users' short fixation counts either increase or decrease. Goldberg and Kotval (1999) showed that a high short fixation count indicates that the user did a lot of searching. Considering the data, short fixation counts increase before users find their targets or guess where they are. Short fixation counts decrease and are replaced by long fixation when users find their targets or are close to completing their tasks (Figure 4.3).

Heatmap

Figure 4.4 is a map of the places on the screen where users focused the most. The central area indicates the most focusing and the surrounding area indicates the least focusing. Other areas on the map indicate areas that were almost not focused on at all. While users were navigating the three-dimensional area, they focused on the middle of the screen. Therefore, the dense area is predominantly in the middle of the screen. Users did not have a tendency to look at the edges.

In particular, when task 3 and task 5 were examined, it was found that the players did not pay attention to the affordances in the game. El-Nasr and Yan (2006, p. 1) state: "many

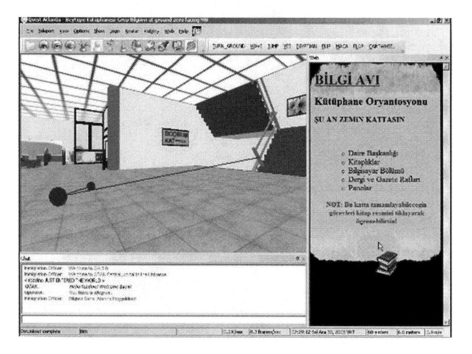

FIGURE 4.2   Eye movements.

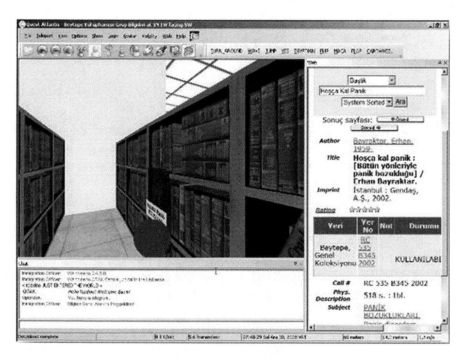

FIGURE 4.3   Short fixation count.

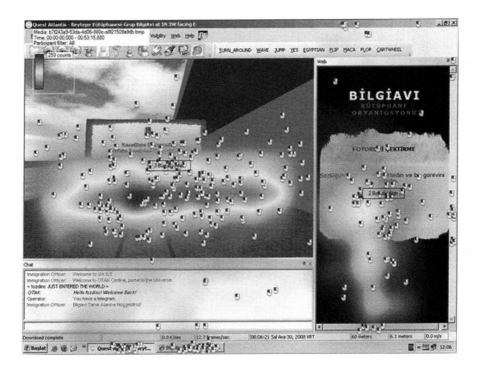

FIGURE 4.4   A section from heatmap.

nongamers get lost in three-dimensional game environments, or they don't pick up an important item because they don't notice it." In addition, in the task of finding the books, they thought that there was a barcode on the book as in the real world and they examined the books to find their barcodes.

CHALLENGES

Users were taken into the laboratory one by one. Since the table on which the computer monitor with eye-tracking technology is located was geostationary, a tall user was not comfortable while playing the game. Since this user was too tall for the table, playing required constant neck bending, and when the user straightened up a bit to feel more comfortable, data loss occurred as the eye-tracking device could not detect the users' eyes.

SOLUTIONS AND RECOMMENDATIONS

Since the game has as its purpose orientation, it was designed for people who had never used the actual library before, used it only a few times, or had just enrolled in the university. However, individuals who had just enrolled could not be included in the research since the usability test was carried out during the semester. In case study 1, nine volunteer students who had never used the library or knew it very little were selected. In case study 2, a Hacettepe University student who was familiar with the library and two other students from other universities who did not know the library were selected. The researchers should implement the three-dimensional orientation about university units (library, dormitories, dining halls, etc.) at the beginning of the academic year, because first time students, who do not have knowledge about university units, will put forward more authentic results. The data set, which is obtained from students who know about the university, will affect the validity of the study.

For usability test 2, the computer laboratory was visited and analyzed by the researchers beforehand, and software problems were detected in the eye-tracking device. These problems were eliminated prior to the test. Data quality was reduced due to one user who constantly looked away from the screen during the data collection process. This user's data was excluded from the analysis done with the Tobii Studio program.

CONCLUSIONS

In this section, results regarding the usability study of three-dimensional library orientation game and suggestions for the development of the system are presented.

The best way to collect information on the actual use of the system is to observe users interacting with the system (Dix et al. 2004). One of the methods used for the observation of users is the "Think-Aloud Method." This method is widely used in usability studies which include people's opinion on the working principles of a product or interface. Supporting this method by asking questions, provides the personal experiences of users in usability studies and their opinion on the functionality of a product/interface. In the studies investigating thinking strategies, Wim et al. (2008) and Hong and Lui (2003) asked players to think aloud during the game. In this way, they aimed to collect some data on how players think in the game. In one of the studies conducted in the medical area, Rudling (2007) has both observed the participants and also noted their comments. He obtained appreciable feedback by allowing participants to speak aloud within a limited time interval. Asking the participants to think aloud provides a more interactive environment than observing them passively. In this study, users worked on a prototype of the system, and usability tests of the system were conducted by observing user behavior. First, observation and survey evaluation techniques were used. Then think-aloud and eye-tracking methods were used in tandem. Bailey (1993) also suggests that more sensitive information can be obtained in the studies conducted in Human–Computer Interaction laboratories.

Both approaches to testing the game's usability observed different implementation processes, results, obstacles, application suggestions, and suggestions for improving usability. Thus, the use of a variety of usability tests during game development and with diverse users enables the detection and solution of different usability problems. Similarly, Johansen et al. (2008) state that presenting quantitative results using statistics, maps, and graphs to supplement more qualitative observation-based results might prove more persuasive than the qualitative results alone.

Case study 1 provided information on the general aspects of the user experience, whereas case study 2 offered the opportunity to examine the experiences of the users in more detail. The participants in case study 1 have a positive approach toward the usability of the game based on the survey. The participants in case study 2 had difficulties playing the game, and the difference is because in the second case, objective information was obtained regarding where and how long people focus on the computer interface, whereas in the first usability test users' subjective answers give an idea to designers about the usability of the game. To improve the usability of the game, both objective and subjective data obtained from users need to be considered, examined, and compared to identify usability problems. This led to the design suggestions given below.

Usability Results and Recommendations for Usability Test 1

Users with positive opinions of the game who encountered several problems with the game revealed several usability issues. Suggestions for those are as follows:

- When the users are navigating to find the dictionary on the lower floor and entering the carrel on the upper floor, since the door shuts immediately after the users open the door, these areas were hard to enter. The door remains open for 4 seconds in these areas. This duration should be extended.

- A map showing where the library is located is used when users first enter the system. When the users click on this map, they enlarge the screen and view the entire map. In order to be able to do this, instructions should be given or the map should be provided on another page. Tüzün et al. (2013) state that menus can be designed in the drop-down style. This method will eliminate the complexity of the menu and it will allow them to reach where they want in a short time.

- When the users search for a book (designated in advance), they are asked to do so on a computer. This search can only be done on one specific computer. This computer has a different screen than the other computers. However, users looked for a sign on the computer. This computer should be indicated, or search should be enabled on all computers.

- Nevertheless, some users were observed to have forgotten the name of the book they were supposed to find when they connected to the catalog search page. This is because the two-dimensional browser where the task is written changes as users changes their location. For this reason, the task should be enabled to be visible during the book search.

- Another reason for the users having difficulties finding the book is not having information on catalog names. This information can be considered within the scope of library orientation training, and providing this information should be considered during design enhancement.

- There is no task that requires the students to navigate on the ground floor. Therefore, students did not navigate much on this floor. Tasks for the ground floor should be developed.

- In a game, when there is a too high or too low a challenge, players may want to leave the game or get bored (Barendregt et al. 2006). Thus, the high number of tasks bored the users. Instead of giving so many tasks, providing a single mission with different tasks for the orientation should be considered as an alternative.

- Controlling a game is one of the most frequently mentioned usability problems in the literature (Barendregt et al. 2006; Olsen et al. 2011; Pinelle et al. 2008). Some users had difficulty controlling the game with the direction keys since they are different from the keys they are accustomed to from other games. It has been observed that although it is possible to change the movement keys in the game (for example, to the QWASD keys used commonly in today's games) users did not know about this feature. An explanation of this issue should be added to the game's help section.

- Some users (especially those who had no information about the library) thought that ground floor was used only as an archive or storage and did not enter this floor for that reason. A well-designed interface should give guidance to users on how to continue the game and should provide feedback to carry out the necessary procedures correctly (Graham et al. 2006). To make it easier for the users to find where to go when performing a task, a map that provides a bird's eye view of the library floors might eliminate such preconceptions.

Usability Results and Recommendations for Usability Test 2

With the new technology that analyzes human–computer interaction using eye movements becoming widespread, better results regarding the usability of ICT (information and communication technologies)-based systems and applications can now be obtained. Research done with eye-tracking technology has been generally conducted in two-dimensional environments. Analyzing the data obtained from three-dimensional environments using this technology is more difficult. Since most fixations take place within the center region, the data obtained from the eye movements should be analyzed qualitatively. Here are this study's conclusions on the data obtained by the eye-tracking device in a three-dimensional environment:

- The game assigns users object finding tasks so they get to know the library (find computer to do search, find carrel to study in, etc.). When the users see the object they are looking for to complete the task, they fixate on that object.

- The user scanned the entire screen when looking for the target in the three-dimensional library orientation game. This situation was recorded as lengthened eye movements by the eye-tracking device. If the lengthening of eye movements is considered as the length of the routes followed by the user to reach a target (Goldberg and Wichansky 2003), then solutions that would take the user to the target from the shortest route possible should be sought. Similarly, the number of short fixation movements increased when the user had difficulty finding the target. Thus the usability of current three-dimensional games can be enhanced by eliminating elements that either distract users or cause them to make mistakes while moving toward the target.

- Contrary to popular belief, an exact correspondence between elements in the actual environment and the design of three-dimensional games does not increase usability. In this study, the lengthening in eye movements and the increase in short movements while the users are looking for the book lending station indicated that users found this task difficult. Thus, the nondescript location of the sign in the real environment of the library emerged as a problem in the usability study. To minimize usability issues inherent in the real environment, the tasks should be facilitated in the game.

- The necessary arrangements emerged from research results and recommendations are expected to improve user satisfaction in the game. Further, the regular repetition of these tests will be important in terms of reflecting changing user needs and expectations of the game.

- In both tests, most users played the game by themselves. Collaborative play should be examined in future studies.

- To minimize user-dependent calibration errors, eye-tracking glasses and headsets should be used in future studies.

REFERENCES

Albert, W. 2002. Do web users actually look at ads? A case study of banner ads and eye-tracking technology. *Annual Meeting for the Usability Professionals' Association*, Orlando, FL.

Bailey, G. 1993. Iterative methodology and designer training in HCI interface design. *Annual Meeting for the InterCHI '93*, New York: ACM, pp. 198–205.

Barendregt, W., Bekker, M., Bouwhuis, D., and Baauw, E. 2006. Identifying usability and fun problems in a computer game during first use and after some practice. *International Journal of Human–Computer Studies* 64:830–846.

Bayraktar, E. and Kaleli, F. 2007. Sanal gerçeklik ve uygulama alanları (Virtual reality on commercial applications). *Annual Meeting for the Academic Computing*, Dumlupınar Üniversitesi, Kütahya, pp. 1–6.

Çağıltay, K. 2011. *Human–Computer Interaction and Usability Engineering: From Theory to Practice.* Ankara: ODTÜ Vakfı Yayıncılık.

Çukurbaşı, B., Bezir, Ç., and Karamete, A. 2011. Üç boyutlu sanal ortamlarda oryantasyon (Orientation of three dimensional virtual environments). *Annual meeting for the 5th International Computer and Instructional Technologies Symposium*, Fırat Üniversitesi, Elazığ.

Deterding, S., Khaled, R., Nacke, L., and Dixon, D. 2011. Gamification: Toward a definition. *Annual Meeting for the CHI 2011 Gamification Workshop Proceedings*, Canada, pp. 12–15.

Dix, A., Finlay, J., Abowd, G., and Beale, R. 2004. *Human–Computer Interaction* (3rd edition). New York: Prentice Hall.

El-Nasr, M. S. and Yan, S. 2006. Visual attention in 3D video games. *2006 ACM SIGCHI International Conference on Advances in Computer Entertainment Technology*, New York: ACM.

Federoff, M. A. 2002. Heuristics and usability guidelines for the creation and evaluation of fun in video games. MS thesis, Department of Telecommunications, Indiana University, Bloomington, IN.

Fitz-Walter, Z., Tjondronegoro, D., and Wyeth, P. 2011. Orientation passport: Using gamification to engage university students. *Annual Meeting for the Australian Computer–Human Interaction Conference*, Australia, pp. 122–125.

Forgues, D. 2007. Why traditional orientation? *Transitions* 2:4.

Goldberg, J. H. and Kotval, X. P. 1999. Computer interface evaluation using eye movements: Methods and constructs. *International Journal of Industrial Ergonomics* 24:631–645.

Goldberg, J. H., Stimson, M. J., Lewenstein, M., Scott, N., and Wichansky, A. M. 2002. Eye tracking in web search tasks: Design implications. *Annual Meeting for the Eye Tracking Research and Applications Symposium*, New Orleans, Louisiana, pp. 51–58.

Goldberg, J. H. and Wichansky, A. M. 2003. Eye tracking in usability evaluation: A practitioner's guide. In *The Mind's Eyes: Cognitive and Applied Aspects of Eye Movement*, eds. J. Hyona, R. Radach and H. Deubel, pp. 493–516. Amsterdam: Elsevier.

Graham, J., Zheng, L., and Gonzalez, C. 2006. A cognitive approach to game usability and design: Mental model development in novice real-time strategy gamers. *CyberPsychology & Behavior* 9(3):361–366.

Granholm, K. 2007. Why online orientation? *Transitions* 2:5–9.

Hong, J. C. and Liu, M. C. 2003. A study on thinking strategy between experts and novices of computer games. *Computers in Human Behavior* 19.2:245–258.

Johansen, S. A., Mie N., and Janus R. 2008. Can eye tracking boost usability evaluation of computer games. *Annual Meeting for the CHI 2008*, Florance, Italy.

Jones, J. G. and Warren, S. J. 2008. Three-dimensional computer-based online learning environments. In *The International Handbook of Information Technology in Primary and Secondary Education*, eds. J. Voogt and G. A. Knezek, pp. 911–920. New York: Springer.

Just, M. A. and Carpenter, P. A. 1976. Eye fixations and cognitive processes. *Cognitive Psychology* 8:441–480.

Kenny, A., Koesling, H., Delaney, D., McLoone, S., and Ward, T. 2005. A preliminary investigation into eye gaze data in a first person shooter game. *Annual Meeting for the European Conference on Modelling and Simulation*, Riga, Latvia, pp. 733–740.

Kumar, J. 2013. Gamification at work: Designing engaging business software. In *Design, User Experience, and Usability. Health, Learning, Playing, Cultural, and Cross-Cultural User Experience Lecture Notes in Computer Science* 8013, ed. A. Marcus, pp. 528–537, Berlin, Heidelberg: Springer-Verlag.

Kutlu, M. 2004. Üniversite öğrencilerinin alıştırma-oryantasyon hizmetlerine ilişkin karşılaştıkları sorunlar ve beklentileri. *Annual Meeting for the Educational Sciences*, Turkey, pp. 1–20.

Maher, M. L., Skow, B., and Cigonani, A. 1999. Designing the virtual campus. *Design Studies* 20:319–342.

Moschini, E. 2006. Designing for the smart player: Usability design and user-centered design in game-based learning. *Digital Creativity* 17:140–147.

Nielsen, J. 2000. *Designing Web Usability*. Indianapolis, IN: New Riders Publishing.

Norman, D. A. 2002. *The Design of Everyday Things*. New York: Basic Books.

Olsen, T., Procci, K., and Bowers, C. 2011. Serious games usability testing: How to ensure proper usability, playability, and effectiveness. In *Design, User Experience, and Usability. Theory, Methods, Tools and Practice*, ed. A. Marcus, pp. 625–634, Berlin, Heidelberg: Springer-Verlag.

Özdinç, F. 2010. Üç-boyutlu çok-kullanıcılı sanal ortamların oryantasyon amaçlı kullanılması (Utilization of three-dimensional multi-user virtual environments for orientation purposes). MS thesis, Hacettepe University, Ankara, Turkey.

Pernice, K. and Nielsen, J. 2009. *How to Conduct Eye Tracking Studies*. Fremont, CA: Nielsen Norman Group.

Pinelle, D., Wong, N., and Stach, T. 2008. Heuristic evaluation for games: Usability principles for video game design. *Annual Meeting for the CHI '08 Proceedings of the SIGCHI Conference on Human Factors in Computing Systems*, pp. 1453–1462, Florence, Italy.

Prensky, M. 2001. Fun, play, and games: What makes games engaging. In *Digital Game-Based Learning*, ed. M. Prensky, New York, NY: McGraw-Hill.

Rouse, R. 2005. *Game Design: Theory & Practice*. Plano, TX: Wordware Publishing, Inc.

Rudling, A. 2007. Multicontrast interaction platform. http://www.utn.uu.se/sts/cms/filarea/0712_arvidrudling.pdf (accessed May 2015).

Sevim, S. A. and Yalçın, İ. 2006. An example of a brief orientation program: Students' adaptation levels of and opinions about the program. *Journal of Faculty of Educational Sciences* 39:217–233.

Tüzün, H. 2010. Dünya üzerine yayılmış çok- kullanıcılı çevrim- içi eğitsel bir bilgisayar oyununun teknik yapısı ve Türkiye'de yaklaşımlar (Technical infrastructure of a world-wide online multi-user educational game). In *Türkiye'de e-öğrenme: Gelişmeler ve uygulamalar (E-learning in Turkey: Progress and Applications)*, eds. G. Telli-Yamamoto, U. Demiray, and M. Kesim, pp. 261–281. Ankara, Turkey: Cem Web Ofset.

Tüzün, H., Akıncı, A., Kurtoğlu, M., Atal, D., and Pala, F. K. 2013. A study on the usability of a university registrar's office web site through the methods of authentic tasks and eye-tracking. *The Turkish Online Journal of Educational Technology* 12:26–38.

Virvou, M. and Katsionis, G. 2008. On the usability and likeability of virtual reality games for education: The case of VR-ENGAGE. *Computers & Education* 50:154–178.

Walsh, J. 2008. The effects of library orientations on student usage of the library. *Library Hi Tech News* 25:27–29.

Wim, L, Quax, P., and Flerackers, E. 2008. Large-scale networked virtual environments: Architecture and applications. *Campus-Wide Information Systems* 25.5:329–341.

LIST OF ADDITIONAL SOURCES

Aycock, H. 1992. Principles of good game design. *Compute* 14(1):94–96.

deFreitas, S. and Maharg, P. 2011. *Digital Games and Learning*. London, New York: Continuum Press.

Hacettepe University Library Web Page, http://library.hacettepe.edu.tr/homepage.

Knapp, K. M. and O'Driscoll, T. 2010. *Learning in 3D*. San Francisco, CA: Pfeiffer.

Vincenti, G. and Braman, J. 2011. Multi-User Virtual Environments for the Classroom: Practical Approaches to Teaching in Virtual Worlds. Hershey, PA: IGI Global.

BIOGRAPHIES

Fatih Özdinç was born in 1983 in Konya, Turkey. He earned his bachelor's degree from the Department of Computer Education and Instructional Technology at Selcuk University in 2007. Later, in 2010 he earned his master's and his doctorate in 2014 at the Computer Education and Instructional Technology Department, Hacettepe University. Dr. Özdinç currently works at Afyon Kocatepe University. His field of interests include multiuser virtual environments, online collaborative learning, programming education, and educational computer games.

Hakan Tüzün is an associate professor in the Department of Computer Education and Instructional Technology at Hacettepe University in Ankara, Turkey. He earned BS and MS in computer education (Gazi University, Ankara, Turkey), and MS and PhD in instructional systems technology (Indiana University, Bloomington, Indiana). In the past, Dr. Tüzün has worked as a computer systems teacher at vocational schools, a research assistant at the university level, a computer systems and network support expert at corporate and military sectors, and as an instructional systems designer in various projects. The work of Dr. Tüzün involves the design of rich learning environments, frequently with the aid of technology but also by considering the culture of the learners and the communities they are part of.

Esin Ergün was born in 1985 in Ankara, Turkey. She graduated from the Department of Computer Education and Instructional Technology at Eskişehir Osmangazi University in 2007. She earned her master's in 2010 and doctorate in 2014 from Computer Education and Instructional Technology Department at Hacettepe University. She was an ICT teacher at primary education for a year. After that, Dr. Ergün has worked with the Department of Computer Education and Instructional Technology at Baskent University between 2009 and 2013. Later, she worked as a teaching assistant in Computer Programming at Karabuk University. She has been an assistant professor since 2014 and also heads the department. Her research interests include online learning, social networks, blended learning, technology integration, and computer games.

Fatma Bayrak was born in 1985 in Van, Turkey. She graduated from the Department of Computer Education and Instructional Technology at Hacettepe University in 2007. She earned her master's in 2010 and her doctorate in 2014 from Computer Education and Instructional Technology Department at Hacettepe University. Dr. Bayrak currently works in the Computer Education and Instructional Technology Department at Hacettepe University since 2009. Her research areas include e-learning, e-assessment, learner characteristics, reflective thinking, and computer games.

Ayşe Kula was born in 1966 in Çorum, Turkey. She graduated from Astronomy and Space Sciences Department at Ankara University. She earned her MSc focusing on instructional computer games in Computer Education and Instructional Technology Department at Hacettepe University. Currently, she is a PhD candidate in Educational Technology Department at Ankara University and studies subject culture in the integration process of information and communication technologies in education. Ayşe Kula started her career as a school teacher at Ministry of National Education (MoNE) and served at the Board of Education (BoE) at MoNE for many years. Then she continued at General Directorate of Innovation and Educational Technologies at MoNE by contributing to various technical projects, mainly the Fatih project. Currently she works as a school teacher at MoNE.

KEY TERMS AND DEFINITIONS

Active Worlds: An online virtual world, developed by Active Worlds Inc. Users assign themselves a name, log into the Active Worlds universe, and explore three-dimensional virtual worlds and environments that others have built. Active Worlds allows users to own worlds and universes, and develop custom three-dimensional content.

Eye tracking: The process of measuring either the point of *gaze* (where one is looking) or the motion of an eye relative to the head. An eye tracker is a device for measuring eye positions and eye movement.

Gaze: To look steadily and intently.

Heatmap: A graphical representation of eye-tracking data where the individual values contained in a matrix are represented as colors.

MUVE: Multiuser virtual environment, has three-dimensional third-person graphics, are accessed over the Internet, allow for many simultaneous users to interact, and represent a persistent virtual world.

Orientation: A period of time at the beginning of the academic year at a university or other tertiary institution during which a variety of events are held to orient and welcome new students.

Think-aloud protocol: A method involving participants thinking aloud as they are performing a set of specified tasks used to gather data in usability testing in product design and development.

CHAPTER 5

In-Game Intoxication

*Demonstrating the Evaluation of the
Audio Experience of Games with a Focus
on Altered States of Consciousness*

Stuart Cunningham, Jonathan Weinel, and Richard Picking

CONTENTS

EXECUTIVE SUMMARY

In this chapter, we consider a particular method of specifically evaluating the user experience of game audio. To provide a domain of game audio to evaluate, we focus on an increasingly occurring phenomenon in games; that of the altered state of consciousness. Our approach seeks to evaluate user experience of game audio from normal gameplay and gameplay that features altered states. As such, a brief background to person-centered approaches to user experience evaluation is presented and then we provide a detailed description of the method that has been adopted in this chapter: the use of personal construct theory via repertory grid interviews.

Subsequently, a scale is proposed, as a product of this investigation that we suggest can be utilized for the audio evaluation of games in user-testing phases. Results from this process include the formulation of a seven-category scale for quickly and efficiently measuring the user experience of game audio. We apply this in the context of game scenarios that feature altered states of consciousness (ASC) versus normal gameplay. It is shown that the devised scale is effective in discriminating between these two different categories and that it has potential to be transferred into a wider range of game evaluation tasks.

ORGANIZATION/INSTITUTION BACKGROUND

The case study took place at Glyndŵr University, which is in Wrexham, Wales, UK. Glyndŵr University has very strong links with the community it serves. Established as a People's College in 1887 and funded initially by the contributions of individual miners, the organization has maintained strong links to industry and its communities throughout its history. In 2008 it won a full university title, adopting the name Glyndŵr University.

The university is an academic institution that delivers higher education, from first degree to doctoral studies, and has close links with regional, national, and international industries. The university has a strong focus on employability and this is at the heart of everything we do. Our aim is to make our graduates as employable as possible. Our degrees are designed for the world of work, and we are proud of our consistently high employability rate.

In particular, the university runs a successful undergraduate degree program in the field of computer game development, which includes, among other things, a course focused on the development and integration of audio in games. As a part of this chapter, and recognizing the issues and challenges highlighted by industrial colleagues, we focus our research on applied solutions to their problems.

CASE STUDY DESCRIPTION: REPERTORY GRID METHODOLOGY

A way to address user experience challenges is to be found in a specific application of personal construct psychology (PCP), known as the repertory grid methodology. PCP is broadly attributed to the work of Kelly (1955) and builds upon the principles of constructivism, most typically associated with the work of Piaget (Wadsworth 1996), and constructivism in a group or collaborative context (Vygotsky 2012). PCP advocates that the most valid descriptions of phenomena encountered by humans are those that they form themselves through experience and by testing and validating descriptions and theories in their own heads and in collaboration and discussion with others. Partially, this explains the diverse and challenging subjective nature of measuring any kind of user experience, but also confirms that the greatest validity of user experience comes via these descriptions. The greatest limitation of such investigation is that validity often comes at the cost of reliability of information, since working with users to elicit constructs is a time consuming and, by inference, financially consuming process. By applying the repertory grid approach in this chapter, we aim to formulate a mechanism and scale that can be applied to evaluate the user experience of game audio.

Audio is a powerful influence and stimulant in games. As will be discussed in this case study, there is significant research about the emotional effect of sound and music and how it contributes to the immersion players perceive in a computer game. It is the direct effects of audio upon the game player that we are interested in evaluating to better understand how sound and music can be utilized in games to enhance the user experience.

The repertory grid method is a specific incidence of PCP that has been designed to strike a balance between the open-ended nature of constructs by applying quantitative measures. It is a participant-dependent research method that typically involves a researcher working one to one with a subject. Traditionally, this takes the form of a semistructured interview and will often utilize techniques such as card sorting and shuffling to facilitate and encourage participation, although latterly online and electronic research tools have become sophisticated enough to support this process at a distance (Grill et al. 2011). It allows participant data to be analyzed and summarized in more efficient ways that balance qualitative descriptions, known as constructs, with quantitative weights, or values, that can be attributed to the subject matter, the domain, under investigation. Particular instances of the domain under investigation, known as elements, are introduced to the subject, which are then described using their constructs and each element rated against each construct using a numerical grade, by way of a semantic differential on a scale with an odd number of points, typically five or seven.

Constructs must be bipolar in nature and so participants are required to define both extremes of the construct; it is common to achieve this through interview and card-sorting techniques of triad and differentiation:

> The triad technique involves providing a participant with three randomly drawn cards, each containing the name of one of the elements. The participant must then group together the two elements they perceive as being most similar. They are then prompted to describe the common feature that relates the two elements in the group and the feature that separates these two from the third; doing so creates a bipolar construct.

> Differentiation is a cruder technique, but it has been found to be effective during interviews where participants struggle with the triad technique or where their responses become repetitive. As the title suggests, differentiation involves the researcher drawing two cards randomly and asking the participant to describe what makes those two elements different from one another. This forms one extreme of a construct and the participant must then be prompted to consider what the opposite term for the construct should be.

To give a brief example of these repertory grid features in action: the domain of investigation is domestic animals; the elements involved are dogs, cats, rabbits, and mice; the bipolar constructs might be *quiet–loud, big–small, short hair–long hair,* and *messy–clean.* The ratings of the elements against constructs, on a 1–5 scale ordered left to right, by a participant could be as shown in Table 5.1.

Subjects each arrive at their own grid following their participation in the repertory grid technique. Owing to the quantitative ratings that are applied by participants, it is possible to carry out data analysis on the elements, constructs, and relationship between elements and constructs in each grid. This can be done simply by ranking and ordering exercises, or

TABLE 5.1   Example Repertory Grid Relating to Animals

1	Dogs	Cats	Rabbits	Mice	5
Quiet	5	3	1	1	*Loud*
Small	5	3	2	1	*Big*
Short hair	3	3	4	1	*Long hair*
Messy	1	5	4	3	*Clean*

in more detail by the application of clustering, through principal component analysis. This allows the researcher to form theories about the nature of the domain. For example, from the fictitious grid used in Table 5.1, it can be hypothesized that: big animals are loud whilst small animals are quiet (the ratings across the elements differ only slightly for rabbits) or that dogs and rabbits are considered very different from one another (their scores are quite far apart over all constructs).

But perhaps the most useful tool in the analysis of repertory grids is in the drawing together of grids from multiple participants. It is common for the researcher to supply participants with a common set of elements and this practice is adopted in the research documented here. This facilitates the concatenation of grids from all participants in a study and the analysis, therefore, of a much larger, ultimately more valid and more reliable data set. Most importantly, this process allows the researcher to determine which constructs are most commonly occurring and thus represent an agreed group norm; the best way(s) in which to describe the elements under investigation, although the ratings supplied might not show the same level of agreement across participants due to their own subjective preferences and likes and dislikes.

CASE STUDY DESCRIPTION: ASC IN GAMES

The representation of ASC is a niche area of video games that has been steadily growing as game developers seek to provide improved levels of realism and exotic gaming experiences. For example, *Dead Space 2* (2011) features representations of hallucination as a central feature of the game narrative, while the *Grand Theft Auto* series contains sequences in which the game character may become psychedelically intoxicated through various methods (Weinel 2010; Blake 2013; Demarque and de Lima 2013). The approaches used by developers to provide these hallucinatory sequences have been gradually improving in sophistication.

In first-person perspective video games, representations of the virtual game environment are mediated by the use of graphics, sound, and game speed. For example, consider a contemporary popular computer game such as Grand Theft Auto 5 (2013), where the player character becomes unknowingly drugged and experiences an extensive "trip." The protagonist character, Michael, experiences a range of strange happenings, which the player is led through by way of cinematic scenes and restricted gameplay. This experience manifests itself as various distorted perceptions of the game world alongside hallucinations. This segment of the game lasts over 5 min and most notably features the player character being probed by a group of aliens in a spaceship and subsequently falling from the alien craft back to Earth. Most notable in this segment of the game is the distortion and oversaturation of the graphics, which is accompanied by the unusual situation, distorted speech and sounds, and trance-like music. As such, ASC features imitate the senses of the game character. For example, a camera is used to imitate sight; stereo game sound imitates hearing; game speed imitates the passing of time in a manner equivalent to human perception. Adjusting properties of graphics, sound, and game speed can therefore allow us to manipulate the way in which sensory perception of the game character is represented.

In previous work, we have been particularly interested in the representation of ASC within games and have sought to deepen our understanding of the phenomenon within games, both from the perspective of the representations themselves and the player's interaction and immersion (Weinel et al. 2014; Weinel, Cunningham, and Griffiths 2014). As such, for the purposes of following through our case study in this chapter, we evaluate the user experience of game audio that feature both ASC and non-ASC segments.

CHALLENGES: EVALUATING GAME USER EXPERIENCE

The usability of interactive computer systems is a long-established measure of their success, both in terms of utility and commercial value. Traditionally, usability is evaluated using a range of methods that can broadly be classified in two ways: those that involve users, and those that do not. Methods involving users include surveys (Chin et al. 1988; Kirakowski and Corbett 1993; Nielsen 1993), interviews, direct observation, and interaction recording (e.g., monitoring user actions). Those methods that do not involve users directly tend to rely on usability experts who conduct studies based on guidelines (Shneiderman 1998; Constantine and Lockwood 1999; Picking et al. 2012) and/or psychological principles (e.g., Wharton et al. 1994). Heuristic guidelines specifically for the usability evaluation of computer games have also been proposed (e.g., Brown 2008). Computer games are also evaluated informally by expert gaming reviewers who usually publish their findings in popular magazines and on gaming websites. However, this approach is arguably "unscientific," not only because of the lack of a methodological approach, but also because of the possibility of personal bias of individual opinions. Nevertheless, such reviews are crucial to the commercial success of computer games.

Whatever methods are employed, a game's quality and popularity ultimately comes down to the users' experience of the game. "User eXperience" (or UX) is a phrase synonymous with usability evaluation, and is currently a popular term in common usage in the field. There are many varying definitions of "user experience," largely depending on the domain of interest (see http://www.allaboutux.org/ux-definitions). One that seems appropriate to the user experience of computer games is proposed by Reiss (2009, p. 1):

> "UX = the sum of a series of interactions. User experience (UX) represents the perception left in someone's mind following a series of interactions between people, devices, and events—or any combination thereof. 'Series' is the operative word."

Reiss goes on to explain the interactions are active (e.g., clicking a button, moving a character on screen), passive (e.g., listening to a beautiful piece of music will cause the user to release dopamine), or secondary to the ultimate experience (e.g., the game experience is good because the designers are talented individuals with a strong track record). He adds that all interactions are open to subjective interpretation. These interactions are constantly experienced by users in real-time environments such as computer game play, and all three types of interaction may exist in parallel, not necessarily in series as Reiss suggests. Such is the immersiveness of computer gaming.

Accurately measuring all user interactions within such a complex experience might be possible, but would probably be inordinately time consuming and expensive. Therefore, it is important to identify the most important elements of the user experience, and target these to maximize the probability of a valid and reliable evaluation.

To do this, it would be sensible to carefully plan a robust approach to any evaluation study. One way of assuring this is to follow a structured process that provides a framework for evaluators to follow. This would enable questions and uncertainties to be identified in advance of the evaluation exercise. For example, which of the aforementioned methods would best be employed to evaluate the user experience of the game of interest? How many users do we need to carry out a credible evaluation? Who are the users—what age, gender, experience, and ability profiles should they have?

One of the simplest established processes for conducting a usability evaluation is known as the "DECIDE framework" (Rogers et al. 2011). DECIDE is an acronym based on the first letter of the first word of each stage of the framework:

- Determine the goals of the evaluation

- Explore the questions

- Choose the evaluation methods and techniques

- Identify the practical issues that must be addressed, such as selecting participants

- Decide how to deal with the ethical issues

- Evaluate, interpret, and present the data

Each stage is relatively self-explanatory, where the evaluator starts by identifying the high-level goals of the evaluation. An example might be to identify whether a new audio score in a game is better than the original version. The next stage would focus on what specific questions need to be asked to achieve the overall goal. For example, do the users prefer the new version, do they spend more time playing it, perhaps we might measure their excitement levels by monitoring biometric responses (heart rate, galvanic skin responses [GSRs], etc.)? If these are the questions, then what methods and techniques are going to help us answer them? This is the third stage of the DECIDE framework. In our case, we might use surveys and interviews to evaluate the users' opinions, and conduct laboratory-based experiments to record excitement levels. It is generally regarded as good practice to employ at least two methods to achieve an element of "triangulation" to improve the validity of the overall evaluation. Once the methods are chosen, it is then a case of making it happen within the scope of the resources available. Practical issues such as selecting and identifying the users are covered in phase four of the framework. Other practical issues such as cost, timing, laboratory availability, and importantly the means of recording collected data, must also be considered. One fundamental issue that needs to be addressed in any study involving humans is the ethical dimension. This is described in the penultimate phase of the framework, and needs to be done of course prior to the evaluation studies taking place. Finally, subsequent to conducting a well-planned study, the results can be evaluated, interpreted, and reported to the wider community.

CHALLENGES: EVALUATING GAME AUDIO

Whilst generic methods such as the DECIDE framework are tried and tested across the usability spectrum, a number of researchers argue that choosing classical methods and techniques (the "C" in DECIDE) does not apply to evaluating computer game experience (Pagulayan et al. 2003; Nacke, Drachen, and Goebel 2010). The argument is that game evaluation is more about "playability" than "usability." Nacke, Drachen, and Goebel (2010) present a comprehensive review of research into playability evaluation. They propose three methodological categories for experiences that surround games: the quality of the product (game system experience), the quality of human–product interaction (individual player experience), and the quality of this interaction in a given social, temporal, spatial, or other context.

This multidimensional phenomenon raises inherent difficulties in attempting to measure and describe user experience in games, especially the experience of game audio, which is often subliminal and is by definition transient, thereby making its evaluation so much more difficult than the more tangible image. The principal challenges are the subjective experience of each user and the use of qualitative data, in the form of language and semantics, for them to communicate their experiences. Utilizing predetermined, quantitative measures such as surveys, Likert, or semantic differential scales, are common methods to overcome these felt difficulties, but come with their own problems, chiefly the danger of lacking depth and validity. This is especially true where the aspect of evaluation does not benefit from any research or inclusive design led tools for measuring subjective perception.

So far, no standardized tool exists for measuring user perception and experience of audio elements within computer games. Research has been done in this area, although surprisingly little, which explores approaches and methods such as that of Nacke, Grimshaw, and Lindley (2010), who consider audio experience specifically, but without any ad hoc or industry-driven standard ever emerging. This is unsurprising, since it can be argued that the field is still relatively in its infancy. This sets user experience of game audio apart, unlike the more technical field perceptual measurement of audio quality, which benefits from a range of application-specific standards (ITU-R 2001, 2003; Bech and Zacharov 2007), it does not benefit from an industry, or even ad hoc, standard. This is not unexpected, but is a noticeable gap. Where research and development has taken place specifically concerned about the user experience of audio, this has typically been in the field of interfaces that utilize sound and evaluation and tends not to be concerned with the actual effect of the audio, but rather its functionality. For example, the work of Gaver (1989) examined the use of sound as an interaction tool and evaluated user experience of this tool to demonstrate the beneficial effect of audio in this capacity.

The computer game industry has grown rapidly and has been commercially driven. In its infancy, audio was nonexistent in games. Its use as a principal driver for interaction, immersion, and gameplay has only come to the fore in the last decade (Roden and Parberry 2005; Liljedahl et al. 2007; Parker and Heerema 2008; Moustakas et al. 2009; Papworth 2010; Chittaro and Zuliani 2013; Östblad et al. 2014). The size of audio teams, focused on design and implementation, in game development are still small compared to their counterparts in departments of animation, graphics, software development, testing, and so on. These factors are compounded by the business-critical and deadline-driven game development environment, which leaves only a short time for detailed evaluation and testing with players, outside of the audio team. Consequently, audio testing is more concerned with integration aspects, such as levels in the mix and audio fidelity, rather than the levels of immersion and enhanced experience of the player.

The theory behind evaluating a player's experience of game audio is similarly limited. Much work has been done around the principles of sound and music design and implementation, focusing on preproduction, production, and postproduction (Gal et al. 2002; Brandon 2005; Collins 2008; Alves and Roque 2010; Stevens and Raybould 2011). But there is little specifically dealing with measuring a player's experience of the resultant game audio. It is reasonable to assume that this too is attributable to the deadline-driven nature of the game development industry and the opaque task of evaluating subjective, individual perception of game players.

Recently, specific game audio user experience evaluation has started to emerge. Mandryk et al. (2006) conducted an investigation into the best methods for evaluating emotive response, such as excitement, boredom, and so on, to entertainment technologies. Their study utilized a computer game as the main focus and took the approach of collecting data via electromyography (EMG) and GSR physiological sensors, which were then cross analyzed with subjective participant ratings. While the results are interesting, the thrust of the work was not upon the user experience of audio in its own right, but rather the overall experience of the computer game.

Sanders and Cairns (2010) conducted two experiments to measure the effect of music in computer games and how it relates to a player's sense of immersion within the game world. Their work utilized subjective participant responses, primarily through the form of questionnaires and ratings in a controlled trial configuration. The results of their research indicate the presence of music in a game positively influences indicators of immersion (in this case time perception of the player). The work also suggests that the presence of music that is preferred by the player will enhance this effect. The approach of Sanders and Cairns is particularly relevant to this case study, since it directly addresses measurement of game involvement, rather than purely trying to measure the mechanics or functions of the game as a piece of software or as an interface.

Demarque and de Lima (2013) carried out a study regarding the fear effects and emotional response to simulated auditory hallucinations. Their work included a case study regarding the implementation of auditory hallucinations in the horror games Silent Hill

(1999), Fatal Frame (2001), F.E.A.R. (2005), and Hotel 626 (2008), and an experiment was undertaken with a bespoke simulation of auditory hallucinations created in Unity. The study used a Likert questionnaire to investigate the user experience of the game with regard to fear emotion, fear behaviors, and immersion. In the study, each participant played the game with and without auditory hallucinations.

The study as a whole sheds light on a relatively unexplored area, and the results of the user study point toward the efficacy of auditory hallucinations in enhancing the "horror" aspects of games. However from a methodological point of view the user study has some limitations, since it relied on a simplistic prototype game with relatively few gameplay elements. One might expect that any additional element in such a simple game would have a significant impact on the user experience, and that the questionnaire for such a comparative study may well have guided the participants somewhat toward the aims of the study. We might therefore judge that the study highlights the need for improved methodological approaches in assessing the diverse qualities that game audio may afford the user, both in the situations produced by actual games and in a less "leading" manner.

The need for more sophisticated means of analyzing the effects of game sound are partly the result of the sophistication with which modern games harness audio as an evocative medium. For example, Bridgett (2013, p. 565) describes the use of dialog, ambience, sound effects, and music in games, to support the overall impression of the game in context; to "...*dramatically heighten emotion and engagement and to cinematize the experience for the player.*" Bridgett emphases that the overall design of sound is critically integrated into the context of the game in question, and moreover that often games also can be seen "...*more as nodes of popular culture than as isolated cultural entities*" (p. 564). As a result, we can see fundamental limitations in evaluating the efficacy of game audio with binary on/off studies. To provide a more meaningful analysis of game audio design, we should seek to analyze it as it occurs within actual games, particularly as these themselves are embedded in a broader cultural landscape that includes films and other media with game audio frequent references, pastiches, and parodies to achieve its effects. Separating the medium from these other factors will certainly have significant effects on the user experience; ways are needed to evaluate real-game audio in real games.

SOLUTIONS AND RECOMMENDATIONS: THE REPERTORY GRID STUDY

In this case study, the repertory grid technique, as broadly described above, was implemented with a group of participants to elicit constructs that will allow for the description of the user experience as it relates to game audio. The purpose of this is therefore to employ a user-centered methodology to create semantic differential scales, rather than to impose scales that might be misunderstood by the user, for game testing that can be specifically used in the audio domain. To this extent, the domain of investigation was ASC and non-ASC game soundscapes and the elements consisted of eight audio clips, created by recording samples of gameplay audio.

Selections of audio were taken from four commercially available, contemporary game titles, namely Batman: Arkham Asylum (2009); Max Payne 3 (2012), *Far Cry 3* (2012), and Grand Theft Auto 5 (2013). All the selected games fall into the broad category of action and adventure, with Far Cry 3 specifically being a first-person shooter game, while the others are predominantly third-person action and/or shooter games. All the games selected feature segments of gameplay in which the player takes control of their avatar while an ASC situation is being represented within the game.

Each audio clip was codified, so as not to influence the constructs produced by participants and to encourage them to focus on listening to the characteristics of the audio. The codes and clip descriptions are shown in Table 5.2.

Participants were guided through the semistructured interview by a researcher and utilizing a digital representation of each element that allowed them to hear each sound when the name of the element was clicked. This was clearly preferential over a paper-based card-sorting technique given the aural nature of the elements involved. Participants were briefed on the nature of the study and introduced to the concept of construct elicitation and scoring of the selected elements using the scale of 1–5 against each construct. A training phase was employed, where participants were able to listen to each of the sound elements and they participated in a scoring exercise on a *dislike–like* construct, which was later discarded for the purposes of analysis. Emulating the card-sorting technique, the choice of sounds was randomized each time a participant was presented with a triad of samples. The sound clips were presented as stand-alone objects and the participant was not viewing any game footage during this time. The only visual cues available during the interviews were the codified names of the current sample selection. Participants were free to listen to each element as many times as they wished during the process. The average time taken for each interview was in the region of 35 min.

A total of six people participated in the repertory grid study. These were mainly university students who consider themselves computer games players. The gender balance was 100% male. A total of 36 constructs were elicited during the process. Participants volunteered each of these constructs during the interviews. The data were analyzed using the OpenRepGrid on Air analysis tool (2014). The resulting repertory grid for all participants is shown in Figure 5.1, in which ratings are shaded with 1 being lightest and 5 being the darkest shade, elements are indicated by code horizontally along the top of the grid, whilst the obtained constructs are shown vertically, with the construct representing the rating 1 on the far left-hand side and the construct representing 5 on the far right-hand side. Each row of the grid represents a pair of bipolar constructs and set of scores obtained from a participant.

Presented in this initial form, it is not intuitive to make particular judgments about relationships between the elements involved in the study or the constructs. However, this initial view of the data obtained illustrates the variety of constructs that have been elicited from the participants and the variation in language and vocabulary that is utilized to describe the qualities of the audio samples. This early inspection does yields some notable observations, for example, the construct *violent* has been used on several occasions, similarly, so have the constructs of *scary* and *horror*.

To explore the data in a deeper way, and determine constructs that may be being used interchangeably by participants, sorting and analysis of the repertory grid data can be performed. Figure 5.2 shows a reordered version of the previous grid. In this visualization, a focus analysis (Shaw 1980; Jankowicz 2004) has been utilized that seeks to reorder the

TABLE 5.2   Descriptions of Audio Elements Used in Repertory Grid Study

Code	Game	ASC	Description
A	*Batman: Arkham Asylum*	Yes	Batman becomes infected by an enemy, Scarecrow's hallucinogenic toxin, and must complete a specific level in order to return to normal consciousness. This sound most notably features the voice of the Scarecrow character that is warped with predelay and reverb effects. In the background there is the presence of some slow, string-based music.
B	*Grand Theft Auto 5*	No	One of the game's main protagonists, Trevor, is in a gunfight with a group of police officers. Multiple instances of incoming and outgoing gunfire are heard, with sirens in the background. The main character is shouting at the police and encouraging them to try to shoot him.
C	*Max Payne 3*	No	The scene is largely sound driven and represents a shootout between the main character, Max Payne, and a group of gangsters. There is slow, string-based background music throughout. Multiple voices of the enemy characters can be heard shouting in a foreign (i.e., non-English) language and this is interspersed with gunfire. There is liberal use of reverb over the diegetic sounds, representing the large space the action takes place in
D	*Far Cry 3*	Yes	The main character, Jason, experiences a heavy drug trip, activated by an earlier interaction with hallucinogenic mushrooms in the forest. There is a cacophony of sounds around the listener like glass shattering in the background. Another voice, processed with predelays and echo, enquires, "*What are you afraid of?*" Screeches are subtly introduced along with a sound similar to a reverse cymbal, which builds to a minor crescendo.
E	*Grand Theft Auto 5*	Yes	The player is in control of another main character, Michael, who has been drugged (unknowingly) by his son. The drug takes effect while the player is controlling Michael driving a car. The sound features mainly dialog from the character, asking what has happened to him and has been time stretched and pitch shifted to make it sound slow and low pitched, although the effect varies over time between the processed speech, normal speech, and back again.
F	*Batman: Arkham Asylum*	No	There is notable dramatic, orchestral music. A voice on a public announcement system is issuing warnings of security breaches. There are some character movement sounds before the music is ducked as we hear the voice of Batman interact with a rescued prison guard who has recently regained consciousness
G	*Max Payne 3*	Yes	Max Payne is able to harness levels of adrenaline accumulated during gameplay to trigger the occurrence of an ASC, which has the effect of slowing down the gameplay. The sample is extracted from a shootout with enemy game characters. The sound begins with instances of gunfire that have been subtly time and pitch stretched, to produce a slowed down effect. There are occasional voices of enemy characters in between the gunshots and weapon reloading sounds. Notably, the background ambience, music, and enemy voices are lower in the mix than during normal gameplay; with the gunfire being high in the mix.
H	*Far Cry 3*	No	There is a brief burst of gunfire, the sound of an animal grunting and then the sounds of movement. There is notable ambience and music, suggesting a jungle scene, before the main character enquires as to the well-being of a rescued colleague

	A	B	C	D	E	F	G	H	
City (1)	3	1	5	2	3	2	3	5	(1) War
Traditional (2)	4	1	2	5	3	4	2	4	(2) Futuristic
Fighting (3)	5	4	1	5	3	5	1	1	(3) Communication
Female voice (4)	5	5	3	5	5	2	3	2	(4) Male Voice
Quiet (5)	4	4	4	5	4	4	5	4	(5) Loud
Control (6)	3	4	2	2	3	4	5	3	(6) Desperation
Question (7)	1	4	3	2	4	1	3	1	(7) Instruction
Human (8)	4	1	3	2	4	1	3	1	(8) Artificial
Negative (9)	2	5	4	3	1	2	5	3	(9) Warfare
Death (10)	4	1	1	5	4	3	2	3	(10) Afraid
Danger (11)	5	1	2	4	3	3	1	4	(11) Intense
Dark (12)	1	5	2	1	4	4	3	3	(12) Energetic
Violent (13)	5	1	1	5	4	3	1	2	(13) Nonviolent
Brave (14)	5	1	3	3	5	4	2	3	(14) Scary
Softer (15)	3	5	5	3	1	2	5	3	(15) Violent
Quiet (16)	4	5	4	3	3	2	4	3	(16) Busy
Clean (17)	5	2	3	5	5	1	3	2	(17) Warped
Relaxed (18)	2	5	3	3	3	4	5	1	(18) Manic
Conscious (19)	3	1	3	4	5	1	2	1	(19) Faint
Urgency (20)	5	1	3	5	3	5	2	4	(20) Atmospheric
Nice (21)	5	2	4	5	2	1	3	3	(21) Eerie
UnNaturalistic (22)	1	3	4	1	2	5	3	4	(22) Naturalistic
Horror (23)	2	5	4	2	3	5	4	3	(23) Action
Busy (24)	4	3	3	5	4	2	3	4	(24) Tinny
NonViolent (25)	2	5	4	3	4	3	4	3	(25) Violent
Not Scary (26)	5	3	3	4	3	4	3	2	(26) Scary
Shallow (27)	4	2	3	3	2	5	3	4	(27) Deep
Slow (28)	2	3	3	2	1	4	3	3	(28) Fast
Nonsuspense (29)	5	2	2	4	3	4	2	3	(29) Suspense
Not noisy (30)	3	4	3	3	3	2	4	2	(30) Noisy
Low-background noise (31)	3	4	3	3	2	4	2	2	(31) High-background noise
Far Away (32)	4	4	3	3	2	3	1	1	(32) Close
Fade (33)	3	4	1	5	2	3	3	4	(33) Flux
Flat (34)	4	5	4	5	4	1	1	3	(34) Layers
Inconsistency (35)	4	2	4	5	3	5	5	2	(35) Consistency
Inconspicuous (36)	2	3	3	2	3	4	5	1	(36) Barrage

FIGURE 5.1 Repertory grid for all participants.

repertory grid so that similar constructs appear visually near to one another and the study elements are also ordered using the same technique.

This reordering now makes an easier task of identifying constructs that may be describing the same listener experience, since rankings are shuffled clustering relationships between them. For example, consider now the constructs *busy–tinny*; *unnaturalistic–naturalistic*; *clean–warped*; and *flat–layers*. We see that the constructs *nonviolent–violent*; *death–afraid*; and *softer–violent*, exhibit a similar series of scores. There is a reasonable degree of consistency in the way that these constructs have been used to rate the study elements, which would suggest that further investigation into these constructs is warranted. This indicates that it may be possible to consolidate these constructs into one. The researcher may execute this consolidation process either by employing construct descriptors already received (if they are similar or identical) or by summarizing him/herself, the quality that is being described. This has been recognized by others using the repertory grid technique as being a particular strength, which is aptly described by Tan and Hunter (2002, p. 42) as being able

	E	A	D	F	H	B	C	G	
War (1)	3	3	4	4	1	5	1	3	(1) City
Fighting (2)	3	5	5	5	1	4	1	1	(2) Communication
Fade (3)	2	3	5	3	4	4	1	3	(3) Flux
Far Away (4)	2	4	3	3	1	4	3	1	(4) Close
Low Background Noise (5)	2	3	3	4	2	4	3	2	(5) High Background Noise
Inconsistency (6)	3	4	5	5	2	2	4	5	(6) Consistency
Not Scary (7)	3	5	4	4	2	3	3	3	(7) Scary
Quiet (8)	4	4	5	4	4	4	4	5	(8) Loud
NonSuspense (9)	3	5	4	4	3	2	2	2	(9) Suspense
Danger (10)	3	5	4	3	4	1	2	1	(10) Intense
Violent (11)	2	4	3	3	3	1	2	2	(11) Nonviolent
Urgency (12)	3	5	5	5	4	1	3	2	(12) Atmospheric
Traditional (13)	3	4	5	4	4	1	2	2	(13) Futuristic
Violent (14)	4	5	5	3	2	1	1	1	(14) Nonviolent
Death (15)	4	4	5	3	3	1	1	2	(15) Afraid
Violent (16)	5	3	3	4	3	1	1	1	(16) Softer
Warfare (17)	5	4	3	4	3	1	2	1	(17) Negative
Brave (18)	5	5	3	4	3	1	3	2	(18) Scary
Noisy (19)	3	3	3	4	4	2	3	2	(19) Not Noisy
Busy (20)	3	2	3	4	3	1	2	2	(20) Quiet
Instruction (21)	2	5	4	5	5	2	3	3	(21) Question
Shallow (22)	2	4	3	5	4	2	3	3	(22) Deep
Fast (23)	5	4	4	2	3	3	3	3	(23) Slow
Busy (24)	4	4	5	2	4	3	3	3	(24) Tinny
Naturalistic (25)	4	5	5	1	2	3	2	3	(25) UnNaturalistic
Clean (26)	5	5	5	1	2	2	3	3	(26) Warped
Flat (27)	4	4	5	1	3	5	4	1	(27) Layers
Female Voice (28)	5	5	5	2	2	5	3	3	(28) Male Voice
Conscious (29)	5	3	4	1	1	1	3	2	(29) Faint
Human (30)	4	4	2	1	1	1	3	3	(30) Artificial
Action (31)	3	4	4	1	3	1	2	2	(31) Horror
Desperation (32)	3	3	4	2	3	2	4	1	(32) Control
Barrage (33)	3	4	4	2	5	3	3	1	(33) Inconspicuous
Manic (34)	3	4	3	2	5	1	3	1	(34) Relaxed
Energetic (35)	2	5	5	2	3	1	4	3	(35) Dark
Nice (36)	2	5	5	1	3	2	4	3	(36) Eerie

FIGURE 5.2 Repertory grid sorted using focus analysis.

to show "... *group norms*" within a sample group of participants, which should be indicative of the wider population that they represent.

To explore the structural aspects of this clustering, the constructs obtained are further analyzed. In the following analysis, construct matches are identified by measuring the Euclidean distance between constructs, over element ratings, and then applying Ward's method for cluster analysis (Ward 1963). As a result, it is possible to produce a more structured form of the constructs, now removed from the traditional repertory grid view, and presented as a dendrogram, as illustrated in Figure 5.3.

From this analysis, it is possible to begin a systematic reduction of constructs and to distil broad categories and descriptors that can be utilized to develop scales to measure the efficacy and qualities of game sound. However, a decision must be made by the person analyzing the data as to which "depth" to work to when deciding upon membership of groups of constructs. This is particularly true as using a very detailed level of construct matching

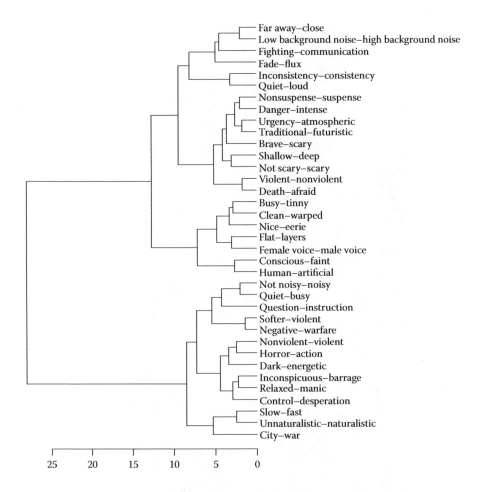

FIGURE 5.3   Cluster analysis of constructs with Euclidean distance and ward clustering.

will yield fewer constructs than obtained from all of the participants, but still result in a significant amount. To assist in this process, there is a final piece of analysis that can be performed upon the original repertory grid data that allows the inclusion of a statistical confidence interval to aid the researcher or developer in identifying significant construct matches. The outcome from this analysis can be seen in Figure 5.4.

This analysis is obtained by the statistical process of bootstrapping (Efron and Tibshirani 1994), which models a measure of accuracy or reliability of a sample. The consequence of this is that confidence intervals can be set at the analysis phase and the data processed to this criterion. The result is that the dendrogram is modified to show where links between constructs are deemed statistically significant. In the case of this analysis, all constructs and groups of constructs that are modeled to have $p < 0.05$ are highlighted by having a box placed around them. This is further expressed in Figure 5.4 by the approximately unbiased (AU) p-value being shown on the top-right edge of construct trees, alongside the bootstrap probability (BP).

By analyzing the data in Figures 5.3 and 5.4, it is therefore possible to consolidate the 36 constructs that were originally elicited into a more concise set. These, it is hypothesized,

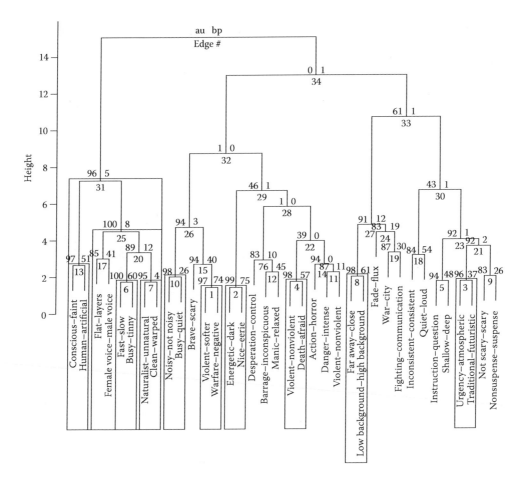

FIGURE 5.4 Cluster analysis of constructs with AU/BP values (Euclidean distance and ward clustering).

can be used to form a common, generally understandable, and applicable scale for measuring user experience of audio in games. The resultant scales are shown in Table 5.3. This set has been arrived at by consolidating the statistically significant construct groups and making flexible use of the variations in constructs that were elicited, along with some interpretation on the part of the researcher to make the scales more fluid. Additionally, a category name has been added that is felt summarizes the particular game audio characteristics that are being described in each of the new scales.

SOLUTIONS AND RECOMMENDATIONS: AN EFFICIENT SCALE TO EVALUATE GAME AUDIO

It is hypothesized that efficacy of the prototype scales will be evidenced by differences in scoring between the ASC and non-ASC elements within the game but that the scales should be equally applicable to both segments of gameplay and easily understood by the user. To provide an initial demonstration of the newly formulated scale being utilized for analysis, we consider the ratings that were obtained earlier in the original repertory grid.

TABLE 5.3   Game Audio-Rating Scales
Resulting from Investigation

Category Name	Construct/Scale	
Valence	*Nonviolent*	*Violent*
Attention	*Atmospheric*	*Urgent*
Distance	*Near*	*Far*
Fear	*Nice*	*Eerie*
Noise	*Quiet*	*Noisy*
Speed	*Slow*	*Fast*
Distortion	*Unnatural*	*Natural*

For the purposes of this analysis, the sound elements used have been separated into two groups: those that are taken from game segments representing ASC and those that do not. The initial constructs are then sorted into the groups associated with the categories presented in Table 5.3. In addition, a number of other constructs with close matching values, or that it seemed should intuitively be mapped, were accounted for within one of the new scale descriptors. The full allocation of all of the original constructs, to the new scales, is shown in Table 5.4. It should be noted that duplication in the constructs occurs where more than one participant presented an identical construct, such as in the Valence category.

TABLE 5.4   Assignment of Constructs to Scale Categories for
Modal Analysis

Category Name	Constructs Used in Modal Analysis
Valence	*Afraid–death*
	Softer–violent
	Nonviolent–violent
Attention	*Traditional–futuristic*
	Urgency–atmospheric
	Nonsuspense–suspense
Distance	*Low-background noise–high-background noise*
	Far away–close
	Fade–flux
Fear	*Energetic–dark*
	Brave–scary
	Nice–eerie
	Not scary–scary
Noise	*Quiet–busy*
	Not noisy–noisy
Speed	*Slow–fast*
	Tinny–busy
Distortion	*Human–artificial*
	Clean–warped
	Conscious–faint
	Naturalistic–unnaturalistic
	Flat–layers

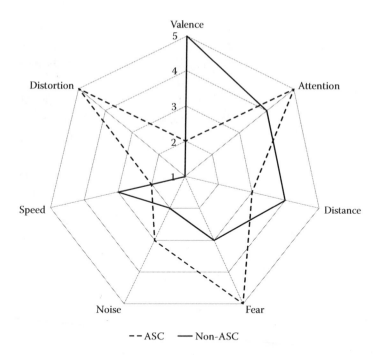

FIGURE 5.5   Modal comparison of ASC and non-ASC game audio ratings.

Since the repertory grid data were gathered using a scale of 1–5, such data are ordinal in nature. To this extent, we carry out modal analysis across the two groups of audio elements, with the intention that such analysis should indicate a difference between the ASC and non-ASC elements. The results from this analysis are plotted in a polar graph, which is shown in Figure 5.5.

The results indicated above are particularly promising. There are distinct differences between the two categories of audio elements over all of the ratings that have been devised. As such, the data suggest that the repertory grid approach has been effective in devising a series of scales that are quickly and easily deployed and can be utilized to measure user experience of a range of game audio attributes effectively. Though it is advocated that further refinement of the scale is required, our research has led us to establish a base framework for the evaluation of game audio, which can be built on in future work from further refining the scale itself and the testing of the efficacy of the scale in gameplay user-testing scenarios.

CONCLUSIONS

In this chapter, we have discussed the lack of focus upon user experience testing in games, particularly in relation to game audio, which often takes a lower priority than other factors in the development of a game, such as gameplay. Recognizing the issue that user testing can be an activity that is resource hungry, we aimed to develop a mechanism that would quickly and effectively allow the measurement of user experience of game audio. Such a tool would be particularly useful for sound designers, composers, and others working within the sound and music teams who are developing games.

This chapter has shown the value that can be gleaned from investing in, what is initially, a time and labor-intensive process, of repertory grid interviews with a range of subjects. However, the benefits are quickly yielded by the formulation of a user-centered method of devising scales and metrics for the evaluation of user experience of audio in games. To demonstrate the value of this approach and the scale that was formulated, it was applied to see if it could determine the presence of subtle game audio differences from segments in games that feature ASC. From the data analysis in this chapter, it was shown that the scale is effective in this capacity.

Although our work here has focused on game audio as a particular domain of interest, it is anticipated that the process would be easily transferrable to other aspects of measuring game user experience. For example, we suggest there is significant use of this approach in evaluating aspects of the game such as control system, immersiveness, graphics, gameplay, narrative, longevity, and so on.

REFERENCES

Alves, V. and L. Roque. 2010. A pattern language for sound design in games. In *Proceedings of the 5th Audio Mostly Conference: A Conference on Interaction with Sound*, Piteå, Sweden, September 15–17, 2010. doi: 10.1145/1859799.1859811.

Bech, S. and N. Zacharov. 2007. *Perceptual Audio Evaluation—Theory, Method and Application*. Chichester: John Wiley & Sons.

Blake, A. 2013. Top 10 hallucinations in video games. *Leviathyn*. http://leviathyn.com/opinion/2013/07/26/top-10-hallucinations-in-video-games/ (accessed May 7, 2014).

Brandon, A. 2005. *Audio for Games: Planning, Process, and Production*. Berkeley, CA: New Riders Games.

Bridgett, R. 2013. Contextualizing game audio aesthetics. In Richardson, J., Gorbman, C., and C. Vernallis (eds.), *The Oxford Handbook of New Audiovisual Aesthetics*. New York, NY: Oxford University Press.

Brown, M. 2008. Evaluating computer game usability: Developing heuristics based on user experience. In *Proceedings of IHCI Conference*, Cork, Ireland, September 19–20, 2008. University College Cork.

Chin, J. P., Diehl, V. A., and K. L. Norman. 1988. Development of an instrument measuring user satisfaction of the human–computer interface. In *Proceedings of the ACM SIGCHI Conference on Human Factors in Computing Systems*, Washington, DC, June 15–19, 1988. doi: 10.1145/57167.57203.

Chittaro, L. and F. Zuliani. 2013. Exploring audio storytelling in mobile exergames to affect the perception of physical exercise. In *7th International Conference on Pervasive Computing Technologies for Healthcare (PervasiveHealth)*, Venice, Italy, May 5–8, 2013. IEEE.

Collins, K. 2008. *Game Sound: An Introduction to the History, Theory, and Practice of Video Game Music and Sound Design*. Cambridge, MA: MIT Press.

Constantine, L. L. and L. A. D. Lockwood. 1999. *Software for Use: A Practical Guide to the Models and Methods of Usage-Centered Design*. Reading, MA: Addison-Wesley.

Demarque, T. C. and E. S. de Lima. 2013. Auditory hallucination: Audiological perspective for horror games. In *Proceedings of SBGames*, São Paulo, Brazil, October 16–18, 2013. Mackenzie Presbyterian University.

Efron, B. and R. Tibshirani. 1994. *An Introduction to the Bootstrap*. New York, NY: Chapman & Hall.

Gal, V., Le Prado, C., Merland, J. B., Natkin, S., and L. Vega. 2002. Processes and tools for sound design in computer games. In *Proceedings International Computer Music Conference*, Gothenburg, Sweden, September 19, 2002. International Computer Music Association.

Gaver, W. W. 1989. The SonicFinder: An interface that uses auditory icons. *Human–Computer Interaction* 4 (1): 67–94.

Goodby, Berlin, and Silverstein. 2008. Hotel 626. Online Flash Game, Doritos.com.

Grill, T., Flexer, A., and S. Cunningham. 2011. Identification of perceptual qualities in textural sounds using the repertory grid method. In *Proceedings of the 6th Audio Mostly Conference: A Conference on Interaction with Sound*, Coimbra, Portugal, September 7–9, 2011. doi: 10.1145/2095667.2095677.

ITU-R. 2001. Recommendation ITU-R BS.1387-1. Method for objective measurements of perceived audio quality. *International Telecommunication Union—Radio Communication Sector (ITU-R)*.

ITU-R. 2003. Recommendation ITU-R BS.1284-1. General methods for the subjective assessment of sound quality. *International Telecommunication Union—Radio communication Sector (ITU-R)*.

Jankowicz, D. 2004. *The Easy Guide to Repertory Grids*. Chichester, West Sussex, England: John Wiley.

Kelly, G. 1955. *The Psychology of Personal Constructs*. New York, NY: Norton.

Kirakowski, J. and M. Corbett. 1993. SUMI: The software usability measurement inventory. *British Journal of Educational Technology* 24 (3): 210–212.

Konami Computer Entertainment Tokyo. 1999. Silent Hill. PlayStation. Konami.

Liljedahl, M., Papworth, N., and S. Lindberg. 2007. Beowulf: An audio mostly game. In *Proceedings of the International Conference on Advances in Computer Entertainment Technology*, Salzburg, Austria, June 15–17, 2007. doi: 10.1145/1255047.1255088.

Mandryk, R. L., Inkpen, K. M., and T. W. Calvert. 2006. Using psychophysiological techniques to measure user experience with entertainment technologies. *Behaviour and Information Technology* 25 (2): 141–158.

Monolith Productions. 2005. *F.E.A.R. First Encounter Assault Recon*, Windows PC. Vivendi Universal.

Moustakas, N., Floros, A., and N. Kanellopoulos. 2009. Eidola: An interactive augmented reality audio-game prototype. In *Audio Engineering Society Convention 127*, New York, USA, October 9–12, 2009. Audio Engineering Society.

Nacke, L. E., Grimshaw, M. N., and C. A. Lindley. 2010. More than a feeling: Measurement of sonic user experience and psychophysiology in a first-person shooter game. *Interacting with Computers* 22 (5): 336–343.

Nacke, L., Drachen, A., and S. Göbel. 2010. Methods for evaluating gameplay experience in a serious gaming context. *International Journal of Computer Science in Sport* 9 (2): 1–12.

Nielsen, J. 1993. *Usability Engineering*. Boston: Academic Press.

OpenRepGrid. 2014. OpenRepGrid on Air. http://www.onair.openrepgrid.org/ (accessed February 6, 2015).

Östblad, P. A., Engström, H., Brusk, J., Backlund, P., and U. Wilhelmsson. 2014. Inclusive game design: Audio interface in a graphical adventure game. In *Proceedings of the 9th Audio Mostly: A Conference on Interaction with Sound*, Aalborg, Denmark, October 1–3, 2014. doi: 10.1145/2636879.2636909.

Pagulayan, R. J., Keeker, K., Fuller, T., Wixon, D., Romero, R. L., and D. V. Gunn. 2003. User centered design in games. In Jacko, J. A. and A. Sears (eds.), *The Human Computer Interaction Handbook: Fundamentals, Evolving Technologies, and Emerging Applications*. New York, NY: L. Erlbaum Associates Inc.

Papworth, N. 2010. iSpooks: An audio focused game design. In *Proceedings of the 5th Audio Mostly Conference: A Conference on Interaction with Sound*, Piteå, Sweden, September 15–17, 2010. doi: 10.1145/1859799.1859810.

Parker, J. R. and J. Heerema. 2008. Audio interaction in computer mediated games. *International Journal of Computer Games Technology* 2008: 1–8.

Picking, R., Grout, V., McGinn, J., Crisp, J., and H. Grout. 2012. Simplicity, consistency, universality, flexibility and familiarity: The SCUFF principles for developing user. *Innovative Applications of Ambient Intelligence: Advances in Smart Systems* 2012: 179–187.

Reiss, E. 2009. A definition of "user experience." http://www.fatdux.com/blog/2009/01/10/a-definition-of-user-experience/ (accessed January 25, 2015).

Rockstar North. 2013. *Grand Theft Auto 5*. Xbox 360, Rockstar Games.

Rockstar Studios. 2012. *Max Payne 3*. Xbox 360, Rockstar Games.

Rocksteady Studios. 2009. *Batman: Arkham Asylum*. Xbox 360, Eidos Interactive and Warner Bros. Interactive Entertainment.

Roden, T. and I. Parberry. 2005. Designing a narrative-based audio only 3D game engine. In *Proceedings of the ACM SIGCHI International Conference on Advances in Computer Entertainment Technology*, Valencia, Spain, June 15–17, 2005. doi: 10.1145/1178477.1178525.

Rogers, Y., Sharp, H., and J. Preece. 2011. *Interaction Design: Beyond Human–Computer Interaction*. New York, NY: John Wiley & Sons.

Sanders, T. and P. Cairns. 2010. Time perception, immersion and music in videogames. In *Proceedings of the 24th BCS Interaction Specialist Group Conference*, Dundee, Scotland, September 6–10, 2010. British Computer Society.

Shaw, M. L. G. 1980. On becoming a personal scientist: Interactive computer programs for developing personal models of the world. PhD thesis. Brunel University, UK.

Shneiderman, B. 1998. *Designing the User Interface: Strategies for Effective Human–Computer Interaction*. 3rd ed. Reading, MA: Addison-Wesley Longman.

Stevens, R. and D. Raybould. 2011. *The Game Audio Tutorial: A Practical Guide to Sound and Music for Interactive Games*. Burlington, MA: Focal Press.

Tan, F. B. and M. G. Hunter. 2002. The repertory grid technique: A method for the study of cognition in information systems. *MIS Quarterly* 26 (1): 39–57.

Tecmo. 2001. *Fatal Frame*. PlayStation 2, Wanadoo.

Ubisoft. 2010. *Far Cry 3*. Xbox 360, Ubisoft.

Vygotsky, L. S. 2012. *Thought and Language*. Cambridge: MIT Press.

Wadsworth, B. J. 1996. *Piaget's Theory of Cognitive and Affective Development: Foundations of Constructivism*. 5th ed. New York, NY: Longman.

Ward Jr., J. H. 1963. Hierarchical grouping to optimize an objective function. *Journal of the American Statistical Association* 58 (301): 236–244.

Weinel, J. 2010. Quake delirium: Remixing psychedelic video games. *Sonic Ideas/Ideas Sonicas* 3 (2): 22–29.

Weinel, J., Cunningham, S., and D. Griffiths. 2014. Sound through the rabbit hole: Sound design based on reports of auditory hallucination. In *Proceedings of the 9th Audio Mostly: A Conference on Interaction with Sound*, Aalborg, Denmark, October 1–3, 2014. doi: 10.1145/2636879.2636883.

Weinel, J., Cunningham, S., Roberts, N., Roberts, S., and D. Griffiths. 2014. EEG as a controller for psychedelic visual music in an immersive dome environment. In *Proceedings of Conference on Electronic Visualisation and the Arts (EVA 2014)*, London, UK, July 8–10, 2014. British Computer Society.

Wharton, C., Rieman, J., Lewis, C., and P. Polson. 1994. The cognitive walkthrough method: A practitioner's guide. In Nielsen, J. and R. L. Mack, (eds.), *Usability Inspection Methods*. New York, NY: John Wiley & Sons, Inc.

LIST OF ADDITIONAL SOURCES

Dix, A., Finlay, J., Gregory, A., and B. Russell. 2004. *Human–Computer Interaction*. England: Pearson Education Ltd.

Calleja, G. 2011. *In-Game: From Immersion to Incorporation*. Cambridge, MA: MIT Press.

Collins, K. 2013. *Playing with Sound: A Theory of Interacting with Sound and Music in Video Games*. Cambridge, MA: MIT Press.

Ekman, I. 2008. Psychologically motivated techniques for emotional sound in computer games. In *Proceedings of Audio Mostly 2008, 3rd Conference on Interaction with Sound*, Piteå, Sweden, October 22–23, 2008. Interactive Institute Sonic Studio.

Fransella, F., Bell, R., and D. Bannister. 2004. *A Manual for Repertory Grid Technique*. New York, NY: John Wiley & Sons.

Grimshaw, M. and T. A. Garner. 2015. *Sonic Virtuality: Sound as Emergent Perception*. New York, NY: Oxford University Press.

Hobson, J. A. 2002. *The Dream Drugstore Chemically Altered States of Consciousness*. Cambridge, MA: MIT Press.

Horowitz, S. and S. R. Looney. 2014. *The Essential Guide to Game Audio: The Theory and Practice of Sound for Games*. New York, NY: Focal Press, Taylor & Francis Group.

Jørgensen, K. 2007. What are those grunts and growls over there? Computer game audio and player action. PhD dissertion, Københavns Universitet, Denmark.

Juslin, P. N. and J. A. Sloboda (eds). 2010. *Handbook of Music and Emotion: Theory, Research, Applications*. Oxford: Oxford University Press.

Newell, A. F., Carmichael, A., Morgan, M., and A. Dickinson. 2006. The use of theatre in requirements gathering and usability studies. *Interacting with Computers* 18 (5): 996–1011.

Sonnenschein, D. 2001. *Sound Design*. California: Michael Wiese Productions.

BIOGRAPHIES

Stuart Cunningham is a senior lecturer in computing at Glyndŵr University. He holds a PhD in similarity-based audio compression from the University of Wales (UK), having previously completed a BSc and MSc at the University of Paisley (UK). His research interests cover a range of computing and creative hybrids, including audio compression; affective technologies; sonic interaction; and sound design. Dr. Cunningham is a Fellow of the British Computer Society (BCS) and a chartered information technology professional (CITP). Dr. Cunningham was a member of the MPEG Music Notation Standards (MPEG-SMR) working group, which developed ISO/IEC 14496-23:2008.

Jonathan Weinel is a sonic artist and researcher. He holds a PhD in music technology, completed at Keele University (UK). Dr. Weinel's main expertise is in audio design and composition of psychedelic music and visual music. He creates sound for sonic arts, video games, and audio–visual projects, and carries out research broadly related to these areas.

Richard Picking is a professor of human–computer interaction at Glyndŵr University. He researches into various aspects of interface accessibility and usability, with a particular emphasis on design for the elderly or disabled. He is a practicing musician and has interests in assessing novel interfaces for sonic interaction. Rich is a Fellow of the BCS and Chair of the BCS Health in the Wales National Committee. Currently, he specializes in user interface design and evaluation, and was a lead designer and technical manager for the FP6 EU-funded program: "EASYLINE + : Low Cost Advanced White Goods for a Longer Independent Life of Elderly People."

KEY TERMS AND DEFINITIONS

ASC: Altered states of consciousness. Describes a state of human consciousness that is not considered "normal" in some regard. Typically this can be indicated by some kind of enhancement and/or impediment to one or more of the human senses, cognitive, or physical ability. States can be induced, for example, by psychoactive substances (such as hallucinogenic drugs), while others may be naturally occurring (such as dreaming).

Game audio: The presence of any kind of sound or music within a computer game situation. Game audio is notably different from time-based, linear audio such as that found in television or film. This is because of the fact that games are interactive and, although they tend to follow a path or guiding structure, they are nonlinear, at least in a time-bound sense. As such, game audio is dynamic and not easy to predict.

Immersion: The notion of the game player, or players, becoming detached from their real-world setting and having the perception that they are actually inside the game world. In essence, the players forget that they are interacting with the game by way of visual, audio, and tactile technologies while being in their own environments and believe they are inside the game and interacting with it in a fluid, intuitive manner.

Personal constructs: The theory of human learning and development that suggests we, as human beings, understand the world around us by our interactions and experiments with it. We formulate our own descriptions and explanations of the features and functions of the world, known as constructs, which are individual to us, though not necessarily unique.

Quantitative and qualitative subjective testing: Game user testing, by nature, involves the elicitation of subjective opinions and views of the participants involved. This information can be gathered in either a quantitative or qualitative form. Quantitative data include any information that can be presented or analyzed in numerical form, such as the number of times users collect an item in the game or a rating they give the game's usability on a scale of 1–5. Qualitative data are any information that takes a descriptive form and will usually be textual (although it could feasibly include pictures, diagrams, or sounds). For example, user descriptions of a game in interviews or focus groups are qualitative.

Repertory grid: A human-centered technique, based on the theory of personal constructs, which involves participants describing the characteristics of a range of elements. These elements typically form a sample from a particular subject or domain of knowledge. Subjects provide a quantitative rating against a series of qualitative constructs to create a matrix of scores and descriptions: the repertory grid.

CHAPTER 6

Tangible and Graphical Game Interfaces

An Experimental Comparison

Zeno Menestrina, Andrea Conci, Adriano Siesser,
Raul Masu, Michele Bianchi, and Antonella De Angeli

CONTENTS

EXECUTIVE SUMMARY

The research presented in this chapter focuses on the study of the advantages and disadvantages of tangible interfaces applied to video games as compared to graphical interfaces. Our work starts from the assumption that tangible interaction (TI) can improve the game immersion, exploiting natural affordances of physical objects and lessening the cognitive effort needed to manipulate graphical interfaces. To validate this hypothesis, the chapter describes the implementation and evaluation of the Radiant[2], a tangible interface to a digital game. The Radiant[2] is an augmented game board: the user interacts with a computer screen by placing tangible blocks on the board and manipulating them. To study how specific interactive features of TI may influence the game experience, we conducted a comparative evaluation of the Radiant[2] with its digital version implemented on a tablet (N = 29). The experience of the users has been assessed through the game experience questionnaire (GEQ) (IJsselsteijn et al. 2008), semistructured interviews, and direct observation. Results suggested that TI provides a higher level of sensory and imaginative immersion, competence, positive effect, and experience. On the other hand, there was no significant impact on flow, challenge, negative effect, and tiredness. These results support the potential of TI for video games design and suggest new design trajectories for the field.

ORGANIZATION BACKGROUND

Research and experiments have been carried out at the Department of Information Engineering and Computer Science. The department, founded in January 2002, covers the primary areas of telecommunications and computer science, with a strong focus on interdisciplinarity.

The work presented in this chapter is part of the research carried out by the human–computer interaction (HCI) (*interAction*) team of the department, and more specifically from the subgroup of *Ludic Design*, whose activity revolves around the exploration of new interactions and experiences in the fields of music, visual art, and gaming.

INTRODUCTION

TI is an area of research that seeks to extend the boundaries of interaction between human and computers with technologically enhanced physical objects. This research approach was pioneered by Ishii, Ullmer, and their colleagues, who aimed at "rejoin(ing) the richness of the physical world in HCI [Human–Computer Interaction]" (Ishii and Ullmer 1997, p. 234), bridging the digital and the real world. The aim of the users' action shifted from digital to tangible objects that, with their physicality, could provide a richer and simpler interaction.

A part of the research on TI has focused on video games, for the purposes of exploiting the features of these interfaces to build more engaging, enjoyable, and social experiences. This interest is not strictly related to the academic community, but also to the game industry, as witnessed, for example, by the "toys to life" (Davis 2014)—Skylanders, Disney Infinity, and Nintendo's Amiibo—or Sifteo Cubes (Merrill et al. 2012).

In this chapter we present a custom-augmented game board called Radiant² that allows the user to act on a digital game by interacting with tangible blocks. The design aimed at creating a close link between the user's physical actions and their effects in the game, thus reducing the gulf (Norman 2002) between the real and the virtual world. The Radiant² is not only a physical means enabling players to perform actions, but it guides them inside the game, favoring the seamless integration of tangible and digital interaction. The challenge of our work has been the exploration of the effects of the TI paradigm on the game experience. Following related work in the area of TI and on classical HCI cognitive frameworks, a greater degree of engagement, enjoyment, and usability was expected. In order to validate our hypothesis, we conducted a comparative evaluation between the Radiant² and its virtual representation implemented on a tablet (N = 29). Results suggest that TI provides a more immersive experience, facilitates more positive feelings, and encourages greater engagement as compared to the digital one. No effects were recorded on other important dimensions of the player experience, such as challenge, negative affect, and flow.

The chapter is organized as follows: first we provide an analysis of the state of the art on TI and related studies applied to game design. Second, we move to present the Radiant² and the video game we designed. Third, we describe our case study and results. Finally, we discuss the outcomes of the evaluation and close the chapter.

STATE OF THE ART

Halfway through the 1990s, the HCI community started to focus its attention on approaches such as *graspable user interfaces* (Fitzmaurice 1996), *tangible user interfaces* (TUIs) (Ishii and Ullmer 1997; Ullmer and Ishii 2000), and TI (Djajadiningrat et al. 2004). This chapter supported the establishment of a more-encompassing research agenda on *embodied interactions* research (Dourish 2004). The focus on TI resulted from a common interest in the investigation of new types of interaction that move digital information off the screen, creating a link between the digital and the physical world.

Fitzmaurice et al. (1995) proposed a system for the control of digital elements through the manipulation of physical blocks (Fitzmaurice et al. 1995), thus laying the foundations of graspable interfaces. This research explored new opportunities for expanding the interaction space of the traditional graphical user interfaces. Ishii and Ullmer (1997) elaborated on this idea, introducing the term TUI and the concept of tangible bits. For the authors, a TUI represents an opportunity to bridge the gaps between the cyberspace and the physical environment: the information moves out of the display boundaries, replacing "painted bits" with "tangible bits," making computing ubiquitous, and augmenting the real world.

A few researchers carried on this experimental investigation in works such as the metaDESK (Ullmer and Ishii 1997), mediaBlocks (Ullmer et al. 1998), and PingPongPlus (Ishii et al. 1999). Ishii and Ullmer (2000) analyzed this emerging trend of computationally mediated interfaces. The authors emphasized how TUIs decrease the edge between representation and control: like the abacus in ancient times, TUIs make no distinction between input and output, establishing a new interaction approach in HCI.

Tangible Interfaces for Games

Research in TI inspired a range of design investigations in various application domains. Some of this research shifted its focus to video games, exploiting the peculiarities of the interaction with the physical world to create more intuitive, engaging, and enjoyable systems.

The research by Cheok et al. (2002), Lee et al. (2005), and more recently by Oswald et al. (2015) focused on the construction of this bridge between cyberspace and the real world. Research on mixed reality, based on TI in "augmented" environments, aimed at testing new gaming experiences, less constrained to screen and controller. People play in the physical world, thinning the line with the game world. These new interfaces increase the user control on the digital game, trying to make the experience more immersive. Expanding the social space, Mandryk and Maranan (2002) presented a hybrid board/video game. Unlike the classic setting "user + display + controller," the board is used as a common space for interaction, shifting the focus of players to a shared "real" environment. Weathergods (Bakker et al. 2007) and Curball (Kern et al. 2006) are other examples of hybrid boards designed to enhance social interaction.

TI was also exploited within the framework of *entertainment education* (Breuer and Bente 2010), with the AlgoBlocks being among the first examples (Suzuki and Kato 1995). These blocks represent a high-level programming environment to introduce the basics of programming to children. By moving part of the information out of the screen and placing it into a shared space, these blocks make programming social and distributed among users. The actions to be performed by the system are communicated by the manipulation of "graspable objects," with which users can establish a more immediate and intuitive relationship. With a similar purpose, Price et al. (2003) exploit TI to create a more enjoyable learning environment. The TUI shifts the attention to the player: the focus is not on the educator, but on the interactive system and the players, who are themselves an integral part of the game world facilitating immersion, engagement, and social interaction.

More recent works like Playte (Christensen et al. 2014) and Touch Wire (Saenz et al. 2015) stressed the continuous interest on the exploration of mixed interaction for entertainment education. The assumption underlying this research is that TI should provide greater usability of the systems and greater player engagement.

The Advantage of TI

Starting from the idea that TI should "create a seamless interaction between the user and the technology [...] allowing us to manipulate digital information with our hands and receive the precepts by our peripheral senses" (Mohebzada and Bhojani 2011, p. 179). Mohebzada and Bhojani (2011) proposed a tangible game-based learning system. These authors attributed the benefits of TI to the reduced cognitive effort needed to understand how to operate the interface when it is more closely related to the physical world. Based on user evaluation results, the authors argue that TI empowers the user with more control over the system and could be used for developing innovative methods of learning and teaching.

Pillias et al. (2014) discuss how tangible interfaces transfer part of the game mechanics into the real world, thus influencing the player experience. They present the design and evaluation of "Fat and Furious," a collaborative tangible video game running on Sifteo Cubes (Merrill et al. 2012). The observation of various game sessions highlighted a few properties that seem to characterize TI:

- Freedom: The physicality of the objects fosters new game strategies.

- Sociability: The physicality of the objects in a shared space fosters more social interaction.

- Learnability: The functions of physical objects do not need to be explained.

- Customization: Playing in the real world, the player has more control over (extra) rules.

A few studies directly investigated TI in comparison to other interaction styles. For example, Xie et al. (2008) studied the differences in the use of physical, graphical, and tangible interfaces with a comparative evaluation of three different versions of a jigsaw puzzle. Although the results did not show any effect of the three interfaces on the game experience, they indicated a preference for the physical game and tangible interfaces due to greater usability as compared to the graphical user interface. Skalski et al. (2010) extended this knowledge, with a study on how the game interface can affect presence and enjoyment. The authors conducted two studies comparing the interaction with directional (joypad), incomplete tangible (Wiimote), and realistic tangible (steering wheel) controllers and analyzed how these conditions affected the game experience. Based on the results of these studies, the authors suggested that higher levels of similarity between the game controller and behavior in real life are conducive to a greater feeling of being inside the game, which leads, in turn, to a more enjoyable and engaging experience. Similarly, Mansor et al. (2009) found that more sophisticated fantasy play occurred when children played with physical rather than virtual toys.

The potential advantage of tangible objects over digital ones can be predicted by several theories and constructs of more traditional HCI. Let us consider for example Norman's theory of action (Norman 2002), which identifies two main *gulfs* in the interaction between users and computers. These gulfs reflect the distance between the mental representations of the user and the states of the computer. The *gulf of execution* refers to the distance between the user's mental goals and the behavioral means of achieving them provided by the interface. The *gulf of evaluation* represents the amount of cognitive effort required to interpret the state of a system after a user action. TUIs have the potential of decreasing both gulfs, by exploiting intrinsic *affordances* of physical objects, and a broad range of stimulation, including tactile and proprioceptive information.

The concept of affordance played a key role in the establishment of the TI paradigm. For many years, this concept has been the focus and the justification of a large amount of HCI research, leading to many interesting contributions but also to broad misconceptions.

Because of this conceptual instability, in this chapter we ground our understanding of affordances on the original conceptualization proposed in ecological psychology (Gibson 2013). According to this influential theory, perception and action are intrinsically linked by affordances: perceptual information that can be picked up by an active organism. These affordances specify the actions an object can support, suggesting its functionality to the observer. Affordances embed the principle of mutuality. They are not intrinsic properties of an object, but relations derived by the encounter between the information of the object and the set of physical actions of the observer. For instance, a stone may afford being thrown by an adult, but rolling by a child.

THE RADIANT² AND OHR

In this section we describe the Radiant², going through its functionalities and characteristics, and OHR (read "ôr"), a video game designed to be played using the Radiant². At the end of the section, we briefly describe the design process that led to the current version of the two artifacts, which have been tested in this chapter.

The Radiant²

The Radiant² is an electronic game board designed to work in conjunction with special elements called Radiant Blocks; furthermore a Nintendo Nunchuk has been used in our case study (Figure 6.1). The Radiant² and the Radiant Blocks have been built from scratch and

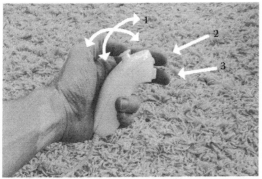

Nunchuk controller

1. The analog stick is used for the horizontal and vertical movements of Spark and the in-game Matrix.

2. The upper button is used for the evocation and disevocation of the in-game Matrix.

3. The lower button is used for jump action of Spark.

Radiant² controller

The Radiant Blocks can be placed on the Radiant². The magnetic attraction and the grooves helps the user in positioning the Block in a specific cell.

Tablet controller

The Radiant Blocks can be dragged on the virtual version of the Radiant². A *snap-to-grid* feature helps the user to position the Block in a specific cell.

FIGURE 6.1 Controllers of the game and their interaction modalities.

designed by the authors taking into account several hardware aspects, such as ergonomics, and software aspects, more related to performance, functionalities, and communication.

The Radiant^2 is a 32-cm square box; its internal structure and sidewalls are made of wood, while its top cover consists of a thin sheet of translucent frosted black plastic. The top cover is divided into 36 areas disposed as a 6 × 6 grid. From now, we will refer to these areas as *cells*. A cell is a physical square of 5 × 5 cm, where a single Radiant Block can be placed. Cells are equipped with electronic contacts that allow communication with the blocks.

A Radiant Block is a 4-cm cube. Its sidewalls, just like those of the Radiant^2, are made of wood and its top cover consists of a thin sheet of white-frosted plastic; its bottom area houses some electrical contacts in order to communicate with the Radiant^2. Both the Radiant^2 and the Radiant Blocks are empowered by the use of microcontrollers and custom electronics boards. Each block is able to communicate with the Radiant^2 and to solve simple computational problems. The Radiant^2 is a collector for all the data coming from the Radiant Blocks: it is used as intercommunications between the blocks and sends information to a computer.

For the purposes of the case study presented in this chapter, six different types of Radiant Block have been used. They can be clustered in two groups: active blocks (Figure 6.2) and passive blocks (Figure 6.3). Active blocks have an input device placed on their top surface, such as a button, a potentiometer, or a switch. Changes to the input device are detected and communicated in real time to the Radiant^2 and have an effect on the game. Conversely, a passive block does not permit any kind of real-time input; they are simple representations of an electronic component such as an LED. The Radiant^2 and the Radiant Blocks are not simply input devices but also communicate information through digital backlights hidden under the top covers (Figure 6.4). These lights can represent any kind of color and level of intensity. When the backlights are on, the top cover is illuminated evenly and highlights the grid's cells. The backlights provide a visual feedback to the user on where to place the blocks.

In order to use the Radiant^2, the player has to place a block on its top. To facilitate placement, each cell presents four L-shaped cuts that are aligned mechanically with the bottom corners of the Radiant Blocks. This mechanical guidance is supported by the use of magnets hidden under the surfaces; the magnetic attraction between cells and Radiant Blocks facilitates the connection and makes the electrical connections more robust. Since the Radiant Blocks are cubic, there are four possible orientations of connection; therefore, the hardware was specifically designed to work regardless of the orientation in which the user places the block.

OHR

OHR is an exploration game based on platform and puzzle mechanics. The game unfolds around the story of Spark, an electronic life form, generated in a wasteland (Figure 6.5). The player controls the character using the Nunchuk: Spark can move on the ground, climb stairs, and jump in order to explore the digital environment displayed on a computer screen and solve puzzles to access new game levels. Puzzles revolve around the theme of electronics. The Radiant^2 provides the tools Spark needs to solve them. By placing these

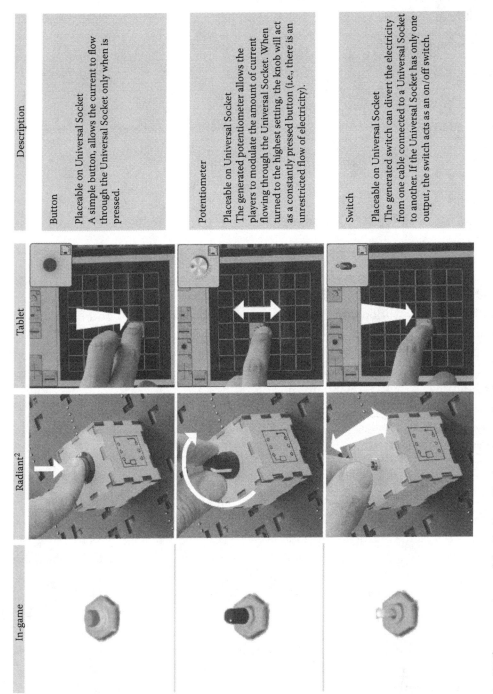

FIGURE 6.2 Different versions of the Radiant Blocks—active (here) and passive (next page)—as represented in game and for both the controllers. In the tablet version, an enlarged view is featured in the upper-right corner of the box.

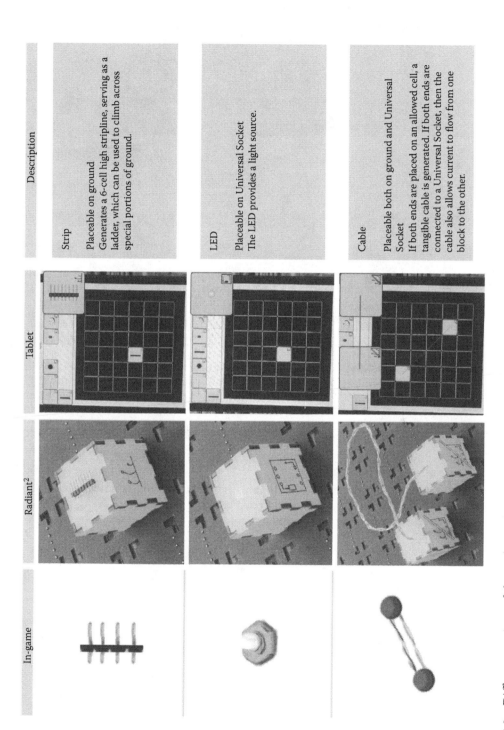

In-game	Radiant²	Tablet	Description
			Strip Placeable on ground Generates a 6-cell high stripline, serving as a ladder, which can be used to climb across special portions of ground.
			LED Placeable on Universal Socket The LED provides a light source.
			Cable Placeable both on ground and Universal Socket If both ends are placed on an allowed cell, a tangible cable is generated. If both ends are connected to a Universal Socket, then the cable also allows current to flow from one block to the other.

FIGURE 6.3   Different versions of the Radiant Blocks—active (previous page) and passive (here)—as represented in game and for both the controllers. In the tablet version, an enlarged view is featured in the upper-right corner of the box.

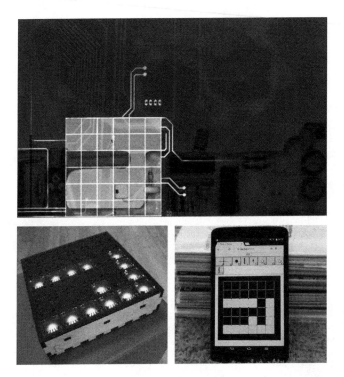

FIGURE 6.4   Different representations of the game world: in-game, Radiant², and tablet version.

tools, in the form electronic components, in the Radiant², the user can build a navigation path to help Spark leave the electronic wasteland.

The most important mechanics of the game is the Matrix Evocation (Figure 6.6). When the Matrix is on, Spark cannot move and the Radiant² can be used to modify the game environment. The Matrix is the digital representation of the Radiant² and is displayed on the computer screen as a 6×6 grid superimposed on the game environment. It can be moved using the Nunchuk, with the limitation that at least one cell of the grid has to stay

FIGURE 6.5   Screenshot of OHR, with Spark exploring the wasteland.

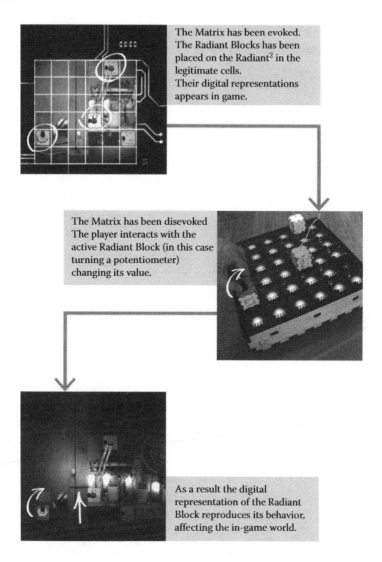

The Matrix has been evoked.
The Radiant Blocks has been
placed on the Radiant^2 in the
legitimate cells.
Their digital representations
appears in game.

The Matrix has been disevoked
The player interacts with the
active Radiant Block (in this case
turning a potentiometer)
changing its value.

As a result the digital
representation of the Radiant
Block reproduces its behavior,
affecting the in-game world.

FIGURE 6.6   Example of the interaction sequence with Radiant^2.

on top of Spark. When the Matrix is active on screen, the Radiant^2 is activated, providing visual information to the players based on the on-screen location. This information is provided with color hints that represent the presence of ground and hotspots called Universal Sockets. While the Matrix is enabled, the players can place the Radiant Blocks; some blocks can be placed only on the ground, others can be placed only on Universal Sockets, and others on both. As soon as the Matrix is disabled, all the electrical components represented by Radiant Blocks (placed on valid cells) are generated in game at the corresponding locations, and the players can interact with them. The elements will remain in game until the Matrix is enabled a second time.

As OHR has been designed to have as much external consistency as possible, all the electronic components represented by the Radiant Blocks have been designed to work as their real-world counterparts. Thanks to this approach the game features puzzles that lend themselves to being solved in different ways by the players (e.g., a switch on the ON position has the same effect of a potentiometer set at its maximum level). In order to better understand how the system works (OHR + Radiant^2), a video presentation can be found at: http://youtu.be/0Gh0tuTHAXk.

Design Process

The design and development of the Radiant^2 and OHR unfolded in parallel, following an iterative user-centered process. This process led to a number of refinements in the hardware and software. The first formative evaluation was run with a medium fidelity prototype and involved a group of interaction designers. As far as the Radiant^2 is concerned, the most relevant feedback regarded the difficulty in the connection between the blocks and the Radiant^2. The first prototype indeed used a mechanical connector, which required a very precise alignment of the Radiant Blocks to work correctly. Furthermore, the physical effort needed to attach and detach the Radiant Blocks was perceived as too high, making the placements of the blocks uncomfortable. These problems were fixed introducing a magnetic guidance system and replacing the mechanical connectors with surface contacts.

Another relevant issue regarded the association between the Radiant^2 and the Matrix cells. Not all players appeared to be able to associate the physical with the virtual grid, and understanding where to position blocks was definitely problematic. These issues were tackled by implementing a system of lights that would help associating the visual display on the screen with that of the Radiant^2. Similarly, the hotspots in the visual game were highlighted. All electrical connections were illuminated and slowly animated to facilitate the association between the Radiant^2 and the virtual game.

The second prototype of the Radiant^2 was presented at the student game competition of the ACM Conference CHI Play 2014 (Menestrina et al. 2014), where it was awarded the first prize. On that occasion, two of the authors collected different feedbacks, which were used to further improve the game. The most relevant feedback indicated an annoying latency in the communication time between the Radiant^2 and the computer running the game. To fix this problem, the USB connection was replaced with an integrated Wi-Fi network. Wi-Fi communications permitted a more reliable data transfer and a dramatic improvement in the responsiveness of the Radiant^2. The comments also indicated a more conceptual problem related to logic underlying the game, as participants struggled to understand the rules about the placement of the Radiant Blocks. To solve this problem we added a distinctive symbol on the side of the blocks. Furthermore, the magnetic guidance was updated, as to permit the collocation of the Radiant Blocks in any of the possible four orientations. As a matter of fact, indeed, users were not comfortable with the previous arrangement, where magnets were asymmetrically oriented to allow only one possible orientation of the blocks. OHR was updated to implement the new Wi-Fi protocols and optimized to increase performances. This preliminary study highlighted that some puzzles in OHR were considered too challenging. Accordingly, the third version of OHR included extra hints in the form of small printed cardboards, which players could rely on to solve the puzzles. A new color coding was introduced in OHR for clearer mapping with the Radiant^2.

CASE STUDY DESCRIPTION

The study was performed in order to evaluate the Radiant^2 in comparison to a graphical interface. We built the experimental hypothesis on related works on TI and HCI, expecting that the Radiant^2 should be capable of decreasing both execution and evaluation gulfs, facilitating a simpler interaction and thus improving the gaming experience. To test this hypothesis, we developed a tablet version of the Radiant^2, implementing all its features through web technologies such as *html5* and *javascript*. Particular attention was made to the visual layout of the Radiant Blocks and their look and feel was reproduced in as much detail as possible. Thus, the Radiant^2 was represented on the tablet screen as a black square with a 36-cell grid highlighted using a dashed white line. The visual representations of the graphical version of the Radiant^2 and the Radiant Blocks were not exactly the same as the tangible version. For example, the backgrounds were in solid colors instead of using a wood texture, avoiding an increased visual complexity that would make their use more difficult. Active and passive Radiant Blocks were represented as gray squares. A digital version of the input devices (e.g., potentiometers, switches, and buttons) was then superimposed on the gray squares, while a graphical representation of the corresponding functional component was superimposed on passive blocks. All Radiant Blocks were placed in a dedicated area above the Radiant^2.

Like the TUI, the graphical version preserved the magnetic guidance feature, replicated with "*drag & drop*" and "*snap to grid*" functionalities. The digital version of the Radiant Blocks could be dragged and dropped on screen; the block was automatically placed on the nearest legitimate cell. Similarly, it could be released by simply dragging it outside the boundaries of the Radiant^2. Both TUI and graphical version implemented the same symbol coding for the blocks. A symbol was added in the right bottom corner of each block, to help users identify the legitimate cells.

When physical actions enacted on the tangible objects could not be implemented on the 2D (two-dimensional) representation, they were replaced with gestures that are largely adopted in touch interfaces. For example, to power switches on and off we used a tap, to turn objects on, as in the case of the potentiometer, we used a swipe. The backlight illumination effects were reproduced by changing each cell's background in real time on tablet screen.

Participants

Data were collected from a sample of 29 students and staff of the University of Trento, 20 males, and nine females, aged between 20 and 47 years (mean 27.2, standard deviation = 5.65) who played OHR. The study focused on the evaluation of two types of interfaces, a graphical version implemented on the tablet and a tangible version implemented on the Radiant^2. Participants were selected among players with different degrees of experience, ranging from beginners to experts. All participants were involved on a voluntary basis.

Design

The study applied a between-subjects design, for the purpose of evaluating the differences in the game experience between the interaction with tangible and digital objects. Each participant used only one type of interface (Figure 6.7).

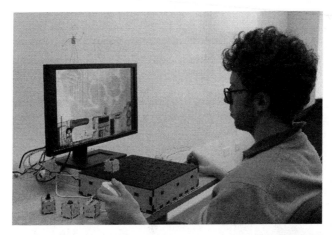

FIGURE 6.7 Two different setups for the evaluation: Radiant^2 on the top, tablet version on the bottom.

Procedure

The experiment was conducted in a quiet room at the Computer Science Department of the University of Trento, Italy, from January 16th to 23rd, 2015. Before starting the experiment, each participant signed a consent form stating that they agreed to be videotaped. The test was divided into two main sections: training and free play (Figure 6.8). At the end of the study, each participant was asked to fill in a questionnaire and answer a seven-question semistructured interview.

Training

At the beginning, each participant was introduced to the interface used during the test. At first, a simple explanation of the functionalities and possible application of each block was provided. The training also included a hand-on phase, where the player was required to try the tablet/Radiant^2, Radiant Blocks, and Nunchuk in order to learn the basic mechanics of the game. During this phase, the player could familiarize with Nunchuk, buttons and movements, block positioning, and explore the different behaviors of the active and passive

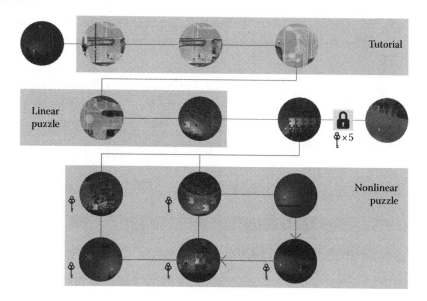

FIGURE 6.8 Structure of the evaluation session in OHR.

Radiant Blocks. The active part of the tutorial was particularly designed to enable players to explore and exploit the capabilities of both interfaces (all types of blocks can be used) and to familiarize with the proposed puzzles. A researcher assisted during the training.

Free Play

This part lasted about 20 min, and each participant played the game at their own pace. In the free-play phase participants were left alone, as to avoid influencing them in any way. They could ask for help only in case of some technical problems with the game or the controller. Three hints for each riddle were printed out on paper: they were presented from the less understandable, which helped the player very little, to the easiest one that revealed the intended solution.

Instruments

In this part of the study, participants were asked to answer the GEQ (IJsselsteijn et al. 2008). GEQ is a specialized tool developed by the Game Experience Lab to measure the experience during and after gameplay. The questionnaire is composed of four independent modules: the core module, the in-game module, the social presence module, and the postgame module. The social presence module that assesses the behavioral and psychological involvement was omitted since OHR does not contain any form of NPC (nonplayer character) or interaction between multiple players such as a "playing online" experience. The in-game module was omitted due to the limited time of free play. The questionnaire items could be answered using a Likert scale ranging from 0 (not agree) to 4 (completely agree), and were averaged in the following indexes:

- *Competence:* A feature that fosters the development of the player skills and makes the player feel as if they are "in control" of the game. An ideal game permits the improvement of the skills and the acquisition of the mechanics in the most enjoyable way. "Being in control" of the game also strengthens the feeling that the players can play their own strategies and not only strategies coming from the game designers.

- *Sensory and imaginative immersion:* Sensory immersion relates to the ability of the game to engage the players and keeps them focused on the game and its stimuli. Imaginative immersion is the ability, typical of role-playing games, to enable the player to use their imagination, empathize, feel, or identify with the characters of the game itself.

- *Flow:* The ability of the game to keep the player fully immersed and concentrated on the game itself. Flow is one of the fundamental dimensions that makes a game an enjoyable experience and keeps the players engaged.

- *Challenge:* A feature that makes the players feel sufficiently challenged during the game. In general, a game must match the player's skill level, and must be able to provide different levels of difficulty to match different levels. A good balance of challenge fosters an immersive experience. A good level of challenge implies the use of motor or/and mental skills, which keeps the player involved.

- *Negative effect:* Any perception of the player during the gameplay that relates to a negative experience, mood, or feeling.

- *Positive effect:* Any perception of the player during the gameplay that relates to a positive experience, mood, or feeling.

- *Positive experience:* The index that measures the extent to which the postgame experience is positive. This component gives an overview of the mood, feeling, or experience that the player feels after the game experience ends.

- *Negative experience:* The index that measures the extent to which the postgame experience is negative. This component gives an overview of what mood, feeling, or experience that the player feels after the game experience ends.

- *Tiredness:* The index that measures the extent to which the player is tired after the activity of playing a video game ends.

The last part of the evaluation consisted of a semistructured interview where participants were invited to elaborate on their feelings, explaining the difficulties encountered and providing their suggestions to improve the game, such as new mechanics, changes in interfaces/controller, or aesthetical preferences.

Results

Data collected with the GEQ questionnaire were analyzed to verify if there were any differences between the two modalities proposed to the participants (the one with tangible objects and the one with digital objects). Negative items were recoded, so that higher values corresponded to positive evaluations and lower values to negative. Each index of the GEQ

TABLE 6.1   Core Module

Dimension	Item	Alpha-Reliability	Mean Radiant (R)	Mean Tablet (T)	Significance
Competence	2, 10, 15, 17, 21	0.93	1.97	1.17	R > T[a]
Sensory and imaginative immersion	3, 12, 18, 19, 27, 30	0.74	2.86	2.21	R > T[a]
Flow	5, 13, 25, 28, 31	0.77	2.89	2.99	NS
Challenge (reduced, reversed scale)	11, 23, (26), 32, 33	0.69	2.46	2.30	NS
Negative effect (reversed scale)	7, 8, 9, 16	0.69	3.71	3.66	NS
Positive effect	1, 4, 6, 14, 20	0.87	3.17	2.60	R > T[b]

Statistical relevance [a]$p < 0.01$; [b]$p < 0.05$; N.S., no significativity.

questionnaire was tested to verify its internal reliability using Chronbach's Alpha. In particular, all the questions showing an item-scale correlation lower than 0.30 were excluded, and indexes that had a Chronbach's Alpha less than 0.69 were not considered valid for the purposes of the analysis. Following this procedure the item "I felt challenged" was omitted by the challenge scale. The two items of the tiredness index reported a strong correlation. The tension index (alpha = 0.23 in the core module) and negative experience (alpha = 0.54 in the postgame module) were not reliable and were disregarded. As other published articles, such as the study (N = 20) by Tan et al. (2013), we chose to compare the results of the GEQ questionnaire using a set of independent samples (T-test analysis) between the Radiant[2] and the tablet (Tables 6.1 and 6.2).

The competence index (alpha = 0.93) showed that participants using the Radiant[2] (M = 1.97, SD = 0.26) had perceived themselves as more competent than the players that used the tablet version (M = 1.17, SD = 0.26). The sensory and imaginative immersion (alpha = 0.74) showed a more engaging experience in conjunction with the Radiant[2] (M = 2.86, SD = 0.21) instead of the tablet (M = 2.21, SD = 0.21); likewise also positive affect (alpha = 0.87) showed a significant advantage of the Radiant[2] (M = 3.17, SD = 0.23) over the tablet (M = 2.60, SD = 0.23). The positive experience (alpha = 0.89) index showed that the feelings of the players and their emotions were more positive with the Radiant[2] (M = 1.74, SD = 0.32) than with its graphical implementation (M = 1.0, SD = 0.32).

TABLE 6.2   Postgame Module

Dimension	Item	Alpha-Reliability	Mean Radiant (R)	Mean Tablet (T)	Significance
Positive experience	1, 5, 7, 8, 12, 16	0.89	1.74	1.00	R > T[a]
Tiredness (reversed scale)	10, 13	0.82	3.73	3.79	N.S.
Negative experience	2, 4, 6, 11, 14, 15	0.54	–	–	–

Statistical relevance [a] $p < 0.05$; N.S., no significativity.

The flow dimension (alpha = 0.77) showed that there were no appreciable differences between the tangible (M = 2.89) and the tablet (M = 2.99), which suggests a very good immersion level (max. 4). Those values also demonstrate that the interfaces used were not affecting the levels of involvement and immersion during gameplay. The challenge dimension (alpha = 0.77) did not show any appreciable difference in the level of challenge: tangible (M = 2.46), tablet (M = 2.30). Negative affect (alpha = 0.69) index highlights that in both interfaces the perceived level of negative feelings and experiences is very low: tangible (M = 3.71) and tablet (M = 3.66). Just like flow, challenge, and negative affect dimensions, tiredness (alpha = 0.82) also showed no relevant difference between tangible and graphical implementations. Challenge, negative effect, and tiredness results were in reversed scale, which means that higher values correspond to a low level of challenge and vice versa.

In general, the statistical analysis highlighted relevant improvements of the TI over the graphical: players were more engaged during the gaming experience and their feelings were in general significantly more positive during and after the playing experience. Other aspects such as tiredness, challenge, negative effect, and flow were not affected by the type of interface used in our case study.

DISCUSSION

The purpose of this research has been the investigation of the advantages and disadvantages of TI in relation to the game experience. This analysis was conducted through a comparative evaluation that allowed the participants, divided into two groups, to try the two different interfaces. The data obtained from the questionnaire, interviews, and observations highlight the differences in the two experiences proposed to the players. In particular, the results show how some characteristics have similar values, while others change significantly.

One common feature is the difficulty perceived by the players. The interviews supported the fact that the use of the two interfaces has always been immediately understood. The same applies to the game mechanics, which were always clear in both cases. Even the perceived level of challenge is equal in the two different versions: the difficulty degree associated with the puzzles was perceived as the same. This is also demonstrated by the performance of the various players during the free play. The analysis of the video in fact shows that just a few users have had particular difficulties in solving the puzzles. Only two players have failed to pass the first gate, while the others, though not always following the same route, have always reached the same puzzles in 20 min. These differences were more due to the design of the game than the design of the two controllers. For example, the two previously mentioned testers simply failed to realize the relationship of cause and effect between a Universal Socket and a door, thus making it impossible to continue through the game level.

The analysis of the data reveals some peculiarities that differentiate the interaction with the two controllers. Players who tried the graphical version reported some difficulties in its use. The rules of the game were clear, but participants were sometimes confused about the right way to interact with the virtual Radiant Blocks. In particular, the potentiometer was not easy to use because there is no immediate relation between the shape of the object and the gesture that activates it ("swipe"). The use of the button, instead, is made difficult by its small size; so much so that some players report that they had to "aim" before using it. Accordingly, their attention was divided between the screen and the game controller, which marks a fundamental difference between the two interfaces. In the graphical version users had to identify the Radiant Blocks before tapping the screen, and only then they could look at the screen to see their effect on the game; in the tangible version this passage can be skipped altogether, since the three-dimensional object is easily identified even without looking away from the screen, and the touch helps the player to grab it in the right way. Similarly, in the graphical version some players were forced to shift their focus to the tablet, to check the correct way to act on active Radiant Blocks, and to avoid moving their fingers on another cell. In the tangible version, the immediate feedback of the physical artifact minimizes this issue.

Taking the case of the potentiometer, while the tangible version provides all the information on how it is turning (thanks to the touch and the physical limit of rotation), the digital version requires the player to look at the tablet to be sure that the interaction is correct. These observations, emerged from the interviews, were reflected by the final data from questionnaires, which highlight that the immersion was more pronounced in the tangible version of the Radiant[2]. This information represents the degree to which the players were involved in the game, identified themselves in the character, and focused on solving the puzzles. Similarly, we can assume that this also influenced the sense of competence, perceived as higher in the tangible version. The tangible controls are easy to use, which influenced the perceived ability to control the game and solve the puzzles. This aspect can be found in the comments regarding the "sensitivity" of the Radiant Blocks. Some players struggled to use the graphical version when it came to interact with small, precise movements. For example, one puzzle whose resolution required setting a certain energy level of the potentiometer, was perceived as particularly difficult by the players who have tried the graphical version. In the tangible counterpart, instead, the real potentiometer guarantees a high level of sensitivity and thus the response to the direct interaction is not mediated by a gesture.

Another significant fact is the desire of the players to explore the TUI, trying different solutions for different puzzles and combining the Radiant Blocks in various combinations. Their closer resemblance—compared to the graphical version—with real objects stimulates a greater desire for interaction and experimentation. In this regard, some players have reported that, even after solving the puzzle, they tried other Radiant Blocks only out of curiosity to see how they influenced the game world. Having a tangible object to interact with fosters a more creative approach to resolve the game riddles. "It was clear which block was the correct one, but I wished to try them all," reported a tester. This kind of thought was not expressed by the users that tried the graphical version. In general, we can assume that the tangible experience is preferable on various aspects that definitely influence the overall game experience.

Compared to the existing literature on TI in games, we believe that this chapter can make a positive contribution to the discussion. This migration of digital information supported by TI seems to positively influence the user experience. Going back to the concepts expressed by Norman, we believe that this type of interface could reduce the gaps related to the *gulf of execution and evaluation*. The "dialogue" with the machine—in other words, the interpretation that the user must give to the interactions with the machine—should be minimized. The Radiant² was designed starting from the idea that the intentions of the players (i.e., what they want to do) should be more related to the actual interaction with the game system (i.e., the set of actions that the system can perform according to their goals).

CHALLENGES

There are some interesting challenges that came out of our experimental study, which could be of interest to other researchers.

The first is the reliability of the system. Nowadays there are extremely powerful and versatile technologies and the development of Radiant² has certainly brought us to "unexplored lands" in the hardware design. There have been many problems (e.g., bugs in the transmission of data between computer and Radiant²) that we mitigated over time and this required a great deal of resources, but we had to be sure that the system was stable enough to conduct our experiments.

Another interesting challenge was the "simplification" of the system. Each game has a certain level of difficulty, otherwise it could not be defined a game. In this regard, Suits defines the lusory attitude, the psychological attitude required of a player, as "the voluntary attempt to overcome unnecessary obstacles" (Suits 2014, p. 55). The difficulty of the game is necessary to make it challenging, but this should be well balanced. In this regard the preliminary design of OHR and Radiant² turned out to be too complex for the first tester (not related to this case study). As described in previous sections, during the planning our system has undergone several changes in order to find a good difficulty level, making it challenging, but not frustrating.

SOLUTIONS AND RECOMMENDATIONS

We believe that there is no perfect answer to the challenges mentioned above, but it seems fair to give the reader some ideas from our reflections.

The system reliability is a crucial issue for those who want to explore the design of new hardware. A greater difficulty in the diagnosis of errors, compared to the debugging of software, and the use of technologies that have not necessarily been designed for the same research purposes impose some limits. Therefore, the most obvious recommendation is to ensure having enough time to make sure that the developed product is reliable enough to not affect the research.

The difficulty of the game is quite an arbitrary matter; so, the recommendation is to not take for granted the difficulty of use of the system. Game designers and programmers can indeed take for granted some factors, but people not closely involved in the design process can perceive these same factors differently. Regarding the game design, preliminary testing is a must.

CONCLUSIONS

This chapter presented a case study based on the evaluation of two different types of interaction, touch and tangible. The research is positioned in the field of TI, specifically in the field of TI applied to video games, an area of HCI that explores the possibility of playing through tangible artifacts.

The ultimate goal was to evaluate if two different types of controllers could offer two types of different gaming experiences. For this purpose, our group has developed a video game and two types of controller, one tangible and one touch. As described, the controller is composed of a tangible game board, called the Radiant[2], and some cubes, the Radiant Blocks; the touch controller is nothing more than its digital counterpart. The types of interaction that characterize them are fundamentally different and the group has evaluated what the differences are with regard to the game experience through a series of tests. From the results obtained it was shown that, even though the experience remains unchanged as regards the difficulty and perceived level of challenge, there are some obvious differences concerning the immersion, the pleasantness, the sense of competence, and the desire to explore and experiment. Our work is not presented as revolutionary, and we do not claim that the results can be generalized without further evaluation. However, we believe that the information obtained confirms that this bridge between the real and virtual worlds may indeed have some advantages. Taking the game industry as an example, the proposed entertainment systems are ever changing, experimenting with innovative interfaces, and proving that the video game experience is not necessarily bound to the screen. In this connection, we believe that TUI can have its own space, showing that a stronger mediation between the virtual and real worlds can be a viable direction for the future of video games.

ACKNOWLEDGMENTS

We would like to thank all the personnel of the MUSE's FabLab (Trento, Italy) and of the electronics lab of the University of Trento (Physics Department) for giving us invaluable suggestions, along with the access to the tools needed to create the Radiant[2]. In addition, we thank Luca Miozzo, who helped us in the usability tests.

REFERENCES

Bakker, S., D. Vorstenbosch, E. van den Hoven, G. Hollemans, and T. Bergman. 2007. Weathergods: Tangible interaction in a digital tabletop game. In *Proceedings of the 1st International Conference on Tangible and Embedded Interaction*, Baton Rouge, LA, pp. 151–2. ACM.

Breuer, J. S. and G. Bente. 2010. Why so serious? On the relation of serious games and learning. *Eludamos. Journal for Computer Game Culture* 4 (1): 7–24.

Cheok, A. D., X. Yang, Z. Z. Ying, M. Billinghurst, and H. Kato. 2002. Touch-space: Mixed reality game space based on ubiquitous, tangible, and social computing. *Personal and Ubiquitous Computing* 6 (5–6): 430–42.

Christensen, D. J., R. Fogh, and H. H. Lund. 2014. Playte, a tangible interface for engaging human–robot interaction. In *Robot and Human Interactive Communication, 2014 RO-MAN: The 23rd IEEE International Symposium on*, Edinburgh, UK, pp. 56–62. IEEE.

Davis, L. 2014. Skylanders and Disney Infinity: How video game toys came to life. *The Independent.* Accessed October 8. http://www.independent.co.uk/life-style/gadgets-and-tech/gaming/skylanders-and-disney-infinity-how-video-game-toys-came-to-life-9782640.html.

Djajadiningrat, T., S. Wensveen, J. Frens, and K. Overbeeke. 2004. Tangible products: Redressing the balance between appearance and action. *Personal and Ubiquitous Computing* 8 (5): 294–309.

Dourish, P. 2004. *Where the Action Is: The Foundations of Embodied Interaction*. MIT Press, Cambridge, MA.

Fitzmaurice, G. W. 1996. *Graspable User Interfaces*. University of Toronto.

Fitzmaurice, G. W., H. Ishii, and W. A. S. Buxton. 1995. Bricks: Laying the foundations for grasp-able user interfaces. In *Proceedings of the SIGCHI Conference on Human Factors in Computing Systems*, Denver, CO, pp. 442–9. ACM Press/Addison-Wesley Publishing Company.

Gibson, J. J. 2013. *The Ecological Approach to Visual Perception*. Psychology Press, Hove, UK.

Ijsselsteijn, W., K. Poels, and Y. A. W. De Kort. 2008. *The Game Experience Questionnaire: Development of a Self-Report Measure to Assess Player Experiences of Digital Games*. TU Eindhoven, Eindhoven, The Netherlands.

Ishii, H. and B. Ullmer. 1997. Tangible bits: Towards seamless interfaces between people, bits and atoms. In *Proceedings of the ACM SIGCHI Conference on Human Factors in Computing Systems*, Atlanta, GA, pp. 234–41. ACM.

Ishii, H., C. Wisneski, J. Orbanes, B. Chun, and J. Paradiso. 1999. PingPongPlus: Design of an ath-letic-tangible interface for computer-supported cooperative play. In *Proceedings of the SIGCHI Conference on Human Factors in Computing Systems*, Pittsburgh, PA, pp. 394–401. ACM.

Kern, D., M. Stringer, G. Fitzpatrick, and A. Schmidt. 2006. Curball—A prototype tangible game for inter-generational play. In *Enabling Technologies: Infrastructure for Collaborative Enterprises, 2006. WETICE'06. 15th IEEE International Workshops on*, Manchester, UK, pp. 412–8. IEEE.

Lee, W., W. Woo, and J. Lee. 2005. Tarboard: Tangible augmented reality system for table-top game environment. In *2nd International Workshop on Pervasive Gaming Applications, PerGames*, Munich, Germany, 5:2.1.

Mandryk, R. L. and D. S. Maranan. 2002. False prophets: Exploring hybrid board/video games. In *CHI'02 Extended Abstracts on Human Factors in Computing Systems*, Minneapolis, MN, pp. 640–1. ACM.

Mansor, E. I., A. De Angeli, and O. De Bruijn. 2009. The fantasy table. In *Proceedings of the 8th International Conference on Interaction Design and Children*, Milano, Italy, pp. 70–9. ACM.

Menestrina, Z., M. Bianchi, A. Siesser, R. Masu, and A. Conci. 2014. OHR. In *Proceedings of the First ACM SIGCHI Annual Symposium on Computer–Human Interaction in Play*, Toronto, ON, Canada, pp. 355–8. ACM.

Merrill, D., E. Sun, and J. Kalanithi. 2012. Sifteo Cubes. In *CHI'12 Extended Abstracts on Human Factors in Computing Systems*, Austin, TX, pp. 1015–8. ACM.

Mohebzada, J. G. and A. H. Bhojani. 2011. The cubes: A tangible game-based learning system. In *Innovations in Information Technology (IIT), 2011 International Conference on*, Abu Dhabi, UAE, pp. 179–84. IEEE.

Norman, D. A. 2002. *The Design of Everyday Things*. Basic Books, Cambridge, MA.

Oswald, P., J. Tost, and R. Wettach. 2015. I. Ge: Exploring new game interaction metaphors with interactive projection. In *Proceedings of the Ninth International Conference on Tangible, Embedded, and Embodied Interaction*, Stanford, CA, pp. 733–8. ACM.

Pillias, C., R. Robert-Bouchard, and G. Levieux. 2014. Designing tangible video games: Lessons learned from the Sifteo Cubes. In *Proceedings of the 32nd Annual ACM Conference on Human Factors in Computing Systems*, Toronto, ON, Canada, pp. 3163–6. ACM.

Price, S., Y. Rogers, M. Scaife, D. Stanton, and H. Neale. 2003. Using "tangibles" to promote novel forms of playful learning. *Interacting with Computers* 15 (2): 169–85.

Saenz, M., J. Strunk, S. L. Chu, and J. H. Seo. 2015. Touch Wire: Interactive tangible electricity game for kids. In *Proceedings of the Ninth International Conference on Tangible, Embedded, and Embodied Interaction*, Stanford, CA, pp. 655–9. ACM.

Skalski, P., R. Tamborini, A. Shelton, M. Buncher, and P. Lindmark. 2010. Mapping the road to fun: Natural video game controllers, presence, and game enjoyment. *New Media and Society* 13 (2), 224–242.

Suits, B. 2014. *The Grasshopper: Games, Life and Utopia*. Broadview Press, Peterborough, ON, Canada.

Suzuki, H. and H. Kato. 1995. Interaction-level support for collaborative learning: AlgoBlock—An open programming language. In *The First International Conference on Computer Support for Collaborative Learning*, pp. 349–55. L. Erlbaum Associates Inc., Bloomington, IN.

Tan, C. T., J. Huang, and Y. Pisan. 2013. Initial perceptions of a touch-based tablet handwriting serious game. In *Entertainment Computing—ICEC 2013*, pp. 172–5. Springer, São Paulo, Brazil.

Ullmer, B. and H. Ishii. 1997. The metaDESK: Models and prototypes for tangible user interfaces. In *Proceedings of the 10th Annual ACM Symposium on User Interface Software and Technology*, Banff, AB, Canada, pp. 223–32. ACM.

Ullmer, B. and H. Ishii. 2000. Emerging frameworks for tangible user interfaces. *IBM Systems Journal* 39 (3.4): 915–31.

Ullmer, B., H. Ishii, and D. Glas. 1998. MediaBlocks: Physical containers, transports, and controls for online media. In *Proceedings of the 25th Annual Conference on Computer Graphics and Interactive Techniques*, Orlando, FL, pp. 379–86. ACM.

Xie, L., A. N. Antle, and N. Motamedi. 2008. Are tangibles more fun? Comparing children's enjoyment and engagement using physical, graphical and tangible user interfaces. In *Proceedings of the 2nd International Conference on Tangible and Embedded Interaction*, Bonn, Germany, pp. 191–8. ACM.

LIST OF ADDITIONAL SOURCES

De Koven, B. 2013. *The Well-Played Game: A Player's Philosophy*. MIT Press, Cambridge, MA.

Falstein, N. and H. Barwood. 2006. Rules worth breaking. Talk at *Game Developers Conference*. San Francisco, CA, USA. http://www.finitearts.com/pages/400page.html. Accessed January 1, 2016.

Fullerton, T., C. Swain, and S. Hoffman. 2004. *Game Design Workshop: Designing, Prototyping, and Playtesting Games*. CRC Press, Boca Raton, FL.

Huizinga, J. 2014. *Homo Ludens Ils 86*. Routledge, London, UK.

MaKey, M. 2015. *An Invention Kit for Everyone*. Accessed June 2. https://vimeo.com/60307041.

Menestrina, Z., A. Conci, A. Siesser, R. Masu, and M. Bianchi. 2015. Super Santos Design. Accessed June 2. http://www.supersantosdesign.org.

OHR + Radiant². 2014. Accessed June 2. https://youtu.be/0Gh0tuTHAXk.

Resnick, M. and E. Rosenbaum. 2013. Designing for tinkerability. In *Design, Make, Play: Growing the Next Generation of STEM Innovators*, M. Honey and D. E. Kanter (eds.), pp. 163–81, Routledge, London, UK.

Schell, J. 2008. *The Art of Game Design: A Book of Lenses*. CRC Press, Boca Raton, FL.

BIOGRAPHIES

Zeno Menestrina graduated in computer science in 2013 at the University of Trento. He studied artificial intelligences at the Universiteit van Amsterdam, with a strong focus on video games. He is currently a PhD candidate both at the Department of Information Engineering and Computer Science at the University of Trento and at the European Institute of Technology ICT Labs Doctoral School. His first-year research was mainly focused on the design of authoring tools for the customization of the behavior of nonplaying characters in the context of serious games. Moreover, he worked on the design and implementation of OHR. He is very passionate about video game development, having spent the last 3 years on various projects on the topic. He is currently working on the design and implementation of a video game for cognitive training and the exercise of executive functions.

Andrea Conci received his master's degree in computer science in 2013 after graduating from the University of Trento, where he developed interests on HCI, tangible interfaces, and participatory design. In 2014, he worked on DALI, a European project focused on the development of a "smart walker" to help elderly people navigating public spaces taking into account social rules. During the same year, he worked on the hardware and software development of OHR, a videogame that explores the tangible interface interaction by using a custom tangible called Radiant[2]. His PhD research is focused on the development of tangible interfaces for the education of young children, in particular how to achieve a trade-off between educational and playfulness aspects during the design.

Adriano Siesser is a researcher with a bachelor's degree in fine arts received from the Academy of Fine Arts in Bologna and a master's degree in graphical art received from the Academy of Fine Arts in Venice. Since March 2014, he collaborates with the *interAction* research group of the Department of Information Engineering and Computer Science, as a member of the *Ludic Design* team. His work is investigating new interactive paradigms between art and technology, especially taking care of the aesthetic side of the team projects. His research interests are in the fields of artistic and technological installations, pedagogy and art didactics, interactive installations for children, and games. During the years, he took courses on sound design, art didactics, graphical art, and aesthetics of the new media.

Raul Masu is studying electronic music with Mauro Graziani and composition with Cosimo Colazzo at the Conservatory of Trento. He attended master classes with Lawrence Casserley, Martin Parker, Agostino DiScipio, Luca Francesconi, Torres Maldonado, and Ivan Vandor. He cofounded the Experiential-Music Lab (University of Trento), a group of study in sonic interaction strategies. His work is published in several international conferences in the fields of music and emotions, sound synthesis and HCI, and in the journal of *Personal and Ubiquitous Computing*. As a member of the Super Santos Design, he won the jury award at the CHI PLAY conference in 2014. He is constantly active as a performer; he played at the MaerzMusic festival in Berlin in the Intonarumori orchestra led by Luciano Chessa. He composed the soundtrack for the documentary "Braids of the University of Trento" and won the second prize at the international composition competition Claxica.

Michele Bianchi is an avid videogame player, a tabletop role-playing games aficionado, and a guy who clearly sleeps too little. He graduated in embedded systems at the University of Trento and got a PhD position there on videogame design for behavior change. He studied computer graphics and game prototyping at Danmarks Tekniske Universitet, worked on a tool to help studying Body Area Networks at TokyoTech, and traveled more to learn as much as he could. If you find yourself stuck in OHR it is his fault: he not only wrote technical papers but he also designed various game mechanics and levels, always arguing that everything was too easy. He is working to pursue his dreams, which he put aside for too much time, looking for more opportunities to learn how to do cool things.

As swift as wind, as silent as a forest, as fierce as fire, and as unshakeable as a mountain.

Antonella De Angeli is an associate professor of HCI at the Department of Information Engineering and Computer Science of the University of Trento in Italy. Her research addresses cognitive, social, and cultural aspects of information technologies with an emphasis on the application of this knowledge to interaction design. She is the head of the

HCI (*interAction*) team of the department, leading a fast-growing group of enthusiastic researchers in interaction design and user experience.

KEY TERMS

Game experience: Game experience is a generic term here used to identify the physical and psychological experience (e.g., positive and negative emotions) of a player playing a video game.

Human–computer interaction: HCI is the discipline related to the study of the interaction between people (users) and computers for the design and development of interactive systems that are usable, reliable, and that support human activities.

Novel interfaces: Novel interfaces are new interfaces whose design extends outside the traditional rules, trying to explore new types of interaction, and new types of experience between the user and the machine.

Tangible interaction: TI is a term that includes approaches that emphasize the interaction with tangible interfaces, a physical embodiment of the data, and the inclusion of the interface in real environments.

Tangible user interface: TUIs are user interfaces that allow interacting with a computer system by manipulating physical tangible objects.

Touch user interface: Touch user interfaces are user interfaces that allow the communication between a user and an electronic device using the sense of touch through a sensitive screen.

Video game: A video game is a game run by an electronic device that allows the player to interact with a digital environment. The term can be referred both to the software or hardware dedicated to a specific game.

CHAPTER 7

Usability Testing of Video Game Controllers

A Case Study

Gareth W. Young, Aidan Kehoe, and David Murphy

CONTENTS

EXECUTIVE SUMMARY

This chapter presents an investigation that compares the performance of game controllers in two-dimensional pointing tasks as defined in the international standard that specifies the requirements for nonkeyboard input devices, ISO 9241-9. In addition, we discuss the evaluation of usability and user experience with these devices during gameplay. We compared performance measurements for controllers while varying the user's exposure to the different feedback elements contained within each controller device. We assessed the performance of the controllers according to the ISO 9241-9 evaluation recommendations. The devices used in the study included a Logitech mouse and keyboard, a Logitech Bluetooth Touchpad and keyboard, a Sony Playstation DualShock 4 controller, and Valve's first-generation Steam controller. Besides performance testing, we measured user experiences with the controllers while playing a popular first-person video game. Participants were asked to complete game levels for each type of controller and answer questions outlining their experience.

ORGANIZATION/INSTITUTION BACKGROUND

The case studies contained within this chapter were undertaken at the Logitech Design Lab in Cork, Ireland, in collaboration with the Department of Computer Science at University College Cork. Logitech is a world leader in products that connect people to the digital experiences they care about. Their products span multiple computing, communication, and entertainment platforms. Logitech-gaming products include mice, keyboards, headsets, and gaming controllers. University College Cork was founded in 1845 and is the academic home of the founder of Boolean Logic, George Boole.

INTRODUCTION

Currently, there is a considerable range of research into the development of contemporary game controllers, while there is relatively little research being conducted to explore the relationship between pointing performance and in-game user experiences (The Entertainment Software Association, 2014). The choice of a controller used can have a major impact on the player's experience of a game (Birk and Mandryk, 2013). The performance of a user while playing a game can also be strongly influenced by the type of controller used (Watson et al., 2013). Certain platforms are synonymous with particular types of controllers, while others are transferrable across platforms. The effects of any one of the varieties of control methods used in a smartphone or tablet device are also potentially viable control methods for new console or PC controller devices. Fortunately, there is a large body of well-documented research in human–computer interaction (HCI) and game console controller analysis, and the associated frameworks and models of these can be applied in the development and evaluation of new forms of game controller interaction.

In terms of in-game control, the relationships between the action–feedback cycle and the central role it has in game play are important aspects of game controller integration. The user must have a sense of control that directly relates to their actions; this in turn works to reduce potential frustrations and enhances the user's participation in the game. The control of a game is after all, the product of a well-designed interaction with game controllers. Historically, the technological limitations of the era were responsible for shaping controller designs. All in-game interactions, such as running, shooting, and kicking, among others, were represented by arbitrary button presses and gestures that were not intrinsic or relatable to the overall gameplay design. In comparison, with today's gesture capabilities, we can now physically manipulate wireless devices to directly control in-game components that may correspond with real-world equivalent operations. This level of correspondence between the artificial and real-world control interactions reduces the learning curve for players, making it more "intuitive" and increases the user's immersion in the game. The mapping of control to in-game actions has been shown to correlate with total immersion experienced by a user (Jennett et al., 2008). Also, the role of interactivity in gaming enjoyment has been observed as declining when efficacy experiences are finite (Klimmt et al., 2007). Therefore, we can conclude that the control mechanisms of gaming interfaces are influential in some way to the greater, overall gaming experience.

BACKGROUND

Early control mechanisms of digital games were simple, as were the games that were used to control. However, contemporary platforms are capable of capturing multiple forms of interaction using sophisticated motion capture sensor technology. Indeed, the spectrum of digital game genres has increased and become quite diverse. This near-endless range of interactive games allows players to experience various different forms of immersion, for example, while waiting on a train or relaxing at home (Thompson et al., 2012). Game designs that were once limited to high-end PCs or specific gaming consoles are now available on mobile devices, online platforms, and are increasingly moving toward an Internet of Things platform for gaming. This opens up the potential for a true ubiquitous "play anywhere, with anyone, at anytime gaming." Examples of this trend include the Grand Theft Auto series, which is now available across a number of very different platforms, from Google Android devices to the Microsoft Xbox console. Increased availability and a variety of gaming platforms presents new challenges, and highlights limitations of both game design and the conventional consumption models, issues that did not exist on older static platforms.

The development of controllers for platform-specific games has historically been restricted by the system's processing power and speed. Consequently, in static gaming, the graphics-processing units of platforms are superior in performance to address the demands of high-end game engines. In comparison, the ability to perform multiple tasks on a mobile device takes precedence over pure gaming performance. For example, a smartphone must possess the ability to make phone calls, text, e-mail, etc., in addition to its game-processing capabilities. The limitations of mobile devices have resulted in the development of novel interaction methods, which are now becoming common in conventional game controller interfaces. For example, the use of virtual thumbstick widgets in lieu of physical thumbstick controllers, touch-sensitive surfaces, and built-in speakers. The compact form factor of mobile devices incorporating a host of various sensors has opened up new and interesting avenues of game interaction. These include, but are not limited to, gesture-controlled touchscreens, accelerometers, gyroscopes, magnetrons, cameras, and microphone interfaces to name a few, which are rarely implemented or to be found in a PC or console platforms (a notable exception to this being the Wii console).

Notwithstanding this array of adaptable input choices for game developers to choose from, there are still some traditional gaming styles that are struggling to adapt to multiple platforms. For example, First- Person Shooter (FPS) games, such as Wolfenstein and Doom (widely considered among the first three-dimensional [3D] FPS games), would have to rethink how user input would control game characters if they were to release the same game today (id Software, 1992, 1993). Control adaptations are increasing in popularity, such as those seen in games like The Drowning (DeNA Co., 2014); however, this can sometimes result in a deviation from traditional FPS physical interfaces and losing the associated affordances of controllers that consumers of this genre have become accustomed to. In addition, specific game genres rely on these standardized and accepted control schemes.

As mentioned earlier, there are several mechanisms that can be used to control games on multiple devices. These too can be influential to the overall gaming experience, specifically, the innate naturalness of user gestures required and their relationship to the actions transpiring on-screen (Skalski, 2011). Players may have certain expectations with controls that they are already familiar with in the real world, for example, steering wheels (McEwan et al., 2012). Using a new controller requires some form of learning; however, this should transpire in a streamlined and continuous manner. This leads to interactions that come naturally to the user when they transfer to alternative platform controllers. This naturalness relates to the user's perception of interactivity based on their previous experiences with interactive technologies and how new control methods need to be predictable, logical, or in line with experientially based expectations. Gamers with prior experience of FPS games will have been conditioned, through repeated measures, to find certain interface paradigms more accessible than others. Players switching to a new platform and/

or controller experience more usability issues and consider themselves more challenged during that transition phase (Gerling, 2011). When designing a new controller, it is very important to consider the users' expectations of device affordances and their applicability to the particular game genre.

Many of the innovative changes in game controller design are associated with a specific gaming platform and in the first generation of commercial controllers, the technological constraints of the platform limited input gestures to small finger movements and button presses. Playing early arcade/video games involved minimum movement to trigger an in-game response. However, recent trends in large-scale controller movements have resulted in comparable levels of engagement and enjoyment in game play. For example, in their work on controller movement, Zhang et al. found that participants responded positively to increased physical exertion in certain gaming conditions (Zhang et al., 2009). Moreover, large-scale actions have been incorporated into popular contemporary games, through the use of advanced controllers, for example, the Microsoft Kinect, Sony Move, and Nintendo Wiimote. However, the size, number, and rate of gestures, bounded by limitations of the controller, the size of the required gesture, and/or the overall level of physical interaction (exertion), do not necessarily have any impact on the gaming experience.

In-game experiments have shown that tilting controls have substantially increased user immersion when applied to associated steering tasks, such as driving (Cairns, 2014). In addition, a slipping mechanism (sliding a finger over a touch-sensitive input device) can achieve deeper immersion than single-touching gestures alone. Participants have been observed moving fingers in sympathy to character motion, suggesting that users were experiencing a direct connection with the game via finger contact. The role of natural mapping, such as these, promotes a deeper immersive experience and is more fun, even if performance is not as good on initial use (Brown et al., 2010). Older gamers have been reported to perform best with a mixed button and gesture controller (such as the Wii) (Pham, 2012). This study showed that the older generation of gamers performed better with a combined button/gesture device in terms of completion time, when compared to these two control elements presented individually. Therefore, when designing new game controller devices, we should consider the importance of combining different modalities of gesture capture as equally important factors.

Further evaluations of gestural control input methods have highlighted a preference for them over classic controllers in the home entertainment environment (Natapov et al., 2009). The Wii controller has been shown to be the most preferable option when undertaking pointing tasks when compared to classically styled controllers (Microsoft Xbox 360 and Sony PlayStation 3). The wider acceptance and intuitive freedom of gesture capture as an input parameter is in fact attributable to the commercial success of this device (ESRB, 2014). Here, the targeting task refers to pointing to a selection on a screen with a cursor or other marked element and selecting it. In comparison, a nonpointing task would be the navigation of an in-game character (or avatar) and is generally performed with an analog joystick/thumbstick, or the "WASD" keys on a keyboard, where WASD is essentially a copy of the arrow keys, for instance, taking the logical mapping and making it available on the nondominant hand.

In most contemporary console game controllers, the inclusion of analog thumbsticks has become an industry standard as the thumbstick naturally implies direction. The through-put (TP) of a thumbstick is generally equivalent to that of the analog joystick. Targeting tasks are common on most nontouchscreen systems and can be interpreted by a device in a number of ways, such as selecting a file to open on a PC or targeting an on-screen enemy during gameplay. Specific to gaming, these two types of tasks (movement and selection) are combined together to create position and rate control of on-screen actions. The ability to accurately point at a target (on a standard X–Y Cartesian plane) and to control the rate of movement (Z plane) has become the norm in gesture design.

CASE STUDY DESCRIPTION: DEVICE EVALUATION TECHNIQUES

The evaluation of nonkeyboard input devices in computing is strongly influenced by the ISO 9241-9 standard (ISO, 2000), a standardized approach to interface evaluation. This includes performance, comfort, and overall analysis techniques for a multitude of potential functions. Fitts' index of performance (Fitts, 1954; MacKenzie, 1992) is used to assess the functionality of a controller and evaluate the effectiveness of its implementation. However, no single-evaluation technique suits the multiparametric control input that occurs during gameplay. Therefore, in our study, a number of validated techniques were included to analyze the individual devices. The assessment of comfort rating, as described in ISO 9241-9, and additional open-ended questioning were used to rate pointing ability, comfort, usability, and user experience.

Multiple experiments that analyze input devices have been used in the validation of ISO 9241-9. Indeed, these findings were used to inform our best-practice methodology in our experimental design. One such evaluation undertaken to assess the techniques incorpo-rated in ISO 9241-9 used comparisons of joystick and Touchpad performance and com-fort, finding a 27% increase in joystick TP over the Touchpad (Douglas et al., 1999). The most important deviations from the ISO standard suggested by Douglas et al. included using 12 participants for between-subject conditions instead of the recommended 25; they suggested that their experiment methods be adopted as an alternative approach; a multi-directional task is more ecologically valid; more open-ended questioning is required for comfort. For our experiments, these factors were considered to be important for the valid-ity of our study. Additional points were also derived from the recommendations made by Soukoreff and MacKenzie (2004). Specifically

1. The Shannon formulation for index of difficulty (ID) should be applied (Equation 7.1).

2. A wide and representative range of ID values are to be used.

3. Error rates should be incorporated for individual ID values.

4. Adjustments for accuracy should be made to convert ID values into index of difficulty with error correction (IDe) (Equations 7.4 and 7.5).

5. Linear regressions should be calculated to ensure a goodness of fit and to verify a small intercept value (<400 ms for positive regressions and >−200 ms for negative, Equation 7.2).

6. No predictions should be made beyond the range of IDe.

7. The dependent measure of TP is to be calculated via the mean of means for each device.

$$ID = Log_2(D/W + 1) \tag{7.1}$$

$$MT = a + b \times log_2(A/W + 1) \tag{7.2}$$

$$TP = ID/MT \tag{7.3}$$

$$IDe = Log_2(D/We + 1) \tag{7.4}$$

$$We = W \times 2.066/z(1 - Err/2) \text{ if } Err > 0.0049\%$$
$$= W \times 0.0589 \text{ otherwise} \tag{7.5}$$

While there are many advantages to using the standardized Fitts' Law and ISO-testing methods, they do not accurately portray targeting tasks in gaming situations (e.g., FPS gaming). Game controllers offer multiparametric controls for translating gestures into on-screen action; accordingly, the analysis of control in these circumstances should be augmented to better fit targeting tasks in three dimensions. Simulation and analysis of 3D Fitts' testing has highlighted increased performance of mice and traditional console controllers over open-gesture capture devices (such as the Microsoft Kinect and Sony Move). These devices were also shown to require a heightened spatial awareness than that of the traditional mouse and controller interface (Zaranek, 2014) and were therefore not considered for our experiment. Here, we have concerned ourselves with the 3D application of control in in-game environments, which also requires consideration of the zero- and first-system ordering of sensor modalities that are distributed between the left and right effectors of the body.

Additional elements of game controller evaluation included in this case study are derived from the theoretical framework provided by McNamara and Kirakowski (2006), providing further insight into human–technology interactions (see Figure 7.1) (McNamara and Kirakowski, 2006). This model has been applied to many human–computer evaluations that have allowed researchers to clearly understand the interactions between humans and controllers. Three codependent factors are modeled to represent these interactions. Specifically, functionality, usability, and user experience measures are used to quantify the various features of an interface and the impact that they may have upon a user.

Functionality tests are performed to determine if the features a device affords are practical, as well as evaluating the performance, consistency, and the robustness of the applied designs. The assessment of usability is used to raise issues of efficiency, effectiveness, and

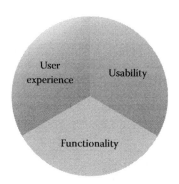

FIGURE 7.1 Functionality, usability, and user experience. (From McNamara N. and J. Kirakowski. Functionality, usability, and user experience: Three areas of concern. *Interactions*, 13(6), 2006: 26–28.)

user satisfaction. Assessing a user's experience is a relatively new and innovative area of investigation within the field of HCI. Measurements are difficult to quantify and can be dependent on a number of contributing factors, including psychological or social factors.

These three types of tests, although unique, do not operate independently of each other. For example, we do not consider usability as a defining-device characteristic. However, the physicality of a device, in terms of its functionality and how the user operates it, directly influences its usability. Also, a system's aesthetic beauty can influence the user's perception of usability and their physical experience with the device before actually using it (Tractinsky et al., 2000). Finally, a device's usability directly influences the user's experience, as poor usability will almost certainly lead to a negative user experience. Therefore, we can see that the assessment of each of these areas of concern is achieved through the application of multiple HCI techniques and is not focused on one alone.

CONTROLLER VARIABLES FOR CONSIDERATION

The cognitive load on users to operate game controllers can be categorized in an increasing order of complexity (Proctor, 2011). Teather and MacKenzie recently found that the order of control is a greater determinant of performance than the actual input method. In their experiment for both position-control modes (tilt and touch), participants reached game levels roughly twice as high as with the velocity-control modes (Teather and MacKenzie, 2014). In addition, human effectors are capable of making gestures that apply either force/torque or displacement/rotation to a control device. The controller responds to each respectively, corresponding to the input gesture applied. An isometric device connects the effector to the controller and its control is derived through the forces or torques applied. In an isometric system, the cursor moves in response to the forces applied to the controller with little or no displacement. The opposite of this is an isotonic device, which operates by capturing this movement alone. In an isotonic system, the cursor moves in direct response to movement of the controller. Many joystick applications are designed to respond to this force/movement with a spring-like resistance that is proportional to the force required to displace it. After the movement is concluded, the joystick returns to a neutral position when this force is removed. This type of system allows the user to perceive proprioceptive and kinaesthetic feedback from the controller in addition to the visual feedback of the cursor moving on-screen. In gaming, the PC keyboard and mouse interface combines the zero-order/positional control of the mouse with the first-order/rate control of the keyboard. However, in console controllers, the minijoysticks operate with only first-order/rate control.

While interaction figures for the mouse may be superior to other pointing control methods, they may not be representative of what is best for game control on differing platforms. A mouse requires a stable surface on which to operate, but most mobile or console-gaming experiences are less fixed, for example, reclining on a sofa or waiting for an appointment. This is conducive toward a home entertainment setting rather than a restrictive desktop arrangement. Even though the mouse is conventionally superior for pointing tasks, it is not necessarily the most appropriate for mobile/home entertainment or console-gaming situations. Recent generations of game consoles have each attempted to introduce some form of spatial gesture capture mechanism. The development of such interfaces has been in response to negative findings from complex user interface (UI) navigation with console game controllers. The need for more affective transparent interfaces (ATIs) has developed in recent times. One potential solution is to use common devices such as smartphones/tablets as controllers for console games. Examples of this type of device adaptation in other domains include the smartphone being used to control home automation, SmartTVs, and other entertainment services. Developers have added certain types of game controller functionalities to smartphones, effectively creating a wireless mobile game controller (Leu and Tung, 2014). As this is an emerging trend, at this moment, there is a lack of appropriate testing frameworks to assess the effectiveness of such virtual controllers.

Another factor to acknowledge between the four control methods is the role of haptic feedback in device operations. When considering haptic sensing and control in a gaming performance context, we have to recognize the importance of the multimodal mediation of all our supporting senses in combination. The amalgamation of visual, proprioceptive, kinaesthetic, and tactile feedback all serve to reinforce the user's ego location, in relation to their own position in space and with respect to other objects or persons around them. The user is now able to orientate, evaluate, regulate, and rectify their gestures to support the output of their input device. The removal of haptics shifts and encumbers the supporting information derived from the visual and proprioceptive senses. This moves away from the input–output arrangement in real-world interactions, to one of reaction, and not interaction. To become interactive, a haptic system must adhere to the expectations of signaling for the human body's various senses.

Multimodal sensation incorporates cues that are derived from cross talk between the various senses, as can be seen in the symbiotic nature of audio–visual and audio–haptic senses. On its own, the haptic sense (primary) can serve to convey a particular degree of information, or in a multimodal arrangement the complexity of the signaling increases but results in more comprehensive information, for example, the concurrent audio–visual sensation of stimuli (secondary). Examples of this can be found in practice, for instance, adding button clicks or other interaction noises to a physical interaction. In addition, the physical characteristics of the system may incorporate the forces required for innate interaction, for example, the force required to activate a key (passive), or feedback that is produced in response to the input action (active), take, for example, a vibratory response.

DESCRIPTION OF CONTROLLERS FOR ANALYSIS

In this study, we compared four types of game controller interfaces: a Logitech G303 Daedalus Apex mouse and Corsair K60 Vengeance keyboard, a prototype Touchpad interface and keyboard combination (Logitech Touchpad T650 and Logitech Ultrathin keyboard), a concept controller (Steam controller), and a familiar console controller (Sony DualShock 4) (see Figure 7.2). Each of the controllers used during this experiment display certain control order and haptic qualities that serve to further distinguish themselves from each other, for a brief description of operation factors (see Figure 7.3).

Logitech G303 Daedalus Apex Mouse and Corsair K60 Vengeance Keyboard

The mouse and keyboard were used in our experiment to serve as a baseline for our analysis. The mouse and keyboard interface is very popular among FPS gamers and has over 50 years of research behind it. The mouse controls the player's X–Y (Cartesian plane) targeting cursor (position rate) and the "WASD" key combination functions to derive the Z direction of travel (control rate). The left and right mouse buttons perform different tasks depending on the game being played, but usually they are primary and secondary weapon fire. The baseline mechanisms of the mouse operate as an isotonic zero-order input device. The mouse is also operated on a solid surface, with its movement controlled not only by the hand, but also in tandem with the wrist, forearm, and shoulder displacement. The combination of multiple joint movements is conducive with increased accuracy and comfort ratings due to our ability to combine small movements in each of these joints for coarse and fine movements during tasks. There is usually very little in terms of tactile indication of task completion during the normal operation of a mouse and a keyboard in gaming systems. However, there are force elements that can affect performance, as are present here in our mouse and mechanical keyboard.

With the mouse, the surface of operation (a wood-veneer desktop in our study here) may cause a noticeable drag upon the smoothness of movement. For the Logitech G303, the glide dynamic coefficient of friction = 0.11 μ (k) and the static coefficient of friction = 0.17 μ (s). In addition, the weight of the mouse is also considered as an important design feature. For the Logitech G303, the mouse-only weight = 87 g, and the mouse plus cable = 127 g. The Logitech mouse and Corsair K60 keyboard also have buttons that display distinct

FIGURE 7.2 Mouse, Steam controller, PlayStation, DualShock 4, and Touchpad concept controller.

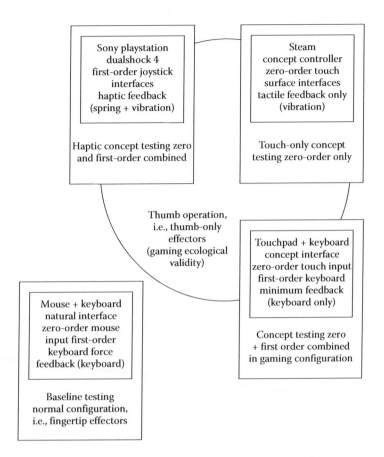

FIGURE 7.3   Summary of controller elements.

"key force" elements. These combine both force and tactile cues to indicate that a button has been pressed or clicked and an activation point has been reached. The forces required to cause a button to travel can be seen in force graphs, which indicate the point of key activation and return. Keyboards with mechanical elements apply springs and dampers to provide users with additional tactile information through clicks or bumps to indicate their activation point. The Logitech G303 mouse contains a metal spring button-tensioning system that keeps the left and right buttons precisely positioned, reducing pretravel, backlash, and delivering optimal response and feel, ensuring that in-game actions remain fast and accurate. The Corsair K60 contains Cherry MX red switches that require only 45 g of force to actuate. The mouse and keyboard are now regarded as the most familiar of all UIs in HCI, with most of all PCs requiring at least one of these interfaces for operation. This increase in familiarity affects the user's ability to complete tasks as they are already acquainted with the device and its operation style.

Logitech Touchpad T650 and Logitech Ultrathin Keyboard

The Logitech Touchpad T650 is a smooth flat glass surface that is touch sensitive. It is multiplatform, including gesture recognition for OSX and Windows 8. It is proficient in terms of precision, comparable to that of most mice, according to Logitech, but is isometric rather than isotonic. It is also customizable within the Logitech SetPoint software. Practical decisions were made to change the normal operational parameters of the device. The Touchpad was arranged and presented to the user as a thumb-operated input device for cursor movements, as opposed to the index finger; it was also to be held in the subject's hands rather than placed on a flat surface. These changes were made to maintain ecological continuity in gesture input styles between the other console-based game controller devices.

The Touchpad and keyboard-combined interface was the first of our concept controller types. It combined an isometric touch surface with a zero-order control process and a first-order keyboard device for Z-plane manipulation. The Cartesian plane was manipulated via thumb motions over the Touchpad surface. The surface itself was sensitive to input across its 134 mm × 129-mm area and has a weight = 210 g. The Touchpad also integrates a "dead zone" that allows the user to rest their finger upon its glass surface without moving the cursor. Because the surface is smooth, the Touchpad relays very little tactile information to the user via the thumb. Users were encouraged to use the tap function for selecting a target. However, it was also possible to "click" the device by pressing down anywhere on its surface. The accompanying Ultrathin keyboard was selected for its slim design (weight = 355 g) and a relatively light button force functionality. For users to locate the WASD keys without looking away from the screen, small rubber domes were applied to tactilely indicate thumb location upon the keyboard. Underneath the keyboard, we added an additional right-click and spacebar button for ease of use during multiparametric operations.

Steam Controller

The Steam controller is the second of the concept controllers tested. This controller is a prototype input device from Valve (Valve Corporation, 2014). The controller incorporates a combination of interfaces that are gesture sensitive and clickable. The most distinctive difference between this device and the traditional controller is the introduction of circular Touchpads instead of joysticks. Steam is attempting to bridge PC and console genres by increasing the fidelity of thumb-based movements to that of those achieved by a mouse in zero-order control input situations. The thumb-operated touch surfaces are 40 mm in diameter, concave, and contain two circular tactile cues for thumb localization. As the input mechanisms on the Steam controller are that of an isometric zero-order control device, Valve has compensated for the reduced force feedback by adding expansive tactile feedback. In addition to the tactile ring indicators displayed on the touch surfaces, the controller is capable of delivering vibrations to the user's Palmer regions. In fact, Valve boasts superior tactile feedback, achieved via dual linear-resonant actuators, the inclusion of which is in response to the reduced kinaesthetic elastic feedback afforded to traditional controllers through spring-loaded thumbsticks. The controller is also configurable, and profiles can be created and edited to support the vast back catalog of games available from Steam. In the configuration menu, it is possible to adjust many parameters of the device. This includes the size of the dead zones in the center of the thumb pads.

Sony DualShock 4

The proliferation of console gaming has led to the familiar form factors and designs used by the Microsoft Xbox and Sony PlayStation (Microsoft, 2014; Sony, 2014). In particular, these console game controller shapes and interface types have become the most recognizable of all game interfaces. These controllers incorporate a combination of joysticks with button and trigger input mechanisms. In the most recent Sony PlayStation controller, the design and construction elements of the gamepad have changed. The concave analog sticks have been upgraded, along with the introduction of a new Touchpad surface between the thumbsticks, with additional accelerometer and gyroscope motion controls. The overall robustness of the PS4 controller has also been improved upon in comparison to previous generations, while maintaining a total weight of 210 g. The DualShock 4 operates as a first-order elastic interface that maintains a spring force upon the thumb during operation. The spring force is directional and relates back to the central return position of the stick at rest. The movement of the thumbstick during operation follows a convex shape. In addition to this force feedback, the DualShock 4 is capable of stimulating the user's tactile system through controlled vibrotactile feedback. The spring and vibrational elements of these gamepads deliver a unique and somewhat controllable haptic feedback to the user.

CASE STUDY 1: FUNCTIONALITY TESTING OF VIDEO GAME CONTROLLERS

The aim of our first experiment was to investigate the targeting performance of the chosen game controllers and compare the functionality, usability, and user experience data that were collected and highlighted to the various controller input configurations. The accuracy of the controllers was measured using a two-dimensional (2D) Fitts' Law assessment and the pointing experience-dependent measures were calculated using validated scales for posttask testing.

Participants

Participants in experiment one (Group A) consisted of 10 males and 2 females. The participants in Group A were aged 22–41 ($M = 28.42$; $SD = 7.08$). All participants in this group had daily experience of using a mouse as a pointing device. Only 50% of participants used a Touchpad every day; 42% once a week; and 8% once a month. 98% of the participants considered themselves as gamers: who play at least every day or once a week (36% respectively); several times a month (18%); and once a month (8%). The preferred platform for gaming was PC gaming (65%), followed by mobile platforms (27%), and finally consoles (8%).

Experimental Procedure

In the first stage of the experiment, participants were asked to target and click on circular objects as they were presented on-screen. To quantify the pointing task evaluations, we used the University of Oregon's WinFitts 2D Fitts' experiment tool (Willson, 2001). This program has been successfully applied to a number of previous experiments that adhere to the ISO 9241 Pointing Device standard [16, 30]. This targeting software is designed for

TABLE 7.1   Experiment Design

Target distance (mm)	40	80	140					
Target diameter (mm)	4	8	16					
Target angle (deg)	0	45	90	135	180	225	270	315

measuring discrete pointing tasks with total time-only measurements, as calibrated in Table 7.1. For all except the mouse, participants were asked to use their right-hand thumb to manipulate the X–Y targeting cursor. Each trial presented all combinations of targeting and selecting $(3 \times 2 \times \delta)$ as can be seen in Table 7.1, with the home square being randomly located on the screen at each step. The experiment consisted of one trial per block, with four blocks in total carried out for each controller. With the preset variables, the modified Shannon formulation was used to calculate the IDe for each block of the experiment (Equations 7.4 and 7.5). Participants were asked to complete a short posttask questionnaire to evaluate the different design aspects of the controller. More open-ended questioning and an informal verbal discussion of their experiences followed this.

RESULTS AND DISCUSSION

The data collected from the WinFitts program and user questioning were used to quantify the functionality of the devices in terms of TP, move time (MT), and errors made. We then performed linear regressions to validate these findings. Participants completed a usability questionnaire to gather posttask usability data. These questions were based on the ISO 9241-9 document mentioned earlier. Finally, users were asked to describe their experience, which was done in two ways. First, users were asked posttask to report on their experiences with each controller type. Second, post experiment verbal questioning was used to elicit more specific user experiences with each of the controller types.

Pointing Task Results

Throughput

User activity with the controller is assessed using a measure of TP in bits per second (bps). For the four devices, we calculated and compared the respective TP rates over the ID derived from the test parameters defined earlier (see Equation 7.3). As expected, the TP rate of the mouse considerably outperformed the other devices as a pointing tool. The mean TP of the devices per IDe value is listed in Table 7.2.

These statistics are illustrated as boxplots in Figure 7.4. As was mentioned earlier, the inclusion of the mouse as a pointing device was to serve as a baseline for comparison. The

TABLE 7.2   Throughput

Device	Number of IDe	Mean (bps)	Standard Deviation (bps)
Mouse	9	3.99	0.21
Touchpad	9	2.27	0.28
Steam controller	9	2.2	0.1
DualShock4	9	1.92	0.12

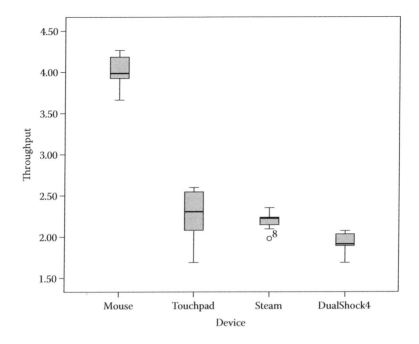

FIGURE 7.4   TP (bps) of each device with outliers marked as circles.

other controllers were evaluated as handheld input devices that did not require a desktop to support them, differentiating them from the mouse in physical operation.

In terms of TP, the other devices performed poorly in comparison to the mouse. The second highest TP was acquired with the Touchpad, with an average TP of 2.27 bps, 43% less bps than the mouse. The Steam controller, with a mean TP of 2.2 bps, 45%, followed this closely less than the mouse and 3% lower than the Touchpad. Finally, the DualShock 4 controller had an average TP of 1.92 bps, 52% lower than the mouse, 15% lower than the Touchpad, and 12% lower than the Steam controller. The reduced TP rate over the IDe range for each of the input devices increased users' dissatisfaction with the device for pointing tasks, as discussed later. This can be seen in the overall user assessment of each controller in Figure 7.8.

A one-way analysis of variance was conducted to explore the impact of input device on TP, as identified in the Fitts' test. There was an overall statistically significant difference at the $p < 0.05$ level in TP between the four controllers: $F(3, 32) = 191.47$, $p < 0.000$. The overall effect size was as large as 0.92, calculated using eta squared. Post hoc comparisons using the Tukey HSD (honest significant difference) test indicated that the mean TP for the mouse was significantly different from the Touchpad, Steam, and DualShock 4 controllers (see Table 7.3). In addition, significant mean differences at the $p < 0.05$ level were noted between the DualShock 4 and the mouse, Touchpad, and Steam controller. Despite reaching an overall statistical difference, post hoc testing has highlighted the small size of the actual differences in mean scores between Touchpad and Steam controllers and hence they were not deemed statistically significant ($p = 0.85$).

TABLE 7.3   Post Hoc Tests for TP

| | | **Tukey HSD Multiple Comparisons** | | | | |
| | | | | | **95% Confidence Interval** | |
(I) Devices	**(J) Devices**	**Mean Difference (I–J)**	**Standard Error**	**Significance**	**Lower Bound**	**Upper Bound**
Mouse	Touchpad	1.71*	0.096	0.00	1.45	1.97
	Steam	1.79*	0.096	0.00	1.53	2.05
	DualShock 4	2.06*	0.096	0.00	1.8	2.33
Touchpad	Mouse	−1.71*	0.096	0.00	−1.97	−1.45
	Steam	0.08	0.096	0.85	−0.18	0.34
	DualShock 4	0.35*	0.096	0.00	0.09	0.61
Steam	Mouse	−1.79*	0.096	0.00	−2.05	−1.53
	Touchpad	−0.08	0.096	0.85	−0.34	0.18
	DualShock 4	0.27*	0.096	0.00	0.01	0.53
DualShock 4	Mouse	−2.06*	0.096	0.00	−2.33	−1.8
	Touchpad	−0.35*	0.096	0.05	−0.61	−0.09
	Steam	−0.27*	0.096	0.04	−0.53	−0.01

* The mean difference is significant at the 0.05 level.

Move Time

The mean MT for each device also followed a similar pattern as seen in the TP results (see Figures 7.5 and 7.6). The mouse outperformed all devices with a mean MT of 954.25 ms across the IDe variables outlined earlier. The Touchpad device followed with an average MT of 1625.65 ms, 70% slower than the mouse. The Steam controller was next,

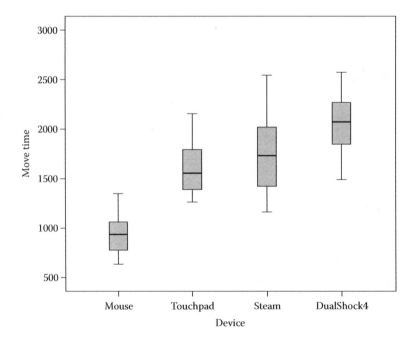

FIGURE 7.5   MT boxplots for each device.

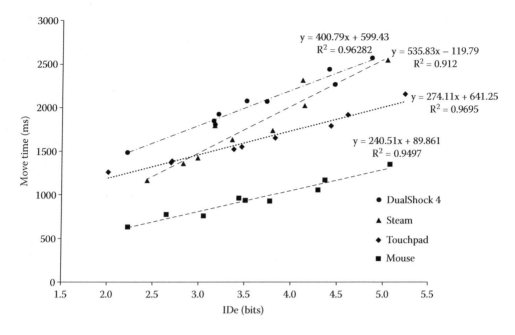

FIGURE 7.6   MT (ms) of all devices by ID (bits).

with an average MT of 1776.09 ms, 86% slower than the mouse and 9% slower than the Touchpad. Finally, the DualShock 4 controller presented an average MT of 2056.52 ms, 116% slower than the mouse, and 27% slower than the Touchpad and 16% slower than the Steam controller. A one-way analysis of variance was carried out to explore the impact of the controller type on MT. A statistically significant difference ($p < 0.05$) was found in MT scores for the four controllers: F (3, 32) = 17.51, $p < 0.000$. The overall effect size, calculated using eta squared, was 0.62. Post hoc comparisons using the Tukey HSD test indicated that the mean MT score for the mouse ($M = 954.25$, $SD = 220.41$) was significantly different from the Touchpad ($M = 1625.65$, $SD = 288.96$, and $p = 0.001$), the Steam controller ($M = 17760.9$, $SD = 452.6$, and $p < 0.000$), and the DualShock 4 ($M = 2056.52$, $SD = 336.78$, and $p < 0.000$) (see Table 7.4). The difference in mean MT scores between Touchpad and DualShock 4 controllers were also significant ($p = 0.048$). The difference in mean MT scores between Steam and DualShock 4 controllers were insignificant ($p = 0.305$).

Errors

The TP and MT measurements from the Fitts' test provided a good measure of the accuracy and time taken by the participants to complete pointing tasks with each controller. However, they do not clearly indicate the success rate of the tasks alone. To accurately evaluate the controllers, the number of errors was measured per ID value and processed using the Shannon formulation. As was seen in the TP and the MT analysis, the mouse outperformed the other devices with the least amount of errors (6%), followed by the Touchpad (8%), then the Steam controller (9%), and finally the DualShock 4 (10%).

TABLE 7.4   Post Hoc Tests for MT

		Tukey HSD Multiple Comparisons			95% Confidence Interval	
(I) Devices	**(J) Devices**	**Mean Difference (I–J)**	**Standard Error**	**Significance**	**Lower Bound**	**Upper Bound**
Mouse	Touchpad	−671.4*	158.18	0.001	−1099.95	−242.84
	Steam	−821.84*	158.18	0.000	−1250.39	−393.29
	DualShock 4	−1102.28*	158.18	0.000	−1530.83	−673.72
Touchpad	Mouse	671.4*	158.18	0.01	242.84	1099.95
	Steam	−150.44	158.18	0.778	−578.99	278.11
	DualShock 4	−430.88*	158.18	0.048	−859.43	−2.32
Steam	Mouse	821.84*	158.18	0.00	393.29	1250.39
	Touchpad	150.44	158.18	0.778	−278.11	578.99
	DualShock 4	−280.44	158.18	0.305	−708.99	148.12
DualShock 4	Mouse	1102.28*	158.18	0.000	673.72	1530.83
	Touchpad	430.88*	158.18	0.048	2.32	859.43
	Steam	280.44	158.18	0.305	−148.12	708.99

* The mean difference is significant at the 0.05 level.

Linear Regression

In addition to the above analyses, we performed a least-squares linear regression to find the intercept and the slope parameters of Equation 7.2. This test highlighted the linear relationship between MT and ID, and validated our results as highly correlated (R^2). For all positive intercept values, we maintained regression values under 400 ms. Negative intercept values did occur, but did not exceed −200 ms. These measurements for each IDe are shown in Tables 7.5 through 7.8.

Usability: Pointing

As well as quantifying the pointing efficiency of the four devices, we also asked users to complete a questionnaire to evaluate usability and user experiences with these controllers for pointing tasks. Almost all participants expressed dissatisfaction with the DualShock 4 as a pointing device, causing some participants to feel that the task was too difficult to complete. Kruskal–Wallis testing revealed some statistically significant differences in question responses across the four different controllers. Four specific usability areas were

TABLE 7.5   Mouse-Pointing Results Including MT Linear Regressions (y–ŷ)

Mouse									
IDe	2.23	3.05	2.64	3.50	3.44	3.77	4.29	4.37	5.07
TP	3.67	4.23	3.66	3.99	3.95	4.27	4.18	3.93	3.99
MT	634.81	763.32	775.71	936.31	962.97	927.22	1062.60	1175.52	1349.77
Error rate	0.02	0.02	0.04	0.04	0.07	0.04	0.07	0.08	0.11
y = 240.51 × +89.861	625.29	823.13	725.79	932.22	916.14	995.67	1121.83	1140.21	1308.06
y–ŷ	15.69	−12.36	8.61	4.23	−58.76	15.78	26.80		
RSQ	0.95								

TABLE 7.6   Touchpad-Pointing Results Including MT Linear Regressions (y–ŷ)

Touchpad									
IDe	2.01	2.71	2.69	3.38	3.82	3.46	4.43	4.60	5.23
TP	1.69	2.00	2.08	2.31	2.31	2.33	2.60	2.55	2.57
MT	1262.36	1390.77	1370.22	1525.92	1653.85	1553.24	1793.90	1923.03	2157.51
Error rate	0.04	0.05	0.06	0.06	0.04	0.07	0.04	0.03	0.05
y = 274.11 × +641.25	573.09	740.47	736.64	901.92	1009.43	922.10	1154.52	1197.16	1347.10
y–ŷ	70.38	8.01	−8.16	−40.83	−35.44	−36.51	−60.75	19.79	83.38
RSQ	0.97								

TABLE 7.7   Steam-Pointing Results Including MT Linear Regressions (y–ŷ)

Steam									
IDe (bps)	2.43	2.98	2.83	3.36	3.16	3.80	4.14	4.12	5.03
MT (ms)	1162.07	1422.92	1360.49	1632.76	1790.28	1734.99	2020.82	2315.77	2544.69
Error rate (%)	0.01	0.03	0.05	0.04	0.11	0.03	0.07	0.11	0.10
TP (bits)	2.26	2.15	2.23	2.24	2.10	2.36	2.21	1.98	2.24
y = 535.83x −119.79	674.91	807.07	769.44	897.08	850.95	1002.86	1084.82	1080.20	1300.20
y–ŷ	−21.57	−55.16	−33.76	−45.86	214.44	−179.29	−76.05	229.20	−32.02
RSQ	0.91								

TABLE 7.8   DualShock 4-Pointing Results Including MT Linear Regressions (y–ŷ)

DualShock 4									
IDe (bps)	2.22	3.15	3.17	3.73	3.21	3.51	4.47	4.40	4.86
MT (ms)	1487.64	1847.29	1807.30	2072.43	1929.84	2079.97	2268.27	2442.71	2573.26
Error rate (%)	0.02	0.03	0.04	0.03	0.17	0.04	0.04	0.09	0.15
TP (bits)	1.79	1.92	2.03	2.08	1.69	1.89	2.05	1.90	1.95
y = 535.83x −119.79	624.00	848.26	852.10	987.25	860.98	934.18	1164.02	1148.41	1259.00
y–ŷ	−1.89	−15.95	−62.34	−22.42	45.40	73.55	−121.16	79.29	25.56
RSQ	0.96								

identified, including smoothness of operation, mental effort exerted during the task, the accuracy of the device in pointing, and the speed of the cursor movement. The overall evaluation of the individual devices showed statistical significance in the answers given for each of the four controllers. A diverging stacked bar chart comparison between these devices for each of the questions can be seen in Figure 7.7. The significance of these differences shall also be discussed (Table 7.9).

Smoothness of Operation
First, significant differences in the users' evaluation of smoothness of operation were measured. The mouse was deemed the smoothest of the four controllers with 67% of users agreeing that it was *fairly* smooth or *too* smooth in its operation. The overall user perception of smoothness decreased from here for the individual controllers. 50% of users found

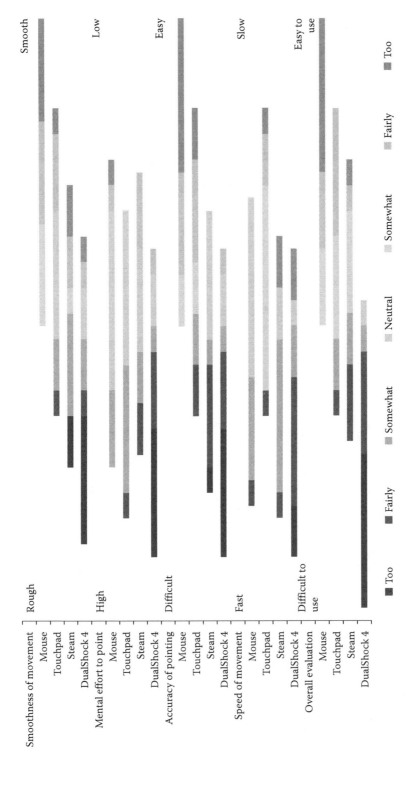

FIGURE 7.7 Statistically significant user ratings from pointing data.

TABLE 7.9 Significant Chi-Squared Results from Pointing Usability Data

Question	Device	Md	x^2 for (3, $n = 47$)	p
Smoothness	Mouse ($n = 12$)	6	13.02	0.05
	Touchpad ($n = 12$)	5		
	Steam ($n = 11$)	3		
	DualShock 4 ($n = 12$)	2.5		
Mental effort	Mouse ($n = 12$)	4	9.82	0.000
	Touchpad ($n = 12$)	3.5		
	Steam ($n = 11$)	4		
	DualShock 4 ($n = 12$)	2		
Accuracy	Mouse ($n = 12$)	6.5	32.84	0.000
	Touchpad ($n = 12$)	5.5		
	Steam ($n = 11$)	3		
	DualShock 4 ($n = 12$)	1		
Speed	Mouse ($n = 12$)	4	9.45	0.025
	Touchpad ($n = 12$)	4		
	Steam ($n = 11$)	4		
	DualShock 4 ($n = 12$)	2		
Overall	Mouse ($n = 12$)	6.5	28.06	0.000
	Touchpad ($n = 12$)	5		
	Steam ($n = 11$)	5		
	DualShock 4 ($n = 12$)	1.5		

that the Touchpad was *somewhat* smooth or *fairly* smooth. User perception of smoothness for the Steam controller was evaluated as *fairly* smooth or *too* smooth by 33% of users. Interestingly, 17% of users thought the movement of the Steam controller was *too* rough. Finally, the DualShock 4 was considered *too* rough or *fairly* rough by 50% of users.

Mental Effort Exerted during the Task

Then, significant differences in the users' evaluation of the mental effort required to point were measured. The mouse received a relatively *neutral* overall rating of 50% for mental effort in operation. The Touchpad received a similar rating, but it was weighted more toward a *somewhat* high rating of mental effort. The Steam controller was more evenly split across the *neutral* or *somewhat* rating of mental effort, with 50% of its user ratings. However, the DualShock 4 received 67% of reports highlighting it as requiring *too* high or *fairly* high amounts of mental effort for pointing tasks.

Accuracy of the Device in Pointing

Next, the significant differences in the users' evaluation of the difficulty in accurately pointing with each of the four controllers were calculated. As with the evaluation of smoothness, the mouse was deemed the easiest of the four controllers for pointing, with 88% of users regarding it as *fairly* easy or *too* easy. The overall user perception of difficulty increased from here respectively for the different controllers. The Touchpad was seen to be *fairly* easy or *too* easy to use by 50% of users. The Steam controller was measured as being *somewhat* difficult or *fairly* difficult by 42% of users. Finally, the DualShock 4 was judged as being *too* difficult for pointing tasks by 83% of users.

Speed of the Cursor Movement

The majority of users evaluated the mouse and Touchpad relatively *neutral* for speed, 42% and 50%, respectively. The Steam controller was deemed to be *somewhat* fast by 50% of participants, but notably, 17% found it *too* slow. The DualShock was evaluated as being either *fairly* fast or *too* fast (59%) by the majority of users; however, some users thought it was *too* slow (17%). The users whose evaluations were deemed *too* slow were further questioned on their answers and they indicated that the process of selecting the target was *too* slow overall, not the actual speed of the task. This may highlight a flaw in the wording of this question in the literature.

Overall Evaluation

Finally, significant differences in the user's overall evaluation of the four controllers at pointing tasks were computed. The final question was a single ease question (SEQ), which was used to establish the user's overall rating of the controller's ease of use. Users clearly preferred the mouse over the other three devices, with 75% of users rating it as *fairly* or *too* easy to use. With respect to the Touchpad and the Steam controller, users indicated a verbal preference for the Steam controller due to their familiarity with similar controller interfaces. When further questioned, users were uncertain of the thumb-based operating style of the Touchpad. This may be attributed to the transparency of these devices in comparison to conventional pointing interfaces—the Touchpad is never operated with a thumb and is very rarely used in gaming. 42% of participants judged the Touchpad as being fairly easy to use and 25% thought it was fairly or somewhat difficult to use. The DualShock 4 was deemed the most difficult to use for pointing tasks, with 88% of users gauging it as *fairly* to *too* difficult to use.

User Experience: Pointing

Participants were asked to evaluate each controller as a pointing device via open-ended questioning (see Figures 7.8, 7.9, and Appendices). The general feedback of the devices followed the trends highlighted above, with the users' order of preference being closely related to each of the device's overall pointing performance. The mouse was evaluated most favorably, with a few users indicating that they would prefer a customizable position resolution (in dots per inch, DPI) for pointing tasks as the cursor sensitivity was too high for them. They also complained that the left-click mechanism was too light and caused them to click unintentionally. The second most-favored device was the Touchpad. Multiple users raised the issue of not being able to accurately move the cursor in one movement, resulting in them having to raise their thumb off the touch surface, place it back down, and sweep toward the target again ("lift-off"). The cursor would either fall short of the target in one thumb sweep or it would overshoot. Users also stated that they were unable to accurately select with the tap-to-click function; this is due to the Touchpad moving the cursor when operated. This movement could be indicative of the "dead-zone" being too small for thumb operation. Similar comments were made about the Steam controller. Selecting small targets with micromovements proved to be difficult for users due to the sensitivity of the Steam controller's touch sensor. In addition, some users expressed

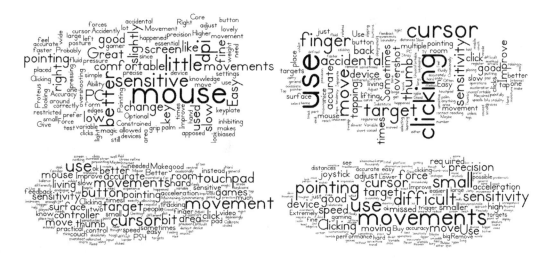

FIGURE 7.8 Tag cloud from questioning for experiment one (left–right; mouse, Touchpad, Steam, and DualShock 4).

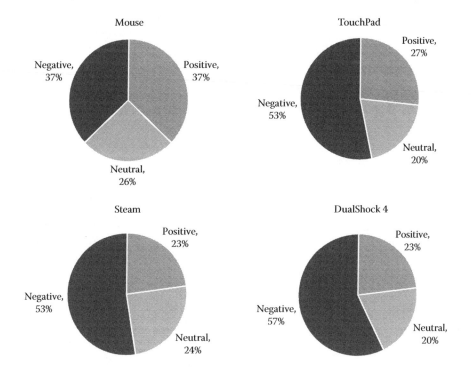

FIGURE 7.9 Analysis of feedback content for pointing tasks.

dissatisfaction with the click mechanism. Finally, the DualShock 4 controller had the greatest user dissatisfaction in pointing tasks. Users found that the sensitivity was unpredictable and unsuitable for small movements. Large or macromovements were easy, but smaller, microadjustments were deemed impossible for some users. Some users were so frustrated with the pointing performance of this controller that they were reluctant to continue the experiment after only two blocks. However, all users rated the click-to-select trigger most favorably.

Further analysis of the feedback questionnaire revealed the following information about how the users experienced pointing with these devices. As can be seen in Figure 7.9, the mouse was the most positively rated for pointing tasks, followed by the Touchpad, with both the Steam and DualShock 4 controllers receiving the same percentage of positive remarks. The DualShock 4 received the highest number of negative comments, jointly followed by the Touchpad and Steam controller, with the mouse receiving the least number of negative comments. Positive and negative remarks toward the devices were reflective of the user ratings mentioned above.

CASE STUDY 2: IN-GAME TESTING OF VIDEO GAME CONTROLLERS

For the second stage of the experiment, participants were asked to use the same controllers in an FPS game. The game "Half Life 2" was used for this study. This game, developed by Valve Corporation, is an FPS with occasional puzzle-based tasks. The user's in-game experiences and self-evaluation were captured at each controller stage via Likert-scale questioning and an open-ended questionnaire. Personal comments were also recorded by the researcher using informal note taking in-game and postgame. The aim of this study was to evaluate the altered in-game usability and user experiences that may have occurred due to the altered state of controller feedback.

Participants

The second group of participants, randomly selected, was composed of seven males and five females. All participants were recruited in Cork (Ireland) and the surrounding community area. The participants in Group B were aged 13–43 ($M = 26.18$; $SD = 8.98$). 42% of participants played video games on a daily basis, 33% once a week, 17% once a month, and 8% played less regularly. The preferred platform for gaming was the PC (33%), followed by the PlayStation and other platforms (25% respectively), and finally the Xbox (17%). The preferred game controller was the mouse and keyboard (42%), followed by the PlayStation controller (25%), while 17% of the participants preferred the Xbox controller, and the same number of participants preferred other interfaces (such as gesture controllers and touchscreens). All participants in Group B were familiar with a range of different game genres, including MMO, FPS, RTS, RPG, sports, and others. There was also no decisive preference of the current favorite game.

Experimental Procedure

The same procedures for posttask user evaluation of usability and experience of Case Study 1 were followed. This stage of the experiment was conducted on a separate date due to the extended time required for both the pointing task and the in-game experiment. Each test period consisted of a 10-min period of adjustment and exploration of key functions, followed by a 15-min block of game play for each controller type. Each of the four blocks of gameplay presented the user with a new controller type, allocated in a counterbalanced order.

IN-GAME RESULTS

Here, we present the results of the study based on the game "Half Life 2." Initially, in-game deaths were recorded to quantify controller functionality, but did not reveal significant differences due to random variations in gameplay stages, and controller functionality was not the focus of this particular study. The counterbalanced ordering of controllers, the individual gamer's previous experiences, and their skill level required the measurement of complex factors such as simultaneous multiparametric control, timing, flow, and previous training. As in Case Study 1, a usability questionnaire was presented to participants to gather posttask usability data. Finally, users were asked to describe their experience after each controller stage using open-ended questioning.

Usability In-Game

Kruskal–Wallis testing revealed some statistically significant differences in question responses across the four different controller stages. Specifically, questions about the forces required for moving and aiming, the accuracy of the controller for moving and aiming, and the overall user evaluation of respective controllers showed statistical significance in answers for each of the four devices. A diverging stacked bar chart comparison between these devices for each of the questions can be seen in Figure 7.10 (Table 7.10).

Evaluation of Physical Force Required for Moving

Kruskal–Wallis testing revealed significant differences in the user's evaluation of physical force required for moving the character and aiming the crosshair. The mouse, Touchpad, and DualShock 4 have shown, on average, to require a relatively neutral amount of force for character movement and aiming. However, the user evaluation of perceived force required for the Steam controller was measured as being fairly *low* or *too* low by 33% of users.

Difficulty in Accurately Moving and Aiming

The same test also revealed significant differences in the user's evaluation of the difficulty in accurately moving and aiming with each of the four controllers. As with the evaluation of force, the mouse was found to be the most accurate of the four controllers for pointing, with 41% of users judging it to be *too* easy to use. The Touchpad followed this, with 50% of users evaluating it as *somewhat* easy to *fairly* easy. The DualShock 4 was evaluated as being *fairly* hard to use for aiming and moving the character by 42% of users. Finally, the Steam controller was assessed as being *too* difficult to use by 58% of users. The statistical importance of the overall user perception of accuracy in-game was particularly interesting as it was also found to have the same importance as in Case Study 1. However, in pointing tasks, the DualShock 4 was found to be significantly *more* difficult to move and aim accurately when compared to the Steam controller.

Overall In-Game Evaluation

Finally, the Kruskal–Wallis test revealed significant differences in the user's overall in-game evaluation of the four controllers. Users clearly preferred the mouse to the other three devices, with 50% of users rating it as either *fairly* easy to use or *too* easy to use.

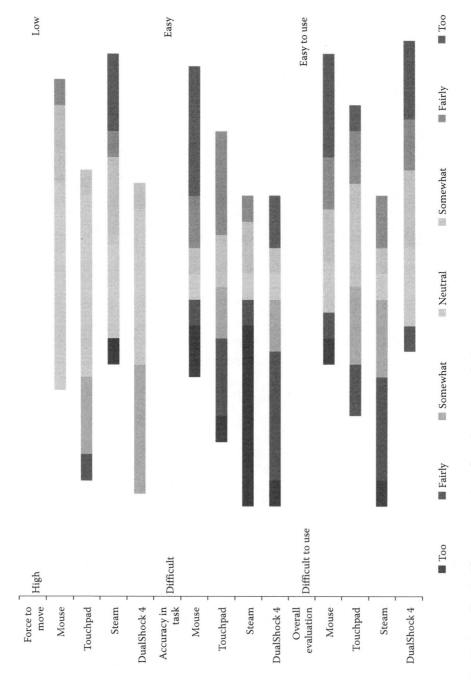

FIGURE 7.10 Statistically significant user ratings from in-game analysis.

TABLE 7.10   Significant Chi-Squared Results from In-Game Usability Data

Question	Device	Md	x^2 for (3, n = 48)	p
Force	Mouse (n = 12)	4	12.35	0.006
	Touchpad (n = 12)	4		
	Steam (n = 11)	5		
	DualShock 4 (n = 12)	4		
Accuracy	Mouse (n = 12)	5.5	8.34	0.04
	Touchpad (n = 12)	4		
	Steam (n = 11)	1		
	DualShock 4 (n = 12)	2.5		
Overall	Mouse (n = 12)	5.5	9.7	0.02
	Touchpad (n = 12)	5		
	Steam (n = 11)	3		
	DualShock 4 (n = 12)	5		

The Touchpad and DualShock 4 controller appeared to be subjected to individual user preference. The Likert scaling for the Touchpad was rated positively by 58% of users and the DualShock 4 received only 29% positive reviews. Moreover, further questioning highlighted the influence of an individual's previous experiences with game controllers. 17% of users rated the DualShock 4 *too* easy to use, as it was their existing controller, which may have biased them somewhat against the Touchpad. The Steam controller was deemed the most difficult to use in-game. 67% of users gave it a negative rating, with 33% of the total ratings deeming it *fairly* difficult to use. These results were also statistically significant in the user evaluation of controllers for pointing tasks. However, the user's ranking of the devices found the Steam controller more favorable than the DualShock 4.

User Experience: In-Game

Test participants were asked to evaluate each controller via open-ended questioning at the end of each in-game testing block. The general feedback for all devices presented notable similarities made apparent in the usability questioning above. In addition, some interesting deviations could also be seen with the user's evaluation of controllers in experiment one. The mouse was evaluated most positively, with users expressing that they found it easy to use for aiming the on-screen crosshair. Some users were unsure about the keyboard arrangement, but they felt that they could quickly adjust and adapt to the new control method. The second most-favored devices were the DualShock 4 and the Touchpad. Several users expressed that they were satisfied with both devices' capability to accurately move and aim the crosshair. Smooth movements were possible with the DualShock 4; however, users noted that they had to glide their right thumb over the Touchpad to look around quickly. In addition, users commented on the lack of ergonomic form in the design of the Touchpad and keyboard combination. These comments possibly represent the current prototype's shortcomings, but should be given greater consideration when further developing the device. Users also commented on the feedback mechanisms of the DualShock 4. The spring mechanisms in the thumbsticks provided users with force feedback information that assisted them in positioning the thumb within its operational area. Several users highlighted that they preferred to use this controller for their own gaming. Finally, the

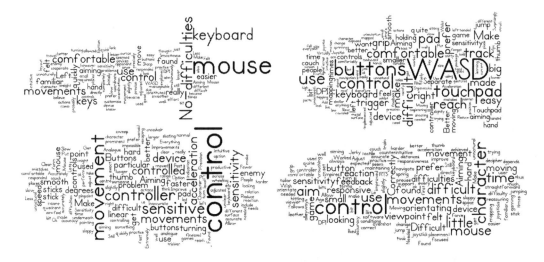

FIGURE 7.11 Tag cloud of open-ended questioning for experiment two (left to right; mouse, Touchpad, Steam, and DualShock 4).

Steam controller registered the greatest user dissatisfaction in in-game operation. Similar comments were made about the Steam controller involving gliding and lift-off. Users were not able to accurately move toward a target, often overshooting. The sensitivity was also commented upon as being too high. Users found that their movements were erratic and jarring for actions that required precision.

An analysis of the questionnaire feedback revealed the following data about how users experienced in-game scenarios with these devices. As can be seen in Figures 7.11, 7.12, and in the Appendices, the mouse was most favorably rated for in-game tasks, followed by the Touchpad, the DualShock 4, and finally the Steam controller. Both the DualShock 4 and the Touchpad received nearly the same percentage of positive remarks. The Steam controller received the highest number of negative comments, followed by the DualShock 4 controller, the Touchpad, and finally the mouse. Positive and negative remarks toward the devices were reflective of the user ratings mentioned above.

DIFFERENCES BETWEEN POINTING AND IN-GAME ANALYSIS

Owing to the noticeable variation in controller evaluations, it was necessary to analyze and compare both sets of data from experiments one and two together. Functionality testing of pointing tasks is easily undertaken; however, these fail to show any meaningful data for the analysis of in-game scenarios. Also, the usability of game controllers for pointing was found to be problematic for game controllers, mainly due to the mixed zero-/first-order input strategies of each of the devices (Table 7.11).

Significant Variations in Usability Testing

Kruskal–Wallis testing was used to discover where variations between pointing and in-game usability testing occurred, as seen in Figure 7.13. For the mouse and Touchpad, no significant variations occurred between user evaluation ratings for each experiment.

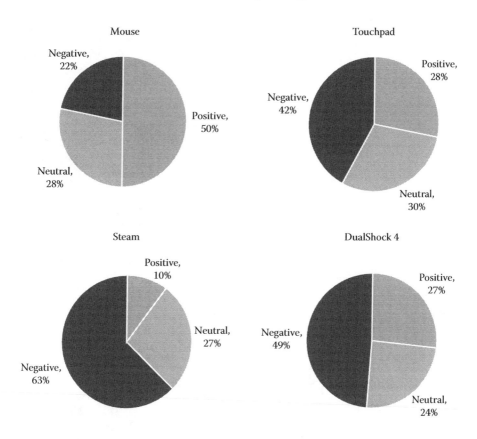

FIGURE 7.12   Analysis of feedback content for in-game tasks.

However, for the Steam controller, a significant variation was found between the user's evaluation of mental effort required for pointing and moving the character/aiming. For the DualShock 4, significant differences were noted between smoothness of operation, perceived accuracy of the device and the speed of operation, finger fatigue, and the overall evaluation of the controller for gaming.

TABLE 7.11   Significant Chi-Squared Variations between Pointing and In-Game Usability Testing

Question	Device	Experiment	Md	x^2 for $(1, n = 23)$	p
Mental effort	Steam	Pointing	4	6.18	0.013
		In-game	6		
Smoothness	DualShock 4	Pointing	2.5	8.34	0.03
		In-game	4.67		
Accuracy	DualShock 4	Pointing	7	11.99	0.01
		In-game	5.5		
Speed	DualShock 4	Pointing	2	5.64	0.02
		In-game	4.5		
Fatigue	DualShock 4	Pointing	4	4.98	0.03
		In-game	1		
Overall	DualShock 4	Pointing	1.5	15.23	0.000
		In-game	5		

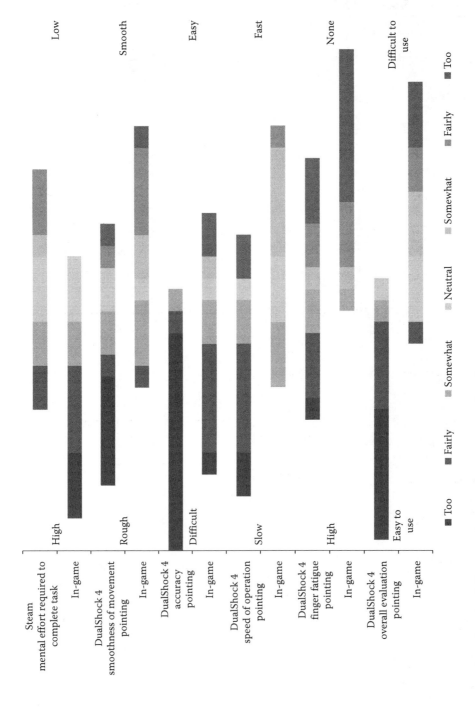

FIGURE 7.13 Significantly different evaluations for pointing task and in-game testing.

Given the changes in user evaluations, it was not unexpected that the overall evaluation of the DualShock 4 controller was significantly different in-game than for pointing tasks.

Significant Variations in User Experience Testing

With respect to the user experience tests, participants were considerably less positive about the Steam controller in the user experience interviews. The Steam controller received a much higher percentage of negative comments and a significantly lower number of positive remarks in the in-game experience reviews compared to the pointing evaluation. Many of the participants were familiar with the DualShock 4 metaphor of game control; some even indicated early on that it was their preferred controller for gaming outside the experiment. However, when questioned about the difficulties that they were experiencing with the Steam controller, many of the participants expressed that they would likely become familiar with the controller if given more time. When evaluating the controllers, novice gamers said that they preferred the Steam device over the other game controllers tested; intermediate players preferred the DualShock 4; and advanced users preferred the mouse and keyboard. This trend may be reflective of the natural affordances of the thumbstick in a console/PC-gaming scenario.

CONCLUSIONS

In this chapter, we have presented two case studies that compared the performance of game controllers in pointing tasks, and collected data pertaining to the usability and user experiences in in-game scenarios. Our main investigation was focused on console-based game controllers and their comparison to a traditional mouse and keyboard. In particular, we focused on a well-known game controller (Sony PlayStation DualShock 4) and two lesser-known models of a handheld game controller. Specifically, Valve's Steam controller and a prototype Touchpad were used to represent emergent controller-based methods of interaction. Our investigation first presented previous research and methodologies of game interaction that were relevant to our examination. We then conducted two experiments that sought to capture functionality, usability, and user experience data to evaluate each controller in tasks that were representative of FPS gaming. In many FPS games, there is "snap to target" assistance, with coarse and fine-grained targeting options. These were removed for the pointing tasks; however, they were retained for the in-game scenario tests.

Case Study 1 measured the subjective-pointing ability of our participants across the four controllers. It was found that the mouse was the most effective targeting device, followed by the Touchpad and Steam controller. The Steam controller and the Touchpad performed comparatively well. The DualShock 4 controller was found to be the least effective at targeting tasks and ranked very low in the usability and user experience data analysis for pointing functionality. The experiment provided a quantifiable measure of each controller's effectiveness when used to seek and select targets that varied in distance, angle, and size. The poor performance of the DualShock 4 may be attributed to the control system ordering of the joystick as a pointing device.

In Case Study 2, we continued our analysis of the same four controllers, but focused our attention to the usability and user experience within game play. We did not collect quantifiable data with this particular experiment, as it would have required a very complex experiment design to account for the numerous subject variables. Usability and user experience data were gathered to give quantitative and qualitative data results. Again, the mouse was rated the most favorable in testing, while the other controllers produced quite different and varied results in usability and user experiences. The DualShock 4 controller was assessed as being superior to both the Steam and Touchpad controllers. This may in part be attributed to the prevalence of console-based FPS games, where participants are already familiar with the control mechanisms used for targeting. Although the Steam and Touchpad were shown to function as superior targeting mechanisms, they were rated less preferable as in-game controllers.

To conclude, we compared the collected data from both experiments and found that these two case studies combined show how the amalgamation of qualitative and quantitative methods, both in and out of gameplay, can be used together to measure functionality, usability, and to better understand the users' overall experience. Specifically, we have shown that functionality testing alone is not sufficient when trying to establish a device's usability and its effects on user experience.

CHALLENGES, SOLUTIONS, AND RECOMMENDATIONS

Limitations in our studies include the relatively short duration of the tests, and the focus being on the initial user experience of the devices. The first experiences of using a new controller can be a predictor of longer-term experience. That said, it is also possible that additional problems and/or opportunities may be revealed with extended use (Karapanos, 2008). As a result, longitudinal use, considering the impact of learning and adaptation over time, are especially important considerations in evaluating new controllers (Kujala et al., 2011).

Another limitation of the studies is the limited consideration of the impact of controller aesthetics. The study involved the use of one prototype device (Touchpad), which was evaluated against other established available controllers. The established controllers have the advantage of optimized ergonomics and refined aesthetics (colors, material textures). Researchers have demonstrated relationships between product usability and product aesthetics (Hassenzahl, 2004; Tractinsky et al., 2000).

The data collected in the studies consist of both data collected from the devices (with logging software), and data collected afterward as participants completed questionnaires. In future, it would be useful to complement this in-game data with biometric and video capture data (with emphasis on facial expressions and body movement). These data may complement the information collected postgame play in the questionnaires, and lead to a more complete understanding of the user experience.

REFERENCES

Birk, M. and R. L. Mandryk. Control your game-self: Effects of controller type on enjoyment, motivation, and personality in game. *CHI'13*, ACM, Paris, France, 2013: 685–694.

Brown, M., A. Kehoe, J. Kirakowski, and I. Pitt. Beyond the gamepad: HCI and game controller design and evaluation. *Evaluating User Experience in Games*, Springer, London, 2010: 209–219.

Cairns, P., J. Li, W. Wang, and A. Imran Nordin. The influence of controllers on immersion in mobile games. In *Proceedings of the 32nd Annual ACM Conference on Human Factors in Computing Systems*, ACM, Vienna, Austria, 2004: 371–380.

DeNA Co., June 20, 2014. www.thedrowning.com.

Douglas, S. A., A. E. Kirkpatrick, and I. S. MacKenzie. Testing pointing device performance and user assessment with the ISO 9241, Part 9 standard. In *Proceedings of the SIGCHI Conference on Human Factors in Computing Systems*, ACM, Pittsburgh, US, 1999: 215–222.

Entertainment Software Association. *Essential Facts about the Computer and Video Game Industry.* June 20, 2014. www.theesa.com/facts.

Entertainment Software Rating Board (ESRB). June 23, 2014. www.esrb.org/about/video-game-industry-statistics.jsp.

Fitts, P. M. The information capacity of the human motor system in controlling the amplitude of movement. *Journal of Experimental Psychology*, 47, 1954: 381–391.

Gerling, K. M., M. Klauser, and J. Niesenhaus. Measuring the impact of game controllers on player experience in FPS games. In *Proceedings of Academic MindTrek Conference: Envisioning Future Media Environments*, ACM, Tampere, Finland, 2011: 83–86.

Hassenzahl, M. The interplay of beauty, goodness, and usability in interactive products. *Human–Computer Interaction*, 19.4, 2004: 319–349.

id Software. Wolfenstein 3D. PC game, 1992.

id Software. Doom. PC game, 1993.

ISO, 9421-9. *Ergonomic Requirements for Office Work with Visual Display Terminals (VDTs)— Part 9: Requirements for Non-Keyboard Input Devices*, International Organisation for Standardisation, London, UK, 2000.

Jennett, C., A. L. Cox, P. Cairns, S. Dhoparee, A. Epps, T. Tijs, and A. Walton. Measuring and defining the experience of immersion in games. *International Journal of Human–Computer Studies*, 66(9), 2008: 641–661.

Karapanos, E., M. Hassenzahl, and J. B. Martens. User experience over time. *CHI'08 Extended Abstracts*, ACM, Florence, Italy, 2008: 3561–3566.

Klimmt, C., T. Hartmann, and A. Frey. Effectance and control as determinants of video game enjoyment. *Cyberpsychology and Behavior*, 10(6), 2007: 845–848.

Kujala, S., V. Roto, K. Väänänen-Vainio-Mattila, E. Karapanos, and A. Sinnelä. UX curve: A method for evaluating long-term user experience. *Interacting with Computers*, 23(5), 2011: 473–483.

Leu, J. S. and N. H. Tung. Design and implementation of a reconfigurable mobile game controller on smartphone. *Wireless Personal Communications (WPC)*, Springer, New York, 74(2): 823–833, January 2014.

MacKenzie, I. S. Fitts' law as a research and design tool in human–computer interaction. *Human–Computer Interaction*, 7(1), 1992: 91–139.

McEwan, M., D. Johnson, P. Wyeth, and A. Blackler. Videogame control device impact on the play experience. In *Proceedings of the 8th Australasian Conference on Interactive Entertainment: Playing the System*, ACM, Auckland, New Zealand, 2012: 18.

McNamara, N. and J. Kirakowski. Functionality, usability, and user experience: Three areas of concern. *Interactions*, 13(6), 2006: 26–28.

Microsoft. Xbox One Wireless Controller. July 2, 2014. http://www.xbox.com/en-IE/xbox-one/accessories/controllers/wireless-controller.

Natapov, D., S. J. Castellucci, and I. S. MacKenzie. ISO 9241-9 evaluation of video game controllers. In *Proceedings of Graphics Interface 2009, Canadian Information Processing Society*, Toronto, Canada, 2009: 223–230.

Pham, T. P. and Y. Theng. Game controllers for older adults: Experimental study on gameplay experiences and preferences. In *Proceedings of FDG 12*, New York, 2012.

Proctor, R. W. and T. V. Zandt., *Human Factors in Simple and Complex Systems*, CRC Press, Boca Raton, FL, 2011.

Skalski, P., R. Tamborini, A. Shelton, M. Buncher, and P. Lindmark. Mapping the road to fun: Natural video game controllers, presence, and game enjoyment. *New Media and Society*, 13(2), 2010: 224–242.

Sony Computer Entertainment America LLC. PS4™ Accessories. July 2, 2014. http://us.playstation.com/ps4/ps4-accessories/.

Soukoreff, R. W. and I. S. MacKenzie. Towards a standard for pointing device evaluation, perspectives on 27 years of Fitts' law research in HCI. *International Journal of Human–Computer Studies*, 61, 2004: 751–789.

Teather, R. J. and I. S. MacKenzie. Comparing order of control for tilt and touch games. In *Proceedings of the 2014 Conference on Interactive Entertainment*, ACM, Newcastle, Australia, 2014: 1–10.

Thompson, M., A. I. Nordin, and P. Cairns. Effect of touch-screen size on game immersion. In *Proceedings of the 26th Annual BCS Interaction Specialist Group Conference on People and Computers*, British Computer Society, Swinton, UK, 2012: 280–285.

Tractinsky, N., A. S. Katz, and D. Ikar. What is beautiful is usable. *Interacting with Computers*, 13.2, 2000: 127–145.

Valve Corporation. Steam controller. July 2, 2014. http://store.steampowered.com/livingroom/SteamController/.

Watson, D., M. Hancock, R. L. Mandryk, and M. Birk. Deconstructing the touch experience. In *Proceedings of the 2013 ACM International Conference on Interactive Tabletops and Surfaces*, ACM, St. Andrews, UK, 2013: 199–208.

Willson, S. K. WinFitts: Two-dimensional Fitts experiments on Win32. January 18, 2001. http://www.cs.uoregon.edu/research/hci/research/winfitts.html.

Zaranek, A., B. Ramoul, H. F. Yu, Y. Yao, and R. J. Teather. Performance of modern gaming input devices in first-person shooter target acquisition. In *CHI'14 Extended Abstracts on Human Factors in Computing Systems*, ACM, Toronto, Canada, 2014: 1495–1500.

Zhang, D., Z. Cai, K. Chen, and B. Nebel. A game controller based on multiple sensors. In *Proceedings of the International Conference on Advances in Computer Entertainment Technology*, ACM, Athens, Greece, 2009: 375–378.

LIST OF ADDITIONAL SOURCES

Cooper, A., R. Reimann, D. Cronin, and C. Noessel. *About Face: The Essentials of Interaction Design*. John Wiley & Sons, New Jersey, US, 2014.

David, T. Y., S. C. Peres, and C. Harper. How well do people rate their performance with different cursor settings? In *Proceedings of the Human Factors and Ergonomics Society Annual Meeting*, 57(1), SAGE Publications, Thousand Oaks, US, 2013: 1561–1564.

Lazar, J., J. H. Feng, and H. Hochheiser. *Research Methods in Human–Computer Interaction*. John Wiley & Sons, New Jersey, US, 2010.

Lidwell, W., K. Holden, and J. Butler. *Universal Principles of Design, Revised and Updated: 125 Ways to Enhance Usability, Influence Perception, Increase Appeal, Make Better Design Decisions, and Teach through Design*. Rockport Publishers, Beverly, US, 2010.

MacKenzie, I. S. *Human–Computer Interaction: An Empirical Research Perspective*. Newnes, Amsterdam, Netherlands, 2012.

Norman, D. A. *The Design of Everyday Things*. Basic Books, New York, 2002.

Preece, J., Y. Rogers, H. Sharp, D. Benyon, S. Holland, and T. Carey. *Human–Computer Interaction*. Addison-Wesley Longman Ltd., Boston, US, 1994.

Rogers, Y., H. Sharp, and J. Preece. *Interaction Design: Beyond Human–Computer Interaction*. John Wiley & Sons, New Jersey, US, 2011.

BIOGRAPHIES

Gareth W. Young is a PhD candidate of digital arts and humanities at University College Cork, Ireland. He earned his MSc in music technology from Dundalk Institute of Technology (2009) and his BEng in sound and broadcast engineering from Glyndŵr University (2008). In addition to his interests in engineering and music technology, Young has a postgraduate certificate in English Language Teaching. He is a part-time composer and has had his work performed at the Hilltown New Music Festival, Ireland, the INTIME Symposium, Coventry, and at both DKIT and UCC schools of music. Young's main topic of research is the design and evaluation of haptic feedback for digital musical instruments. You can find further information about his career, compositions, recordings, and research at garethyoung.org.

Aidan Kehoe is a principal UX designer at Logitech Design Laboratory in Cork, Ireland. He studied for his PhD in the Computer Science Department at University College Cork, and has published papers in the areas of speech interaction and gaming. He is also the coauthor of several patents relating to game controller interaction.

David Murphy is a lecturer and researcher at the Department of Computer Science, University College Cork, Ireland. He is also a director of the Interactive Media Laboratory, UCC. David is the program director of both the MSc and postgraduate diploma in interactive media, and a codirector of the BA in digital humanities and information technology, UCC. His research interests include spatial sound, serious games, and virtual reality.

KEY TERMS AND DEFINITIONS

First-order control: Where one or two actions are required to manipulate the velocity of display change or system response, for example, when using a thumbstick or joystick.

Fitts' Law: Used in HCI to describe the relationships between movement time, distance, and target size when performing rapid aimed movements. According to Fitts, the time it takes to move and point to a target of a specified width and distance is a logarithmic function of the spatial relative error.

Functionality: Refers to the capabilities, features, actions, and/or services of a device. During evaluation of the product, functionality of the device is evaluated for usability, effectiveness, reliability, usefulness, etc. Such evaluations may also highlight some additional desired functionality that should be incorporated in the device.

Isometric: A device that presents with a constant shape or is nonmoving (including pressure and force devices). An isometric device is a UI that senses force but does not perceptibly move. An example of an isometric controller would be the IBM TrackPoint.

Isotonic: A device that presents constant tension in operation (including displacement, free moving, or unloaded devices). An ideal isotonic device has zero or constant resistance. An example of an isotonic controller would be a mouse.

Throughput: Originally presented by Fitts as an index of performance (IP), "The average rate of information generated by a series of movements is the average information per movement divided by the time per movement." However, it is more commonly referred to as TP, measured in bits per second (bps), in most contemporary experimentation involving these types of measurement.

Usability: An analysis that seeks to measure the interaction between the user and the device to ascertain if the device is capable of undertaking the tasks it is supposed to. Usability assessment is used to measure a device's effectiveness, efficiency, and user satisfaction. Further descriptions of device transparency, learnability, and feedback mechanisms can be drawn from analyzing these data. The measure of usability is defined in ISO 9241-11 as "quality in use."

User experience: Assessing a user's experience can be somewhat problematic as the evocative nature of the relationship a user develops with certain types of technology can be idiosyncratic and diverse in its formative stages. Measurements are difficult to quantify and can be dependent on a number of contributing influences, such as psychological or social factors. An example might include personal opinions on aesthetics, a user's exposure to advertising, or the social desirability of certain technologies.

Zero-order control: Where a single input action is required to directly manipulate the display position or other system response, for example, interactions that involve mice or Touchpads.

APPENDICES

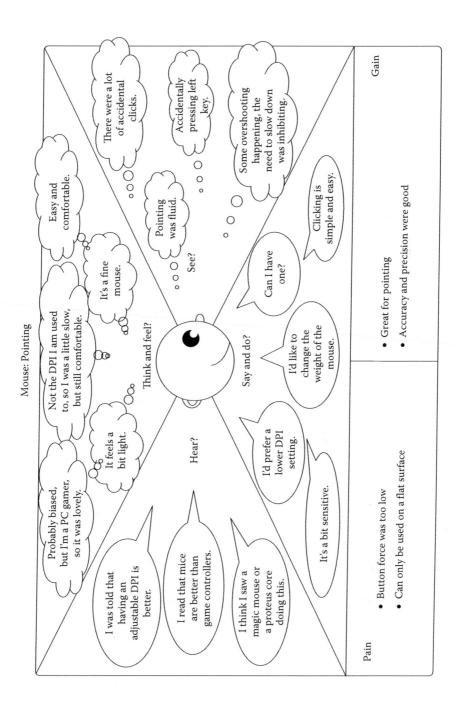

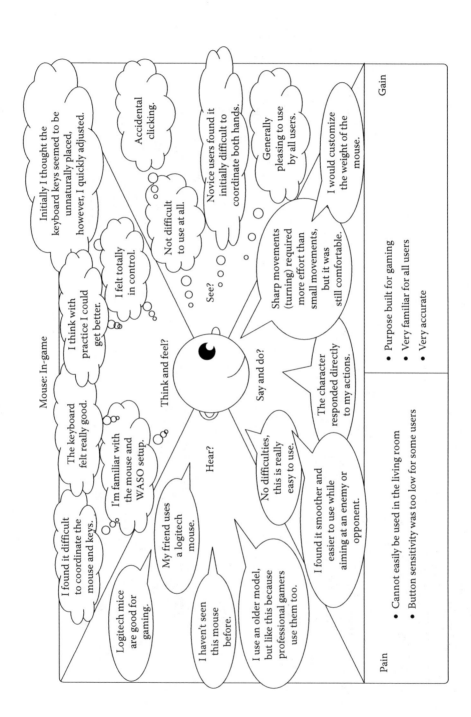

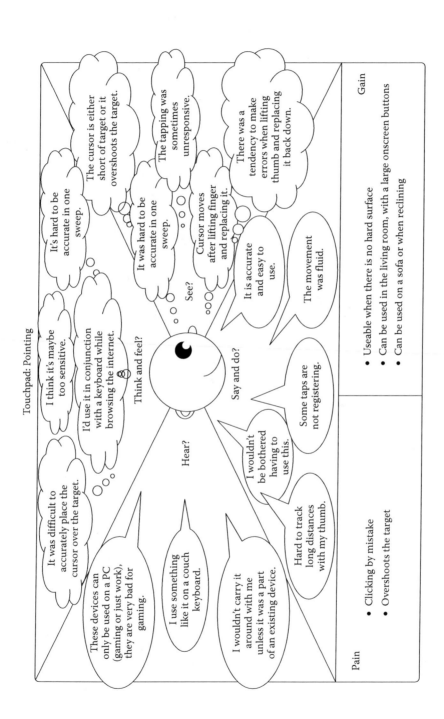

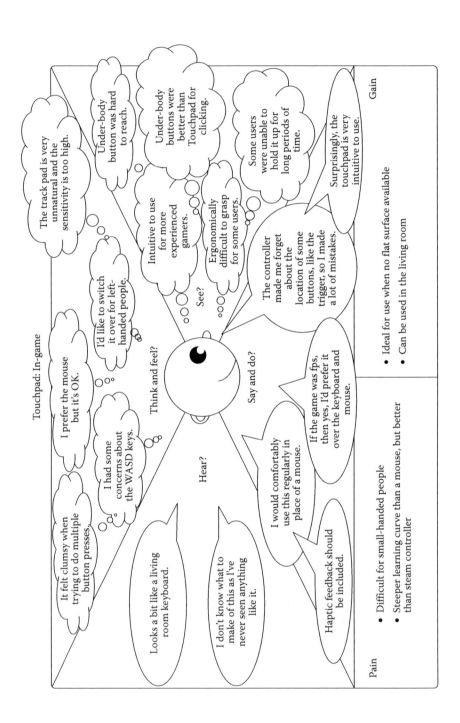

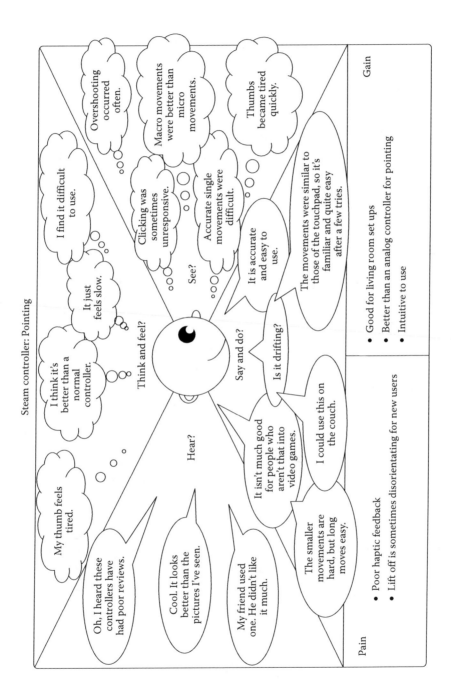

Steam controller: Pointing

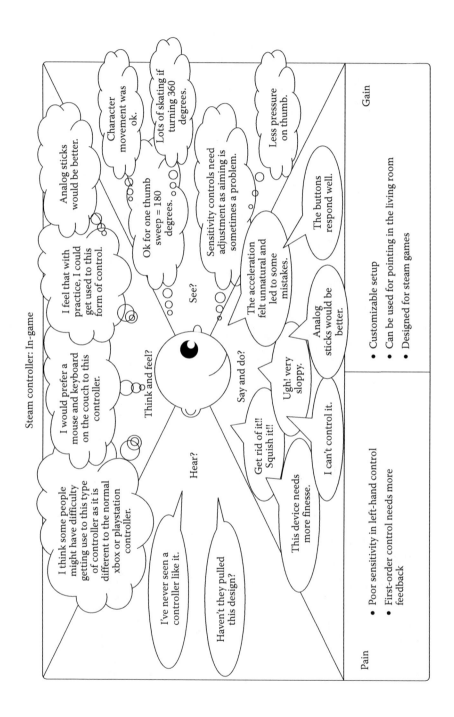

DualShock 4: Pointing

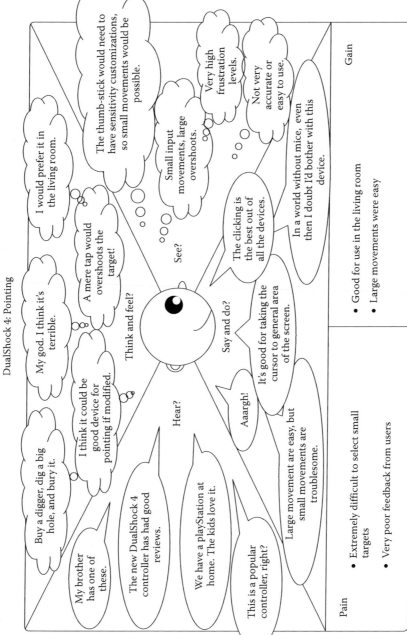

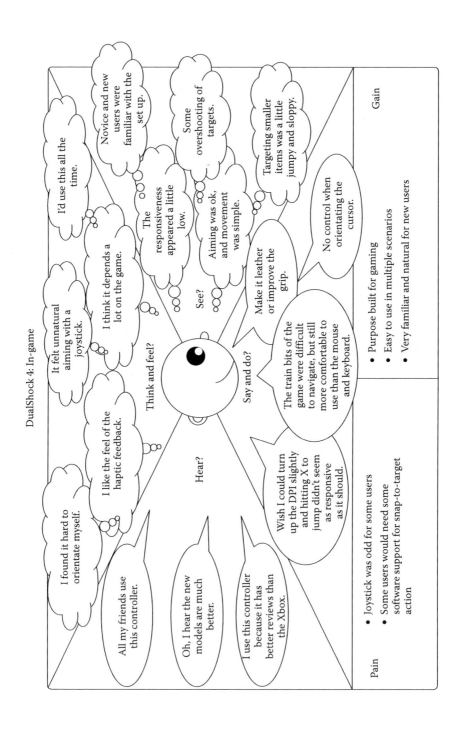

CHAPTER 8

Business Models within Mobile Gaming Experience

Claudia Lucinda Hernandez Luna and David Golightly

CONTENTS

EXECUTIVE SUMMARY

This chapter is an exploration of mobile games, and how the business models used in mobile games can affect enjoyment. Two business models are analyzed in this project: Freemium and Advergaming. The chapter reviews game enjoyment, focusing on the concept of the flow and the Gameflow model, using this framework to consider how different business models may impact the enjoyment and experience of mobile gaming. This is followed by an evaluation case study with 15 gamers of different games with different business models. The results showed that business models can affect enjoyment in games in several ways. Enjoyment can be easily interrupted or disturbed by business models in games. Some in-game strategies are more accepted than others. Also, the business models are not a reason to abandon a game when they are applied in a moderated way. We recommend that, with adaptations, flow and the Gameflow tool provide useful perspectives for understanding mobile gaming and the influence of business models of gaming experience.

ORGANIZATION BACKGROUND

The University of Nottingham Human Factors Research Group (HFRG) conducts theoretical and applied research on the topic of people and their interactions with complex systems. Areas covered include virtual and augmented reality, transport, health and industrial systems, physical ergonomics and product design, and consumer technology. This work has been funded by the UK government and the European Union, but also includes direct collaboration with industry and government sectors, to deliver insight into effective user-centered design and technology deployment. Regarding consumer technology, the HFRG has explored an array of topics relevant to user experience, with a particular interest in mobile technologies and ubiquitous computing related to interactive consumer products, aesthetic and emotional design, games, in-car technologies, and visitor experiences.

INTRODUCTION

> We are pretty much all gamers now....
>
> *NEW YORK TIMES*, 2011

Mobile gaming is a growing industry. Mobile games revenue is predicted to be somewhere between 20 and 30 billion dollars, amounting for about 25% of the total video game industry's profits expected to hit 110$ in 2015 (Forbes, 2015).

As extant game companies try to adapt themselves to the change that mobile phones represent in the industry, and new specialized mobile game companies and independent developers appear, they all have been releasing mobile game titles under modified business models. "In-app" purchases, for example, are now a common part of the gaming experience. These features might be critical for generating revenue, but might also impede the game playing experience, for example, with interruptions that prompt the user to pay to continue their gaming. This is a user experience question, a financial question, and an ethical/legal issue. While, the motivation of the in-app purchase is to make it integral to the enjoyment of the game, it is not unusual for people (often children) to end up spending substantial sums of money, with many examples in the media of people running up large bills (*Guardian*, 2013, 2014). While tighter regulations and clear pricing has steadily been adopted by the mobile gaming industry, it is not clear how much of a distraction or disruptive influence these business models are—how they impinge on the game experience, or whether gamers are overtly concerned.

The following study explored how game experience might be influenced by these newer business models. The Gameflow (Sweetser and Wyeth, 2005) methodology is used in both a review of games, and as part of an evaluation with regular gamers. This evaluation was coupled with qualitative interview data to understand how business models were perceived and could influence gamers. This study can add to our understanding of business models as a critical aspect of contemporary gaming experience. It also gives an example of the useful application of the Gameflow model in the context of mobile business models.

Background

Enjoyment can be described as a positive affective state that reflects feelings such as pleasure, liking, and fun (Motl et al., 2001). Blythe et al. (2004) affirm that studies of enjoyment in the field of human–computer interaction (HCI) are relatively recent, because of the more historical emphasis on reducing frustration and increasing usability when people use computer systems. Designers are now striving not only to reduce frustration, but to create positive reactions and experiences for their users (Goh and Karimi, 2014; Frederick et al., 2015), with enjoyment being one of the user experience goals key to the creation of consumer technology.

Flow, by Csikszentmihalyi (1991), is one of the most important psychological theories to explain enjoyment not only in games, but for activities in general. According to Nakamura and Csikszentmihalyi (2002, p. 90) "Being 'in flow' is the way that some interviewees described the experience of engaging just-manageable challenges by tackling a series of goals, continuously processing feedback about progress, and adjusting action based on this feedback." The flow experience is so gratifying that people will do activities with little concern for what they can get out of it, with the activity being intrinsically rewarding and autotelic (Csikszentmihalyi, 1991). An important precursor of flow experience is a match between the person's skills and challenges of the tasks performed over a certain level, so most flow experiences are goal-directed. Finally, flow activities provide a sense of discovery and a feeling of being transported into a new reality (Csikszentmihalyi, 1991).

Some researchers have used flow as a framework to measure enjoyment in games. Chen (2007) affirms that most of video games include and leverage the components of flow. Chen also states that a balance between challenge of the activity and the players' ability should be reached, in order to maintain flow. Otherwise, users may feel anxious or bored. This idea is supported by Chiang et al. (2011), who defined four flow states applicable for players: flow, boredom, anxiety, and apathy. Zhou (2013) conducted a study to determine the aspects that can affect flow in mobile games. The results showed that perceived ease of use, connection quality, and content quality affect flow, content quality having the largest effect.

In 2005, Sweetser and Wyeth (2005) synthesized existing literature on computer games and developed the model of "Gameflow" to help designers to measure enjoyment in games. The Gameflow model has eight core elements that are based in the eight elements of flow stated by Csikszentmihalyi (1991). Sweetser and Wyeth state that games must keep the player's concentration through high workload, and at the same time give the player tasks that are sufficiently challenging to be enjoyable. Also, the tasks must have clear goals, so the player can complete them, and receive feedback on the progress of completing the tasks. In this way, the players should feel they have control over the task.

Gameflow guidelines could be used for expert reviews or as a base to construct other types of evaluations, like player testing. The complete Gameflow criteria developed by Sweetser and Wyeth (2005) can be found in Table 8.1.

TABLE 8.1   Gameflow Elements and Example Criteria

Element	Example Criteria
Concentration Games should require concentration and the player should be able to concentrate on the game	Games should provide a stimuli from different sources Games must provide stimuli that are worth attending to
Challenge Games should be sufficiently challenging and match the player's skill level	Challenges in games must match the players' skill levels Games should provide different levels of challenge for different players
Player Skills Games must support player skill development and mastery	Players should be able to start playing the game without reading the manual Learning the game should not be boring, but be part of the fun
Control Players should feel a sense of control over their actions in the game	Players should feel a sense of control over their characters or units and their movements and interactions in the game world Players should feel a sense of control over the game interface and input devices
Clear Goals Games should provide the player with clear goals at appropriate times	Overriding goals should be clear and presented early Intermediate goals should be clear and presented at appropriate times
Feedback Players must receive appropriate feedback at appropriate times	Players should receive feedback on progress toward their goals Players should receive immediate feedback on their actions
Immersion Players should experience deep but effortless involvement in the game	Players should become less aware of their surroundings Players should become less self-aware and less worried about everyday life or self
Social Interaction Games should support and create opportunities for social interaction	Games should support competition and cooperation between players Games should support social interaction between players (chat, etc.)

CASE STUDY DESCRIPTION

A wide variety of literature has been published about the changes in the nature of games as they are being adapted for mobile devices. The majority of authors on the topic affirm that mobile games are played as "casual games" (Finn, 2005; Fritsch et al., 2006; *New York Times,* 2006; Paavilainen et al., 2009; Engl and Nacke, 2013; Trenta, 2013; Zhou, 2013). As such, mobile games act as a secondary activity, in that a parallel activity can often encroach or claim priority, such as an incoming call or message. Also, the physical availability of games on mobile devices may mean that games may be played in short spaces of free time, for example, while travelling on trains (Jain and Lyons, 2008). Therefore, users may prefer games that do not require high attention (Paavilainen et al., 2009), and successful casual games should fit efficiently into the lifestyle of the users (Pagulayan et al., 2002). As a result, Paavilainen et al. (2009, p. 11) affirm that "the change of player groups and play habits continue transforming the field of digital games, broadening the consumer base and play environments."

An important aspect that has contributed to the rise of mobile gaming has been the business models in which games are managed, since mobile games are usually offered in accessible ways to users. The business model concept refers to the model that describes the design or architecture of the value creation, delivery, and capture mechanisms it employs (Teece, 2010). As the game industry has evolved, constant changes in the business models it uses are generated, and casual games' characteristics allowed the experimentation of new models that have generated revenues for game publishers (Trenta, 2013). Game publishers have adapted existing business models that work successfully in other platforms and software into mobile gaming, offering alternatives to the conventional "premium" (i.e., one-off, up-front purchase) model that might be less appealing to the casual gamer.

The dominant business models in mobile games are Freemium and Advergaming (Mueller-Veerse and Vocke, 2011; Feijoo et al., 2012; Trenta, 2013). It is important to note that these models may be used in combination. We also note that these models are not unique to mobile games. For example, in game advertising is as common on PC and dedicated games platforms as it is on mobile platforms, for example, with the licensing of real models and marques of cars to be used in driving games.

The Freemium business model has emerged combining "free" and "premium" consumption in association with a product or service (Niculescu and Wu 2011). Mobile publishers offer additional paid content for their games, enticing users to buy more of what they need to expand their game experience (Fields, 2014). According to Forbes (2014), the genre of Freemium has managed to change the habits of gamers around the world, who nowadays expect mobile games to be available for free to download and playable without making any purchase. For Trenta (2013) the reason why the Freemium business model is so successful is that the user is free to decide how they want to consume the content chosen and how far they want to commit to the game. Freemium strategies include

- Selling virtual goods, referring to digital objects and other premium content that only exist within online worlds (Frieling, 2013; Trenta, 2013).

- Boosters that allow players to accelerate their progress in the game by making micropayments, or increase skill or special abilities (Fields, 2014).

- "Time waiting"—letting players use the game for free until they have to wait for certain period of time to continue playing. However, users have the option of a micropayment to allow them to play without experiencing a delay (Finn, 2005).

- Pay per play—the first levels or worlds in the game are unlocked and free, but players must pay to continue playing (Trenta, 2013).

An alternative model is Advergaming. In this business model the mobile games can be available for users without any cost. However, during the whole experience of the game, the players are exposed to advertising in several ways. There are generally two strategies of execution in the Advergaming model: in-game advertising and around-game advertising (Crandall and Sidak, 2006; Trenta, 2013). The in-game advertising strategy features brand names throughout the game. This type of advertising has an objective: to position a product or a brand inside a game, a similar strategy as the one used in movies (Tina and Buckner, 2006; Trenta, 2013). This kind of advertising can increase the realism of the virtual world, mostly when the brands and products are included in the gameplay experience (Crandall and Sidak, 2006; Trenta, 2013). Trenta (2013) divides this kind of advertising in interactive and static. Interactive in-game advertising consists in inserting elements or products with which the players can interact (e.g., the characters may drink a certain kind of beverage with a real brand on it). Static in-game advertising consists in insert static elements in the game, with which the user cannot interact directly (e.g., an advertisement in a billboard on a Football game).

Around-game advertising essentially refers to banners and advertisements around the gameplay window. Advertisements also can be shown at the beginning of a game, at the end, or between games or levels (Trenta, 2013). There are also some cases where the players have the option of seeing advertising videos to obtain rewards, like game credits, boosters, or virtual goods.

CHALLENGE

Pulling together both the topic of enjoyment, and business models, it is clear that there might be tension between these two areas. The challenge is therefore to understand how the type of business model might influence the perception of the game. The kind of strategy employed in the business model might be a conscious attempt to interrupt the flow and experience of the game, which can only be reinstated by some form of purchase (Freemium) or by distracting the gamer from the core game experience to advertise other products or games (Advergaming). To explain how enjoyment is affected by Freemium and Advergaming, both business models were compared with the eight elements of Gameflow (Sweetser and Wyeth, 2005).

The analysis presented explains the specific actions that the business models perform in games that can affect enjoyment, in relation to the eight main concepts of the Gameflow model (Sweetser and Wyeth, 2005) outlined in Table 8.1. For consistency and accuracy, the analysis presented here was also reviewed with an expert gamer who has also worked in the video games industry for more than 5 years, in this research he acted as a subject matter expert, evaluating the Gameflow criteria in a mobile games context.

Concentration

Gameflow (Sweetser and Wyeth, 2005) states that concentration in enjoyable games is required; players must be able to concentrate and the attention of the players should be maintained through the game.

With the Freemium model, maintaining the attention of players can be difficult if the game is interrupted by time waiting restrictions or limited contents (attention is interrupted when the game is interrupted). In Advergaming, concentration in the games can also be broken in several ways. Some games that use this business model are suddenly interrupted by static ads or videos, and this stimuli is not worth the users' attention. Also, concentration can break when advertising is invasive, too striking, or when it includes sounds or animation. Accidentally clicking on around-game advertising can also constitute a nonrelated game task that can distract players from the tasks that they need to concentrate on.

Challenge

Gameflow (Sweetser and Wyeth, 2005) mentions that challenges in games must match the players' skill levels. When a game is managed by the Freemium business model this condition is not always fulfilled, because the game may block some contents that have adequate challenges for the players' skill levels for a certain period of time, or block contents that are exclusively for players that pay. Gameflow (Sweetser and Wyeth, 2005) also mentions that games should provide new challenges at an appropriate pace, and that the level of challenge should increase as the player progresses in the game; in Freemium, the level of difficulty for each user cannot be reached in some cases without making micropayments.

Fields (2014) mentions that in some cases, users have to make virtual goods purchases or perform a set of repetitive tasks in the game to progress. These repetitive tasks do not always have an appropriate level of challenge for players. The result may be apathy (Johnson and Wiles, 2003, as cited in Sweetser and Wyeth, 2005) or boredom (Chen, 2007). Thus, flow may be interrupted.

Player Skills

In player skills, Sweetser and Wyeth (2005) mention that the players must be rewarded appropriately for continued play. However, some Freemium games do not reward users appropriately in order to persuade them to make micropayments. The time waiting strategy is an example of this. Players are not rewarded by continued play, but forced to wait a certain amount of time to continue, unless they make a micropayment.

Control

Control is also an element that can be affected by business models in several ways. One of the important guidelines in this element is "players should not be able to make errors that are detrimental to the game and should be supported in recovering from errors" (Sweetser and Wyeth, 2005, p. 5). This guideline can be affected both by Freemium and Advergaming models. In the case of Advergaming, when advertising is used, users may click banners or videos and be sent to an unknown internet direction that interrupts the game; this usually happens without the appearance of a warning message for the users to know they are taken out of the game. In Freemium, the players sometimes are not warned that they are being taken out of the game interface to take them to the store. This is especially problematic, since there have been recent cases where people do not realize they are making real payments in games (*Guardian*, 2013; *Washington Post*, 2011). As a result, Apple has begun paying compensations to parents whose children ran up high bills by playing mobile games, as ordered by The Federal Trade Commission of the United States (*Guardian*, 2014).

Advergaming can affect other aspects of control as well. Gameflow states that "players should feel a sense of control over their movements and interactions in the game world" (Sweetser and Wyeth, 2005, p. 5), and Advergaming may make this impossible, since users could feel they do not have total control of their interactions if advertising tends to appear suddenly. Gameflow also states that the players should feel a sense of control over the game interface. This can be affected in some games where suddenly the game is suspended to show advertising.

Freemium can affect control as well. Players may feel they do not have control over the game if the time waiting strategy is used, because they are not able to progress in the game. Also, users may feel their actions are not totally shaping the game world, as Gameflow states, because some contents may be blocked if they do not make micropayments. However, Freemium can support control in one way, in that it makes the user free to decide how they want to consume the content chosen and how far they want to commit to the game (Trenta, 2013), which is one of the guidelines of Gameflow: "players should feel that they are free to play the game the way they want (not simply discovering actions and strategies planned by the game developers)" (Sweetser and Wyeth, 2005, p. 5).

Clear Goals

This element of Gameflow (Sweetser and Wyeth, 2005) should not be affected by the business models, since it refers mostly how goals are explained to the players by presenting a storyline, and Advergaming and Freemium models usually do not interrupt or cause any distractions if the game is presenting a story or a goal.

Feedback

The feedback element explains that players must receive appropriate feedback at appropriate times in the game (Sweetser and Wyeth, 2005). This element is also one of the least affected by the business models, since it can produce an effect of disconcerting users if they are not informed of what is happening in the game they are playing. Gameflow states that "In-game interfaces and sound can be used to deliver necessary status feedback" (Pagulayan et al., 2002; Federoff 2002 as cited in Sweetser and Wyeth, 2005, p. 9). In this case, if around-game advertising contains sounds, it can interrupt the feedback indicated by sounds to the users.

Immersion

About immersion, Gameflow mentions that "players should become less aware of their surroundings" (Sweetser and Wyeth, 2005, p. 6), this guideline may not be met when both Advergaming and Freemium models are used. Around-game advertising can interrupt immersion, since it provides a link between the game and everyday life, so can the Freemium model by providing a link outside of the immediate game experience when the game offers users the acquisition of virtual goods. Immersion can also be interrupted when time restrictions in Freemium business models are used; this strategy breaks immersion by taking the player out of the game for certain periods of time.

Social Interaction

Gameflow (p. 10) clarifies that "social interaction is not an element of flow, and often can interrupt the immersion in games, as real people provide a link to the real world that can knock players out of their fantasy game worlds." However, Gameflow also explains that social interaction is a strong element of enjoyment in games, they also explain that "to support social interaction, games should create opportunities for player competition, cooperation, and connection" (Pagulayan et al., 2002 as cited in Sweetser and Wyeth, 2005, p. 10).

It is important to understand that some mobile games support social interaction in games by using social media or by other services (e.g., the GameCenter by Apple). The social interaction should not be conditioned by business models in mobile games, because it creates competition and cooperation between players, which can bring benefits to the game developers.

SOLUTION

The solution to the challenge of understanding the relevance of business model to enjoyment was to conduct a user evaluation with gamers to understand the perception of Freemium and Advergaming business models in mobile games. The evaluation study is described in detail below.

Method

Participants and Ethics

Fifteen adult participants were recruited for the study (9 males and 6 females). The range of ages of the sample was from 19 to 30 years old, and the mean age was 24 years old. The majority of the participants are postgraduate or undergraduate students, with the exception of two participants who graduated from university less than 3 years ago.

All the participants of the sample were familiar with mobile gaming, having installed more than three games on their mobile phones and playing them at least 15 minutes/day. This characteristic was a requirement to participate in the study. The recruitment strategies used for the study included social media postings (e.g., Facebook), and email. Before the recruitment of participants, an ethics application was approved by the University of Nottingham Ethics Committee.

Procedure

The study was divided into three steps, first an interview about previous experience of the participants toward mobile games and business models was conducted, second, the evaluation of the three games selected for the project, and finally another short interview about their experience with the games of the project and the business models they used. In total, the participants took 40–50 minutes to complete the study. An information sheet that was handed to the participants contained basic information about the study: a brief description of the objectives, the name and contact details of the researcher and supervisor of the project, the duration of the study, what the participant will have to do, the research methods that will be used, how the data will be collected and its confidentiality, and the right to withdraw from the study at any time. The consent form formalized the agreement of the participants and the researcher.

The interviews were semi-structured, which means the questions asked were planned before the study. However, in this kind of interview, the interviewer can ask questions on the go, depending on the responses of the participants. The goal of semi-structured interviews, as Lazar et al. (2010) describe, is to dig through the interviewee's comments, looking for opportunities to gain additional insight and understanding.

The total duration of the first interview stage was 15 minutes and it was mainly conducted with the aim of finding out the perceptions of business models in mobile games. The questions planned for this first interview stage were divided into three topics: general information about participants habits in mobile gaming, Advergaming business model perceptions, and Freemium business model perception.

After this phase of the interview was complete, the evaluation of the games started. This process consisted in giving the users the three games selected for the study for a total of 5 minutes each. A postgame questionnaire was handed to them between the games, so they could answer it according to their perceptions of each game.

The questionnaire handed to the participants was based in Gameflow (Sweetser and Wyeth, 2005). The majority of guidelines for gameplay enjoyment described in Gameflow were converted into statements listed in the postgame questionnaire. The questionnaire is divided by sections, each of them being an element of Gameflow (Sweetser and Wyeth, 2005); according to Lazar et al. (2010) questions should be asked in order to make sense in the context of the research. This also reduces the cognitive load on respondents and allows them to think more deeply about the topic about which they are answering.

Once the participants finished evaluating the games, a short semi-structured interview was made to collect data about the business models in the games they evaluated. The planned questions for this interview stage were divided in two main topics: gameplay experience and business models experience. Though not originally planned, questions to collect information about the interruption of enjoyment caused by the business models were asked as well, depending on the responses and activity of the participants. It should be noted that the final evaluation was only partially about the games themselves, and as much about using the experience of business models as played in the games as a reminder or cue to the gamers' more general experience with each of the business models.

The study was not performed in a laboratory, but at "informal" locations in the University of Nottingham (e.g., a library, a cafe, a hall). The intention was to emulate as much as possible the settings where casual games are played. According to Kjeldskov and Graham (2003), mobility and dynamism of changing context are difficult to emulate in laboratory settings, which is why field studies are ideal for the study of rich real-world cases. However, places where major distractions are likely to occur were not selected, like a city bus or the street. The informal places are helpful to provide good conditions to conduct the interviews, fill the questionnaires, and make the participants feel comfortable at the same time.

The full study with each participant was audio recorded, to ensure the data collected was complete and reliable. Appropriate sections particularly around the opening and closing phases of interview (i.e., not during the game evaluation) were transcribed.

Games

To assist in this analysis, three real games were evaluated to understand how the actual implementation of different business models influenced the gamer experience. These games were selected because they typified the business models, one representing each business model, and one with both. The games were also selected because they rated highly on the Apple and Google Play stores. This was important as it was desirable that comments from gamers focused on the business models and not on negative aspects of a poor quality game.

Game 1—Make them jump (MTJ) is a casual game developed by Ketchapp. In this game, the screen is divided vertically in two parts, each part with a character running; the objective is to make the characters jump in different times, so they can avoid the obstacles that appear in the way. The game finishes when any of the two characters hit the obstacles. The game is managed entirely by the Advergaming business model, which appears both while the users are actively playing and between games. Around-game advertising is shown while the users are playing. Additionally, when the users lose in the game and they are sent to the main menu of the game, ads are likely to appear while they are interacting with it.

Game 2—Banana Kong (BK) is an action game developed by FDG Entertainment GmbH & Co.KG. It was selected because it has a good rating in both Google Play and the Apple Store and also because it is managed by a complete Freemium business model, without advertising. In this game, users can win game credits (bananas) every time they play, since they have to collect them in the game. The game has a store where users can acquire virtual goods like hats or parachutes by paying with the game credits that were previously collected while playing the game. On the other hand, some of the virtual goods cannot be acquired with game credits, only by making micropayments.

Game 3—Robot unicorn attack (RUA) is a game developed by Adultswim games. The game is managed by a combination of Freemium and Advergaming business models. The objective of the game is to run as much as possible while overcoming obstacles by jumping or swiping. The distance covered is counted as a score of the game. Like in BK, in RUA the players can collect game credits (diamonds) while they are playing. The diamonds can be either collected in the game, or bought by packs in the store by making a micropayment. The diamonds acquire different kinds of virtual goods, like accessories to customize the main character, or boosters.

The platform chosen for the study was a mobile phone, an iPhone, by Apple. The reason why this device was selected instead of other types of devices such as tablets, is to make more evident the effects of the business models and mobile phones characteristics, particularly in the case of Advergaming, which can use banners in the gameplay window; since the screen of the mobile phone is smaller than in the tablet, it would be more likely for the users to click the banners in a small screen.

Analysis

The analysis presented here centers on the qualitative output from across all stages of the study, that is, the perceptions of business models is as much derived from gamers experience (as expressed in the preevaluation and postevaluation interview) as it is from the specific evaluation of the games themselves. This is indicated by the nature of comments and quotes offered here, which do not only relate to the specific games being evaluated.

Regarding the results of the qualitative data obtained in the study, the opinions were very divided about the preference of the business models applied in mobile games. The results of the study showed that mobile games can create flow, and that gamers were aware and understood the general elements of the Gameflow model (Sweetser and Wyeth, 2005). Some users described elements of flow while talking about enjoyment or business models. The most mentioned elements were immersion and concentration. Participant 4 said "I am in a universe of superheroes, and suddenly I have an advert, that's not consistent, it takes me out of this reality where I am living in this moment." Participant 12 stated "The ads are distracting, because they break the concentration in the game before you ever started playing."

Also, players are aware of the existence of business models in mobile gaming, which can actually affect enjoyment in several ways. The findings about overall perceptions and enjoyment are explained further.

Enjoyment

It is important to mention that, when asking the users about their evaluation responses, they would mention design characteristics (such as colors, characters, etc.) of the games that could affect their judgment of a game. Specifically, Game 1 and Game 3 presented some general usability issues that made the users feel lost when trying to select an option in the menu, or by trying to play the game. These flaws and issues of the interface were mentioned in the interviews about the evaluation, but the business models were rarely identified as a reason to give a game a low score in a Gameflow element.

Only two participants were observed to abandon a game due enjoyment disruptions, like Participant 7, who mentioned "I stopped playing because it is just too annoying.

Sometimes there is advertising over the game so you just can't keep playing, it's pointless." Other users reported to accept the business model, even if it interrupts enjoyment from time to time; they are aware of how the business models work, thus, they accept them and tolerate them. The comments of participants indicated that the level of engagement in a game is the most important aspect considered by users when deciding to accept a business model in a game or not. If the game is attractive and engaging enough for the users to keep playing regularly, the business model will be accepted by the users, and be considered as an option to make micropayments. Thus, overall, the presence and characteristics of the business models did not come across as being as relevant to gamer user experience as other, more general aspects of gameplay.

Business Models

Nonetheless, the majority of the participants have negative perceptions of both business models, since they described negative emotions (like anxiety or anger) when talking about them. Participant 2 mentioned "The advertising makes me angry. Sometimes when I lose in the game I just want to try again faster, but I find advertising, and this somehow makes me angry." However, as mentioned before, the business models are tolerated and accepted in most of their strategies or ways of application. The participants were asked about these different strategies inside business models individually. The results are presented below.

ADVERGAMING

The participants described in their own words some negative effects that advertising can have in games, this indicates that Advergaming can actually affect enjoyment in games. Participant 2 of the study mentioned "I ignore the advertising in the games because it breaks the continuity of playing"; participant 7 said "I have a game where every 2 levels or 3, and ad pops up every time, and I hate it, because I have to press the X to close it, and sometimes I can't press it and I press the ad, it is irritating."

Qualitative analysis about the preference of the business models showed that the less preferred way of implementing of Advergaming is when advertisements interrupt the gameplay. Also, a marked preference toward the positioning where the ads should be placed favored the banners in the gameplay window rather than the ads in the menus of the game; 14 of the 15 participants affirmed the banners in the gameplay window do not cause negative perceptions of advertising, even if they take space of the screen while they are playing, since they are mostly ignored by the users. In this case, the banners in the screen compete with the game to gain attention from the users; the games capture the most attention, as a consequence, the ads in the same screen are practically ignored. Participant 7 mentioned "Banners (in the gameplay window) do not block my view from the screen, there are only images there when you are playing, you can see them there and it's ok, it doesn't matter, but the ads in the menus are more annoying because you have to press X to close it." This result is somewhat surprising, given that the device used was an iPhone which, though with a reasonable screen size for a mobile phone, still offers limited screen space. Nonetheless, users did not feel that devoting space to adverts impinged significantly on the quality of their gaming experience.

Actually, in all strategies of Advergaming, the majority of users reported to ignore advertisements. Participant 3 mentioned "there has not been a single time that I am interested in an ad that I see, they are all about something I would not buy." The majority of participants that reported to ignore advertisements stated that they do it because the ads are about products that they are not interested in buying. Participant 5 affirms "When the ads are from Google or something like that, I don't even look at them." However, 8 participants of 15 reported they have paid attention to ads when they are about other games. Thus, it can be stated that this strategy may lead to better results of the Advergaming model.

The strategy of showing advertising in the game to get rewards is widely accepted. Participants mentioned that they would see advertising videos to get additional game credits or power ups. Participant 6 mentioned "The game that I play everyday gives you a diamond every day if you watch trailers for other games, I watch them just to get the diamonds for free." Also, participant 7 affirmed "I saw a different ad, it was about another game! like 'if you download that game, you're going to get 10 hints instead of 5, so I download the other game just to get the extra hints.'"

Advergaming is mostly tolerated by the users if the game where it is implemented is free, or if it is really engaging; participant 4 of the study mentions "If the game is worth it, you can get along with the advertising, it is still annoying, but if you want to play you will play." Also, half of the participants tolerate around and in-game advertising because they consider it is acceptable for game developers to release a free game, while making profits placing advertisements in their games. Participant 10 stated "I'm ok with the advertising, I don't mind if it is a cheap game, they (the game developers) have to fund the game somehow…." Participant 8 mentioned "Sometimes ads can be annoying, depends of how it is implemented; I think is necessary because they (the game developers) need to make money of it, that's the whole idea." This attitude toward around-game advertising in games is completely different when participants have paid upfront for games, in this case most of the participants consider the appearance of advertising in games unfair.

On the other hand, in-game advertising is accepted because it does not interrupt gameplay, and makes the games realistic; which confirms the statement of Crandall and Sidak (2006). The majority of users affirmed to accept advertising in free games as long as it appears in a moderated way and it does not interrupt the game they are playing, also, none of the participants remembered abandoning a game because advertising caused a negative effect on them.

FREEMIUM

The Freemium business model, as Advergaming, has a negative perception among users. The main reason is that users do not like hidden costs in their games. Participant 10 mentioned "(Freemium) kind of annoys me because if they want me to pay for a game, they should have made it like you have to buy it, I don't like hidden costs. They want you to pay more and they are pretending they don't." Also, participant 9 mentioned "there are many games in which they [game developers] only want to sell, so in the game you cannot do anything if you don't buy something."

An important thing to observe is that only a few of the mobile games players are willing to make a micropayment in a mobile game. Users that are not willing to make in-app purchases affirm that the main reason not to do it is the casual nature of mobile games themselves; players are not willing to spend money on a game that they will play only in short amounts of time. Participant 6 affirms "I haven't purchased anything because I believe it is not something serious, or something important that I have to pay for." Price is also another reason why users do not consider purchasing in a mobile game. Participant 1 said "who is going to pay 1 pound for 100 coins? I wouldn't pay ever, but if you say 1 pound for 1000 coins, ok I will, because it's a big offer."

From the whole sample chosen for the study, only a few users accepted they have made in-app purchases in games before; these users reported they have made a purchase of game credits or boosters to accelerate their progress in the game.

The users that make in-app purchases agreed on the fact of giving importance to the story lines of the games. They are more attracted to make a purchase in games that have several levels to beat or more challenges to overcome, than the games that only have one level to beat, for example. Participant 2 affirmed that he would feel more attracted to make in-app purchases in Game 3 than in Game 1 or Game 2, because Game 3 has more levels to beat, thus, it will take more time to complete. He mentions "you can play maybe for 1 month because it has a story, and you want to know what will happen. In the other games you just have to jump. I will lose interest."

About the strategies of Freemium, purchasing boosters or virtual goods are acceptable by the majority of users. On the other hand, the time waiting strategy is the less accepted from Freemium, and users generally have negative perceptions about it because it interrupts gameplay. Participant 4 states "time mechanisms are kind of contradictory; they would not let you play because you failed." However, this strategy is the one that pushes the users to make in-app purchases more than other strategies of Freemium. The majority of users that have made in-app purchases mentioned that they have made it because they did not want to wait to keep playing. Also, users that have paid for games stated that they feel more inclined to do so when games allow social interaction with other players.

BUSINESS MODELS PREFERENCE

The preference of Advergaming or Freemium business models are divided. Advergaming was the most preferred by 9 of the 15 participants, while the other 6 affirmed they liked Freemium the most.

Advergaming is preferred because users do not like hidden costs in the games they play. Most of them agreed on the fact that they have never made a purchase in a game. The main reason to dislike Freemium is that it breaks the continuity of a game, while the advertising could just be ignored. Participant 11 affirms "I prefer advertising in games than the option of buying things, because you can just ignore advertising, the other option interrupts the progress or won't let you continue. Advertising seems a little bit more passive, you can choose to ignore it if you want."

About Freemium, the participants who prefer it over Advergaming stated that it is a better option because advertising also breaks the continuity of games, but in a different way.

Advergaming can affect enjoyment when it interrupts the game while users are playing, different to Freemium, which can break the continuity of games by blocking content that do not let the participants progress in game levels, or will ask them to wait after a certain time of playing. Participant 5 mentioned "the worst advertisements are the ones that would not let you play until you close it; it's ok if they (the game developers) want to put some ads in there, but do not pause it, do not interrupt my moment with the game." Participant 13 also affirms "I do not like advertisements in games because they can change your mood completely when playing, you have to quit and do other activity, like closing the window that just popped up, or come back to the game."

RECOMMENDATIONS

This project aimed to discover if enjoyment in mobile games is affected particularly by Freemium and Advergaming business models. The results of this research showed a variety of results that are relevant to explain the preferences and perceptions of mobile gamers in the application of business models in mobile games.

Freemium and Advergaming business models do affect enjoyment in mobile games, and the work presented here sheds light on the mechanisms through which this might occur. The disruptions in enjoyment can vary according to the type of business model the games use, the mechanics proper of the game that is played, and the context in which the game is played. The results of the study showed that the disruptions generated by the business models cause generally bad impressions in users. However, the disruptions are mainly tolerated in the majority of their applications, and were secondary to other concerns about usability and quality of gameplay. It is important to highlight again that these impressions were not drawn just from the games evaluated, but from the gamers general experience and comments on gaming.

About perceptions, the results showed that the opinions can vary according to each individual strategy of the business models; each one is perceived differently by users and their acceptance can vary according to how the strategies are applied. Users have a preference for Advergaming over the Freemium business model, because Advergaming does not break the continuity of the game as Freemium does; thus, players are not obligated to pay to continue playing. Interestingly, gamers appeared more tolerant of Advergaming when it had a direct relation to the game.

In terms of the Gameflow model therefore, not only does Freemium affect more of the elements for flow within games, it does so in a manner that often cannot be avoided. Advergaming, on the other hand, affects fewer elements but also is ostensibly ignored by gamers so that its effects are further reduced.

Value of Gameflow

Overall, flow and Gameflow proved valuable tools for understanding the mechanisms through which the business model influences user experience. Gameflow was also a practical, easily accessible tool that gamers themselves rapidly came to terms with and could use as part of their dialogue with the researcher to describe different game elements. The usefulness of Gameflow in the current study demonstrates that other researches in the field of both mobile gaming and business models could use this approach to potentially great effect, both as an exploratory tool and as an inventory in evaluations such as A/B testing (Andersen et al., 2011).

That said, a limitation was that the Gameflow guidelines (Sweetser and Wyeth, 2005) were developed for games played on PCs and consoles. As a consequence, some of the guidelines in Gameflow do not apply correctly to mobile gaming. To overcome this problem, some of the guidelines were modified or deleted in the postgame questionnaire that was used to evaluate the games. Items less relevant in the player skills element include "players should be able to start playing the game without reading the manual" and "games should include online help so players don't need to exit the game"; casual games do not provide manuals or online help to teach users how to play, since their complexity is much less than console or PC games. Also, in the social interaction element, the guidelines "games should support social interaction between players (chat, etc.)" and "games should support social communities inside and outside the game" were less relevant because the social interactions in casual games are usually less prominent than in console and PCs games. However, some questions from the element of social interaction are worth including because they make reference to the integration of social media in mobile games, which is the most common social characteristic that these games include. We would note though that none of these limitations relate to business models and, in terms of business models analysis, Gameflow has provided a highly effective lens through which to consider the impact of business models on gaming experience.

Another limitation was time. The initial idea of the second part of the study was to let the participants play the three chosen games for more than 5 minutes each, so they could experience a more complete interaction with the three variations of the business models. However, the study time was reduced to accommodate a longer preevaluation and postevaluation interview. To increase the quality of responses about the experience of the participants with the business models, qualitative and more specific questions about the topic were added to the interviews. It would however be desirable to study gamers over longer periods of interactions, particularly with games where they have invested considerable time (and potentially money!).

Also, the participants included primarily the younger demographic, including gamers who had moderate levels of familiarity with gaming. One of the interesting characteristics of mobile casual games is that they potentially appeal to a much wider demographic than typical games. It would need to be verified whether the results and attitudes expressed would extend out to this broader population.

Finally, the study here has viewed business models purely as a user experience consideration, not in terms of actual financial transactions, that is whether over time the business models would actually lead to spending or purchases. A next step could be to use survey work to see whether game characteristics really do relate to actual purchasing behavior.

ACKNOWLEDGMENTS

The first author was funded by the Mexican National Council for Science and Technology (CONACyT). The second author was supported by RCUK through Horizon Digital Economy Research (EP/G065802/1).

REFERENCES

Andersen, E., Liu, Y., Snider, R., Szeto, and Popović, Z. 2011. Placing a value on aesthetics in online casual games. In *Proceedings of the SIGCHI Conference on Human Factors in Computing Systems*. Vancouver, BC, Canada, ACM, pp. 1275–1278.

Blythe, M. A., Overbeeke, K., Monk, A. F., and Wright, P. 2004. *Funology: From Usability to Enjoyment*, Vol. 3. Norwell, MA: Springer.

Chen, J. 2007. Flow in games (and everything else). *Communications of the ACM*. 50(4): 31–34.

Chiang, Y., Lin, S., Cheng, Y., and E. Z.-F. Liu. 2011. Exploring online game players' flow experiences and positive affect. *Turkish Online Journal of Educational Technology-TOJET*. 10(1): 106–114.

Crandall, R. W. and J. G. Sidak. 2006. *Video games: Serious business for America's economy*. Entertainment Software Association. http://ssrn.com/abstract = 969728.

Csikszentmihalyi, M. 1991. *Flow: The Psychology of Optimal Experience*, Vol. 41. New York: Harper Perennial.

Engl, S. and L. E. Nacke. 2013. Contextual influences on mobile player experience—A game user experience model. *Entertainment Computing* 4(1): 83–91.

Federoff, M. A. 2002. Heuristics and usability guidelines for the creation and evaluation of fun in video games. PhD dissertation, Indiana University.

Feijoo, C., Gómez-Barroso, J. L., Aguado, J. M., and S. Ramos. 2012. Mobile gaming: Industry challenges and policy implications. *Telecommunications Policy* 36(3): 212–221.

Fields, T. 2014. *Mobile & Social Game Design: Monetization Methods and Mechanics*. Boca Raton, FL: CRC Press.

Finn, M. 2005. Gaming goes mobile: Issues and implications. *Australian Journal of Emerging Technologies and Society* 3(1): 31–42.

Forbes. 2014. Freemium is the new shareware, as in app purchasing matches traditional conversion rates. March 1. Accessed August 12, 2014. http://www.forbes.com/sites/ewanspence/2014/03/01/Freemium-is-the-new-shareware-as-in-app-purchasing-matches-traditional-conversion-rates/.

Forbes. 2015. Digital drug of choice: Mobile games. April 29. Accessed May 20, 2015. http://www.forbes.com/sites/archenemy/2015/04/29/digital-drug-of-choice-mobile-games-2/.

Frederick, D., Mohler, J., Vorvoranu, M., and R. Glotzbach. 2015. The effects of parallax scrolling on user experience in web design. *Journal of Usability Studies* 10(2): 87–95. http://uxpajournal.org/the-effects-of-parallax-scrolling-on-user-experience-in-web-design/.

Frieling, J. 2013. Virtual goods in online worlds: Basics, characteristics and monetization. In *Proceedings of GI Jahrestagung 2013*, Koblenz, Germany. pp. 3097–3107. Available at http://subs.emis.de/LNI/Proceedings/Proceedings220/3097.pdf.

Fritsch, T., Ritter, H., and J. Schiller. 2006. User case study and network evolution in the mobile phone sector (a study on current mobile phone applications). In *Proceedings of the 2006 ACM SIGCHI International Conference on Advances in Computer Entertainment Technology*, Hollywood, California. 10. Doi: 10.1145/1178823.1178836.

Goh, J. and F. Karimi. 2014. Towards the development of a "user-experience" technology adoption model for the interactive mobile technology. In *HCI in Business*. Fiona Fui-Hoon Nah (Ed.), Springer International Publishing, pp. 620–630.

Guardian. 2013. Apple's in-app game charges: How my kids ran up huge bills. March 26. Accessed July 12, 2014. http://www.theguardian.com/technology/shortcuts/2013/mar/26/apples-in-app-game-charges-kids-bills.

Guardian. 2014. Apple to pay $32.5m over practice that let children make in-app purchases. Jan 15. Accessed July 12, 2014. http://www.theguardian.com/technology/2014/jan/15/apple-practice-children-make-in-app-purchases.

Jain, J. and G. Lyons. 2008. The gift of travel time. *Journal of Transport Geography* 16(2): 81–89.

Johnson, D. and J. Wiles. 2003. Effective affective user interface design in games. *Ergonomics* 46(13–14): 1332–1345.

Kjeldskov, J. and C. Graham. 2003. A review of mobile HCI research methods. In *Human–Computer Interaction with Mobile Devices and Services*. Luca Chittaro (Ed.), Berlin: Springer, pp. 317–335.

Lazar, J., Heidi Feng, J. H., and H. Hochheiser. 2010. *Research Methods in Human–Computer Interaction*. Chichester, UK: John Wiley & Sons.

Motl, R. W., Dishman, R. K., Saunders, R., Dowda, M., Felton, G., and R. R. Pate. 2001. Measuring enjoyment of physical activity in adolescent girls. *American Journal of Preventive Medicine* 21(2): 110–117.

Mueller-Veerse, F. and J. Vocke. 2011. Online, social, and mobile: The future of the video games industry. Cartagena-Capital. http://www.cartagena-capital.com/news-and-events/news/256-online-social-and-mobile-the-future-of-the-video-gamesindustry.

Nakamura, J. and M. Csikszentmihalyi. 2002. The concept of flow. *Handbook of Positive Psychology.* 89–105.

New York Times. 2006. Mobile games await for a better platforms. Dec 10. Accessed August 9, 2014. http://www.nytimes.com/2006/12/10/technology/10iht-wireless11.html?_r=0.

New York Times. 2011. With smartphone games, downtime becomes a pastime. Jun 8. Accessed August 10, 2014. http://www.nytimes.com/2011/06/09/technology/personaltech/09GAMES.html.

Niculescu, M. F. and D. J. Wu. 2011. When should software firms commercialize new products via Freemium business models? Under Review.

Paavilainen, J., Kultima, A., Kuittinen, J., Mäyrä, F., Saarenpää, H., and J. Niemelä. 2009. *GameSpace: Methods and Evaluation for Casual Mobile Multiplayer Games*. University of Tampere, Hypermedia Laboratory, 2009. Available at http://tampub.uta.fi/haekokoversio.php?id=293.

Pagulayan, R. J., Keeker, K., Wixon, D., Romero, R. L., and T. Fuller. 2002. User-centered design in games. In *Human–Computer Interaction: Designing for Diverse Users and Domains*. Boca Raton, FL: CRC Press, pp. 217–233.

Sweetser, P. and P. Wyeth. 2005. GameFlow: A model for evaluating player enjoyment in games. *Computers in Entertainment (CIE)*. 3(3): 3–3.

Teece, D. J. 2010. Business models, business strategy and innovation. *Long Range Planning* 43(2): 172–194.

Tina, W. and K. Buckner. 2006. Receptiveness of gamers to embedded brand messages in adver-games: Attitudes towards product placement. *Journal of Interactive Advertising* 7(1): 3–32.

Trenta, M. 2013. Modelos de negocio emergentes en la industria del videojuego [Emerging business models in the videogames industry]. *Revista ICONO14. Revista Científica de Comunicación y Tecnologías Emergentes* 12(1): 347–373.

Washington Post. 2011. In-app purchases in iPad, iPhone, iPod kids' games touch off parental firestorm. Feb 8. Accessed July 12, 2014. http://www.washingtonpost.com/wp-dyn/content/article/2011/02/07/AR2011020706073.html.

Zhou, T. 2013. Understanding the effect of flow on user adoption of mobile games. *Personal and Ubiquitous Computing* 17(4): 741–748.

LIST OF ADDITIONAL RESOURCES

Bell, M., Chalmers, M., Barkhuus, L., Hall, M., Sherwood, S., Tennent, P., Brown, B. et al. 2006. Interweaving mobile games with everyday life. In *Proceedings of the SIGCHI conference on Human Factors in Computing Systems*. Québec, Canada, ACM, pp. 417–426.

Coursaris, C. K. and D. J. Kim. 2011. A meta-analytical review of empirical mobile usability studies. *Journal of Usability Studies* 6(3): 117–171.

Ha, I., Youngseog, Y., and M. Choi. 2007. Determinants of adoption of mobile games under mobile broadband wireless access environment. *Information & Management* 44(3): 276–286.

Lin, H.-F. 2014. The effect of product placement on persuasion for mobile phone games. *International Journal of Advertising* 33(1): 37–60.

Mack, Z. and S. Sharples. 2009. The importance of usability in product choice: A mobile phone case study. *Ergonomics* 52(12): 1514–1528.

Nelson, M. R. 2005 *Exploring Consumer Response to "Advergaming."* Mahwah, NJ: Erlbaum.

Salo, J. and H. Karjaluoto. 2007. Mobile games as an advertising medium: Towards a new research agenda. *Innovative Marketing* 3(1): 71–82.

Wright, P. C. and A. F. Monk. 1991. A cost-effective evaluation method for use by designers. *International Journal of Man–Machine Studies* 35(6): 891–912.

BIOGRAPHIES

Claudia Lucinda Hernández Luna is a user experience architect; she earned an MSc in human computer interaction from the University of Nottingham and a bachelor's degree in visual design from the Universidad Autónoma de Nuevo León (UANL). Hernández Luna has worked as a professional in the areas of user experience design, usability, and information architecture. Her current research interests are: human computer interaction, ubiquitous computing, mobile contexts and devices, and agile methodology. Her particular interest is bridging the gap between business, design, and technology.

David Golightly holds a PhD in psychology, with a specialization in human–computer interaction. He has worked in commercial usability services for both mobile and financial services, before joining the Human Factors Research Group in 2007. In his role as senior research fellow, Golightly studies how people interact with technology to engage in work and leisure activities, and how knowledge and experience shapes their understanding of the world.

KEY TERMS

Advergaming: Business model used in mobile games; the games can be available for users without any cost. However, during the whole experience of the game, the players are exposed to advertising in several ways.

Business models: The manner through which a product such as a game is able to derive revenue.

Enjoyment: A positive affective state that reflects feelings such as pleasure, liking, and fun.

Freemium: Business model commonly used in video games; the model allows the players to play games for free, but has the option of buying extra content to enrich the experience in the games.

Gameflow: Model developed by Sweetser and Wyeth in 2005 to help designers measure enjoyment in games. The Gameflow model has eight core elements that are based in the eight elements of the theory of flow.

Mobile games: Video games designed specially for mobile devices, like smartphones or tablets.

Mobile phones: Wireless handset whose main functions are to make calls, receive messages, and internet navigation.

CHAPTER 9

NerdHerder

Designing Colocated Physical–Digital Games with Sociological Theories

Yan Xu and Blair MacIntyre

CONTENTS

EXECUTIVE SUMMARY

We developed and evaluated a multiplayer mobile-augmented reality (MAR) game, *NerdHerder*, to research social play in a shared physical–digital space. *NerdHerder* is inspired by the recent innovations in physical game interfaces, such as Wii and Kinect. These interfaces enable a hybrid physical–digital gaming space by mapping physical actions to digital game controls. But current multiplayer games designed for the hybrid game space often involve players standing next to each other, yet staring at their own character and activities on the screen. This kind of parallel play is limiting—people play next to each other, but do not try to influence one another's behavior. We believe that digital games have the potential to bring more engaging and cooperative social experience to players. To achieve this goal, we adapt sociological theories to the specific domain of colocated hybrid physical–digital games. Using the research method of research through design (RtD), the goal of our case study is to explore the dynamics between sociological theories, the game design that embodies these theories, game interfaces that enable such a design, and social play behaviors that emerge from gameplay. In our work, we first turn sociological theories into design guidelines based on existing games and research, and then we implement a subset of them in *NerdHerder*. We conduct a user study on *NerdHerder* to see if the theory-based design affects social interaction as we anticipated or not. Finally, based on our design process and empirical data, we reflect on the core framing constructs that are uniquely important for colocated social play in a hybrid physical–digital gaming space and provide design implications based on these constructs. Our case study aspires to stimulate more in-depth discussions with researchers and designers who are also interested in social play experience in the space of physical–digital games.

ORGANIZATION BACKGROUND

The case study was conducted in the Augmented Environments Lab (AEL) at the Georgia Institute of Technology. The AEL is a multidisciplinary lab founded by Professor Blair MacIntyre, where novel user experiences are created by combining the latest augmented reality (AR) technology with creative design. We have been designing, developing, evaluating, and teaching AR games since 2008. From 2010 to 2012, we ran the Qualcomm Augmented Reality Game Studio* to bring together students with technical and design backgrounds to create novel AR games. This game studio was a collaborative effort between the Georgia Institute of Technology and the Savannah College of Art and Design. Our case study, *NerdHerder*, is one of the projects created in the game studio to explore how to design games with a MAR interface to support social play.

Beyond the goal of making a fun game, *NerdHerder* was created as a research platform to explore sociological theories and generate empirical data on social play. Therefore, our design process is different from many other digital games in the industry. We will discuss our research method and design process in further detail in the next section.

INTRODUCTION

Motivation

In recent years, physical interfaces have changed the landscape of the video game industry, exemplified by the success of Nintendo Wii and Microsoft Kinect. Research shows that physical game interfaces can increase engagement (Bianchi-Berthouze et al. 2007) and the amount and enjoyment of social interaction (Lindley et al. 2008). However, designing for social play in a shared hybrid physical–digital space is still challenging. First, the players' attention is distributed between both the physical and digital media, and individual and group activities. Especially when a game keeps players busy with individual tasks, players may not have the bandwidth to attend to other players' states nor engage in social play. For example, observations of movement-based console games, such as *Dance Central* (on Xbox Kinect) and *Just Dance* (on Wii), show that players were mostly staring at their own avatar on the screen rather than paying close attention to others' moves (Isbister 2012). A second pitfall is to equate colocation with being social. The proximity between people (or their digital representations) does not guarantee social experience; the amount of social presence and awareness may vary (de Kort and Ijsselsteijn 2008). In other words, without proper design, people may play "alone together" (Turkle 2012). For example, researchers found that players stayed in their "private sphere" of gaming rather than using the mobile game as a medium for having fun together, even though they were physically sitting close to each other (Szentgyorgyi et al. 2008). To address these challenges and explore design opportunities, we take a theory-driven design approach that learns from sociological theories and build a game prototype based on theory-driven guidelines.

---

* Qualcomm Augmented Reality Game Studio, http://ael.gatech.edu/argamestudio/, accessed on January 31, 2015.

Methodology

We use the RtD method to guide the design and study of our multiplayer AR games. RtD recognizes interaction design as a core knowledge inquiry activity (Zimmerman et al. 2007). Multidisciplinary efforts from ethnography, engineering, and sociology are embodied in the design, while the user experience of the resulting design provides new insights. Our case study, *NerdHerder*, is a design artifact that combines several different types of knowledge. It was designed with the guidelines we generate from existing sociological theories that focus on colocated social interaction. We also leveraged our years of experience in understanding the affordances and constraints of AR interfaces and how to implement them through collaboration among engineers, artists, and user researchers.

In recent years, RtD has been recognized by the human–computer interaction (HCI) community as a novel way to understand the process and thinking of interaction design. Similarly, it is hard (if even possible) to discuss the relationship between game interfaces and player experience without having designed products that embody that relationship. RtD is a good fit for the creative design of games. In contrast to "engineering design," which focuses on solving well-defined problems, creative design focuses on the interplay between problem setting and problem solving (Wolf et al. 2006). Our design process uses social games experiments with different game mechanics and rules. The RtD method acknowledges this kind of explorative process.

CASE STUDY DESCRIPTION

Gameplay

We designed, implemented, iterated, and evaluated a multiplayer MAR game, *NerdHerder* (see Figure 9.1). The multiplayer *NerdHerder* is a 2-versus-2 team-based competitive MAR game. In the game, the goal is to feed the donuts to the nonplayer character of the Donut King, who patrols the game board. The goal is to get five points before the other team. In the game, players need to use their virtual fishing rod, which extends from their camera phone to the scene, to hook donuts that are scattered on the board and to put them in the mouth of the Donut King. The donuts spawn periodically. The Donut King occasionally opens his mouth to be fed. When the Donut King eats a donut from a player's fishing hook, his/her team gains one point. Two Nerds, dressed in blue and red, wander around on the board. Each Nerd belongs to one team. The Nerds are naturally attracted to donuts and move toward them. When the Donut King gets a "sugar high" after eating four donuts, he starts charging at the Nerds and tries to squash them. If this happens, the corresponding team loses one point.

There are two kinds of power-ups that periodically spawn on the game board. The *shake* power-up makes the other team's player's hook randomly jitter for 2 seconds. The *stealth* power-up allows players to sneak up on the other player's hook, and steal their donut. Both power-ups have a limited influence range, which requires players to get close to the other person's hook to shake them or steal from them.

FIGURE 9.1 Screenshots of NerdHerder game. In the top picture, the Donut King opened his mouth and players can feed the donut into his mouth; in the bottom picture, the Donut King is in the attack phase and chasing after the Nerds. Players lead the Nerds away from Donut King with donuts on their fishing line.

Game Control, Mechanism, and Rules

The core game control in *NerdHerder* is the fishing hook, which dangles from the digital fishing rod that extends from the camera phone device that users are holding. Players' spatial and physical movement is directly mapped to the fishing hook's movement in the game world. Because we use an AR interface, the digital game board overlaps with the physical game board, which is a piece of paper with trackable patterns on it. The game characters (the Nerds and the Donut King) walk on the game board as if they are walking on the physical paper.

For the social play aspect of the game, we used sociological theory-based guidelines. The game mechanics and rules encouraged players to interact with each other, in the digital and physical game space. For example, we introduce dependency between teammates, direct conflict between teams, and leverage shared emotion to encourage the interaction between teammates and also among all players. Besides theory-based design, the specific design and aesthetic of multiplayer *NerdHerder* is influenced by cooperative games (e.g., *Left4Dead*), team-based sports (e.g., *Curling*), and board games (e.g., *Hungry Hungry Hippos*).

System Configuration

Nerdherder was developed using the Unity game engine combined with Qualcomm's Vuforia AR SDK plugin. The networking between different devices used the Player.IO

Unity API, a client–server network structure that used a cloud server (provided as a service of Player.IO) to synchronize game state between the phones. One of the players' phones function as an authoritative host that decides the physics and game logic; the rest of the phones function as clients that render data as requested by the host. The server functions as a conduit and passes data between the clients and the host. If the host player quits the game in the middle of a session, the server will choose one of the remaining phones as a host and continue the game seamlessly. The game runs on android phones equipped with 1-GHz processors or higher. It also runs on iOS smartphones and tablets.

Adapting Sociological Theories to Social Games

Similar to designing other digital games, we designed *NerdHerder* through iterative cycles of playtesting, analysis, redesign, and implementation. But different from most games, we also designed *NerdHerder* to be a research platform for exploring sociological theories. We want to test these theories and see how user behaviors unfold in a colocated game context, which is a different context than originally conceived for these sociological theories.

Prior research shows that social play is influenced by many factors, including the game design, players and their relationships, and the context of play. To understand such a complicated and emergent phenomenon, we turned to sociological theories that have long explored the question of "*what makes social interaction more enjoyable.*" Out of the vast amount of literature, we choose interaction ritual (IR) theory as the main framework. Collin's IR theory (Collins 2004) is a synthesizing theory that analyzes several ingredients that contribute to the success or failure of social interactions. We chose this theory because (1) it originates from research understanding face-to-face social interactions, which aligns perfectly with the social and spatial settings in colocated games; (2) it is an overarching theory that synthesizes much existing sociological research into one cohesive model.

IR theory was created to understand the elementary processes that underpin all social interactions; this theory analyzes the ingredients and outcomes of successful social interactions of small groups in mundane everyday life. Collins points out four key ingredients for successful social interactions in his book—bodily copresence (physically assembling in the same space), barrier to outsiders (a sense of who is taking part and who is excluded), mutual focus of attention (awareness of each other's attention focusing on a common object), and synchronization of emotions (common mood or emotional experience that gets elevated during the interactions). These factors are interlinked: bodily presence and boundary to outsiders allow people to keep track of a certain range of people's actions and reactions, which forms a foundation for them to gain awareness of each other's actions and attention. When they have mutual focus of attention, participants express and share their emotional reactions. As their emotions are observed, they stimulate more responses, forming a feedback loop that tends to intensify the shared experience among people.

Successful rituals produce a sense of group solidarity, which is represented in symbolic emblems. Individuals will want to repeat this interaction again with enthusiasm and confidence (which is referred to as emotional energy [EE] in the IR theory). The group tends to develop moral standards of what is right or wrong, punishing those who violate its symbolic code.

In his book, Collins recognizes that games are natural rituals. He also insightfully points out that game designers "unconsciously or nondeliberately bring about the ingredients for a successful ritual…and they bring together a community that has no other coherence, and no other purpose, than the experience of the peaks of ritual emotion itself" (Collins 2004, p. 59). In the following four subsections, we use IR theory as a lens to analyze the design and gameplay experience of existing social games and to generate a list of design guidelines for colocated digital games. These guidelines are grounded in both theory and existing social game design.

Bodily Copresence
In IR theory, bodily copresence is the beginning of the IR process. People can naturally keep track of each other, even when other people are not their direct focus of attention (Goffman 1967). For example, in board games and card games, such as Mafia and Little Max (as analyzed in Salen and Zimmerman 2004, pp. 467–472), to win the game, a player needs to observe other players' body language and facial expression to guess cards or recognize bluffing.

The interpersonal spatial arrangement during board games makes it easy to observe others and to be observed. Players sit around a table facing each other, causing players to form an F-formation circle in which each participant has equal and maximized ability to observe others (Kendon 1970). However, the close spatial arrangement among players does not always lead to social play. In Szentgyorgyi et al.'s study on Nintendo DS games, they found that players did not have much social interaction during multiplayer games with handheld devices. Interestingly, they also found that players tended to sit next to each other, even though the network connection works over a much larger range, and players arranged their body orientation to form a semicircle that allowed them to have face-to-face interaction. The above study shows that although players naturally form a social configuration that can possibly allow them to leverage bodily copresence, their attention is consumed by the digital screen and dynamic game content, rather than by other players. One solution to this problem is to leverage the physical interface so that players reveal more game-related information through physical actions, which may motivate observation of other players and further communication and interaction. Lindley et al.'s comparative experiment of people playing Donkey Konga with the Bongo interface or GameCube controllers found that players have higher frequency of verbal, nonverbal, and gestural interaction using the physical Bongo interface. They explain that with a reality-based interface, "players display information about their interactions with a game through their movement, making their use of the device a rich source of consequential communications." The consequential effect of body movement is also found in our previous study of the AR multiplayer game of *BragFish* (Xu et al. 2008). We found that some players adopted the strategy of guessing other player's intentions by observing their body movement. With the natural mapping between players' physical movement and their avatar's actions, players can easily leverage their bodily presence to perform game events and also observe others' progress through both physical movement and digital representations.

In summary, to fully leverage players' physical presence in social games, game designers can (1) map the players' physical movement to their in-game state, so that it is easier for players to display their game state and perceive others' game state through bodily movements and (2) motivate players to pay close attention to other's physical presence (e.g., movement, gestures, facial expressions, and conversations) through the game reward system.

Barrier to Outsiders

The participants, by committing to be part of the activity, form a circle that has entry barriers for outsiders. Games have a clear beginning and end of an activity. People choose to join a game or become a spectator. Here we take a closer look at how games gather a group of players with the same interest.

In pickup basketball games, being at the same location of the basketball court is a clear indicator of interest. Researchers also found that players use "ritualized scripts" to join and exit a game (Jimerson 1999). The player community generates and regulates these scripts among themselves according to social norms. To support players initiating an ad hoc digital game with strangers, we need to have some signaling mechanism and well-understood social etiquette. Designers can start to experiment with different ways to do so, such as wearing DS buttons (a physical button produced by a third party that displays distinct logos tied to backpacks, clothes, jackets) and carrying their Nintendo DS visibly to indicate an interest in joining an ad hoc Nintendo DS multiplayer game. In more recent Nintendo 3DS games (e.g., the use Wii Street Pass), game devices have the ability to automatically connect with other devices. A player can turn this capability on or off. These emerging ways of connecting handheld game players shows an interesting shift. Instead of relying on socially accepted conventions (e.g., breaking the ice by a ritualized script), players use the game equipment's physical presence (including symbols of the game device) and its digital presence to initiate ad hoc gameplay.

Different from the barrier to outsiders in everyday life social interactions, many games engage outsiders as spectators, like the audiences surrounding street chess players and the sports fans cheering for their team in a stadium. In recent years, the indie game community has started to explore the design space of including spectators in face-to-face interaction with digital games, such as Johann Sebastian Joust (Die Gute Fabrik Game Studio), a digitally enabled physical play game that players need to jostle opponents' PlayStation Move controllers while avoiding their own controller being jostled. Part of the reason why these games are successful is because they are fun to watch. Even if the audiences were not playing, they laugh together with the players and cheer them on, increasing the enjoyment and social interaction. In these games, physical movements are meaningful actions in the game, and can be easily observed and understood by the audience. Learning from these designs, we want to provide mechanisms that leverage high physical enactment to engage the audience.

Mutual Focus of Attention

Mutual focus of attention means more than paying attention to the same object or activity; rather, it is about being aware of others' attention toward the same target (Mead 1925). By doing so, people can understand each other's actions and emotions. Moreover, this allows people to try to ascribe a sense of intention to the others, which precedes their actions (Tomasello 1999).

By analyzing existing social games, we found three ways to join players' attention toward each other. First, they may share a common game object that is independent of individual actions. For example, rhythm games (e.g., *Rock Band* [on Xbox], *Just Dance* [on Wii], and *Dance Central* [on Xbox Kinect]) directs players' attention to a common object of melody which synchronizes the actions of multiple players. Players coordinate with each other through the shared object of rhythm rather than by directly observing each other.

Second, games can direct players' attention to shared objects and activities that can be directly influenced by individual players' actions. Seif El-Nasr et al.'s empirical study on cooperative games summarized a dozen design patterns that may lead to cooperative game behaviors (Seif El-Nasr et al. 2010). Among these patterns, "interacting with the same object," "shared goals," "shared characters," and "shared puzzles" fall into this category. Although their discussion is under the context of colocated cooperative games, these patterns are useful to other types of social games (i.e., competitive and team-based competitive games) because they support players' joint attention and consequential interaction. When players focus on the same object/goal/character/puzzle, they negotiate with each other to interact with the common target. In some cases, this introduces direct competition to gain control of the common objects. For example, team sports often include a game object that players fight for, such as a basketball or football. In other cases, players work out strategies and division of labor to perform more efficiently as a team.

A third approach to join players' attention is to direct their attention to other players or their avatars. In digital games, their attention is often directed to a player's avatar, while in nondigital games, it is directed to the other player. For example, during a board game, players take turns to perform their actions while other players are watching. This means that players take turns being a performer (during their own turn) and a spectator (at others' turns). The group joins their attention on the performing player during their turn.

Compared to board games, where players get the full attention of other players during their turn, digital games often claim more attention from players within the digital interactive world. To motivate players to pay more attention to other players or their in-game avatars, design patterns of cooperative games, such as "complementarity" (complementing each other's activities), "synergies between abilities" (assisting or enhancing capabilities of other players), and "abilities that can only be used on another player" (Rocha et al. 2008) have been created to increase the dependency between players (and their avatars), thus motivating players to pay attention to each other in cooperative games.

In summary, we discuss three ways that a designer can support mutual focus of attention among players: (1) through shared game objects that are independent of players, (2) through common objects and activities that can be affected by individual players, and (3) by motivating players to direct their attention to other players. Each of these methods fosters qualitatively different social experiences.

Shared Mood

When people start to engage in social interaction, they get more caught up in the shared rhythm and mood. According to IR theory, shared mood and mutual focus of attention reinforce each other. Emotion is a central ingredient and outcome of IRs. Collins emphasized that "*what makes or breaks a ritual is the extent to which the group builds up a strong collective emotion.*" The shared mood can be empirically shown as shared laughter, conversational rhythms, and synchronized movements.

Shared mood is what a good social interaction and a good social game have in common. Both indicate synchronization between participations. The difference is that, in most of the natural rituals of social interaction such as a conversation, shared mood is an emergent pattern between participants while in social games the emotioneering (Freeman 2004) of the game design plays a critical role in supporting and fostering the shared mood between players. Learning from existing games, we discuss several game mechanics that foster shared mood.

One of the most common emotional indicators during gameplay is laughter, so shared laughter is often included in metrics for cooperative game behaviors. Seif et al. found that shared laughter in a cooperative game is most likely to happen because of the animations, cut scenes, or special elements that are specific to one game. Other causes for shared laughter include shared goals, complementarity, shared puzzles, and shared characters. Similar findings were also found for board games (Seif El-Nasr et al. 2010). Xu et al.'s video analysis on board games found that shared laughter is evoked by game-content-related jokes, humorous comments on previous moves, shared game history, and exaggerated physical actions (Xu et al. 2011). Sometimes the jokes do not even look to be funny from the researchers' eyes as an outsider, but they become amusing because the players have their shared experience and their mood to build on, getting tuned together enough that the fun is magnified. In some cases, players' conversations and laughter overlapped repeatedly. Without finishing a sentence, others already understood the joke based on the shared game history, and immediately followed it by laughter or another joke. Jokes, comments, and laughter build on top of each other, and are an indicator of a high level of synchronization.

In IR theory, mutual focus of attention and shared mood reinforce each other. In the above findings from studies on board games and console games, game designs that effectively support shared moods all provide a common target that players are aware of, whether it is game-based (such as cut scenes, funny animations, creative narratives, and shared goals/characters) or player-generated (such as shared history built through multiple game experiences and other out-of-game shared history).

Outcomes of Repeated IR

A successful IR leads to individual and group level enjoyment. As individuals, they have more EE associated with these kinds of IRs. Players who enjoyed a good game together usually feel their time well spent. They will want to repeat this experience by choosing the game over other methods of entertainment. They will probably prefer to play again with the same group because of the social bond created from the shared game enjoyment. These social bonds may turn into stronger social relationships between players. This process of creating and reinforcing social relationships is defined as transformative play by Salen and Zimmerman (2004). A group that has been successful in such games will start to build their identity, especially in highly competitive team-based games, such as teams in MLG (major league gaming).

Theory-Based Design Guidelines

Using IR theory as a lens, we have analyzed many different genres of social games. The following table summarizes the theory-based guidelines for colocated physical–digital games (Table 9.1).

NerdHerder: Theory-Based Design

The design and iteration of *NerdHerder* is based on the above design guidelines. We choose a subset of them that are highly relevant to the colocated physical–digital game scenarios (see Table 9.2), and implement them as specific design choices in the multiplayer version of *NerdHerder*. In addition to using the theory-based design guidelines, we also design the game based on other threads of research, such as the lessons we learned from our previous multiplayer AR game design and user studies, the affordances and constraints of the MAR

TABLE 9.1 Sociological Theory-Based Design Guidelines for Colocated Multiplayer Games

Sociological Theory-Based Design Guidelines for Colocated Social Games	
Bodily presence	Natural mapping: Map body movements and gestures to game state changes, e.g., swinging a Wii controller is mapped to swinging a tennis racket.
	Motivating the use of bodily presence in the game: Encourage players to use their bodily and social skills in the game through the reward system, e.g., players need to pay close attention to others' intonation and facial expressions to win a Mafia card game.
The circle of play	Signaling: Initialize a game through in-game and out-of-game signals, e.g., Wii StreetPass on Nintendo 3DS enables players to initiate ad hoc games.
	Displaying information to spectators through bodily enacting: Digital display is not the only way that information is presented. In the social context, facial expressions and body movements can reveal information observable to spectators, e.g., in card games, much tension is shown through the performance of players while their cards are secret.
Mutual focus of attention	Common game objects that are independent of players: Objects that every player can get synchronized to, e.g., the melody in rhythm games.
	Shared game objects/activities that are affected by players: When players interact with the common object or activity, they will have consequential social interactions around them, e.g., solving a shared puzzle can concentrate players' attention to the same goal and they are likely to help each other.
	Motivating players to pay attention to each other: Players can become the common focus of attention, e.g., with the turn-based structure of board games, players take turns to become performers and spectators. When in their turn, players exclusively claim everyone else's attention.
Shared mood	Game-generated shared target: Shared content, cut scene, fun animation, good dialogue can all become the moments that players laugh together. Players may also generate shared mood in the process of going through similar challenges.
	Player-generated shared experience: Players' shared in-game and out-of-game experience may evoke similar emotions among players, e.g., commenting on the in-game spot when the players were defeated last time.

TABLE 9.2   Subset of Chosen Design Guidelines for NerdHerder and Their Implementations

Theory-Based Design for *NerdHerder*

Bodily presence	1. Blending physical and digital game worlds: Using AR interface to leverage players' physical movement and social skills when they share a physical–digital space.
	2. Constructing the shared awareness by the hybrid colocation: Using the physical positions of multiple camera views to construct shared awareness among players; motivating players to observe other's physical position to compensate for the loss of digital information.
Mutual focus of attention	1. Joining players' attention onto common targets: Directing players' attention together to the common objects (e.g., shared goals and characters between team members) and the activities around these common objects.
	2. Dependency on the teammate: Tuning the game so that it is hard for a player to win by themselves; motivating players to coordinate actions between teammates.
	3. Conflict with the other team: Inducing competition around certain objects and timing. The power-ups are designed for players to pay close attention to others' physical and digital presence.
Shared mood	1. Shared enemy: Leveraging the dramatic anticipation created by the Donut King's "rage" period, during which he tries to squash the Nerd characters of both teams.
	2. Humorous content: Providing cross-team shared topics to communicate and laugh about.

interfaces, and the technical opportunities supported by the cutting-edge technology and hardware.

MAR interfaces track the device position and orientation in relation to the physical world, typically through computer vision algorithms. This enables the game to react to the players' physical movement. This feature opens up the design space for social games because players can observe others' physical position and movement and generate conversations and strategies based on those observations. In *NerdHerder*, the basic game control is to move the fishing rod around the game board. The virtual fishing rod is attached to the players' device, dangling with simulated gravity as if it were real. We intentionally keep the fishing rod visible, reinforcing the feeling that the digital world coexists in the same space as our physical world. This game control naturally maps players' physical movement to the fishing rod's movement. Based on this mapping, players can leverage their existing bodily and physics-based skills (i.e., acceleration, distance, orientation, and gravity) in the game. Moreover, they see where the others players are and what their movements are, and they can infer others' in-game state accordingly. This common ground is the foundation for a shared awareness—when players coordinate their actions in relation to others, they can have a reasonable prediction of other players' and game characters' movements and timing.

Although AR interfaces provide natural mapping as a basis for social interaction, the game needs to motivate players to truly leverage their bodily presence. For example, the power-up design in the game, including the "shake" and "stealth," require players' hooks to be in near proximity to take effect. Therefore, players need to pay attention to others' digital and physical position. Moreover, the "stealth" power-up was designed to encourage players to pay attention to others' physical movement. When a player gets the "stealth" power-up, they become invisible for 5 seconds, during which this player can steal donuts from others by getting close to them. While the other players have lost the ability to see the player digitally, they still can observe them in the physical world and try to avoid getting close to them to prevent their donuts getting stolen. Through these motivations, we expect to see more competition strategy emerge around the target objects of power-ups.

NerdHerder: User Study

The primary purpose of the user study is to understand *what* player behaviors emerge from multiplayer *NerdHerder*, and *how* these behaviors are triggered or supported by our theory-driven design. To support detailed analysis of gameplay sessions, we video recorded the sessions from multiple perspectives, logged game events with time stamps, asked users to fill out feedback questionnaires, and interviewed the groups of players.

Study Procedure and Setting

The user study included four parts. First, participants filled out a player demographics questionnaire after they signed the consent forms. Second, we walked through how to play the games and let each user try out the game controls and familiarize themselves with the goals, power-ups, and game events. Third, after everyone agreed that they understood the game, they played the multiplayer game twice. Fourth, after the gameplay was complete, the participants filled out two questionnaires designed to measure their social presence and game experience. The questionnaires were designed based on prior work on social presence (Biocca et al. 2003, de Kort et al. 2007). Finally, a semi-structured interview was conducted with the group to understand more about their experience. The user study was set up in a research lab as follows (Figure 9.2).

To capture and synchronize the video of play behavior and game events, we set up four cameras. Cameras 2 and 3 were set to capture the facial expressions of the players. Camera 1 hung above the table to capture players' movements in the space. Camera 4 takes a side view and was used as a backup camera.

Participants

In total, eight groups of four players (32) joined the user study. They were recruited through fliers, word-of-mouth, and mailing lists distributed at our university. Nine participants (28.1%) were female. The average age was 21.7 (*Min* = 16; *Max* = 38; *SD* = 5.4). Five participants (15.6%) had experience with AR interfaces prior to the user study. All participants had played games with physical interfaces before, such as Wii or Xbox Kinect. Two participants self-reported 60 hours of gaming per week. For the remaining 30 participants, their median weekly game time was 4.0 hours, with an average of 5.9 hours.

Group Composition

Prior work has shown that existing social relationships affect social play experience and enjoyment. People tend to be more expressive in the presence of a friend than in the presence of a stranger. Therefore, we recruited pairs of participants or a group of four. All players showed up in teams of two or four except Groups 4 and 7. Group 4 was made of two groups of friends. One group showed up with three participants; one of them became a

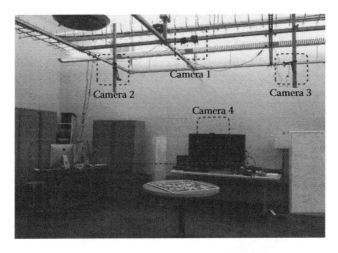

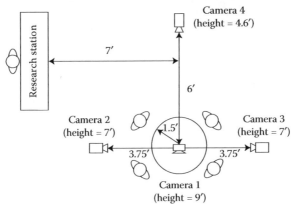

FIGURE 9.2   User study setup. The top image shows the study space; the bottom figure shows the camera positions and distances.

spectator of gameplay. In Group 7, one group showed up with a third friend while the other group was missing one (Table 9.3).

Data Analysis

We collected four types of data: the questionnaire data about users' feedback on game experience and social interaction; video recordings of the gameplay; game logs that show events in the game; and interview data from semi-structured interview after gameplay. The most time consuming part of our data analysis is the qualitative data analysis. Our goal is to analyze the relationship between the design elements and the players' social interaction behavior. The main sources of data are the video recordings of gameplay and the after-game interviews. We transcribed and coded these data. When events were observed from the video recordings, we referred to the game log to understand what happened in the digital game world. We also analyzed the after-game questionnaires about social play and the game experience.

In the following writing, we referred to the participants by their group number and player ID. For example, G1P1 means player 1 in the first group. Pseudonyms are used to

TABLE 9.3   Group Composition and Social Relationships among Participants

ID	Female/Total	Social Relationships among Participants in Each Group
1	0/4	A group of classmates from the same class.
2	2/4	Two pairs of friends. One pair had been friends since elementary school; the other pair includes two roommates from the undergraduate student dormitory.
3	0/4	A group of friends from the same church. Two of them share the same occupation.
4	1/5	Two groups of friends. One group is made of graduate students from the same lab; the other group includes three summer interns who are in the second year of high school.
5	1/4	Two pairs of friends. One group is made of grad school friends; the other group includes two roommates from the undergraduate student dormitory.
6	2/4	A group of friends who all come from the same university in another state. They are in Atlanta for a summer intern program. This group lives in the same building during the summer.
7	0/4	Three participants are long-term friends who just graduated from high school together. One undergrad student was scheduled to come together with his friend, but his friend did not show up because of a last-minute emergency.
8	3/4	Two pairs of friends. One pair is made of friends who met in grad school; the other pair is two sisters.

replace real names in conversations. R and B represents whether a player is in the red team or the blue team.

Findings

Feedback on Social Game Experience

Overall, *NerdHerder* gameplay was enjoyable and social for participants. On a 1–7 Likert scale, the average game enjoyment was 5.94 (SD = 1.41). Players enjoyed social interactions during the game (mean = 5.94, SD = 1.25). Players considered the game easy to learn (mean = 5.95, SD = 1.06). When asked to compare *NerdHerder* with other colocated games, participants often compare *NerdHerder* with other games with physical interfaces. For example, G7P2 compared the social interactions in *NerdHerder* with her past experience with Dance Central on Xbox Kinect.

G7P2: "This (NerdHerder) was more social. I don't talk to my sister while we are dancing. At the end, we are like, oh, look at your picture…oh, whatever, you know… If you heard us [during the game], we were talking, 'oh nerd, move away…,' we were all laughing…"

Players attributed the sociable gameplay of *NerdHerder* to the "physical movement" (G3P2, G2P3, G5P4), "more intimate setting" (G1P1, G2P3), "communication" (G5P4), "casual gameplay" (G2P1, G7P2, G7P4), and "collaboration" (G2P2, G2P3). In the following quote, G5P4 considered *NerdHerder* more social than colocated console games where everyone stares at the screen, or than some slow paced board games.

G5P4: "I like it from a social aspect, because, one, there is a lot of movement; two, there is a lot interaction with other people, as opposed to some sort of board game, which is slow paced. You have to wait for the dice, or the turn-based system. Everybody is facing each other, and playing at the same time, and communicating, so I think it adds a lot more social value…even if you have a four player game on a PlayStation, something that everybody is looking at the screen and focusing on that, whereas everybody is facing each other (during NerdHerder)."

In summary, *NerdHerder* provided a social and enjoyable game experience for most players. The following analysis will focus more on play behaviors triggered or supported by theory-based design based on qualitative data analysis.

Physics and Bodily Skills Integrated in Social Play

Enabled by the AR interface, our design overlays the digital world on the physical world; both worlds share the same coordinate system. Our design intent is for a player to use their existing physical and bodily skills, such as their intuitive understanding of distance, speed, position, and direction. We observed a variety of ways that players use these skills. For example, players pointed at spots on the physical game board to remind their teammate about resources (see Figure 9.3) or danger.

In competition, players frequently charge at the other team by moving closer, and the other team counteracts by moving further away, forming an interesting dance-battle-like movement pattern (as shown in Figure 9.4). Note that in this sequence, P3 and P4 get further and closer in a sequence of competitive moves.

Movement and positions were also used strategically. In the following example, one player talked about his strategy of saving the power-up to maximize its value, and he secured this resource by positioning himself physically closer to it.

G4P5: It's important to save up the power-ups…we did this a couple of times… You save the "stealth" to when they try to keep it away, like, in the middle of it [the Donut King's attack phase], they are going to lose two points, because you stole it.

Interviewer: But if you keep it, the other team could potentially get it.

G4P5: Yeah…They [other players] were all on the other side of the board. I saw a "stealth" over there. I am just going to move there and wait. If it's like there is one in the

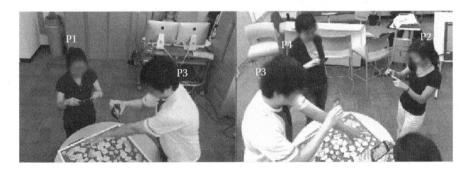

FIGURE 9.3   G8P2 asked for a donut, her teammate G8P3 pointed his hand to the donut's position on the board.

(1) 6:57—P4 got a "Shake" power-up

(2) 7:00—P4 moved toward P3, P3 moved further away; 7:02—the log shows that P4 shook P3's hook

(3) 7:00—P3 and P4 both moved toward the power-up of "Stealth," P3 started giggling: 7:09—the log shows that P4, who was closer to the power-up, got it

(4) 7:10—P3 and P4 laughed, and P1 started smiling; the log shows that P4 stole a donut from P1

(5) 7:10—P3 and P4 both moved toward the "Shake" power-up; they laughed louder together; 7:16—the log shows that P3 got the power-up this time

FIGURE 9.4 A sequence of physical movements because of power-ups in Group 6. (1) P4 got a "shake" power-up; (2) P4 moved toward P3, P3 moved away. Two seconds later, P4 shook P3's hook; (3) P3 and P4 both move toward a "stealth" power-up, P3 started giggling. P4 got the power-up. (4) P4 stole a donut from P1. P3 and P4 laughed and P1 smiled; (5) P3 and P4 competed over the same power-up again. They both laughed out loud.

middle of everybody, there is no point of saving it. If one pop over the corner, just go over there and wait.

Using this kind of strategy requires players to keep track of others physical distances, judge the time required to reach a target (for himself and for other players), and decide the right timing to use the power-up. The player was able to decide whether a power-up was worthwhile saving based on its position in relation to other players.

In summary, with the intuitive mapping between physical and digital space, players were able to use existing physical and bodily skills for collaboration and competition.

Multiple Communication Channels for Awareness

The design of *NerdHerder* provides several incentives for players to keep track of their teammate and opponents. The user study showed that players constructed a shared awareness of the game through verbal communication, observation of in-game activities, and physical movements.

Overall, physical movements were frequently used as counteraction and strategic play, as shown in the last section. But we did see the ineffectiveness caused by the imprecise mapping between the physical and digital object positions. The design of the "stealth" power-up, which makes the player's hook disappear on the other team's screens and enables the player to steal, is intended to test if players can use their awareness in the physical space to compensate for the loss of information in the digital space. The players liked this feature for its drama and power, even though they were usually not able to avoid having their donut stolen due to the difficulty of precisely inferring another player's location simply by observing their physical movements.

G1P2: I feel like the coordination that I did, was power-up based. It's like, "OK, who just got the Ninja (Stealth power-up)?" If it was my teammate, don't have to worry. If it's the other teammate, oh boy, watch out! I save my donut up here (gesturing that he lifted the camera phone up high)

G1P1: There is not much you can do…

G1P2: Well, I started to pull my donuts up here…while wait for him (the Donut King) to have his mouth open (so that one could score),

G1P4: I did the same thing.

Interviewer: The hook was invisible on the screen after they got the power-up. How do you know where they are?

G1P1: Well, you don't.

G1P3: You just assume they are coming after you.

(Group laughter)

G1P4: Paranoia works as a strategy.

(Group laughter)

G1P1: Yeah, the Ninjia thing is probably the best part, that asymmetrical information. But one thing you can't really perform right on the screen, it's really invisible.

G1P2: Yeah.

G1P1: If you look at them, you will be like, oh, they are looking over here. It's not really going to help…So you can get a feel by looking at the person and see where they point their phone, but it's not accurate.

G1P2: By the time you look at the person back to the phone, your donut could be gone.

This conversation showed that players did try to leverage their observation of other players to infer where their hooks are—"you can get a feel by looking at the person and see where they point their phones"—but the mapping between the hook and players' device (where the digital fishing hook dangles from) is a rough approximation. Therefore, being aware of other's physical movement did not give them perfect information of what that player was doing in the game, creating tension and suspense as we intended.

Another frequent communication was calling out the game state based on players' observations of in-game state, including: reporting the hook state (whether it had donut or needed one, when their donut got stolen), calling out danger for the Nerd, reporting scores for both teams, and talking about game characters' movement and state. The importance of verbal communication is shown as follows.

G3P1: If you didn't communicate, you lost. That one time I switched partner and I didn't communicate, I lost. Basically calling out how many more donuts you need; you know, calling out…

G3P2: It's like working in the kitchen…Because we are chefs, all around communicating in the kitchen, If not, someone has a hot pan… you have to do that, or somebody gets stabbed.

The frequency and importance of verbal communication was related to using the camera as the player's controller, which was one of the goals of the design. When a player gets closer to the board (to get a donut or to guide Nerds), their field of view is reduced proportionally. Since they are unable to keep the big picture of the game state, players needed to rely on communication with teammates during the game, as shown in the interview:

G5P2: I think it is a lot harder to watch with your teammate and other people playing since your camera is your controls, and then you start shocking things…

G5P3: Yeah, you really kind of focus on you are doing.

G5P1: That's why communication is important.

G5P2: It is.

However, as verbal communication occurred in a public space, the other team could overhear it and take counteractions, as shown in the following example.

G5P2: One of the down side of communicating… like they were doing a good job with communicating, what it did a really good job of was telling me the strategies that I haven't just thought of.

G5P4: Argh, it's funny.

G5P2: So I had everything I was thinking of, plus all their inputs as well, which didn't seem to help (since the other group did not win that time).

In summary, our game incentives were effective to motivate players to keep track of what is going on through multiple communication channels. We also found two challenges:

- Imprecise mapping between physical and digital may hinder transferring social awareness across the boundary of physical and digital worlds.

- Verbal communication may leak strategy to other players.

Common Objects as Hot Spots for Interactions

To support players forming mutual focus of attention, we designed several shared objects, including the common goal of feeding the Donut King, the shared Nerd for the two team-mates to protect, and the power-ups for everyone. The user study demonstrated that these common objects became hot spots that attract attention and activity.

Players observed others' actions around the Donut King, commented on them, and developed strategies. Three players from three groups developed an unexpected strategy, repurposing the power-ups as gatekeepers to the goal (the Donut King's mouth). Instead of using the power-up against other players directly, they hovered the Shake or Stealth power-up on top of the Donut King's mouth.

G7P1: "Stealth" is my favorite one. Because you guys will be all waiting, like, try to feed him, right when he was about to open up again. Then I will just steal it (the donut) (Laughter).

This strategy shows that some players were able to turn the observation of the shared goal of the Donut King to their advantage. Moreover, they combined it with the distance-based power-ups. This emergent strategy turned out to be effective.

Similarly, the shared character of the Nerds gathered players' interest in multiple occa-sions. Between teammates, sometimes players divided the tasks to make sure someone was protecting the Nerd and to keep them away from the Donut King. Most groups (seven out of the eight) constantly used the strategy of leading the other team's Nerd into the Donut King. The following example shows how players fought head to head for the control over one Nerd. The competition often increased emotional intensity and lead to shared laughter or faster pace of communication.

G5P2(R): Jake, strategy number two, we are at zero points, so lure their blue guy into him.
G5P1(B): chuckled
G5P2(R): because we don't lose anything. Get him smashed!
G5P4(R): yeah, bring them down to zero
G5P1(B): no…no…no (raised voice)
G5P2(R): come here blue guy
G5P4(R): come here blue guy, come here blue guy. (Laughter) He (the blue Nerd) is so confused.

Since both teams could use a donut to lead either Nerd, players can choose to spend their time protecting their own Nerd or to leading the other team's Nerd into danger.

In summary, the common objects we designed motivated the interactions between teammates and the two teams. The activities on the same object required paying close attention to what others were doing with it, which created joint attention among players.

Common Enemy as Emotional Stimuli for All

Players in the same team share the same goal and to need to protect the same Nerd, which forms a strong basis for sharing emotion within the team. To bring out shared emotion between the competing teams, we designed the common enemy of the Donut King. In the game, the Donut King charges at both of the Nerd characters every time he eats four donuts. We also put in a few seconds of delay for players to prepare for the attack phase and increase the intensity of the emotion by "dramatic anticipation." The burst of emotions frequently happened during the Donut King's attack phase.

In the user study, the competing teams shared similar kind of frustration when both of their Nerds got attacked. When the two Nerds are close together, they get run over by the Donut King together. Players raised their voices, cursed together, and laughed together.

(During the game, both Nerds just got stepped on)
G5P4(B): Are you serious? Are you serious?
G5P1(B): (loud laughter)
G5P2(R): I think there should be a third team, with one person, that's the Donut King.
G5P4(B): Yeah…(laughter)
G5P1(B): (Smile) I agree. That would be awesome.

Some players observed this problem of clustered Nerds and spent time keeping the two Nerds separate. But one team chose a different path—they decided to collaborate with the other team disregarding the preset game rules.

(During the game, both Nerds got stepped on)
G2P2(R): what? I was right there… (frustrated tone)
G2P1(R): (chuckle) "squish"… "squish" (the sound effect when the Nerds stepped on by the
  Donut King)
(Group laughter)
G2P4(B): Is he just going back over in the same track over and over again?
G2P1(R): Yes. That … was awful.
G2P2(R): That is.
G2P3(B): Do we want to try to just work together to get the objective completed?
G2P1(R): I think so.
(Both the Nerds get squashed again)
G2P(R), P2(R), P4(B): Urgh, OK… (at the same time)
G2P4(B): I was trying to lure him away…
G2P1(R): It's not…working.
G2P3(B): OK, let's take care of the Nerds.

FIGURE 9.5   High-five between two teams in Group 2.

The collaboration was suggested by P3 when both the Nerds were squashed together. One member of the other team (P1) verbally agreed. But the group did not have a plan yet, and their Nerds continued to be squashed. But this group quickly figured out what went wrong. After the communication above, they agreed upon which team they wanted to support to win, which players should be in charge of scoring, and which players should protect the Nerds. With communication and adjustment, they won the game as a group together. They burst into big laughter and had high-fives between the two teams (see Figure 9.5).

In summary, the shared enemy of the Donut King created a shared mood among players. It helped to get players to synchronize their emotions despite the team division. In one group, it even motivated players to change game rules from competition to collaboration.

Summary

The user study showed that *NerdHerder* is a fun and social game. Moreover, it showed a great variety of emergent social play. We observed that players leveraged their bodily and social skills in for both gameplay strategy and communication. These behaviors are expressed through verbal communication, nonverbal utterance, bursts of emotions, and body movements and gestures. In *NerdHerder*, players leveraged their bodily skills for various purposes—they changed interpersonal distance with other players during the competition; they occupied physical–digital locations by positioning themselves appropriately; they pointed at spots containing resources on the game board using hand gestures; they controlled the camera view by moving the camera phone closer to or further away from the game board. This variety shows that body actions are not only used as game inputs in a reality-based computing environment, but also as external displays of in-game game states for other players in the hybrid social space. At the same time, players can observe the others' body movement and guess their intentions. For example, players understood that when someone got a "shake" power-up and started to move toward them, they had the intention of shaking your hook. Players responded to this with dodging movements.

Players formed strategies using their spatial awareness and timed their actions based on the distances involved. They also formed interesting strategies around the shared objects of Nerds and power-ups. The game generated emotional highlights that were shared among players. Even though players were supposed to compete with the other team, they created their own rules based on the shared emotion toward to the shared enemy of Donut King. Through the design process and user study, we confirm that sociological theory-based design guidelines are very useful when designing games that foster enjoyable and emergent social play.

CHALLENGE

It is worth noting that theory-based design guidelines do not automatically lead to specific design choices. The challenge is that we often do not get the design right on the first try. In fact, the design team brainstormed, developed, and playtested many different versions of game control and mechanics before we found the ones presented here. Figure 9.6 shows one of the playtesting sessions that we did with summer camp high-school students. Because social play is complicated phenomena that can be affected by many factors, pinpointing specific designs that may lead to certain social interaction is very difficult. Moreover, because of the emergent nature of social play, two groups of players may have different behaviors that are related to the same game design choices.

SOLUTION

To address the challenge of how to get the design right, we find sociological theories are most valuable in understanding playtesting feedback, which we use to iterate and improve our design. Theories give us clues how to decipher the seemingly mysterious player behaviors, especially when players did not appear to be socially engaged with each other. For example, one of our playtesting sessions had very little social interaction even among friends—four players talked to each other less than 10 times. Without the theories pointing out potential directions, it would have been difficult to understand what went wrong and how to improve the design.

For example, we added the Donut King's periodic "sugar high" after our first round of playtesting. Initially, each team faces two challenges, feeding the Donut King, and making sure that their Nerd is not squashed. With these two challenges, we hoped teammates would coordinate to manage these two goals. However, we found that most players

FIGURE 9.6 Playtesting NerdHerder with a group of four high-school students.

preferred the task of feeding the Donut King themselves rather than leading the Nerd. Because most players were frantically feeding the Donut King, they did not even notice when their Nerd was stepped on. Needless to say, there was little coordination between teammates. Informed by the sociological theories, we realize that players' attention was not gathered on their shared team character, the Nerd. Even though we designed the character with the goal of have an object of mutual focus of attention, players ignored it because other tasks seemed to be more important or interesting to them. When a player could engage in a game without paying attention to their teammate, even if it was not the best strategy, they did not have the motivation for team coordination.

In the new design, we made the following changes. First, we increased the importance of protecting the Nerd. We changed the artificial intelligence of the Donut King, so that he always charges toward the Nerds rather than randomly roaming around. If the players do not do anything to protecting the Nerd, their team will lose points. Second, we added a moment of delay before the Donut King charged the Nerds, to leave time for teammates to coordinate their team actions. When the Donut King periodically gets the sugar high, he stops eating or roaming, makes a roaring sound, stomps twice, pauses for 4 seconds, and then charges directly at the Nerds. This pause is important because it allows players to anticipate what is about the happen and have time to coordinate their next actions. Third, we do not allow players to feed the Donut King all the time. When the Donut King charges at the Nerds, he closes his mouth. By separating the two challenges (feeding and protecting the Nerds), we increase the importance of communication and coordination between players for multitasking. Every single detail of the Donut King's sugar high has a purpose. As seen in our final user study, the sugar high activity generated much shared laughter and excitement among the players.

RECOMMENDATIONS

Reflecting on the design, iteration, and user study of *NerdHerder*, we share the following recommendations with fellow designers and researchers for colocated social play:

- Provide game incentives for players to leverage copresence in the shared hybrid space

- Do not overcrowd players' attention

- Design mapping mechanisms to reveal or hide game state

- Consider the role of camera control in supporting shared awareness

In our case study, we find the above aspects are fundamental to the cognitive, behavioral, and emotional aspects of social play. We hope to open up the design space for colocated hybrid games, and inspire other designers to envision and create novel social games.

Provide Game Incentives for Players to Leverage Copresence in the Shared Hybrid Space

The sense of copresence ("being there together") can be supported through bodily and mediated communication channels. While much technical effort focuses on supporting more channels for communication and interaction, the design lessons from *NerdHerder* show the importance of designing game incentives that encourage users to leverage copresence for social play. As shown in our playtesting, we learned that players were used to playing individually, even if collaborating with teammates could have been more strategic. So we added game mechanics to make sure teammate collaboration is not just an option, but a necessity. The resulting experience did increase the collaboration and strategy coordination between teammates.

In colocated games, even if it is convenient and natural to leverage bodily copresence, it does not happen automatically but heavily depends on the incentives in the game. This seems to be counterintuitive, considering both Collins and Hutchings stated that bodily copresence happens immediately when people are in the same space. We believe it has to do with attention allocation during the game, discussed in the next section.

Do Not Overcrowd Players' Attention

Attention is the cognitive process of selectively concentrating on one aspect of the environment while ignoring other things. It is referred to as "the allocation of processing resources" (Anderson 1990). Unfortunately, there are too many things competing for player's attention in modern multiplayer games. Especially in a shared hybrid game, the players' attention splits between their own digital and physical realms, and between individual and group activities. For example, during the gameplay of *NerdHerder*, the players' attention is split between the mobile screen where game events and activity is shown, the physical space where players move, and the sound space of verbal communication and nonverbal utterance. Engaging in screen-based individual activity may compete for players' attention with social interaction.

During our own iterative design process, the hardest part is to design for less individual activities on the screen, and leave time and space for interpersonal interaction. Designers need to be aware that designing for social play is different from designing for individual flow during which skills and challenges grow together (Csikszentmihalyi 1997). Game designers have refined the art of engaging players as individuals in single player games. We need more games and game research that engages players with each other in multiplayer digital games. The indie game "Journey" (Thatgamecompany) is an excellent example of minimizing the distraction and bringing together players through a solitary environment with shared challenges. In our game *NerdHerder*, we dedicate moments of pausing for players to prepare for the upcoming challenge and coordinate teamwork. We also slowed down the game pace compared to the early versions, by lowering resource respawn rates, slowing down object movement, and adding wait time. These adjustments allow players pay attention to activities involving the more complicated cognitive process of observing and responding to other players, such as coordination, competition, and assistance.

Social play is a "co-liberation," a balance between oneself and the group, escaping from alienation (too much "me") and conformity (too much "we") (DeKoven 1978). Through *NerdHerder*, we find that shared enemy, shared objects, and dedicated time periods for interaction are effective means to guide players attention to the "we" moments during the gameplay.

Design Mapping Mechanisms to Reveal or Hide Game State

In HCI, a natural mapping (Norman 1988) takes advantage of physical analogies and cultural standards and leads to immediate understanding. But in the context of social games, a mapping mechanism may support or block "immediate understanding" for players. Players *discern* others' behaviors by observation (e.g., physical movements, verbal or nonverbal utterances, and facial expressions). But how they *interpret* these behaviors in the meaning system of games depends on the mapping mechanism. On one hand, designers need to encourage players to pay attention to each other; on the other hand, there needs to be some ambiguity in the mapping between actions and in-game state changes. Interesting social play behaviors, such as bluffing and guessing, rely on such ambiguity.

In *NerdHerder*, we experiment with the balance through the fishing rod and line game interface. There are two implications to this interface. First, the fishing rod and line has a fixed length, meaning that a player's in-game position has a predictable location relative to their real world position. We saw that players develop strategies based on that information. For example, some players "saved" power-ups when they are obviously the closest to them. The second implication is that there is some ambiguity of players' position in game because the digital fishing line is flexible. There is not a rigid mapping between the player's phone position and their hook position when the phone is moving (and the hook swings). In the user study, some users commented that the imprecise mapping between device movement and the digital object movement makes it less effective to infer where other players' hooks were, reducing their motivation in inferring the others' position. We could change this aspect of *NerdHerder* by reconsidering the balance between revealing game state information and requiring playful guesswork.

In summary, the mapping mechanism in social games is more complicated than just implementing straightforward natural mappings. It needs to strike a delicate balance between motivating players to pay attention to others to find their state, and leaving enough space for players to hide their game state when needed.

Consider the Role of Camera Control in Shared Awareness

"The camera is the window through which the player interacts with the simulated world" (Giors 2004, p. 1). Camera control in digital games is highly interactive and is critical to the rest of the game experience. Examples of types of camera control in digital games include: first person, third person, and action replay (Christie et al. 2008). The AR interface in *NerdHerder* ties the players' motion control to the camera view and the action upon the digital world. In other words, the camera is the controller. It combines a first-person view with a top-down perspective view (which is more common in third-person view games). With this camera control, players need to understand the alignment of coordinate systems in the digital and physical worlds, and expect the physics in the digital world would work identically to the physical world. This section focuses on discussing the role of camera control in constructing shared awareness among players.

In the user study, many players realized that their physical motions (e.g., moving and rotating the camera phone) changed the field of view when they move closer or further from the game board. With the small screen through which a player views the digital world, it is hard to maintain a view of the whole game board. Players commented that to compensate for the limit of the small screen and constantly moving camera they needed to rely more on communication to keep track of the game events. Players were constantly talking out loud about their actions (e.g., scoring, having a donut stolen, protecting the Nerd, etc.) and calling out what they observed (e.g., the Donut King chasing the Nerd, the other team scoring, etc.). Players also pointed out resources for their teammate when he/she appeared on a part of the game board that they could not see.

In first-person shooter games, this kind of limited and constantly moving camera control is common and players communicate their game state with each other even when they have split screens accessible to multiple colocated players. However, designers need to create different mechanisms that enable players to keep track of the game state and the state of other players. In many first-person shooter games the radar view shows the teammates' position in relation to the player. In some other games, the camera control forced the players' avatars to be spatially near each other in the digital space to proceed. These games rely on the players' shared mental model of the digital space to construct shared awareness through multiple camera views. In contrast, in *NerdHerder*, players are aware of others' perspectives because players see the physical position of other players' camera in the real world, which is mapped to an overlapping coordinate system in the game world. This makes it easier to understand the others' perspectives and integrate them in the gameplay. This intuitive approach to shared awareness is one advantage for AR games.

CONCLUSION

In the case study of *NerdHerder*, we explore how to design colocated hybrid physical–digital games that truly integrate players' physical and bodily interaction to support enjoyable social play. We create a colocated multiplayer AR game based on the guidelines generated from sociology theories, and report the lessons we learned through designing and studying the game. In addition to trying to design a fun and social game, we designed *NerdHerder* as a research platform for social play. Sociological theories of face-to-face social interaction are the foundation of our case study. As we have shown, these theories were effective lenses when we analyzed empirical data from existing social games, iteratively designed our own game, and interpreted user behaviors.

Designing for emergent social play is challenging, because we designers cannot predict the social dynamics each time the game is played. Sociological theories provide us the key ingredients to help predict and understand complicated social play behaviors. Our case study is a new application of theory into a different design space: multiplayer games where players share a hybrid physical–social space. We see that unique player behaviors and creative strategies emerge when players try to make good use of their physical presence in the digital game space. We reflect on our empirical data and share our understanding of the core framing constructs in this design space. Based on our design lessons and user study, we provide recommendations to designers that we find critical for designing colocated social play experiences. We aspire to stimulate more meaningful discussions with game researchers/designers who are also interested in the space of physical–digital games.

REFERENCES

Anderson, J. R. 1990. *Cognitive Psychology and Its Implications*. New York: W.H. Freeman.

Bianchi-Berthouze, N., W. W. Kim, and D. Patel. 2007. Does body movement engage you more in digital game play? And why? In *Affective Computing and Intelligent Interaction*, A. C. R. Paiva, R. Prada, and R. W. Picard (Eds), pp. 102–13. New York: Springer.

Biocca, F., C. Harms, and J. Burgoon. 2003. Toward a more robust theory and measure of social presence: Review and suggested criteria. *Presence: Teleoperators and Virtual Environments* 12 (5): 456–80.

Booth, M. 2009. Replayable cooperative game design: Left 4 dead. *Presented at Game Developers Conference*, San Francisco, USA.

Christie, M., P. Olivier, and J.-M. Normand. 2008. Camera control in computer graphics. *Computer Graphics Forum* 27: 2197–218. Wiley Online Library.

Collins, R. 2004. *Interaction Ritual Chains*. Princeton: Princeton University Press.

Csikszentmihalyi, M. 1997. *Finding Flow: The Psychology of Engagement with Everyday Life*. New York: Basic Books.

de Kort, Y. A. W. and W. A. Ijsselsteijn. 2008. People, places, and play: Player experience in a socio-spatial context. *Computers in Entertainment* 6 (2): 11, Article 18. ACM.

de Kort, Y. A., IJsselsteijn, W. A., and Poels, K. 2007. Digital games as social presence technology: Development of the Social Presence in Gaming Questionnaire (SPGQ). Paper presented at: *Proceedings of PRESENCE: The 10th International Workshop on Presence*, Barcelona, Spain.

DeKoven, B. 1978. *The Well-Played Game: A Player's Philosophy*. Norwell: The Anchor Press.

Die Gute Fabrik Game Studio. Johann Sebastian Joust, http://www.jsjoust.com/, accessed on January 31, 2015.

Freeman, D. 2004. Creating emotion in games: The craft and art of emotioneering. *Computers in Entertainment* 2 (3): 11, Article 8a. ACM.

Giors, J. 2004. The full spectrum warrior camera system. *Paper presented at GDC'04: Game Developers Conference*, San Jose, USA.

Goffman, E. 1967. *Interaction Ritual: Essays in Face to Face Behavior*. Piscataway: Aldine Transaction.

Hatfield, E. and J. T. Cacioppo. 1994. *Emotional Contagion*. Cambridge: Cambridge University Press.

Isbister, K. 2012. How to stop being a Buzzkill: Designing Yamove!, a mobile tech mash-up to truly augment social play. In *Proceedings of the 14th International Conference on Human–Computer Interaction with Mobile Devices and Services Companion*, San Francisco, USA, pp. 1–4. ACM.

Jimerson, J. B. 1999. "Who has next?" The symbolic, rational, and methical use of norms in pickup basketball. *Social Psychology Quarterly* 62 (2): 136–56.

Kendon, A. 1970. Movement coordination in social interaction: Some examples described. *Acta Psychologica* 32: 101–25.

Lindley, S. E., J. Le Couteur, and N. L. Berthouze. 2008. Stirring up experience through movement in game play: Effects on engagement and social behaviour. In *Proceedings of the SIGCHI Conference on Human Factors in Computing Systems*, Florence, Italy, pp. 511–4. ACM.

Mead, G. H. 1925. The genesis of the self and social control. *International Journal of Ethics* 35 (3): 251–77.

Norman, D. A. 1988. *The Design of Everyday Things*. New York: Basic Books.

Rocha, J. B., S. Mascarenhas, and R. Prada. 2008. Game mechanics for cooperative games. *ZON Digital Games* 2: 72–80.

Salen, K. and E. Zimmerman. 2004. *Rules of Play: Game Design Fundamentals*. Cambridge: MIT Press.

Seif El-Nasr, M., B. Aghabeigi, D. Milam, M. Erfani, B. Lameman, H. Maygoli, and S. Mah. 2010. Understanding and evaluating cooperative games. In *Proceedings of the SIGCHI Conference on Human Factors in Computing Systems*, Atlanta, USA, pp. 253–62. ACM.

Szentgyorgyi, C., M. Terry, and E. Lank. 2008. Renegade gaming: Practices surrounding social use of the Nintendo DS handheld gaming system. In *Proceedings of the SIGCHI Conference on Human Factors in Computing Systems*, Florence, Italy, pp. 1463–72. ACM.

Thatgamecompany. Journey, http://thatgamecompany.com/games/journey/, accessed on January 31, 2015.

Tomasello, M. 1999. *The Cultural Origins of Human Cognition*. Cambridge: Harvard University Press.

Turkle, S. 2012. *Alone Together: Why We Expect More from Technology and Less from Each Other*. New York: Basic Books.

Voida, A., S. Carpendale, and S. Greenberg. 2010. The individual and the group in console gaming. In *Proceedings of the 2010 ACM Conference on Computer Supported Cooperative Work*, Savannah, USA, pp. 371–80. ACM.

Wagner, H. L. and J. Smith. 1991. Facial expression in the presence of friends and strangers. *Journal of Nonverbal Behavior* 15 (4): 201–14.

Wolf, T., J. Rode, J. Sussman, and W. Kellogg. 2006. Dispelling "design" as the black art of CHI. In *Proceedings of the SIGCHI Conference on Human Factors in Computing Systems*, Quebec, Canada, pp. 521–30. ACM.

Xu, Y., E. Barba, I. Radu, M. Gandy, and B. MacIntyre. 2011. Chores are fun: Understanding social play in board games for digital tabletop game design. *Paper presented at the Fifth International Conference of the Digital Research Association (DIGRA)*, Hilversum, Netherlands.

Xu, Y., M. Gandy, S. Deen, B. Schrank, K. Spreen, M. Gorbsky, T. White et al. 2008. BragFish: Exploring physical and social interaction in co-located handheld augmented reality games. In *Proceedings of the 2008 International Conference on Advances in Computer Entertainment Technology*, Yokohama, Japan, pp. 276–83. ACM.

Zimmerman, J., J. Forlizzi, and S. Evenson. 2007. Research through design as a method for interaction design research in HCI. In *Proceedings of the SIGCHI Conference on Human Factors in Computing Systems*, San Jose, USA, pp. 493–502. ACM.

LIST OF ADDITIONAL SOURCES

Billinghurst, M. and H. Kato. 2002. Collaborative augmented reality. *Communications of the ACM* 45 (7):64–70.

Billinghurst, M., A. Clark, and G. Lee. 2005. A survey of augmented reality. *Foundations and Trend in Human–Computer Interaction* 8 (1):1–202.

Craig, A. B. 2013. *Understanding Augmented Reality: Concepts and Applications*. Burlington: Morgan Kaufmann.

Fine, G. A. 2002. *Shared Fantasy: Role Playing Games as Social Worlds*. Chicago: University of Chicago Press.

Huynh, D.-N. T., K. Raveendran, Y. Xu, K. Spreen, and B. MacIntyre. 2009. Art of defense: A collaborative handheld augmented reality board game. In *Proceedings of the 2009 ACM SIGGRAPH Symposium on Video Games*, New Orleans, USA, pp. 135–42. ACM.

Kendon, A. 1990. Conducting Interaction: Patterns of Behavior in Focused Encounters. Cambridge: Cambridge University Press.

Lemert, C. and A. Branaman, eds. 1997. *The Goffman Reader*. Hoboken: Wiley-Blackwell.

Parten, M. B. 1932. Social participation among pre-school children. *Journal of Abnormal and Social Psychology* 27 (3): 243–69.

Van Krevelen, D. W. F. and R. Poelman. 2010. A survey of augmented reality technologies, applications and limitations. *International Journal of Virtual Reality* 9 (2): 1–20.

Wagner, D. and D. Schmalstieg. 2003. First steps towards handheld augmented reality. In *Proceedings of the Seventh IEEE International Symposium on Wearable Computers*, White Plains, USA, pp. 27–135. IEEE.

Xu, Y., E. Barba, I. Radu, M. Gandy, R. Shemaka, B. Schrank, B. MacIntyre, and T.-M. Tseng. Pre-patterns for designing embodied interactions in handheld augmented reality games. In *Proceedings of the IEEE International Symposium on Mixed and Augmented Reality-Arts, Media, and Humanities (ISMAR-AMH)*, Basel, Switzerland, pp. 19–28. IEEE.

BIOGRAPHIES

Yan Xu is a researcher in Computational Imaging Group in Intel Labs. Her current research focuses on designing and developing novel user experiences for computational photography with depth cameras and camera arrays. Prior to joining Intel Labs, Dr. Xu earned her PhD in human-centered computing program at Georgia Institute of Technology. Motivated to bring better social play to digital games, her PhD thesis focuses on understanding and designing social play for colocated physical–digital games. Her work is multidisciplinary, bringing together different research fields, such as HCI, sociology, and game research. Her research on AR games is recognized by the research community, including two best-paper awards from ACM and IEEE conferences. Dr. Xu is an active author, volunteer, and reviewer for the ACM SIGCHI community since 2006. She also served on the Program Committee of IEEE International Symposium on Mixed and Augmented Reality 2013.

Blair MacIntyre is a professor in the School of Interactive Computing at the Georgia Institute of Technology, and directs the GVU Center's Augmented Environments Lab. His research focuses on developing the potential of AR as a novel technology and new medium for games, entertainment, education, and work. He has published more than 100 research papers, is actively involved with industry as a consultant, and is regularly interviewed in the media about AR, games, and mobile technology. Dr. MacIntyre earned PhD from Columbia University in 1998, and BMath and MMath degrees from the University of Waterloo in 1989 and 1991. He is the recipient of an NSERC Postgraduate Scholarship and an NSF CAREER award.

KEY WORDS AND THEIR DEFINITIONS

Augmented reality: AR is a type of interface that overlays the digital graphics on top of the real world in real time. On smart phone and tablet devices, AR interface usually superimposes or composites digital graphics on the video stream of camera feed from the device.

F-formation: F-formations are spatial arrangement patterns emerged among people during interaction. It was brought forward by Adam Kendon, stating that "an F-formation arises whenever two or more people sustain a spatial and orientational relationship in which the space between them is one to which they have equal, direct, and exclusive access" (Kendon 1990, p. 210). He also summarizes several shapes of F-formation (o-space, p-space, and r-space).

Interaction ritual theory: IR focuses on the interactions and the emotional input and feedback of individuals within those interactions. This theory analyzes the ingredients and outcome of social interactions. The key ingredients include bodily copresence, barrier to outsiders, mutual focus of attention, and shared mood.

The key outcomes include group solidarity, EE, symbols of relationship, and standard of morality. Drawing on the work of many other sociologists, including Emile Durkheim and Erving Goffman, the theory is formally posited by Randall Collins.

Mutual focus of attention: The awareness to tell whether the other person is paying attention to the same object as oneself or not. It is also referred to as "joint attention" in Randall Collins' book *Interaction Ritual Chains*.

Physical user interfaces (UIs): Physical UIs take users' physical movements as input to interact with digital information. These bodily movements are mapped spatially from the physical world to the digital world. When used in games, physical interfaces recognize or track natural movements that players are familiar with in real life and map them to the actions of avatars or characters in the game. For example, swinging a game controller is mapped to swinging a tennis racket in a Wii Sports game.

Research through design: RtD is a research method that recognizes interaction design as a core knowledge inquiry activity. It was introduced to HCI research by John Zimmerman et al. RtD recognizes the coevolution between problem and solution. It brings together multidisciplinary efforts, such as ethnography, engineering, psychology, and sociology. All these efforts are embodied in the design, while the user experience of the resulting design provides new insights into this existing knowledge.

Social play: Social play is any play when people interact with each other. There are different types of social play. According to developmental science, there are four stages of play (the latter three are social play). The required social skills for these plays are learned by children as they grow. They are solitary play (exploring objects and the world), parallel play (play next to each other yet do not try to change others' behavior), associative play (still play independently but interact with others, such as talking or borrowing toys), and cooperative play (interact with each other for the purpose of play, share ideas, and coordinate actions).

CHAPTER 10

Testing the Usability, Usefulness, and User Experience of TableTalk Poker, a Social Game for Seniors

Karyn Moffatt, Nicholas Shim, Jeremy Birnholtz, and Ronald M. Baecker

CONTENTS

EXECUTIVE SUMMARY

As they age, many older adults experience shrinking social networks and limited opportunities for fostering new social relationships. We postulate that games can be used to enhance social opportunities for seniors via social media. To test this hypothesis, we designed TableTalk Poker, an augmented poker game designed to encourage greater peer interaction via support for conversation and collaboration between a playing and a nonplaying partner.

In this chapter, we describe our experiences designing and testing the usability, usefulness, and user experience of TableTalk Poker. Our design approach began with exploratory field observations, which helped us to recognize the importance of playing with a partner and for supporting a range of player and nonplayer roles. We then used an iterative design process that included paper prototyping and user testing to fine-tune our design and address accessibility and usability concerns. Finally, to test the user experience of our resulting design, we studied its impact on social engagement, by observing play both with and without a partner.

Our design process was instrumental in helping us to understand how games could be designed as social media for seniors. Our final evaluation confirmed that playing with a partner supported greater social interaction and conversation. Playing with a partner also seemed to lead to more advanced forms of game play and the use of more advanced strategies such as folding more strategically, betting more aggressively, and bluffing more often.

ORGANIZATION BACKGROUND

Demographic shifts in the structure of the world's population are leading to a dramatically aging society. As of 2014, over 10 million Canadians were 50 years of age or older, representing almost 30% of the population overall; while those 65 years of age and older total 5.6 million or 16% of the population (Stats Canada 2014). Comparable trends have been observed across industrialized nations. Older adults today are healthier, better educated, and more financially secure than any group of elders before them. Nonetheless, most people will experience some degree of cognitive, motor, and sensory decline with age, and correspondingly a shift in their abilities, needs, and preferences.

Older adults are quickly becoming diverse and savvy users of a broad range of technologies. Of adults age 65 and over, 47.5% were online as of 2012, an increase of almost 20% since 2010 (Stats Canada 2013a). Of these Internet users, nearly one in three has adopted social media and just over one in four play games online (Stats Canada 2013b). Though uptake remains low compared to that of younger generations (e.g., 93.4% of 16–24 year olds use social networking sites and 56.9% play online games), it is growing dramatically. These trends are encouraging because computer technologies offer great potential to support individuals as they age—by compensating for cognitive and sensory impairments, by supporting independent living, and by promoting social interaction.

In this project, we worked with seniors recruited through a variety of organizations, but mainly via Ryerson University's LIFE Institute, a continuing education program for adults 50+, that partnered with us for this project. The LIFE Institute offers courses on a broad range of topics and a rich social environment through which seniors can engage in volunteering and outreach activities. In addition to facilitating recruitment from their computer club, they also provided us with access to their computer lab.

CASE STUDY DESCRIPTION

Social engagement—the maintenance of social connections and the participation in social activities (Bassuk et al. 1999)—has been positively associated with a number of health outcomes, particularly for older adults. Socially engaged seniors tend to live longer (Glass et al. 1999; Reblin and Uchino 2008), experience fewer depressive symptoms (Glass et al. 2006), self-report lower levels of disability (Mendes de Leon et al. 2003), and demonstrate both higher levels of cognitive function (Bassuk et al. 1999; Krueger et al. 2009) and lower incidence rates for dementia (Saczynski et al. 2006; Crooks et al. 2008). Unfortunately given all of these benefits, many seniors face shrinking social networks and reduced opportunities for fostering new relationships, hindering their ability to remain socially engaged throughout later life.

In response to this challenge, numerous technological efforts have sought to increase opportunities for social engagement. However, most of these initiatives have targeted family connections (e.g., Mynatt et al. 2001; Khoo et al. 2009; Judge et al. 2010; Lindley et al. 2010). Although socioemotional selectivity theory suggests individuals will tend to concentrate on close family relationships in later life (Carstensen 1992), not all individuals will have such options available. Moreover, some evidence suggests that the number of social connections a person has may affect health, with larger networks leading to better outcomes (Bassuk et al. 1999; Crooks et al. 2008).

To date, very little HCI (human–computer interaction) research has been directed at technologies to support peer interaction among seniors (two exceptions include work by Mubin et al. (2008), and Keyani et al. (2005) on colocated recreation for seniors). Although inconsistencies in the web such as the varying terminology, organization, and navigation among sites (Goodman et al. 2003) exacerbate age-related cognitive, sensory, and motor losses (Craik and Salthouse 2000), seniors today seem willing to embrace new technology—provided the potential benefits are perceived to outweigh the costs (Melenhorst 2002). They are increasingly active online, with over half (53%) of adults 65+ identifying as Internet or email users, and with 39% reporting broadband access at home (up from just 8% in 2005) (Zickuhr and Madden 2012). Moreover, they are increasingly active on social networking sites such as Facebook, with 34% of online adults 65+ reporting use (Zickuhr and Madden 2012). They have also demonstrated an interest in games (Lenhart et al. 2008), including those designed for mental (Thompson and Foth 2005) and physical (Stach et al. 2009) fitness. Unfortunately, today's computer games mostly cater to young audiences and generally have poor support for conversation and relationship building (Shim et al. 2010). Our work seeks to address this problem, and to study and evaluate the impact of social gaming systems on seniors.

One challenge for usability practitioners interested in social games is that to fully appreciate their potential, they must be played within the social context for which they were designed. This has prompted many researchers to focus on understanding the sociability of existing games and established gaming systems. For instance, Jung et al. (2009) conducted a six-week field experiment in a long-term care facility on the impact of playing Nintendo Wii games and found that playing had a positive impact on overall well-being. Other work has sought to extend game evaluation heuristics to account for the unique qualities of social games (Paavilainen 2010), and to extend the Technology Acceptance Model (TAM) by adding factors for social influences and flow experiences (Hsu and Lu 2004).

In designing computer games for seniors, usability is often driven by a concern for accessibility, and the extent to which the game meets the needs of a population with diverse cognitive, sensory, and motor abilities (Ijsselsteijn et al. 2007; Gerling et al. 2011). Usability testing has also explored questions of seniors' perception and acceptance of social games (Theng et al. 2009). Much work on seniors and gaming has looked to games as a means for achieving some other goal, such as rehabilitation (Uzor and Baillie 2013), exercise (Gerling et al. 2013), or cognitive stimulation (Jung et al. 2009). As such, evaluation often focuses more on these factors than on establishing the core usability of the game.

We conjecture that online games, if designed as social media, could serve as a platform for enhancing peer social interaction among seniors, and we sought to develop a social gaming environment to test our ideas. The remainder of this chapter describes the process we used to develop our game, TableTalk Poker, and our final evaluation which sought to assess how well our resulting design supported socializing around game play.

Formative Evaluation: Understanding Seniors at Play

Social media have been defined as those that allow users to interact and connect with one another, via such services as social networking sites (e.g., Facebook), virtual worlds (e.g., Second Life) and communication systems (e.g., Skype) (Kaplan and Haenlein 2010). We argue there is merit in thinking about games for seniors as a form of social media; that is, we urge designers of games for seniors to provide opportunities for interaction and forming relationships. Nonetheless, the benefits and viability of this idea remain open questions. Nap et al. (2009) reported the results of two focus groups and four contextual inquiries in which seniors mention playing games mainly for fun and relaxation, and express a preference for single-player games. Seniors in an experiment conducted by Gajadhar et al. (2010) were found to experience less enjoyment in online coplay compared to playing together with people in the same room or playing online against a computer.

Yet De Schutter (2010) and De Schutter and Vanden Abeele (2010) reported on surveys, interviews, and observations with seniors suggesting that "fostering connectedness" is an important source of the meaning of game play for seniors, and that social interaction is the most important predictor of playing time. Favorite aspects of Everquest for players surveyed by Griffiths et al. (2004) were the social aspects, even more so for older players than for adolescents. Adult gamers (aged 35–73) interviewed by Quandt et al. (2009) placed a special emphasis on the opportunities to meet other players and develop social contacts through a game; online interactions sometimes led to real-life relationships. Montola and Waern (2006) suggested that nonplayers be invited into games, and group such participants as spectators, who passively participate in the game, and bystanders, who watch but do not participate. Finally, Voida and Greenberg (2009) found that console gaming can serve as a "computational meeting place" for a wide variety of relationship structures, including peer relationships among seniors. Nonplayer roles are starting to gain wider recognition, with companies like Twitch starting to capitalize on tools to support video game spectators (Meyer 2014).

To complement the above findings from the literature, we conducted a series of three formative activities to gain a better understanding of how games are learned and played by seniors (Shim et al. 2010). In our first activity, we conducted field observations at Yee Hong, a long-term care facility for seniors in the Greater Toronto area to help us better understand group dynamics of seniors at play. In our second formative activity, we observed a healthy woman in her late 50s play online games for the first time on *Yahoo! Games*. Finally, in our third activity, we ran a structured learning session, in which we paired novice poker players with an advisor and observed them playing a traditional in person poker game. The remainder of this section provides a brief overview of the outcomes of these activities.

Our field observations at a long-term care facility for seniors echoed many of the themes from the literature. What was most interesting about a Wii bowling event we watched was that while nearly 30 residents attended, only 4 actively played the game. Although the rest were only spectators, they seemed to enjoy the game as much as the players did. Spectators cheered on the competitors, clapping, and commenting on their play. Some even playfully taunted players by verbally betting on whether they would get a strike or not. These observations motivated us to build nonplayer roles into our system; such support is mostly missing from currently available online games.

In our second formative activity, we observed the challenges older novice gamers encounter when learning new games. The games' terminologies were unclear to our participant, so simply jumping in and playing a game was difficult. She was presented with a series of choices used to customize the game experience. Although likely a nice feature for experienced gamers, the added choice caused confusion without producing engagement or a sense of reward for this novice participant.

This experience reflects a broader observation. Although computer games are a notable pastime for nearly a quarter of older adults (Lenhart et al. 2008), some games are hindered by usability challenges and design deficiencies that deter participation. Most games are designed for a younger audience and do not take into consideration the needs and preferences of seniors (Iyengar and Lepper 2000; Shim et al. 2010). These factors have led some to perceive few benefits to playing games online (Ijsselsteijn et al. 2007). Even the Nintendo Wii—often praised for its accessibility—has met with mixed results when evaluated with seniors. One study found the Wii too complex and challenging for elderly players (Gerling and Masuch 2011), while another identified physical and coordination problems with using the Wii (Neufeldt 2009).

Isbister (2010) suggested that observing game play can provide coaching and critical commentary that substantially improves the game experience for players, and bases her analysis on Bandura's (1977) theory of social learning. In our third activity, we noted social learning while observing a traditional card-based poker game, where each player was partnered with an advisor. In these sessions, participants reported that what they liked about playing with a partner is that it provided a gradual learning experience that increased their confidence and comfort. They also enjoyed being able to ask the teachers and advisors for the motivations behind their actions.

Iterative Design: Developing TableTalk Poker

From our formative fieldwork and review of the research literature, we found support for the importance of engaging players and of enriching the play experience through opportunities for social interaction. We, therefore, embarked on paper prototyping and then user-centered iterative design of a novel online poker environment called TableTalk Poker.

Texas Hold 'em Poker

We chose Texas Hold 'em poker as the game for our environment, as it is a multiplayer game that is inherently social when played face-to-face. Moreover, we felt it represented a good balance between opportunities for learning and familiarity. Though quite well-known, it is sufficiently complex that even regular players can improve their skill and expertise.

Poker was also an interesting focus for our exploration because, although numerous online poker environments exist, none are well suited to the needs of older adults. Current sites focus only on card play, neglecting the subtleties in gestures, facial expressions, and conversation. Some sites have tried to compensate for this missing human element by allowing users to manually select emotions but this tends to be very unnatural as tells are generally inadvertent in the physical game. In general, nonverbal communication (facial expression, body language) is essential in poker, both in terms of the game play and in terms of the sociability of the game (Golder and Donath 2004). On top of this, hands in many online environments start and end very quickly. This high speed of play further limits possibilities for social interaction. There is no time to chat or make friends. In effect, existing online poker environments have not yet capitalized on the social potential of this game.

In Texas Hold 'em, a poker hand consists of two cards dealt face down to each player and five community cards placed face up in the middle for all players. The five community cards are placed on the table in three rounds (the *flop*, in which three cards are placed on the table; the *turn*, and the *river*). After each round, users have the option of betting. The winner of a hand is determined by the best five-card hand that can be made from a combination of the players' two cards and the five cards in the middle that are available to all hands. Since success in Poker is measured in the long-term, users need to be strategic when deciding when to bet more of their cash on a hand (*raise*), stay in the hand by matching the current bet (*call*), or abandon the hand (*fold*).

Early Design Feedback

The design of our system went through several iterations. Cognizant of the cognitive, sensory, and physical limitations of seniors, we wanted to provide hinting and sought to reduce extraneous clutter. Furthermore, we wanted to promote conversation. Although many of the online games we reviewed offered text communication via chat windows alongside the main game window, we considered the idea of chat bubbles integrated into the main view to denote who spoke and potentially help draw attention to the conversation. However, when we showed an early design (Figure 10.1) to an avid poker player in her mid-50s, her first reaction was "this is intimidating," and noted that our design was not much different than existing systems in terms of complexity and clutter.

Paper Prototyping

We thus took a step back from our original design ideas and turned to paper prototyping, which allowed us to work more closely with users and better understand the interaction challenges. Noting the difficulties of prototyping with seniors reported by Massimi et al. (2007), we instead worked with three adult women aged between 25 and 55 with no online gaming experience. Although these women were generally younger than our target demographic, we engaged them as proxies based on their lack of familiarity with online games. We used a layered elaboration technique similar to Walsh et al. (2010), where at each layer, only one salient item was drawn: table, players, cards, prompts, or chat. We used transparencies, water-soluble markers, and sticky notes to dynamically create prototype interfaces and define desired user interactions (see Figure 10.2).

FIGURE 10.1 Early design mock-up.

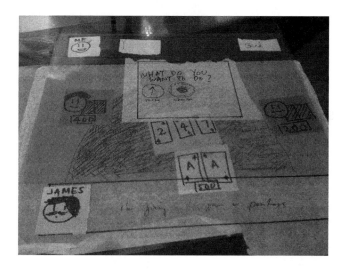

FIGURE 10.2 Paper prototype of TableTalk Poker using layers of transparencies, augmented with sticky notes and markers.

For the prototyping sessions, we first created three rough variants of the system. Before we began, the participants were given a briefing on the basics of poker, ensuring that they all understood the betting rounds, potential actions, and goal of the game. We simulated playing the game with sticky notes and asked participants to perform the following tasks: join a game, raise a bet, check, call, fold, and chat to another player. Participants were encouraged to move the interface elements around and to add buttons, text, and screens on the fly. They were asked to think aloud as they worked, while we watched for gaps in the interaction and noted any desired changes in the layout. We repeated this process for all three designs.

The participants enjoyed the experience and found it very engaging. The use of paper made it easier to iterate on ideas and reduced attachment to particular designs. The participants found this extremely useful, as it allowed them to easily mix and match elements or create their own, while building on ideas, such as the table layout, that they already favored.

Through discussion with each other and the researchers, the participants reached a consensus on a final design. This interface had elements from all three initial variants with heavy influence from the ideas of our participants.

Usability Testing

We then worked with five older adults from Ryerson University's LIFE Institute. The participants' ages ranged from 72 to 86 and their experience with online poker varied from avid player to complete novice. All, however, were enthusiastic at the prospect of a gaming environment that would provide opportunities for mental stimulation and social interaction.

Over the course of a month, we held sessions weekly for 1 h, and revised our interface each week based on the feedback received. Participants played against the computer, against each other, or with each other (virtually or physically). We voice-recorded each session and also took handwritten notes on the problems users encountered, subtle dynamics when players worked together, conversations that arose, and functionality used (or not used). Informal discussions with the group of players revealed what features they would like to see added and how these features might appear and be used.

Through this testing, we discovered and corrected bugs in the system, and improved design to account for diverse abilities and game skill. For instance, one of the participants had developed tremors in her hands over the years, and finer movements like mouse dragging (which we were using for a raise slider) were very difficult for her. We instead opted for a button approach that was easier for her to perform.

Another reoccurring usability theme involved the poker language. Terms such as check, raise, call, and fold, though standard to the game of poker, were not as obvious as we anticipated. Participants would often forget what terms meant and the implication of their actions. This led us to building in hinting on mouse hovers (i.e., tooltips), and also simplifying the language whenever possible by, for example, changing "raise" to "bet."

The most interesting results came from observing the social dynamics between players and the strategies they employed in the games. Looking at the chat history archived by the system, we observed that beginner players ignored the public chat all together, while experienced online gamers engaged with the chat feature much more frequently. From conversations with the players, we realized that beginner players were too focused on the game itself to additionally attend to the chat interface.

We also found early evidence that the dynamics drastically changed when participants were paired with a more experienced, similarly experienced, or less experienced player. The more experienced player tended to lead the strategy more often than not, while the learner passively accepted the decisions. The learners surprisingly did not seem to mind this. One subject was too scared to do the wrong thing as a player, and too embarrassed to ask a "stupid" question, but enjoyed watching and learning from someone else. Among peers, a negotiation process tended to arise. It appeared that these behaviors were directly correlated to confidence. Relationships evolved to be more peer–peer like as users became more comfortable with the game each week. These findings foreshadow the results from our summative evaluation presented in the next section.

We also found that there were often lulls between games, as players would get caught up in unrelated conversations. We found this to be beneficial toward our goal of promoting social interaction and this encouraged us to enforce breaks between games to facilitate this. A 20-second break time is awarded after each hand and 5-minute breaks awarded every 30 hands. This contrasts with the no breaks/rest time typically found in online games.

Final Prototype

The resulting design, which incorporated feedback from our usability testing, is shown in Figure 10.3. The player's own hand is placed in the lower middle of the screen and is enlarged for emphasis (Figure 10.3a). Opponents are seated around the table as in a traditional game (Figure 10.3b), maximizing space for player's cards and community cards. We adopted a minimalistic approach, whereby only pertinent items are visible, and audio is used selectively for denoting the player's turn and the start of a new betting round. Animations were intentionally avoided to reduce distractions.

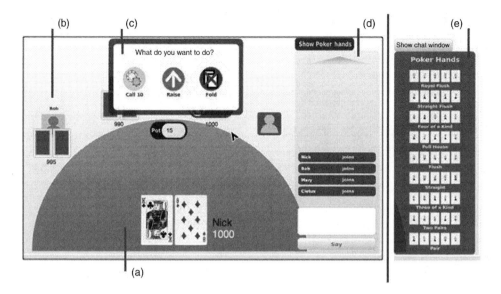

FIGURE 10.3 Final design featuring a quasi-first person perspective that emphasizes the player's own hand (a), relative to the other hands (b). Game play options are presented in the foreground (c) to guide novice players; only options that make sense contextually are presented in the dialogue. On the right, users can toggle between a chat window (d) and a poker hand reference (shown separately in (e)).

Questions are posed to users in the foreground (Figure 10.3c), guiding them and prompting for actions. To ease decision-making, the system only presents game play options that make sense contextually. For example, we remove the fold button if consistent with the game's rules, the current betting scenario offers the option to check (that is, to remain in the game without adding additional money to the pool).

A panel on the right allows users to switch between a chat window (Figure 10.3d) and a reminder sheet displaying the hierarchy of hands (Figure 10.3e). In addition to supporting messaging among all the players (including nonplaying partners), the chat window displays in the stream significant game event updates, such as when a new person joins or a hand is won. The alternative reminder sheet summarizes hand strength, with weakest hands at the bottom and strongest hands at the top, allowing novice players to jump in without having to first memorize all the rules.

Summative Evaluation: Comparing Play with and without a Partner

To assess the extent to which our resulting design encourages social interaction, we conducted a study of social gaming experiences by observing two groups of seniors playing TableTalk poker. We were especially interested in examining the impact of nonplayer roles on social interaction during game play; thus, in one group, participants played in remote pairs, while in the other, they played independently. TableTalk Poker included the following features to promote social interaction:

Different types of participation: Upon signing into the system, users are given the option to play or team up. The latter option allows a user to select someone with whom to partner.

When playing as partners, one person takes the active role of player and has control over the game play, while the other has a more passive role, and can act as an advisor, collaborator, or observer. Partners share the exact same view of the system, and share a voice chat (over Skype) so they are able to converse and consult with one another. A text-based group chat (visible to all players and partners) enables communication with opponents. TableTalk Poker also supports a *spectator* role, but we disabled this role for the study as we felt we could not make it engaging at our sample size. Spectators can see everyone's hands and also the probability of winning as can be seen in some TV poker broadcasts. Aside from watching and commenting, spectators can also be allowed to guess on the outcome.

Making space for conversation: A key difference between playing poker in a traditional face-to-face setting and online is the speed of play. In a face-to-face setting, shuffling and dealing physical cards creates a natural lull in the game play for conversation to occur. In an online environment, shuffling and dealing can be done instantaneously, and as such, online poker games tend to proceed much faster, with less room for conversation. To increase opportunities for social interaction, we slowed down the pace in TableTalk Poker with enforced one-minute breaks between rounds designed to mimic the time required to shuffle a physical card deck.

Research Questions

Our research was guided by the following research questions:

1. How does playing with a partner impact the *social experience* of playing an online game? That is, we were interested in understanding whether playing with a partner would lead to greater social interaction, and what that interaction might look like. We were also interested in exploring how nonplaying partners would define their role (i.e., Would they act as teachers, learners, collaborators, or a mix of these roles?).

2. How does playing with a partner impact the *game experience* for both the players and their nonplaying counterparts? Does playing with a partner increase the player's engagement with the game relative to playing alone? Are nonplayers as engaged with the game as players are?

3. How does playing with a partner impact *game play*? Does it lead to the use of better or different strategies? Does it lead to greater confidence in game decisions? Do partners share knowledge and help each other learn?

Method

Participants were randomly assigned to either play alone (*solo-play*) or with a partner (*partner-play*). In both groups, players competed against each other and communicated with opponents via a group text chat. In the partner-play group, participants were further assigned the role of *playing partner* or *nonplaying partner*. Each pair played together as a team, but only the *playing partner* had active control over the gameplay. Nonplaying partners had the same view of the interface, but could not control it other than to contribute to the group text chat. In addition, each pair could consult with each other privately over voice chat. Thus, there were three distinct participant categories, which we refer to as *solo players*, *playing partners*, and *nonplaying partners*. For consistency, we also use the term *partner* to refer generally to either half of a player–nonplayer dyad, and *player* to refer broadly to a solo- or partnered-player.

Each group completed two 4-hour sessions of game play. In the first session, researchers began by briefing the participants over a group lunch, after which participants filled out a series of questionnaires (personality, background, and poker knowledge). Participants were then asked to choose a seat; for the partner-play group, partners were randomly paired according to their seat selection. At the start of the second session, these pairings were randomly changed to enable a wider mix of personalities and skills.

For both sessions, the bulk of time was spent playing TableTalk Poker. Participants were given a 15-minute break every hour, or upon request. At the end of each session, the partner-play group was given a questionnaire to assess their relationship with their partner for that session. At the end of the study, participants in both groups filled out a final set of questionnaires (poker knowledge and game engagement), and each participant met briefly with a researcher for a 10-minute semi-structured interview.

Participants

Thirteen older adults ranging from 50 to 86 years of age (M = 67, SD = 8.79, 7 female) were recruited from Ryerson's LIFE Institute, 8 were assigned to the partner-play group (yielding 4 pairs), and 5 to the solo-play group. Participants had at least a high school education, were competent in English, and had varying experience with computers and online games. Lunch and transportation costs were provided. To motivate game play, we offered a cash prize of $100 to the top-performing player in each group.* (In the partner-play group, the top-performing partner was also awarded $100.)

As participants were recruited from a limited number of sources, some had preexisting relationships with each other. Given the relatively small sample size, it is perhaps not surprising that this was apparent in our pairings even though pairs were randomly assigned. In fact, only one team in the first session did not already know each other (as reported in the exit interview). No pair in the second session knew each other before hand. We consider the impact of these relationships in interpreting our results.

Setup

The study was conducted in a computer laboratory at Ryerson University. Conducting the study in a single environment enabled us to directly observe all participants, but meant that participants were not fully isolated from each other, as would be the case online. To minimize the impact of this setting, we deterred face-to-face communication by separating participants by at least one computer on either side (see Figure 10.4), and grouping players and partners at opposite ends of the room. The solo-play group was additionally given noise-canceling headphones. Each participant played on a desktop PC, equipped with a mouse and keyboard, voice chats in the partner-play group used Skype 4.2, and were recorded with MP3 Skype Recorder.

---

* In the solo-play group, the winner declined the prize and asked that it be divided among all players.

FIGURE 10.4 Participant seating arrangement. Left: dark circles denote players and gray circles, nonplayers. Right: the partner-play group. The solo-play layout was the same, but without the nonplayers.

Analysis

We collected data from a number of sources to triangulate on our research questions. Inductive analysis of transcripts of the partner-player voice chats and the player–opponent text chats serve as our main data source, and were used to identify major themes. We drew on additional data to complement the transcripts, and clarify the themes identified. These sources include:

- Observational field notes, collected by two researchers who rotated through the group, sitting behind each player to observe factors, such as body language, behavior, and usability.

- A 10-minute semi-structured exit interview to capture individual reflections on the experience of using the system.

- A measure of *engagement* (Table 10.1), modeled on the dimensions of perceived attention and intrinsic interest in Csikszentmihalyi's flow theory (Csikszentmihalyi 1990), with questions on usability inspired by the work of O'Brien and Toms (2010).

TABLE 10.1 Game Engagement

1. I forgot about my immediate surroundings while playing on this website.
2. I was drawn into the game-playing experience.
3. I enjoyed playing TableTalk Poker.
4. The game playing experience was fun.
5. I found TableTalk Poker very easy to use.
6. I felt frustrated while playing on TableTalk Poker.

Note: Respondents rated their agreement with the following statements on a 5-point Likert scale (from 1 strongly disagree to 5 strongly agree). Engagement is the average of the responses. (A reliability analysis revealed they were measuring the same construct, Cronbach's? = 0.941.)

- For the partner-play group, a measure of *social attraction* between partners, measured at the end of each session using the social attraction component of McCroskey and McCain's (1974) survey of interpersonal attraction.[*]

- A pre- and poststudy poker quiz to provide baseline data on poker knowledge and assess whether or not knowledge increased over the course of the study.

- Log data of all actions in the system (bets, folds, calls, and raises), used to calculate risk aversion, recklessness, aggressive play, and bluffing behavior.

We additionally collected background data to characterize our participant population. As part of this, we administered an abbreviated Big-Five personality assessment (Gosling et al., 2003). We had hoped the personality data would yield additional insight into our results; however, given our small sample size it did not.

Results

In presenting our results, we begin by describing the themes that emerged during our analysis of the transcripts, grouped according to our three main research questions. We bring in secondary results—from the questionnaires, exit interviews, and observational notes—as needed to complement the main findings. We focus our attention on the experience of the partner-play group, using the solo-play group as a point of comparison. We then examine the influence of our design on game play, relying more heavily on the log file data to drive the investigation, and using the transcripts to clarify and contextualize these results. We then conclude our discussion of the results by relating our findings back to our research questions. Note that pseudonyms are used to reference individual participants.

Effect of Playing with a Partner on the Social Experience of Play

Among the solo players, there was little evidence of ongoing conversations. The text-based chat (the only communication channel available) was little used aside from a few one-off congratulatory messages like "nice hand." Though solo-play participants occasionally took off their headphones and yelled to each other—despite our instructions to the contrary and perhaps highlighting the inadequacy of text chat—there was little evidence of ongoing conversation, interaction, or self-disclosure during solo-play.

Overwhelmingly, playing with a partner led to more social interaction. Though the partner-play group similarly ignored the group text-chat, they made extensive use of the private voice chat between partners, indicating that this channel provided a social outlet not afforded to the solo-play group. Over this channel conversation flowed easily and prolonged silences were rare. That participants generally enjoyed playing with a partner was also evident from the questionnaire results. The social attraction scale

---

[*] Participants completed the social and task attraction components. Only social attraction is included in our analyses; task attraction yielded no interesting findings. We did not administer the third component, physical attraction, as it is not relevant to audio-only communication.

data indicated that participants generally liked their partners, with an overall mean interpersonal attraction score of 3.71 (SD = 0.97) on the 5-point scale. Those who had a preexisting relationship rated their partners somewhat higher than those who did not (familiar: M = 4.42, SD = 0.27; unfamiliar: M = 3.29, SD = 1.92), but we did not have the power to test this difference statistically. When asked whether they would have preferred playing alone, the mean was 2.5 (SD = 1.91). As a mean rating of three or less indicated disagreement, this result indicates that on average, had a slight preference for playing with a partner. To be clear, this result aggregates across the experiences of all participants, which were varied. As we will discuss shortly, some experienced conflict with their partners, and correspondingly, were less positive about playing with a partner.

For some pairs, conversation moved to more personal topics, indicating that they were starting to develop a friendship. Self-disclosure is known to be a key element of the formation of personal relationships and trust (Derlega et al. 1993); thus, personally revealing conversations can be seen as early evidence of the formation of friendship. For example, in the following dialogue, Ernie (playing-partner) and Louise (pseudonyms), with no preexisting relationship, talk about their grandchildren and the use of webcams to connect with distant family members.

Ernie: Did you have the microphone one too? A camera?
Louise: Yes, we also had the camera.
Ernie: The webcam.
Louise: Yeah, we could see them on holidays. They would take us to the table with them [grandchildren]. And I would be sitting there crying, but at least you see them growing up.
Ernie: Especially, when they are that far away. That's for sure.

Notice in particular how Louise shares not only the basic details of the experience, but also her emotional reaction to seeing her grandchildren over video.

Playing with a partner meant that players in the partner-play condition had someone whom they could confide in, celebrate with, or help guide them, and though our sample size was small, we witnessed several examples of these different roles. For example, in the following quote Maverick (playing-partner) consults George's poker expertise, and George takes on the role of a teacher:

Maverick: Nine nine ten jack. What is higher, a straight or a flush?
George: A flush.
Maverick: A flush is higher, ok.

Solo players had to instead consult the poker hand reference (on the side bar of the interface, as shown previously in Figure 10.3), which we frequently observed them do. However, for more advanced knowledge, solo players were left to learn by trial and error, unlike partnered-players. For example, in the next quote, Boyle gives Kitty (playing-partner) tips on strategy, going beyond what can be included in a cheat sheet:

Boyle: Three cards are gone and they tell you in poker, if you don't have a chance after the first three cards, then get out.
Kitty: Oh, ok.

Similarly, teachers could provide rationale and explanation as shown in the next quote, also between Kitty and Boyle:

Kitty: So what do I do?
Boyle: Fold.
Kitty: Fold?
Boyle: You see why? You don't need to chase it.
Kitty: Ok.
Boyle: A three would have helped you but you have no chance of getting a three, you can't get a flush.
Kitty: laughs… I am enjoying this you know.

Nonplayers adopting a teaching role could also reinforce learning by highlighting key points. For example, in the following quote George (nonplaying partner) comments on Kitty's last hand to ensure she recognized its strength:

George: So did you realize that you were almost a hundred percent guaranteed to win that?
Kitty: No. [laughs]
George: OK. You gotta recognize when you have a good hand here. You were almost guaranteed to win that one.
Kitty: Mm.
George: That's why you gotta bet.
Kitty: Yeah.
George: It was extremely unlikely that you and I were gonna get beaten on that hand.
Kitty: Is it because I had the five spades?
George: Yes, yeah, yes, and the point is you had the highest one in your hand. Nobody could beat you. Even if somebody had a flush.

When the playing partner was instead the more experienced player, the teacher–learner relationship would flip, and the nonplaying partner would take on the role of an apprentice. In the following quote, Ernie explains his moves to Rosa (nonplaying partner), thus involving her in the game and enabling her to learn from his actions:

Ernie: Do you see my hand here? It's not a bad hand, it's not a great hand but it's a great place to start so we will see what happens. We are going to stay in this game until we see what happens on the next hand

Rosa: So have we got anything?
Ernie: Well it's my turn now, what do I want to do, I am going to stay in this game so I am going to call. So I call. So what do I want to do now? I want to raise; I am raising $100.
Rosa: You're bold.

Rosa took advantage of this opportunity to learn more about the game, asking Ernie questions throughout the game as shown in the following excerpt:

Rosa: What does call mean?
Ernie: Call means we will just stay in the game. We won't [put in] any more money. We will just stay in the game.

In some cases both partners had similar poker experience. When this occurred, partners tended to act as cooperative allies as demonstrated in the following quote from Maverick (playing-partner) and George:

George: Probably wasn't help for anybody else.
Maverick: Not unless they happen to have a couple of diamonds.
George: Yeah we'll see what they do and if it's not too expensive maybe stick around. If it costs you much then you get out.
Maverick: Yeah okay.

Nonplayers were also often a source of social support. In this excerpt, for example, Maverick (playing-partner) relies on Rosa for support as he bluffs and then celebrates victory:

Maverick: Yeah I put in a hundred…people probably think we have a pair of kings, which we don't.
Rosa: [laughs] Foolin' around, hey?
Maverick: Ok, well, we got a one in four chance of getting a diamond but that's just uh… oh, we won that.
Rosa: Aah, we won that?
Maverick: And nobody sees what we had, because everyone folded. YAY!

In the last excerpt, Rosa's use of the term "we" also suggests that she perceived herself to be part of a team with Maverick, even though she didn't have control over the game. Our analysis of the transcripts yielded several positive examples of partners sharing closely in the experience of playing the game and engaging as a cohesive unit. In this next example, Ernie (playing-partner) and Louise use language such as "we" and "let's" that suggests that they perceived themselves as a unit. This was observed frequently in participant conversations:

Louise: I've never seen so many low cards in my life!
Ernie: We are getting them all.
Louise: Yeah.
Ernie: Oh well…
Louise: Oh my goodness!

Ernie: Let's survive until the cards turn around
Louise: Yeah.

Most commonly, we saw evidence of engagement in the negotiations of hands. Because poker has elements of chance and trickery, there are moments where the decision-making can become rather stressful. Partners often shared this stress, again demonstrating a perception of playing as a single cohesive unit. In his example, George and Maverick (playing-partner) have just completed their straight, only to be trumped by a flush.

George: I think you've got to stay; with the pot being 5000. There's your eight.
Maverick: Eight, nine, ten, jack, wait seven, eight, nine, ten, jack.
George: Yeah.
Maverick: Now if they've got a flush we're toast.
George: I don't think there's a flush there. Well, I think you've got to go in. No flush.
Maverick: Ok.
George: User nine is going to call. Oh my god, yeah.
Maverick: Ace high flush.
George: Yeah shoot ace high flush. [laughs]
Maverick: [laughs] Wow.

This again points to the level at which partners were engaged with the game, and highlights that alternative roles, such as partners, can be a viable method of involving additional individuals, perhaps especially those lacking the confidence or skill to play on their own.

Though most pairs worked well together, for a few, there was evidence of conflict. Maverick (playing-partner), for example, noted in his poststudy interview that he was repeatedly frustrated with his partner Rosa's inexperience with the game, and found her advice and cheerleading to be distracting:

> There was zero contribution, in fact negative. She'd say some distracting things. … When the three cards were dealt, she'd say "those are great!" but [she didn't understand that] everyone gets those cards.

Rosa, on the other hand, reported feeling a lack of respect and frustration when Maverick did not follow her advice.

In another case, Selma (playing-partner) and Boyle disagreed repeatedly on strategy. Boyle was frustrated when Selma did not consult him prior to acting, and felt she did not fully consider his perspective on playing the odds. This excerpt, in which Selma wants to "see the flop" (i.e., the first round of three community cards), even though she holds a very weak starting hand highlights the tension that was present throughout their experience:

Selma: I'll see the first one.
Boyle: No, no, no.
Selma: Well I can't take it back.
Boyle: Why do you do it?

Selma: Well if these numbers come out then we have three of a kind.
Boyle: You have a useless hand.
Selma: I'll fold this time.
Boyle: This is about five times though, you've done it.

When probed during the exit interview, participants attributed successful partnerships to prior relationships and personality. Rosa, for example, said she enjoyed playing with Ernie more because she knew him. Similarly, Ernie seemed to accept Rosa's lack of knowledge, attempting to explain things to her and involve her in the decision-making process, this extra patience likely stemming from their preexisting relationship. Even Kitty who performed equally well with both her partners and rated them both highly (4.23 and 4.69) suggested that, "(the researchers) should do a better job pairing people together, not people who get really frustrated when you don't win. You have to pair personalities better." This suggests, as was noted by many of our participants, that the enjoyment of playing with a partner stemmed more from the social relationship than from the availability of expertise, per se.

While we did not explicitly study gender in this study—and no participant identified it as a factor—it is interesting to note that these two instances of conflict occurred in mixed-gender pairings. Gender and expertise have been previously found to impact power dynamics in conversation (Leet-Pellegrini 1980), and research with children has suggested computer-sharing dynamics are influenced by gender (Inkpen et al. 1997). We only explored one control protocol (i.e., one person held complete control), but other protocols are possible. Examining more collaborative sharing protocols could serve as an interesting area for further exploration.

Effect of Playing with a Partner on Game Engagement

On the whole, participants were engaged with the game in both conditions, and generally reported liking the game. For example, when one participant in the solo-play condition joked to the researcher "you can just leave us here, we'll play through the weekend," the others laughed and nodded in agreement. Questionnaire results lend further support, with mean engagement scores above 4 out of 5 for all participant groups (solo players: M = 4.63, SD = 0.41; partnered-players M = 4.33, SD = 0.19; and nonplayers: M = 4.04, SD = 1.19). Though, we did not have sufficient power to perform rigorous statistical analyses, the slightly lower means in the partner-play group may reflect that for these individuals the game was not the only factor contributing to their experience, with social interaction also playing a role. It is, however, noteworthy that the nonplaying partners reported comparable game engagement to the other groups. This is consistent with the transcript data reported above which seemed to indicate that despite having no direct control over the game play, they were engaged with it and considered themselves a cohesive unit with the playing partner.

Effect of Playing with a Partner on Game Play

Playing a new game with a partner should provide a ready source of knowledge and information, and boost confidence. We, therefore, investigated the extent to which participants

TABLE 10.2   Summary of Pre- and Posttest Poker Knowledge Scores
in the Two Conditions ($N = 13$)

	Pretest Mean (SD)	Posttest Mean (SD)
Partner play ($N = 8$)	6.75 (3.10)	7.37 (3.06)
Solo play ($N = 5$)	6.60 (1.94)	6.60 (1.51)

in the two groups developed poker skills over the course of the study, and the ways in which playing with a partner affected game play. In terms of the poker skills test (see Table 10.2), there was some evidence that participants in the partner-play group improved between the pre- and posttest, but this difference was not large enough to test statistically at our sample size.

The more interesting results were, however, the ways in which playing with a partner affected how the game was played. The game log data and chat transcripts suggest important differences between the two conditions in style of play and range of strategies employed. In particular, we found that the partnered-players were more aggressive than the solo players. They raised more often and checked less. They also bet more when raising, putting more pressure on their opponents. When they folded, they folded earlier, thereby investing less in weak hands. Finally, they also bluffed more successfully.

Table 10.3 shows the distribution of actions for each group. Solo players opted to check (pass; instead of raising) 35% of the time, as compared with partnered-players, who did so 18% of the time. Poker strategy (e.g., Harrington and Robertie 2004) suggests that such frequent checking is not optimal. Raising the cost to the opponents to stay in the hand makes the decision to call, and potentially strengthen one's hand, much more difficult. Solo players only opted to raise 13% of the time, as contrasted with 24% in the partner-play condition. Solo players were also more conservative with their betting, raising on average 85.4 units (SD = 21.7), while partnered-players raised by 135.1 units (SD = 11.5) on average. This shows greater risk taking by the partnered-players, and suggests that they perhaps had better understanding of pot odds.[*]

As shown in Table 10.4, solo players opted to fold their hand after seeing the flop (i.e., the first round of community cards) 30% of the time, as contrasted with 42% in the partner-play condition. That is, the solo players were willing to invest more money to see the turn and river cards (i.e., the second and third rounds of community cards), only to fold later. Conventional poker strategy suggests folding is the best move if the flop does not improve

TABLE 10.3   Distribution of Actions across the Two Groups, by Count (#) and by Proportion (%) ($N = 9$)

	Check		Calls		Raise		Fold	
	#	%	#	%	#	%	#	%
Solo play	998	35	956	33	388	13	545	19
Partner play	426	18	935	39	581	24	433	18

---

[*] In poker, pot odds refer to the size of the pot relative to the cost to call; e.g., with $20 in the pot and a cost of $1 to stay in the hand, it is worthwhile to call any hand with at least a 1/20 chance of winning.

TABLE 10.4   Distribution of Rounds in Which Participants Folded across the Two Groups, by Count (#) and by Proportion (%) (N = 9)

	Pre Flop		Flop		Turn		River	
	#	%	#	%	#	#	#	%
Solo play	170	31	163	30	98	18	114	21
Partner play	138	32	183	42	74	17	38	9

one's hand. This periodically came up in partner-play dialogue, as we saw in the earlier excerpt where Boyle advises Kitty to fold (p. 26).

Finally, Table 10.5 summarizes the bluffing behaviors of the two groups. Bluffing misleads opponents to believe that one's hand is strong, with the goal of winning the pot through strong betting. We define a successful bluff as a win when the probability of winning (based on the cards held) is less than 50%. In the solo-play condition, 191 total hands were played, of which there were 30 (16%) in which the winner did not have the absolute best hand. Of those 30 hands, the participant was bluffing (by our definition) in only 14 cases (7%). In contrast, of the 176 hands played in the experimental condition, 70 hands (40%) were won without the absolute best hand and in 38 cases (22%) the player–partner pair was bluffing.

To better understand these differences in risk-taking behavior, we returned to the chat transcripts. One clear theme in participant conversations was that playing with a partner seemed to improve player confidence and expand participants' range of strategies. In this excerpt, for example, Ernie wants to call a raise of 100, but realizes his chances of hitting the straight are low. He turns to Louise to reaffirm his decision:

Louise: We just need a nine!

Ernie: Yea, I know, we have been up with a pair of hearts and all. 100 bucks for a possible straight. Is it worth the money or not?

Louise: I don't know. Do you want to see one more?

Ernie: Yeah, I am going to see one more. Call it; just see what's called. We got our card, we got our card!

Louise: Yea, I know!

TABLE 10.5   Summary of Bluffing Behavior

	Solo Play		Partner Play	
	#	%	#	%
Total hands played	191		176	
Hands won without best hand (<100% probability of win)	30	16	70	40
Hands won with bluffing (<50% probability of win)	14	7	38	22

Note: The table shows the total hands played, hands won without the best hand (i.e., the winning hand was not the strongest dealt), and hands won where the probability of winning was less than 50% (i.e., bluffing). In all other cases (not shown), the winning hand was the strongest hand dealt (N = 9).

This continual reaffirmation of the correct play and improved understanding of the game seemed to bolster the confidence of players in this condition, and helps explain their more assertive decision-making and game play strategies. In his interview, Maverick reflects on this:

> It was really good because the first time (with George), he knew how to play and he could coach me and then it was fine and after a while I was at a level where I was comfortable playing on my own.

We also observed evidence of partners suggesting new strategies that players would not normally adopt. Kitty mentions for example that, "I used to check a lot, but with George I don't. Right away I start betting. He taught me to be more aggressive." In this excerpt, George urges Kitty to bluff, bringing her attention to the community cards and how it might be an opportunity to scare their opponents off.

George: Alright, make a big bet here. Since your cards are not so good there I'd say betting 500 would be good.
Kitty: You think so?
George: Yeah, cause there's no way that card helped them. It's very unlikely.

In all of these ways playing with a partner seemed to have a clear effect on how participants played the game and the extent to which they engaged in risk-taking and a wider range of strategies. These effects seem to stem from having readily available expertise and knowledge, and from mutual reinforcement through dialogue.

Discussion

Our first research question asked how playing with a partner impacts the social experience of playing an online game. We found that nonplayers adopted a range of roles, including mentor and peer collaborator, that participants generally enjoyed playing with a partner, and that overwhelmingly, playing with a partner led to greater social interaction. While very little conversation occurred during solo-play, conversation was abundant for the partner-play group. Not all the interaction was positive, however. Some pairings experienced conflict, suggesting further work is needed to determine how to best match partners and balance power.

In response to our second research question, game engagement ratings were high for all participants, including solo players, partnered-players, and nonplayers alike. Importantly, nonplayers were as engaged with the game as their partners, with pairs acting as cohesive units and using inclusive language such as "we" and "let's" when discussing game play. Nonplayers were generally involved in the decision-making, and shared in the joy of wins and the disappointment of losses.

For our final question, we found that playing with a partner led to very different game play. Partnered-players used more advanced strategies. When they folded, they folded early, and when they stayed in the game, they played more aggressively, raising and bluffing more often. The chat transcripts suggest that the partners were integral to this difference, providing both a source of knowledge and a source of encouragement.

CHALLENGES

The work presented here represents a first step in exploring games as social media. However, more work is needed to fully understand the potential of this space. Our study was done in an artificial setting, for a relatively short duration, and with a small sample size. Moreover, our between subjects design limited our ability to compare the experiences of playing with and without a partner—a within-subjects evaluation would enable more direct comparison. In addition, we have focused thus far, on just one game, poker. As such, personal preferences for poker are surely confounded in our results. We chose poker because it is a familiar multiplayer game that is inherently social when played face-to-face, but a different game choice may have yielded different results.

One of the biggest challenges we encountered in this project was simultaneously addressing diverse needs. While the primary focus of our work was to explore the ways in which games could support the social needs of seniors, the game clearly needed to additionally address cognitive, sensory, and physical needs or it would fail regardless of the potential for social support. Barriers to adoption were numerous. Some of the seniors we worked with had very little previous computer experience and were unfamiliar with standard metaphors. Lack of familiarity with games and common gaming components such as text chat was particularly challenging during the formative stages. With little experience with computers and digital games, it was beyond the capabilities of some of our participants to envision new social gaming environments.

A final challenge was designing a robust summative evaluation in the context of a multiplayer social game. Ideally, our summative evaluation would have involved multiple play sessions with different groups of participants. However, each play session required substantial effort, particularly in terms of recruitment. Moreover, individual personalities clearly impacted group dynamics, particularly within pairs, and our design did not enable us to tease out these effects.

SOLUTIONS AND RECOMMENDATIONS

In terms of solutions and recommendations, we offer both our recommendations for working with seniors to develop digital games, and specific design guidelines for developing social gaming environments for seniors.

Designing for Social Engagement and Seniors

Designing a social game for seniors highlighted a multitude of access barriers and these were particularly evident during our iterative design process. One way in which we addressed this challenge was to seek input from a variety of sources, which included but were not limited to older adults. For example, some of the participants in our paper prototyping activities were not senior, and even those that were, were on the younger end of the spectrum. However, all were novices to online gaming. This enabled us to separate the challenges of designing games for novice players from the compounded challenges of addressing age-related needs. We then revisited age-related needs in the next round of user testing, which did involve older adults.

This is not to say that working with older adults was not important. Perhaps, the only reason we were able to effectively work with proxies during one stage of our design is that we are so extensively worked with older adults from the earliest stages of the project. Our formative observations, in particular, provided insight into the ways in which seniors approached games, which proved indispensible in the later stages of the design. These experiences also helped us to better frame what success means in this context. Common usability metrics such as speed and efficiency take on a slightly different meaning in the context of aging. Faster is not always better and slower does not necessarily indicate a flaw or inferior design. It was only through direct interactions across a variety of activities that we were truly able to appreciate these differences.

Design Guidelines

Our experience suggests several design guidelines for improving the social capabilities of gaming environments targeted at seniors:

Social games for seniors should offer opportunities for interaction during game play. We saw that playing poker together provided a starting point for conversations and building relationships, and that interacting with others seemed to impact the perceived engagement of the game for our participants. They generally enjoyed interacting with each other. This also resulted in some inexperienced players learning more about poker. We, therefore, recommend that games provide opportunities for general-purpose (i.e., not necessarily game-focused) social interaction between players. Our experience suggested further that audio communication seemed to be used more frequently and more effectively than text-based chat for our participants. However, not all seniors will want greater social interaction, and not all pairings or groupings of seniors will be successful as we saw with some of the pairings in our study. Thus, it is important that features to support social interaction be designed such that they are available for those who want them and can be ignored by those who do not.

Social games for seniors should support a variety of roles and kinds of participation. While technical features that enabled players to interact with each other were helpful in forming relationships and getting players to interact with each other, it was not until we assigned them partners that we saw substantial use of these features. Putting players in pairs got them talking to each other, meant that less experienced players could learn from more experienced ones, and resulted in the use of a greater range of game strategies. We, therefore, recommend that social games for seniors allow for multiple forms of participation. In some cases, these features could support self-assignment to roles within groups already known to each other. In others, the system could pair strangers with each other. Our experiences suggest that such pairing could be improved with cognizance of potential personality and skill level similarities or differences.

Social game interfaces for seniors should account for diverse abilities and needs. We saw interaction and nascent relationships between participants with varying levels of technical and poker experience. Our iterative development strategy that involved participants in the design of the game helped ensure that the game was accessible. Without these steps, some participants may have had difficulty using the game and not benefited from the social opportunities that it offered them. We, therefore, urge designers to consider the unique needs of seniors in designing social games, and to recognize that these principles apply with equal importance both to the interface elements for gameplay and to those for social interaction.

Social games for seniors should support learning. Seniors may often be playing games as much for the social interaction opportunities as for the games themselves. This means that they may frequently play games with which they have little experience, in fact, many are eager to learn new games and skills. Opportunities for learning can come from features that support interaction and playing multiple roles (see above), as well as from those supporting screen or (in the case of poker) hand/card sharing. One could also imagine automatic pairing of more and less experienced players.

CONCLUSIONS

In this chapter, we described our experiences developing TableTalk Poker, a social gaming environment designed to address the unique social and accessibility needs of seniors. We first employed a number of exploratory activities, which in combination with a literature review helped us to better understand how older adults socialize over game play and how current gaming environments fall short of meeting their needs. We then used an iterative design approach to develop TableTalk Poker. This process included a wide variety of techniques, including presenting early design sketches to target users, conducting prototyping activities with proxy users, and finally performing a series of informal user testing sessions with seniors to refine our design and gather early insight into how it supported social interaction. We finally conducted a comparative evaluation to tease out the impact of playing with a partner. Individual differences played a large role in the experience of playing with a partner. Good player–partner compatibility enhanced engagement, but mismatches highlighted the need for control over with whom one plays and whether one plays with a partner. A larger study, beyond the resources we had available, would be needed to fully understand the role of personalities and to provide insight on how to match partners.

Nonetheless, our study was on the whole, successful. Participants in both groups (with and without a partner) had a great time playing TableTalk Poker, reporting that the system was easy to use and very engaging. Pairing players with partners afforded numerous avenues for interaction. It allowed for existing friends to bond over an activity, acted as a formidable icebreaker, supported teacher–learner interactions, and encouraged apprenticeship and cheerleading. We saw during game play the start of relationships with the potential to grow into meaningful friendships. Nonplayers were as engaged in the game as players themselves, and pairs often saw themselves as one unit. Finally, playing with a partner influences mastery: those in our partner-play group played better, exhibiting more advanced strategies.

In conclusion, Isbister (2010) emphasized the need for more work on design and evaluation for enhancing social play in digital games. This work is a response to that call, contributing to the understanding of how implementing online games as social media can enhance seniors' social experience, game experience, and quality of game play. As the use of social networking sites becomes more common among seniors, there will be a wealth of opportunities for doing more research on new game designs and new ways to enable communication and collaboration among game players and nonplaying participants.

REFERENCES

Bandura, A. 1977. *Social Learning Theory*. New York: General Learning Press.

Bassuk, S. S., Glass, T. A., and Berkman, L. F. 1999. Social disengagement and incident cognitive decline in community-dwelling elderly persons. *Annals of Internal Medicine* 131(3):165–173.

Carstensen, L. L. 1992. Motivation for social contact across the life span: A theory of socioemotional selectivity. In *Nebraska Symposium on Motivation*, ed. J.E. Jacobs, 209–254. Lincoln, NE: University of Nebraska Press.

Craik, F. I. M. and Salthouse, T. A. eds. 2000. *The Handbook of Aging and Cognition*. Mahwah, NJ: Lawrence Erlbaum Associates.

Crooks, V., Lubben, J., Petitti, D. B., Little, D., and Chiu, V. 2008. Social network, cognitive function, and dementia incidence among elderly women. *American Journal of Public Health* 98(7):1221–1227.

Csikszentmihalyi, M. 1990. *Flow: The Psychology of Optimal Experience*. New York: Harper & Row.

De Schutter, B. 2010. Never too old to play: The appeal of digital games to an older audience. *Games and Culture* 6(2):155–170.

De Schutter, B. and Vanden Abeele, V. 2010. Designing meaningful play within the psycho-social context of older adults. In *Proceedings of the 3rd International Conference on Fun and Games (FnG'10)*, 84–93. New York: ACM.

Derlega, V. J., Metts, S., Petronio, S., and Margulis, S. T. 1993. *Self-Disclosure. (Sage Series on Close Relationships)*. Thousand Oaks, CA: Sage Publications.

Gajadhar, B. J., Nap, H. H., de Kort, Y., and Ijsselsteijn, W. 2010. Out of sight, out of mind: Co-player effects on seniors' player experience. In *Proceedings of the 3rd International Conference on Fun and Games (FnG'10)*, 74–83. New York: ACM.

Gerling, K. and Masuch, M. 2011. When Gaming is not suitable for everyone: Play testing Wii games with frail elderly. Paper presented at the *1st Workshop on Game Accessibility: Xtreme Interaction Design*, Bordeaux, France.

Gerling, K. M., Mandryk, R. L., and Kalyn, M. R. 2013. Wheelchair-based game design for older adults. In *Proceedings of the 15th ACM SIGACCESS International Conference on Computers and Accessibility (ASSETS 2013)*, 27:1–27:8. New York: ACM.

Gerling, K. M., Schulte, F. P., and Masuch, M. 2011. Designing and evaluating digital games for frail elderly persons. In *Proceedings of the 8th International Conference on Advances in Computer Entertainment Technology (ACE '11)*, Article 62, 8 pages. New York: ACM.

Glass, T. A., Mendes De Leon, C. F., Bassuk, S. S., and Berkman, L. F. 2006. Social engagement and depressive symptoms in late life: Longitudinal findings. *Journal of Aging and Health* 18:604–628.

Glass, T. A., Mendes De Leon, C. F., Marottoli, R. A., and Berkman, L. F. 1999. Population based study of social and productive activities as predictors of survival among elderly Americans. *British Journal of Medicine* 319:478–483.

Golder, S. A. and Donath, J. 2004. Hiding and revealing in online poker games. In *Proceedings of the 2004 ACM Conference on Computer Supported Cooperative Work (CSCW'04)*, 370–373. New York: ACM.

Goodman, J., Syme, A., and Eisma, R. 2003. Older adults' use of computers: A survey. In *Proceedings the 17th Annual Conference on Human–Computer Interaction: Designing for Society*, 8–12. Bath, UK: Springer.

Gosling, S. D., Rentfrow, P. J., and Swann, W. B. 2003. A very brief measure of the big-five personality domains. *Journal of Research in Personality* 37(6):504–528.

Griffiths, M. D., Davies, M. N. O., and Chappell, D. 2004. Online computer gaming: A comparison of adolescent and adult gamers. *Journal of Adolescence* 27(1):87–96.

Harrington, D. and Robertie, B. 2004. *Harrington on Hold 'em: Expert Strategy for No-Limit Tournaments, Volume I: Strategic Play*. Las Vegas, NV: Two Plus Two Publications.

Hsu, C. L. and Lu, H. P. 2004. Why do people play on-line games? An extended TAM with social influences and flow experience. *Information & Management* 41(7):853–868.

Ijsselsteijn, W., Nap, H. H., de Kort, Y., and Poels, K. 2007. Digital game design for elderly users. In *Proceedings of the 2007 Conference on Future Play (FuturePlay'07)*, 17–22. New York: ACM.

Inkpen, K., McGrenere, J., Booth, K. S., and Klawe, M. 1997. The effect of turn-taking protocols on children's learning in mouse-driven collaborative environments. In *Proceedings of Graphics Interface 1997 (GI'97)*, 138–145. Toronto, ON: Canadian Information Processing Society.

Isbister, K. 2010. Enabling social play: A framework for design and evaluation. In *Evaluating User Experience in Games*, ed. R. Bernhaupt, 11–22. London: Springer-Verlag.

Iyengar, S. S. and Lepper, M. 2000. When choice is demotivating: Can one desire too much of a good thing? *Journal of Personality and Social Psychology* 79:995–1006.

Judge, T. K., Neustaedter, C., and Kurtz, A. F. 2010. The family window: The design and evaluation of a domestic media space. In *Proceedings of the SIGCHI Conference on Human Factors in Computing Systems (CHI '10)*, 2361–2370. New York: ACM.

Jung, Y., Li, K. J., Janissa, N. S., Gladys, W. L. C., and Lee, K. M. 2009. Games for a better life: Effects of playing Wii games on the well-being of seniors in a long-term care facility. In *Proceedings of the Sixth Australasian Conference on Interactive Entertainment (IE '09)*, 5:1–5:6A. New York: ACM.

Kaplan, A. M. and Haenlein, M. 2010. Users of the world, unite! The challenges and opportunities of social media. *Business Horizons* 53(1):59–68.

Keyani, P., Hsieh, G., Mutlu, B., Easterday, M., and Forlizzi, J. 2005. DanceAlong: Supporting positive social exchange and exercise for the elderly through dance. In *Extended Abstracts of the SIGCHI Conference on Human Factors in Computing Systems (CHI-EA'05)*, 1541–1544. New York: ACM.

Khoo, E. T., Merritt, T., and Cheok, A. D. 2009. Designing physical and social intergenerational family entertainment. *Interacting with Computers* 21(1–2):76–87.

Krueger, K. R., Wilson, R. S., Kamenetsky, J. M., Barnes, L. L., Bienias, J. L., and Bennett, D. A. 2009. Social engagement and cognitive function in old age. *Experimental Aging Research* 35(1):45–60.

Leet-Pellegrini, H. M. 1980. Conversational dominance as a function of gender and expertise. In *Language Social Psychological Perspectives*, eds. H. Giles, W. P. Robinson, and P. M. Smith, 97–104. Oxford: Pergamon Press.

Lenhart, A., Jones, S., and Macgill, R. 2008. *Video Games: Adults are Players Too*. Washington, DC: Pew Foundation.

Lindley, S. E., Harper, R., and Sellen, A. 2010. Designing a technological playground: A field study of the emergence of play in household messaging. In *Proceedings of the SIGCHI Conference on Human Factors in Computing Systems (CHI '10)*, 2351–2360. New York: ACM.

Massimi, M., Baecker, R. M., and Wu, M. 2007. Using participatory activities with seniors to critique, build, and evaluate mobile phones. In *Proceedings of the 9th International ACM SIGACCESS Conference on Computers and Accessibility (ASSETS'07)*, 155–162. New York: ACM.

McCroskey, J. C. and McCain, T. A. 1974. The measurement of interpersonal attraction. *Speech Monographs* 41(3):261–266.

Melenhorst, A. S. 2002. Adopting communication technology in later life: The decisive role of benefits. PhD dissertation, Eindhoven University of Technology.

Mendes De Leon, C. F., Glass, T. A., and Berkman, L. F. 2003. Social engagement and disability in a community population of older adults: The New Haven EPESE. *American Journal of Epidemiology* 157(7):633–642.

Meyer, R. 2014. It's totally normal to watch other people play video games. *The Atlantic*, September 3.

Montola, M. and Waern, A. 2006. Participant roles in socially expanded games. In *Proceedings of the Third International Workshop on Pervasive Gaming Applications (PerGames'06)*, eds. C. Magerkurth, M. Chalmers, S. Bjoerk, and L. Schäfer, 165–173. Sankt Augustin, Germany: Fraunhofer FIT.

Mubin, O., Shahid, S., and Mahmud, A. A. 2008. Walk 2 Win: Towards designing a mobile game for elderly's social engagement. In *Proceedings of the 22nd British HCI Group Annual Conference on People and Computers: Culture, Creativity, Interaction—Volume 2 (BCS-HCI '08)*, 11–14. Swinton, UK: British Computer Society.

Mynatt, E. D., Rowan, J., Craighill, S., and Jacobs, A. 2001. Digital family portraits: Supporting peace of mind for extended family members. In *Proceedings of the SIGCHI Conference on Human Factors in Computing Systems (CHI'01)*, 333–340. New York: ACM.

Nap, H. H., de Kort, Y., and Ijsselsteijn, W. 2009. Senior gamers: Preferences, motivations and needs. *Gerontechnology* 8(4):247–262.

Neufeldt, C. 2009. Wii play with elderly people. *International Reports on Socio-Informatics* 6(3):50–59.

O'Brien, H. L. and Toms, E. G. 2010. The development and evaluation of a survey to measure user engagement in e-commerce environments. *Journal of the American Society for Information Science & Technology* 61(1):50–69.

Paavilainen, J. 2010. Critical review on video game evaluation heuristics: Social games perspective. In *Proceedings of the International Academic Conference on the Future of Game Design and Technology (Futureplay'10)*, 56–65. New York: ACM.

Quandt, T., Grueninger, H., and Wimmer, J. 2009. The gray haired gaming generation: Findings from an explorative interview study on older computer gamers. *Games and Culture* 4(1):27–46.

Reblin, M. and Uchino, B. N. 2008. Social and emotional support and its implication for health. *Current Opinion in Psychiatry* 21(2):201–205.

Saczynski, J. S., Pfeifer, L. A., Masaki, K., Korf, E. S. C., Laurin, D., White, L., and Launer, L. J. 2006. The effect of social engagement on incident dementia: The Honolulu–Asia aging study. *American Journal of Epidemiology* 163(5):433–440.

Shim, N., Baecker, R. M., Birnholtz, J., and Moffatt, K. 2010. TableTalk Poker: An online social gaming environment for seniors. In *Proceedings of the 2010 Conference on the Future of Game Design and Technology (FuturePlay'10)*, 98–104. New York: ACM.

Stach, T., Graham, T. C., Yim, J., and Rhodes, R. E. 2009. Heart rate control of exercise video games. In *Proceedings of Graphics Interface 2009 (GI'09)*, 125–132. Toronto, ON: Canadian Information Processing Society.

Statistics Canada. 2013a. Table 358-0154—Canadian Internet use survey, Internet use, by location of use, household income and age group for Canada and regions, occasional (percent), CANSIM (database) (accessed: February 25, 2015).

Statistics Canada. 2013b. Table 358-0153—Canadian Internet use survey, Internet use, by age group, Internet activity, sex, level of education and household income, occasional (percent), CANSIM (database) (accessed: February 25, 2015).

Statistics Canada. 2014. Table 051-0001—Estimates of population, by age group and sex for July 1, Canada, provinces and territories, annual (persons unless otherwise noted), CANSIM (database) (accessed: February 25, 2015).

Theng, Y. L., Dahlan, A. B., Akmal, M. L., and Myint, T. Z. 2009. An exploratory study on senior citizens' perceptions of the Nintendo Wii: The case of Singapore. In *Proceedings of the 3rd International Convention on Rehabilitation Engineering & Assistive Technology (i-CREATe'09)*, Article 10, 5 p. New York: ACM.

Thompson, G. and Foth, D. 2005. Cognitive-training programs for older adults: What are they and can they enhance mental fitness? *Educational Gerontology* 31(8):603–626.

Uzor, S. and Baillie, L. 2013. Exploring & designing tools to enhance falls rehabilitation in the home. In *Proceedings of the SIGCHI Conference on Human Factors in Computing Systems (CHI'13)*, 1233–1242. New York: ACM.

Vasconcelos, A., Silva, P. A., Caseiro, J., Nunes, F., and Teixeira, L. F. 2012. Designing tablet-based games for seniors: The example of CogniPlay, a cognitive gaming platform. In *Proceedings of the 4th International Conference on Fun and Games (FnG'12)*, 1–10. New York: ACM.

Voida, A. and Greenberg, S. 2009. Wii all play: The console game as a computational meeting place. In *Proceedings of the 27th International Conference on Human Factors in Computing Systems (CHI '09)*, 1559–1568. New York: ACM.

Walsh, G., Druin, A., Guha, M., Foss, E., Golub, E., Hatley, L., Bonsignore, E., and Franckel, S. 2010. Layered elaboration: A new technique for co-design with children. In *Proceedings of the 28th International Conference on Human Factors in Computing Systems (CHI'10)*, 1237–1240. New York: ACM.

Zickuhr, K. and Madden, M. 2012. *Older Adults and Internet Use*. Washington, DC: Pew Foundation.

LIST OF ADDITIONAL SOURCES

The LIFE Institute, Ryerson University. 2015. Welcome to the LIFE Institute. https://www.thelifeinstitute.ca/ (accessed May 5, 2015).

Yee Hong Centre For Geriatric Care. 2015. Welcome to Yee Hong— a Caring Community for Seniors. http://www.yeehong.com/ (accessed May 5, 2015).

BIOGRAPHIES

Ronald M. Baecker is an emeritus professor of computer science, emeritus Bell chair in human–computer interaction, and founder and director of the Technologies for Aging Gracefully lab (TAGlab) at the University of Toronto. He has been named one of the 60 pioneers of computer graphics by ACM SIGGRAPH, has been elected to the CHI (Computers and Human Interaction) Academy by ACM SIGCHI, has been given the Canadian Human Computer Communications Society Achievement Award, has been named an ACM Fellow, was given a Canadian Digital Media Pioneer Award, and recently received a Lifetime Achievement Award from the Canadian Association of Computer Science, the National Organization of Canadian Computer Science Departments/Schools/Faculties. He is editor of the *Synthesis Lectures on Assistive, Rehabilitative, and Health-preserving Technologies* (Morgan & Claypool Publisher).

Jeremy Birnholtz is an associate professor in the Departments of Communication Studies and Electrical Engineering and Computer Science at Northwestern University. His research aims to improve the usefulness and usability of communication and collaboration tools, via a focus on understanding and exploiting mechanisms of human attention and identity management. Birnholtz's work has been published in the *ACM CHI, CSCW*, and *Group Proceedings*, as well as in *Organization Science, HCI, JASIST, JCMC*, and *Computers in Human Behavior*. His research has been supported by the National Science Foundation, Google, Facebook, and the U.S. Department of Agriculture.

Karyn Moffatt is an assistant professor in the School of Information Studies at McGill University. Her research in human computer interaction explores how technology can be designed to meet the social and information needs of older adults and people with disabilities. Her work has led to a number of publications in top-tier international venues and has been recognized with awards at *ACM ASSETS 2007, ACM CHI 2009*, and *ACM CSCW 2014*. Her research is supported by grants from NSERC, FQRNT, Google Inc., GRAND NCE, and AGE-WELL NCE.

Nicholas Shim is a researcher and engineer from Sago Sago Toys, working on titles such as Sago Mini Pet Cafe and Monsters. He earned an MSc in human computer interaction from the University of Toronto and leads Sago's research with kids and parents. Shim is an experienced usability tester who has worked with gamers as young as 2 and as seasoned as 86. Prior to joining Sago he worked at Electronic Arts as a software engineer, developing console games for the NBA Live and FIFA franchises.

KEY TERMS AND DEFINITIONS

Nonplaying partner: We use the term nonplaying partner to refer to the player within a paired team that does not have control over the game. Nonplaying partners have the same view of the interface as playing partners but cannot control the game play. They participate by providing suggestions, making observations, or otherwise communicating with the playing partner via voice chat.

Partner-play: We use the term partner-play to refer to playing our game collaboratively with a partner as a team. Each pair of partners competes with other partners or individuals in the game.

Playing partner: We use the term playing-partner2 to refer to the player within a paired team that has active control over the game.

Seniors: In this chapter, we use the term seniors to describe adults aged 50 and over. Although a threshold of 65 years is more typically used in HCI research, in this work we needed to respect the definitions and norms of our partner organization, Ryerson University's LIFE program. Regardless of the threshold used, it is important to note that age alone does not define what it means to be a senior citizen or to hold preferences and values common to that group.

Social media: Services as social networking sites (e.g., Facebook), virtual worlds (e.g., Second Life) and communication systems (e.g., Skype) that allow users to interact and connect with one another (Kaplan and Haenlein 2010).

Solo-play: We use the term solo-play to refer to playing our game individually, without a collaborating partner. Solo-play nonetheless involves interacting with other players as competitors.

CHAPTER 11

Usability Testing of Serious Games

The Experience of the IHCLab

Pedro C. Santana-Mancilla, Laura S. Gaytán-Lugo, and Miguel A. Rodríguez-Ortiz

CONTENTS

EXECUTIVE SUMMARY

The usability evaluation of new technologies is a key factor for their success, ensuring that heterogeneous populations of users will be able to easily interact with these technological tools (Moreno-Ger et al. 2012). While usability testing methods applied to general purpose software are varied, evaluating the usability of video games requires special characteristics. If additionally, the games to be evaluated are those that have a purpose beyond entertainment (serious games), the challenge is greater.

In this chapter, we present a methodology designed for evaluating the usability of serious games, developed at the IHCLab research group at the University of Colima, Mexico. This methodology has been applied in several case studies of serious games; these games were created in order to improve different skills in students. The methodology and selected case studies are presented below.

INSTITUTION BACKGROUND

The University of Colima (http://www.ucol.mx) is an institution of higher education with 75 years of history and is composed of 12,099 undergraduate students, 13,496 high school students, and 739 graduate students.

The School of Telematics is a school at the University of Colima that offers four educational programs in the area of information and communication technologies (ICT): two undergraduate and two graduate. Three of these programs are nationally recognized for their excellence. The school's academic staff is composed of 23 full time professors and 47 lecturers that attend a student population of 510. The aim of the School of Telematics is to graduate efficient, competitive, and socially committed professionals.

The IHCLab Research Group is an interinstitutional research group started at the School of Telematics in collaboration with researchers at the University of Guadalajara, Mexico and Algoma University, Canada. The IHCLab Research Group integrates research and education, providing students (both undergraduate and graduate) with a project-based learning environment.

INTRODUCTION

Serious Games

Serious games are defined as a type of video games but with a serious purpose. They are used for training, advertisement, simulation, or education. In fact, serious games allow students to experiment with situations that are impossible or difficult to happen in the real world for different reasons, such as security, cost, or time (Zapusek et al. 2011). Serious games are not only intended just for entertainment, but also for serious activities, as Ling He et al. (2011) explain, serious games can help players to get professional skills in vocational skill training. Furthermore, serious games use instruction in the gameplay experience in order to develop a specific skill (Bellotti et al. 2009). As Zyda (2005) explains, a serious game is a mental contest that is executed on a computer, contains specific rules, and uses entertainment to further government or corporate training, education, health, public policy, and strategic communication objectives. After a wide review of literature, Marsh (2011) proposes a well-used definition of serious game as digital games, simulations, virtual environments, and mixed reality that provide opportunities to engage in activities through responsive story, game play, or encounters to inform, impact, or for well-being. Marsh explains that the quality or success of serious games is characterized by the degree to which their purpose has been fulfilled.

Today, serious games are receiving interest from researchers because of their multiple advantages (Vangsnes et al. 2012). In Mexico, this interest is more evident in academia (Armería-Zavala and Hernández-Gallardo 2012; Armería-Zavala et al. 2013; García-García et al. 2012; Garcia-Ruiz and Tashiro 2011; García-García et al. 2013; Gaytán-Lugo and Hernández-Gallardo 2012; González-Calleros et al. 2014; Gaytán-Lugo et al. 2015; Palacio et al. 2012; Ruiz et al. 2014; Santana 2011) since they have started to take advantages of the benefits of serious games for different purposes.

Some Numbers about Video Games

Since the first boom in the 1980s, the video game industry has maintained an important place in the world market. According to the website of the (Entertainment Software Association 2012), the annual growth rate from 2009 to 2012 increased by more than 9% in size—four times the growth rate of the U.S. economy during the same period. The use of serious games has grown significantly in recent years. A few facts of this situation are as follows: about 100 is the number of Global Fortune 500 companies that have used serious games for learning or training purposes in 2012. In addition, 64 million is the number of children between 2 and 17 years old who are currently gamers, and there was 8.07% increase in students' math test score numbers after playing the Dimension M game over an 18-week period, compared to an increase of 3.74 points for the control group (Entertainment Software Association 2012).

Meanwhile, the Mexican video game industry had an average annual growth of 18.7% during 2007–2010. In 2010, the Mexican market was worth $757 million USD, placing the country among the top 15 video game markets, being the first one in Latin America (ProMexico 2012), these numbers show that video games are already part of our culture just as other types of technology.

Serious Games and Education

Many sectors and organizations support the idea that serious games can transform the way people learn and make such learning more enjoyable (Marsh 2011). Video games offer pedagogical benefits over traditional methods of teaching and learning, for an increasingly diverse student population, with different backgrounds and skills (Connolly et al. 2009).

This statement is also supported by Squire (2004), who explains that video games encourage a way of learning that transcends traditional disciplinary boundaries and emphasizes integrated problem solving. Brown (2008) mentions that the appearance of video games in classrooms represents an important institutional credit to the new media.

Baker and Mayer (1999), Robertson and Howells (2008), and Watson et al. (2011) found that video games encourage skills related with teamwork, competence, collaboration, critical thinking, and communication. In fact, there are researchers who explain advantages of the use of video game in schools as an educational tool in different fields. In 2003, researchers from Massachusetts Institute of Technology (MIT) and Wisconsin University, including Henry Jenkins, James Gee, and Kurt Squire, formed Arcade Education, an association whose mission is to explore social, cultural, and educational potential gaming by starting new game development projects, coordinating interdisciplinary research, and information through public talks on the use of these emerging technologies in education (Brown 2008). This is why many educational organizations are considering the potential of serious games to support learning (Marsh 2011).

Methodology for Testing Usability of Serious Games

The IHCLab has ventured into the use of serious games applied to education since 2010, with the aim of achieving an increase in student skills, improving students' focusing, and the association of both concrete and abstract concepts. Based on the gained knowledge when developing our first serious games, we created a methodology to assess usability and thus to create games that are easy to use and at the same time attractive to users. Next, we will describe the elements on the methodology called "IHCLab Usability Test for Serious Games" and through three case studies, we will show its validity.

Evaluation Type

The evaluation is summative because it focuses on evaluating finished serious games.

Stage

The evaluation should be carried out in a laboratory or in an adequate space to function as such. This configuration can be used to do the evaluation with all participants simultaneously.

Figure 11.1 shows the laboratory configuration. The circles represent persons: (1) observers, (2) moderator, and (3) users. Triangles are cameras recording the user face. Rounded-rectangles are computers, and the pentagon a multimedia projector. The game must be installed on each computer when the laboratory is set up.

Study Sample

The size sample must be determined by following the recommendation of Nielsen (2000), who indicated that it is better to distribute the budget for user testing across many small tests instead of blowing everything on a single elaborated study. Therefore, we recommend a study sample of 5–20 users.

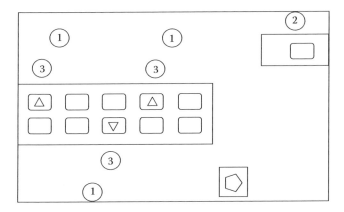

FIGURE 11.1   Laboratory configuration.

Method

The evaluation session should last between an hour and hour and a half (depending on the complexity of the task). The evaluation includes the following phases:

Phase 1: The moderator opens the session with a 10-minute introduction and applies a general questionnaire for user characterization.

Phase 2: A live demo is carried out using the multimedia projector; this demo must show the participants the features of the serious game. The aim of the demo is to put the use of the game controllers into context to the users.

Phase 3: The participants should be given a task list to complete in the game.

Phase 4: In this phase, the evaluation team can select among three questionnaires to collect the opinions of the participants: (1) game heuristics questionnaire; (2) game experience questionnaire (GEQ); and (3) use for learning survey. These questionnaires can be applied one by one or as a combination of the three.

Questionnaires

Game heuristic questionnaire: We adapted and generalized game heuristics reported in the literature (Desurvire et al. 2004, 2007), thus the resulting heuristics are listed below:

H1: Does the game react in a consistent way to the player's actions?

H2: Could you customize the profile, music, video, the game difficulty, and speed?

H3: Could you find a predictable and reasonable behavior of the controls?

H4: Does the game provide information about an action to take?

H5: Can the player skip not-playable content (i.e., videos or texts) to return to the game?

H6: Are the controls intuitive and customizable?

H7: Are the game controls consistent within the game?

H8: Does the game present information about the game status?

H9: Does the game provide instructions, help, and training?

H10: Are the status score indicators seamless, obvious, available, and do not interfere with the game play?

Game experience questionnaire: The GEQ is divided into two dimensions: (1) four questions, where the learners had to give a grade from 1 to 10, where 10 is the most significant and (2) seven questions that measured some important indicators with a 5 Likert scale. The first dimension of the GEQ includes the next questions:

Q1: Did you find the game fun?

Q2: Was it difficult to adapt to the game control?

Q3: Did you find the game exciting?

Q4: How easy it was to fulfill the objective of the game?

As mentioned, the second dimension measures seven indicators:

1. Efficiency

2. Effectiveness

3. Immersion

4. Motivation

5. Emotion

6. Fluency

7. Learning curve

The use for learning survey: As a final step, the use for learning survey can be applied with two questions to gain knowledge about users' perception about the game and its use as educational material:

Q1. How do you feel using the game?

Q2. Do you feel motivated to use a game like this for educational purposes?

Case Study Description

At the ICHLab, this methodology has been applied to seven serious games. The following three case studies will show the use of the methodology. Each case will demonstrate how to describe the results of one part of the questionnaires with the intention of not repeating the same situation several times to the reader.

La Leyenda de Dasha (the Dasha Legend)

La Leyenda de Dasha is a serious game intended to support and improve reading comprehension skills in third graders (aged 8–9 years) from Mexico.

Participants

Participants of the study were 20 learners, 55% males and 45% females. All of them were third graders with an age average of 8 years.

Game Heuristic Questionnaire

Participants found that the game controls are consistent, predictable, intuitive (with reasonable behavior), and customizable (see Figure 11.2). In addition, they believed that the game presented quality and usable information, the actions to take were clear, and provided useful instructions, help, and training.

Two heuristics got bad results: H2 and H5. H2 is related to game customization; players found few options for customizing the game. This is a good area of opportunity for improving the game's usability. H5 is about skipping the nonplayable content; this game was developed to improve the reading comprehension of children and in a large part of the gameplay, the user had to read several paragraphs of text. To achieve this goal, it is important not to skip these texts.

Game Experience Questionnaire

Regarding game experience found in the GEQ results (we call it first dimension), kids found the game fun and exciting, with a low difficulty to adapt to the game control; but they believed that the game objective was slightly difficult to fulfill (see Figure 11.3). The four questions got an average grade above 9.

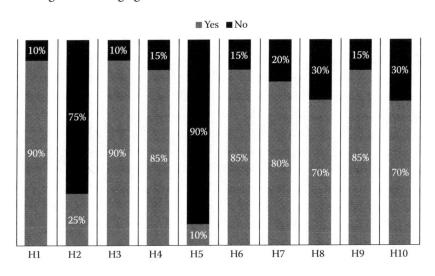

FIGURE 11.2 Game heuristics questionnaire.

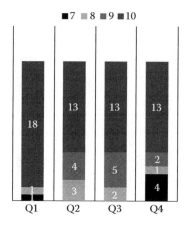

FIGURE 11.3   GEQ first dimension.

FallBox

FallBox is a serious game to teach human–computer interaction (HCI) to undergraduate students. The game uses multimodal interaction by using a keyboard and head tracking.

Participants

The subjects of study were 20 people, 11 males and 9 females, with an age range from 14 to 29 years. In all, 70% of the subjects had previous experience in playing computer games.

Game Experience Questionnaire

Figure 11.4 shows the results of the second dimension of the GEQ. The subjects identified lack of effectiveness with the head-tracking device as the main (and only) potential obstacle. In addition, the participants found the head-tracking technology (in relation to

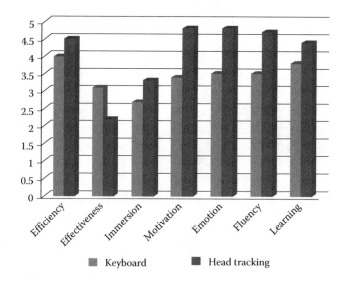

FIGURE 11.4   GEQ second dimension.

the keyboard) more efficient, immersive, inspiring, exciting, smooth, and easy to learn, which indicates that they indeed wanted to use the head-tracking device.

El Encanto

El Encanto is a serious game intended for social work students to learn about community intervention.

Participants

The subjects of study were 7 people, 4 males and 3 females. All of them were undergraduate students who studied intervention methods in communities as part of their classes. In this instance, 71% had previous experience playing video games, spending an average of 2 hours a day; they play games on consoles or personal computers (PCs) mainly at home.

Use for Learning Survey

When we asked the Q1 from the use for learning survey, 71% of the students reported that they felt comfortable with the serious game, while the rest (29%) commented as follows:

- "I felt actually a little nervous because I do not play video games, but after a while I felt better and it was nice to play the game."

- "I felt a little stressed. I am not addicted to games."

Finally, regarding Q2, we found that 100% of the students were motivated to use the game for educational purposes. They made a number of positive comments, including:

- "It is a very good tool for training students dedicated to the interaction in actual communities."

- "It would allow a great learning experience."

- "I liked it."

Challenges

Having a specific methodology to evaluate the usability of video games is very important because video games require a range of specific characteristics, unlike other types of software. Furthermore, it is important to remark that the proposed methodology was specially designed for serious games, which are different from other types of video games. Although we succeeded in applying and validating this methodology in several different cases, we know that we have to keep working in order to improve the methodology to enhance the user experience of serious games.

Solutions and Recommendations

The use of this methodology has improved the user experience of serious games developed at the IHCLab Research Group. In addition, the case studies presented in this chapter helped to create a set of testing guidelines for future development of serious games.

The importance of usability testing is about the necessity of measuring the ease of use and the users' acceptance of serious games. Therefore, this methodology will be useful for academics and practitioners developing serious games.

CONCLUSIONS

The use of serious games applied to education has brought us an enjoyable way of acquiring knowledge, since games offer constant challenges that must be overcome by players (learners). This is the way that students learn through our serious games. In addition, as with any other software, usability testing of video games is very important. This chapter presents a methodology for evaluating such usability, and the three different case studies demonstrate that our methodology has been successfully implemented. The case studies described in this chapter will serve as a clear example to the reader of the use of our methodology.

REFERENCES

Armería-Zavala, L. and S.C. Hernández-Gallardo. 2012. Development of number sense in third grade of elementary school using serious game. In *Proceedings of the 20th International Conference on Computers in Education ICCE 2012*, 29–31. Singapore.

Armería-Zavala, L., S.C. Hernández-Gallardo, and M.Á. García-Ruíz. 2013. Designing interactive activities within Scratch 2.0 for improving abilities to identify numerical sequences. In *Proceedings of the 12th International Conference on Interaction Design and Children*, 423–426. ACM Press. http://dl.acm.org/citation.cfm?doid=2485760.2485831.

Baker, E.L. and R.E. Mayer. 1999. Computer-based assessment of problem solving. *Computers in Human Behavior*, 15(3–4), (May): 269–282.

Bellotti, F., R. Berta, A. De Gloria, and L. Primavera. 2009. Adaptive experience engine for serious games. *IEEE Transactions on Computational Intelligence and AI in Games*, 1(4), (December): 264–280.

Brown, H.J. 2008. *Video Games and Education. History, Humanities, and New Technology*. Armonk, NY: M.E. Sharpe.

Connolly, T., M. Stansfield, and L. Boyle, eds. 2009. *Games-Based Learning Advancements for Multi-Sensory Human Computer Interfaces: Techniques and Effective Practices*. IGI Global. http://services.igi-global.com/resolvedoi/resolve.aspx?doi=10.4018/978-1-60566-360-9.

Desurvire, H., M. Caplan, and J.A. Toth. 2004. Using heuristics to evaluate the playability of games. In *CHI '04 Extended Abstracts on Human Factors in Computing Systems*, 1509. ACM Press. http://portal.acm.org/citation.cfm?doid=985921.986102.

Desurvire, H., Jegers, K., and Wiberg, C. 2007. Evaluating fun and entertainment: Developing a conceptual framework design of evaluation methods. In *First Workshop on Design Principles for Software that Engages Its Users*, FUN 2007.

Entertainment Software Association. 2012. *The U.S. Video Game Industry's Economic Impact*. ESA Newsletters. http://www.theesa.com/article/u-s-video-game-industrys-economic-impact/.

García-García, C., J.L. Fernández-Robles, V. Larios-Rosillo, and H. Luga. 2012. ALFIL: A crowd simulation serious game for massive evacuation training and awareness. *International Journal of Game-Based Learning*, 2(3): 71–86.

García-García, C., V. Larios-Rosillo, and H. Luga. 2013. Agent behaviour modeling using personality profile characterization for emergency evacuation serious games. In *Intelligent Computer Graphics 2012*, eds. D. Plemenos and G. Miaoulis, 441:107–128. Berlin, Heidelberg: Springer. http://link.springer.com/10.1007/978-3-642-31745-3_6.

Garcia-Ruiz, M. A., J. Tashiro, B. Kapralos, and M. Vargas Martin. 2011. Crouching tangents, hidden danger: Assessing development of dangerous misconceptions within serious games for healthcare education. *Virtual Immersive and 3D Learning Spaces: Emerging Technologies and Trends*, 269–306.

Gaytán-Lugo, L.S. and S.C. Hernández-Gallardo. 2012. Towards improving reading comprehension skills in third graders with a serious game. In *Proceedings of the 20th International Conference on Computers in Education ICCE* 2012, Singapore.

Gaytán-Lugo, L.S., P.C. Santana-Mancilla, A. Santarrosa-García, A. Medina-Anguiano, S.C. Hernández-Gallardo, and M.Á. Garcia-Ruiz. 2015. Developing a serious game to improve reading comprehension skills in third graders. *Research in Computing Science*, 89: 71–79.

González-Calleros, J., J. Guerrero-García, H. Escamilla, and J. Muñoz-Arteaga. 2014. Towards model-game-based rehabilitation information system. In *Proceedings of the 5th Mexican Conference on Human–Computer Interaction*, 15–21. ACM Press. http://dl.acm.org/citation.cfm?doid=2676690.2676693.

Ling He, Xiaoqiang Hu, and Dandan Wei. 2011. The case analysis of serious game in community vocational education. In *Proceedings of the 2011 International Conference on Computer Science and Network Technology (ICCSNT)*, 3: 1863–1866. Harbin: IEEE. http://ieeexplore.ieee.org/lpdocs/epic03/wrapper.htm?arnumber=6182333.

Marsh, T. 2011. Serious games continuum: Between games for purpose and experiential environments for purpose. *Entertainment Computing* 2(2), (January): 61–68.

Moreno-Ger, P., J. Torrente, Y.G. Hsieh, and W.T. Lester. 2012. Usability testing for serious games: Making informed design decisions with user data. *Advances in Human–Computer Interaction*, 2012: 1–13.

Nielsen, J. 2000. Why You Only Need to Test with 5 Users. http://www.nngroup.com/articles/why-you-only-need-to-test-with-5-users/.

Palacio, R.R., C.O. Acosta, A.L. Morán, and J. Cortez. 2012. Towards video game design guidelines to promote significant leisure activities in Mexican older adults. In *Proceedings of the 4th Mexican Conference on Human–Computer Interaction*, 43. New York: ACM Press. http://dl.acm.org/citation.cfm?doid=2382176.2382186.

ProMexico. 2012. Industrias Creativas En México. http://mim.promexico.gob.mx/wb/mim/ind_perfil_del_sector.

Robertson, J. and C. Howells. 2008. Computer game design: Opportunities for successful learning. *Computers & Education*, 50(2), (February): 559–578.

Ruiz, J.G., E.M. Cano, F.L. Orozco, and L.D. Huerta. 2014. Evaluating the communicability of a video game prototype: A simple and low-cost method. In *Proceedings of the 5th Mexican Conference on Human–Computer Interaction*, 30–33. ACM Press. http://dl.acm.org/citation.cfm?doid=2676690.2676698.

Santana, P.C. 2011. Arquitectura Para Interacción Multimodal En Los Juegos Por Computadora. In *Memorias Del 4to. Congreso Internacional En Ciencias Computacionales CiComp 2011*. Ensenada, México: UABC.

Squire, K. 2004. Replaying History: Learning World through Playing Civilization II. Doctoral thesis, University of Indiana.

Vangsnes, V., N.T. Gram Økland, and R. Krumsvik. 2012. Computer games in pre-school settings: Didactical challenges when commercial educational computer games are implemented in kindergartens. *Computers & Education*, 58(4), (May): 1138–1148.

Watson, W.R., C.J. Mong, and C.A. Harris. 2011. A case study of the in-class use of a video game for teaching high school history. *Computers & Education*, 56(2), (February): 466–474.

Zapusek, M., S. Cerar, and J. Rugelj. 2011. Serious computer games as instructional technology. In *2011 Proceedings of the 34th International Convention MIPRO*, 1056–1058. Rijeka, Croatia: IEEE.

Zyda, M. 2005. From visual simulation to virtual reality to games. *Computer*, 38(9), (September): 25–32.

LIST OF ADDITIONAL SOURCES

García Ruiz, M.Á. and P.C. Santana Mancilla. 2015. Introducción a la Usabilidad de los Videojuegos. In *La Interacción Humano-Computadora En México*, eds. J. Muñoz Arteaga, J.M. González Calleros, and A. Sánchez Huitrón. Naucalpan de Juárez, México: Pearson.

Gaytán-Lugo, L.S., S.C. Hernández-Gallardo, P.C. Santana-Mancilla, and M.A. Garcia-Ruiz. 2014. A contextual study and usability testing of video games to inform the design of a serious game to improve reading comprehension. In *Memoria Del Encuentro Nacional de Ciencias de La Computación*. Oaxaca, Mexico.

Rodríguez-Ortiz, M.A., P.-C. Santana Mancilla, and M.A. Garcia-Ruiz. 2013. El Encanto: Juego Serio Para El Aprendizaje de Intervención Comunitaria Para Estudiantes de Trabajo Social. In *Memorias Del XII Congreso Nacional de Investigación Educativa (COMIE 2013)*. Guanajuato, Mexico. 1–12.

Tullis, T. and B. Albert. 2008. Measuring the user experience: collecting, analyzing, and presenting usability metrics. *The Morgan Kaufmann Interactive Technologies Series*. Amsterdam; Boston: Elsevier/Morgan Kaufmann.

BIOGRAPHIES

Pedro C. Santana-Mancilla is a research professor at the School of Telematics at the University of Colima in Mexico. His research interest focuses in human–computer interaction, serious games, and learning technology. In 2012, he earned an IBM Faculty Award to support his research in intelligent environments for education. He is a senior member of the IEEE (Institute of Electrical and Electronic Engineering). Santana-Mancilla is also a member of the Mexican Association on Human Computer Interaction (AMexIHC), the Mexican Society of Computer Science (SMCC), the Association for Computing Machinery (ACM), and ACM SIGCHI Officer of the Mexican Chapter.

Laura S. Gaytán-Lugo is an analytical, imaginative, enthusiastic, methodical, and productive computer systems engineer. She lectures systems design, numerical methods, and mathematical logic, among other courses, at the School of Mechanical and Electrical Engineering of the University of Colima, Mexico. Her research interest lies on human–computer interaction and educational technology. She has been collaborating in different research projects on serious games, crowd–computer interaction, interaction styles, virtual environments, item response theory, group testing, and reading comprehension. Currently, she is a PhD candidate at the Universidad de Guadalajara, Mexico, where her research project focuses on how to improve global reading comprehension in Mexican third graders through a serious game.

Miguel A. Rodríguez-Ortiz is currently the production manager of the General Office of Educational Resources, lecturer at the School of Telematics, and member of the IHCLab Research Group of the University of Colima, Mexico. He has been working on the design and development of educational software since 2001. During his master's degree studies, he worked in the production and usability evaluation of an educational video game for the School of Social Work of the National Autonomous University of Mexico, which was very well received. Rodríguez-Ortiz also collaborates in educational serious game development projects at the General Office of Educational Resources.

KEY TERMS AND DEFINITIONS

Heuristic evaluation: Heuristic evaluation is a usability inspection method that helps to identify usability problems in the user interface (UI) design from digital products. Expert evaluators generally examine the UI judging its compliance with recognized usability principles called heuristics. Heuristic evaluation is studied and practiced in software development and UI design.

Human–computer interaction (HCI): It involves the planning, study, and design of the interaction between computers and users. It is generally considered as the intersection of computer science, design, behavioral sciences, and other fields of study.

Serious games: Serious games are video games that can include simulations of real-world events or processes, designed with the purpose of educating and solving a problem, beyond entertainment. Serious games may have other purposes, such as supporting marketing. Serious games will sometimes deliberately sacrifice entertainment and fun in order to achieve a desired player progress.

Usability: The learnability and ease of use of a human-made object. The object of use can be a digital product such as a website, video game, or anything a human interacts with.

Usability testing: A user-centered interaction design technique to evaluate a digital product by testing it on users. This practice gives input on how people use a digital system.

Index